INLANDIA

A Literary Journey through California's Inland Empire

Edited by Gayle Wattawa
With an introduction by Susan Straight

Santa Clara University, Santa Clara, California
Heyday Books, Berkeley, California

This book is made possible in part by a generous grant from The James Irvine Foundation. Further funding was supplied by the National Endowments for the Arts.

© 2006 by Heyday Books
Introduction © 2006 by Susan Straight

Library of Congress Cataloging-in-Publication Data
Inlandia : a literary journey through California's Inland Empire / edited by Gayle Wattawa ; with an introduction by Susan Straight.
    p. cm. — (A California legacy book.)
Includes index.
 ISBN 1-59714-037-6 (pbk. : alk. paper)
 ISBN 978-1-59714-037-9
 1. California—Literary collections. 2. American literature—California—San Bernardino County. 3. American literature—California—Riverside County. 4. American literature—21st century. I. Wattawa, Gayle.
 PS571.C2I55 2006
 810.8'0979495--dc22
                          2006029658

Cover photo by John Ortega
Cover design by Lorraine Rath
Interior design by Rebecca LeGates
Maps by Ben Pease
Printing and binding: McNaughton & Gunn, Saline, MI

Orders, inquiries, and correspondence should be addressed to:
        Heyday Books
        P. O. Box 9145, Berkeley, CA 94709
        (510) 549-3564, Fax (510) 549-1889
        www.heydaybooks.com

Printed in the United States of America on recycled paper (50% post-consumer waste). ♻

10 9 8 7 6 5 4 3 2

Contents

Acknowledgments

First and foremost, my warmest thanks to The James Irvine Foundation for the generous grant that made this book possible, and to the National Endowment for the Arts.

I am deeply grateful to the advisory committee for this book: Kevin Hallaran (Riverside Municipal Museum), Heather King (University of Redlands), Kathryn Morton (Riverside Public Library), and Ruth Nolan (College of the Desert). Excellent suggestions for writers whose work I should look at came from Jeff Green, Michael Jayme, Susan Straight, Dwight Yates, Sholeh Wolpé, and Ann Japenga, who also generously provided a wealth of historical and background material. The University of Redlands, Heather King, and Charlotte Burgess deserve special thanks for their extraordinary support of the book, as well as the Riverside Public Library for arranging to launch the book with such exuberance.

A heartfelt thanks to Juan Felipe Herrera, who not only named the anthology *Inlandia*, but lent me the talented and resourceful members of one of his creative writing classes to help collect material: Karina Angel, Jason Aviña, Levi Bailey, Kristin Barnes, Greg Boytos, Andrew Conniff, Danielle Davis, Lauren Eash, Violeta Esparza, Diana Franco, Julia Fullman, Veronica Galvan, Kennisha Green, Michael Haight, Marlene Hoffman, Madison Jennings, Michelle Johnson, Jasmyne Jones, Priscilla De Loera, Violeta Loreto, Tiffany Medley, Shreya Mehta, Eri Mendoza, Veronica Reveles, Brittany Roberts, Dominique Sassani, Matthew Sawyer, Marcus Scott, Chris Sedhom, Nemo Simmons, Herlinda Tin, Casey Weiant, and Patrick Wu.

For initial ideas and enthusiasm, I am grateful to Ellen Estilai (Riverside Arts Council), Brenda Focht (Riverside Municipal Museum), Laura Kalpakian, Cheryl Klein (Poets & Writers), H. Vincent Moses (Riverside Municipal Museum), Valerie Reinke, Susan Rice (San Bernardino Arts Council), and Lynn Voorheis (Riverside Municipal Museum). Interns

Emily Elrod, Jordan MacKay, and Marie Olivier devoted numerous hours between them to this anthology and deserve many thanks.

I am grateful to Malcolm Margolin for the opportunity to work on such a challenging and rewarding project. I also thank my parents, sisters, grandparents, and Jennifer for listening patiently and with encouragement to the ins and outs of this project, and Erin for his love and support.

Gayle Wattawa
Berkeley, September 2006

Inland Empire and Environs

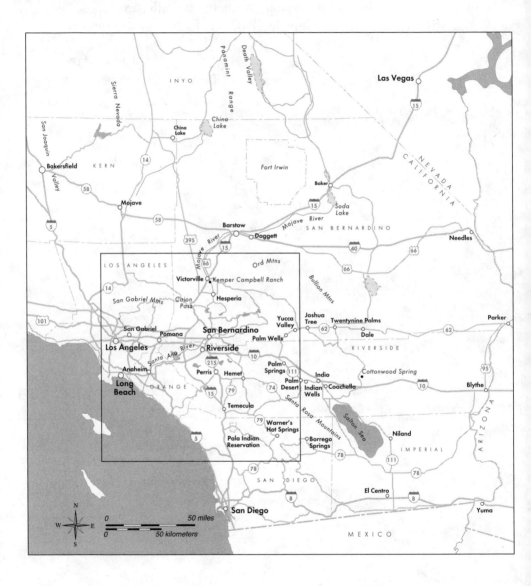

Inset

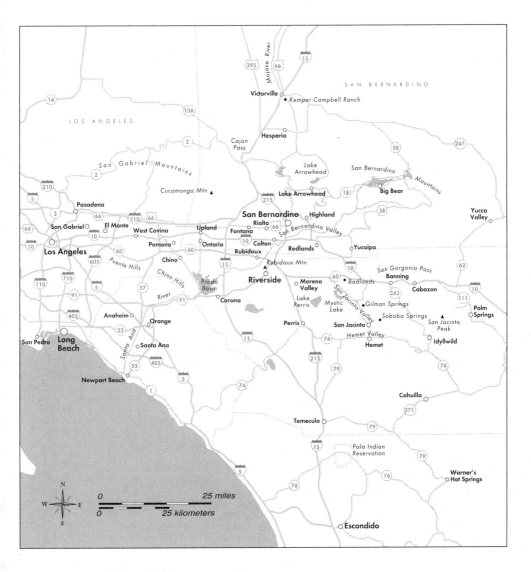

Introduction

Susan Straight

We had forests. As a child, I read of Sherwood Forest in England, where men could be lost to sight for years; of haunted woods in Europe, like those where my mother was born, where wolves and witches and darkness reigned amid the huge firs; of rain forests in South America where birds and monkeys screamed amid the dripping branches; of the chestnut and hickory and dogwood of Appalachia and the wilderness of trees in the great eastern forests of America.

And though no one knew it, in my part of Southern California, the inland reaches of terrain where most of us see only smog-shrouded hills and dried wild oats and mazes of freeway, we had magical, mythical woods as well—thousands and thousands of acres planted in orange and lemon and grapefruit trees that covered much of Riverside and San Bernardino and Redlands. Apricots and olive groves in Hemet, the date palm groves in Mecca and Indio, walnut trees in Elsinore, and cherries and apples in Cherry Valley and Oak Glen. Between them, in the wild San Gorgonio and San Jacinto Mountains, on the rolling hills of Temecula, we had pines and oaks that had lived for centuries. Along the riverbeds were cottonwoods and willows, and in the desert Joshua trees made their own eerie forests, and smoke trees rose from the sand. All my life, here in this place, we have had our own myths and legends and stories, but they were not heard very often outside in the world.

I live in a house three blocks from Riverside Community Hospital, where I was born, where my brothers, my ex-husband, and his siblings were born, and most of our friends and all of our children.

I have always lived here, except for my college years, and I have seen nearly every mile of land in the region which this new anthology calls "Inlandia." When I was a child and people from elsewhere asked adults about where we lived, I remember hearing again and again that we were an hour from the mountains, an hour from the desert, an hour from the ocean, and an hour from Los Angeles. And I always thought, when I was a child, But why would we want to leave?

We had everything, in my eyes. The endless forests of cultivation, the lush wildflowers of the desert in spring, the date groves and pine forests. Trout from mountain lakes, lemons and oranges and avocados all winter, and as children we didn't care when smog veiled the hills in the summer. We mined the foothills near our house for fool's gold and rose quartz, and then we lay panting in an orange grove, and swam in the swift waters of the canal, where grass waved on the bottom as though in a true stream.

In fact, I realized as I grew older, everyone wanted to come here, to the inland region. Everyone's parents had come from somewhere else. My own mother was from Switzerland; her parents had moved from their small valley to seek their fortunes. They did not find them in Ontario, Canada, or northern Florida, but then they saw the ultimate pictures of prosperity and success, the land of milk and honey as represented in decades past: the postcards of purpled, snow-covered mountains in the distance, and orange trees in the foreground, all golden in the sun.

That is truly what we saw, growing up here, all winter. It was paradise, though I have since learned that the rest of the world might not recognize it.

In elementary school and junior high, I found that nearly everyone's parents had immigrated here—from Louisiana and Oklahoma and Mississippi, from Michoacán and Zacatecas and Guanajuato, from the Philippines and Germany and Japan. I had friends whose fathers were military men and whose mothers were immigrant brides from those countries. I had other friends whose fathers were military men and who'd returned to the South and vowed never to live in poverty and segregation again. All settled in Riverside, in San Bernardino, in Victorville—wherever there were military bases. And their children grew up in the Inland Empire—a new people. They played with the children of the Okies who'd broken down here, with my mother-in-law's people, who'd broken down in Calexico and whose sons became some of the first black Border Patrol agents.

I lived in a neighborhood called Okietown for the first three years of my life, and then my mother married my stepfather, who had also found his promised land here, having left New Brunswick, Canada. We moved to Riverside, and they have never left.

We ran freely as children, to the foothills and groves and river, and my parents, who loved this landscape with the passion of those raised in snow, took us camping everywhere. We knew every mile of Inlandia.

The dinosaurs of Cabazon, where people could eat hamburgers inside the head of a brontosaurus. The date palm groves in Mecca and Oasis and Indio, where even the names were exotic, and where I stood under the gray-green fronds arching above me, touching the etched trunks and the golden sprays of dates cascading overhead, and knew it was really a cathedral. The heat was so intense, and the cicadas' song filled my forehead, and the smell of water in the irrigation furrows was silver. On the way home, we got date shakes in Indio and watched the famous movie—*The Sex Life of the Date.*

I love every mile of my homeland. The fields of watermelon and cantaloupe in Blythe and Ripley, where my foster brothers and sisters came from. The savanna-like golden grasses in the Temecula Valley, with the oaks gathered like black clouds in the distance. The steep entrance of the Cajon Pass, where the mountains are purple in winter dusk and the wind is so fierce it will throw trucks like toys. The dunes outside Palm Springs and Whitewater, where the sand is white and soft as cake flour, and the smoke trees rise like ghosts in the distance. (My ex-husband once worked at a juvenile correction facility in Whitewater, and when Los Angeles boys tried to run away, he followed them in that desert, as they trudged with suitcases and radios through the creosote and rabbitbrush and hot sand, until they gave up in what they considered a particularly impersonal hell.)

I love the tiny communities that only we in this place know— Rubidoux, named for a pioneer of the area, and Belltown, where our cousins live near the Santa Ana River; Agua Mansa and La Placita, where New Mexicans came to grow grapes along that river and build adobe houses, marked now only by a cemetery and a few scattered homes; the old Cucamonga, where vineyards flourished and my parents bought wine; and Muscoy, on the outskirts of San Bernardino, where my brother liked to check out fighting roosters.

For twenty-five years I have written about this region and tried to infuse my work with love and desire and the fierceness we retain in these small places where people loved their own with the vehemence, the stubborn and suspicious and inventive qualities required to survive in this part of Southern California. It was a place where the land and sun and smog and violence and people could be forbidding, but the same land and sun and people offered survival and love and tungsten-hard loyalty to each other.

And for all these years, I have wanted to see my place represented in literature, in a wide-ranging collection of all the communities and voices and landscapes I've known.

Here it is.

The oranges, the Washington navel and Valencias I've tasted all my life, the ones my brother grew for many years, descendants of the tree which I drive past often and always nod to in obeisance. They are here, in John Jakes's excerpt and in the narratives by Harry Lawton and Mary Paik Lee of those Chinese and Korean men and women who harvested the fruit.

The legends of Tahquitz, the angry god whose stories I heard as a child when I was afraid to hike in his canyon above Palm Springs, and the stories of Mukat and his children, who lived in the desert. Malcolm Margolin's account of the expulsion of the Cupa people from Warner Springs, less known than the famous tale of Ramona, but sadder to me because I knew Gordon Johnson, a descendant of one of the women wailing as she left her home. Johnson's stories of humor and heartbreak on Pala, where his ancestors persevered, bring the story full circle.

The forbidding, alluring desert is here, in Erle Stanley Gardner's excerpt: "I went to sleep with the sand making little whispering noises that sounded more and more like words." I have heard so many times those whispers, in Cabazon and Palm Desert, and have been trapped in a truck while the raging winter sandstorms blasted the paint off the hood. Erle Stanley Gardner wrote in the inland area, sometimes at the Mission Inn, where Carrie Jacobs-Bond wrote her poem included here, and where I wrote parts of all my novels.

Sometimes I believe we have an advantage here in our land, because even the very words used to describe us are lovely: pomegranate and pyracantha, bougainvillea and jacaranda, granite and ghostly coyotes and eucalyptus. Even our smog makes the sunset vivid as dangerous passion.

The writers I read for inspiration as a young author are here. I always admired Laura Kalpakian's fictional St. Elmo, her creation of a place much like San Bernardino, and how, as the excerpt in this anthology shows, she knew the people here so well. Route 66 was a mythical place in our history, and no one wrote about it like John Steinbeck; not until I read *The Grapes of Wrath* did I understand the refusal of many of my elderly neighbors to get rid of a carburetor or radiator or even an old tire.

Recent statistics reveal, several years in a row, that the many disparate communities of my city, my region, my landscape—once fairly small in population—have been transformed into the fastest-growing counties in America. Hundreds of thousands of people, drawn by affordable housing, have left Los Angeles and Orange and San Diego Counties to move to this area.

The new voices in *Inlandia* represent the best of my hopes and dreams and literary desires, the eloquent renderings of how the old worlds and new have collided and melded in this place like no other. Alex Espinoza has made his native Colton into Agua Mansa, a tender and heartbreaking and hopeful place. The Riverside landscape of Michael David Egelin, the Highland of Keenan Norris, the Blythe of E. J. Jones, and the Salton Sea of Gayle Brandeis are all places I have always wanted to see in print, the mirages and neighborhoods and voices I missed before.

When I left Riverside to attend university in Los Angeles, I was already fully formed, stubborn and fierce and suspicious as my inland compatriots. As I'd expected, my universe was ridiculed. "You're from Riverside? The Inland Empire? What do you have out there? Cows? Oranges, right?"

To answer the people from Pasadena and Los Angeles and Orange County and San Francisco, I had many responses. My land has had the distinction of being the capital of many things in the past—arson, smog, urban sprawl, methamphetamine, biker gangs, and yes, citrus and dairy. We have always been a rural place where people grow things to make their fortunes, and sometimes they grew hamburgers and Hell's Angels, as in Eric Schlosser's examination of the MacDonald brothers and San Bernardino. M. F. K. Fisher gave up on growing anything but haunting memories. People grew desire for gold, they grew insane. I knew the Harada house, where a Japanese American woman grew courage.

Now many of the groves—walnuts and apricots and oranges—are gone. Now people in this region grow houses, and mortgages, and more and more children.

But in the past, sometimes people who came to inland Southern California grew nothing but false hope.

In college, as a seventeen-year-old freshman, I was assigned to read Joan Didion's essay "Some Dreamers of the Golden Dream." Her depictions of inland life were stunning and at the same time painful to me. "This is a story about love and death in the golden land," she begins, and describes what was to most people "an alien place…a harsher California…this ominous country." I had never read a phrase like "talismanic fruit," and I stayed up all night with my fingers turning the pages, knowing she was exactly who I wanted to be, that I wanted to write like that. But I had never seen anyone examine my own world, the Santa Ana winds, the lemon groves bordered with river-rock walls, and it was through those words that I now learned how others saw us: "the country of the teased hair and the Capris and the girls for whom all life's promise comes down to a waltz-length white wedding dress and the birth of a Kimberly or a Sherry or a Debbi and a Tijuana divorce and a return to hair-dressers' school.…Here is where the hot wind blows and the old ways do not seem relevant, where the divorce rate is double the national average and where one person in every thirty-eight lives in a trailer. Here is the last stop for all those who come from somewhere else, for all those who drifted away from the cold and the past and the old ways."

I lay awake all night, thinking of my friends and their parents. My future husband's parents, who fled Mississippi and Oklahoma but who'd brought their cooking and voices and ways with them. My neighbors, born in Japan and the Philippines and Germany, now married to white and black and Mexican American servicemen, whose children I had always known. My own mother, who had left the cold behind and whose husband left her amid a dust storm in Glen Avon with me at three and a new baby, when the dirt sifted under the windowsill and covered everything.

I went home the next day and tried to tell my mother about the piece, and about writing, and about how it made me feel. Didion had said, recalling one of our great scandals, "Here is where they are trying to find a new life style, trying to find it in the only places they know to look: the movies and the newspapers. The case of Lucille Marie Maxwell Miller is a tabloid monument to that new life style." My mother frowned and said, "Lucille Miller? Oh, your Aunt Beverly lived on her street. The one who killed her husband. Beverly always said that woman was capable of murder."

I didn't know what to feel then. I was one of those people Joan Didion knew everything about. I drove to Ontario, the neighborhood in the essay, where my father and his siblings had struggled to survive when their parents, who'd immigrated from Colorado, left them. To Fontana, where my grandmother worked at Kaiser, the now-closed steel plant which was our lifeline. To San Bernardino, where my mother had her first job. To Muscoy, a tiny place of dirt roads and clapboard houses where my stepfather had bought a one-room shack with no bathroom. His first property. I drove home to my neighborhood in Riverside, which made the places in Didion's piece look good by comparison.

I wanted to someday know the code of her elegance and precision and genius, the prose I admired so much, but I wanted to read about my dreamers in their smog-shrouded pale asphalt streets, in their orange groves where the white blossoms fell around us like stars when the sun was going down, in their canyons where the gods of the mountains, like Tahquitz, waited for revenge, in their silver-hot vineyards and the date groves of Mecca where dark men cut grapes and put paper bags around the date clusters.

And now it is here. Inlandia.

INLANDIA

Katherine Saubel

Born in 1920 on the Los Coyotes Reservation and raised in Palm Springs, Katherine Saubel is a Cahuilla elder and president of the Malki Museum, a museum of Cahuilla culture on the Morongo Reservation. She is the author of several books on Cahuilla culture and language. The Women's Hall of Fame, the Smithsonian Institution, and the National Museum of the American Indian have all honored Saubel for her invaluable insight into numerous aspects of Cahuilla culture. She lives on the Morongo Reservation.

Saubel translated this version of the Cahuilla creation story from a recording made by a shaman, Perfecto Segundo, more than half a century ago. It is included in Deborah Dozier's *The Heart Is Fire: The World of the Cahuilla Indians of Southern California*. The story usually takes an entire night to relate and has been greatly edited. Italics were added for clarity. The " ' " character represents a glottal stop, similar to the break in sound in "uh-oh."

from *The Heart Is Fire*

The story goes like this. There was night, only darkness. When they were going to appear, the night shook, the night vibrated. The night rang and then it quieted down. And then they appeared, just out of nothing. Just out in mid-air they hung. There was nothing to hold them up. They were just suspended in the air. Then they disappeared. That is when they say it was a miscarriage. And then it happened again. They appeared like they did, and they disappeared. And then they hung again, suspended in air. Then the thing they were suspended in dried. Then they moved. They moved and they stretched. They grew and they stretched some more.

In this way, the two gods, Mukat and Témayawet, were born from an embryo formed by primordial forces associated with darkness and the night, Tookmeoot and 'amna'a. Mukat and Témayawet argue with each other about which of them was born first. Then they climb to the top of the centricle of the world. They draw the earth from their hearts, then the ocean and the sky. They connect the earth and the sky by fixing the centricle in the middle.

And then Témayawet asks again, "What are we going to do now?" And Mukat says, "You should know but you don't. So now we will create the people." Then they started to create the people. They did not get them out of their mouths, but they worked them from the mud. It was in the dark that they did all this. Témayawet created his creatures in a hurry and carelessly. Then he was finished. Mukat made his people slowly, everything was done slowly and everything was done perfectly. It was not like Témayawet had created his people, with webbed feet and webbed hands, with two faces—one in the back and one in the front. Mukat created them beautiful, just the way they are now with their hands, their feet, their eyes—everything beautiful, perfect.

And then Mukat said, "I wonder why Témayawet is finished. I wonder why he has done everything so quickly?" And then Témayawet told him, "How are we going to know? How are we going to see what we are doing? This is all in the dark. And so our hearts will bring out the stars and we will spray them up to the sky: and then we will have light. And we will do this now." They started to shake. Their powers shook them. They vibrated, they thundered, and then the stars came out of their mouths. "Now we shall create the sun rays. Now we shall create the rays—the gray, the white rays of the sun." And they shook, their hearts shook. They quivered from their power. Then they brought out the sun.

When everything they had done was complete Mukat knew that Témayawet's creations were not too good. When the light shown on them, then Témayawet knew that he wasn't doing things the right way. The people were not formed the right way. Mukat told Témayawet, "You were older and yet you didn't do a very good job with your creatures, with your faces that look both ways, with their stomachs both ways, their hands all closed and webbed." It wasn't like the hands that Mukat made, with the fingers, the toes. "You said you were older," he said. "How are they going to carry? How are they going to carry their baskets? How are they going to carry their load, when they have a back on each side?" Mukat said, "When they gather or when they get and go and carry their game, they will have no place to carry it."

Then Témayawet said, "This way, when they go, they don't have to turn around, they don't have to do anything. Just do it both sides, both ways, and it will save them a lot of time."

But Mukat said, "Well, look at my creatures. They can close their fingers when they are going to carry water or hold something in their hands. They can turn around, they can look around, there is nothing in the way. They can carry anything on their shoulders."

Then Témayawet said, "Our creations won't die, they will live forever."

And Mukat said, "No, they will crowd the world. That cannot be. We will have people to cure illnesses, but everyone must die."

When he sees how fine Mukat's creations are, Témayawet is ashamed of his own. He goes underground, taking his creatures with him, causing great earthquakes. But, Ménill the Moon stays with Mukat.

Ménill stayed with him. Moon Maiden, he called her. The Moon Maiden took care of the creations. She took them and showed them games, how to make this from that, painted them and colored them. She put designs on them and made them dance. She just trained them in everything she could find. Then she would sing the songs to them. They would dance and they would kneel down and touch down. It was all of them together, not just one or two. She would make them do this.

But these beings were not ordinary people. They were beings that were supernatural. They had strength, they had power. And then there was the Moon Maiden. Then Mukat passed by Ménill, the Moon Maiden. The story says that Mukat overshadowed her. Moon Maiden had the feeling that something bad had happened. She could feel it. She felt bad. She never said a word to anyone, she didn't tell him she was going to leave them. But in the night, she left and went up to the sky. She never told anyone, she just left without telling them where she was going. The next morning, they looked for the one that she took care of. They looked for her. They cried. They went here and there and looked for her but they couldn't find her. There was a pool of water. They looked and saw her in the water, and they all jumped in there. But she disappeared. They saw her reflection from the sky. They looked up and saw her. They called her down. They told her, "When you were here we were happy. Everything was beautiful and wonderful and we miss you. Come on down." She just smiled at them.

Mukat becomes a menace rather than a help to his people. He has already put death into the world, and now he gives Poison to the rattlesnake. He invents the bow and arrow and tricks people into shooting at one another. *The souls of the dead wander, lost, to the four directions, until a super being comes and shows them the way to Telmikish, the land of the dead, and he shows the people the mourning rituals for the dead. The people become angry with Mukat.*

They gathered together and they talked about how he was probably going to destroy us. They discussed this among themselves and decided they were going to get rid of him before something drastic happened to them. That was not just a few people, there was a lot of people at the time. They all agreed to do away with him.

The rituals for mourning the dead come from the Cahuilla creation myth. It concludes with an elaborate description of the death of the creator god, Mukat. No one now living is able to retell the myth in the traditional manner in the Cahuilla language.

At the beginning, the words are different. The ancient words that tell this story are different, it is deeper than what we are saying now. The ancient words were said before. "My children, my creatures, my created beings," he told each and every one, "I guess I am going to die," he said. He said, "My heart is getting cooler, my hands are getting colder." He was getting worse when he said this. Then he sang this song, "I guess I am going to die."

Mukat's long death scene takes up a major part of the myth. Much of Cahuilla ritual life connected to mourning and burial ceremonies is included in this part of the story. In his death song, Mukat enumerates all of his acts of creation and recites the names of all the plants and animals he has created. He teaches the people the sacred traditions that they are to live by.

"I feel it. I feel it. I am going to die." He was getting weaker and weaker. He said this to his creatures. Then he started to sing the song. He sang this and explained to them. He was saying this as he was singing this. His creatures sang with him. And they were singing for him as he was lying down and getting worse and worse.

Mukat is dead. This is where it ends. He is singing the song. "It is dropping on me, he is falling on me. It getting old on me," he says, as he sings. "It is getting old on me, it is getting old on me. It is falling on me. It is singing, naming all the plants, falling on me. It is dying on me." This is where it ends.

The people burn Mukat's abandoned body. From Mukat's ashes, all the food plants grow—acorns, squash, chia, sage, all the food of the Cahuilla. In his death, Mukat has given his people their way of life, their laws, customs and ceremonies, and their food.

Francisco Patencio

Francisco Patencio, a Kauisik Cahuilla of the Agua Caliente Band of
Palm Springs, was born in Chino Canyon in 1856. He became a
noted elder, religious leader, and storyteller, and his *Stories and
Legends of the Palm Springs Indians* was published in 1943. A revised
and updated version of the book, including newly discovered material, is being edited by Lowell Bean and will be published by the Agua
Caliente Cultural Center in 2007. Patencio died in 1947.

This excerpt, which tells the story of fantastical migrations of
early natives in the Inland Empire, is from *Stories and Legends of
the Palm Springs Indians*.

Some of the Early People *(Mo moh pechem)*

These people before us, they are gone. We do not know their color,
nor how they may have been, but this we know: that they were people of much power. They did not walk, if they did not want to do so,
because they had the power to rise and go through the air. They were
men like us, and had families the same as we today—only they had
much more power and could fly.

These people lived on the mountains, and called themselves *Mo moh
pechem*, which means "moaning in pain." But this does not mean that
they were sick at all—it was only a tribe name.

Now these people could not fly anywhere at any time. No, but only
after long prayer till the time came were they given the power. They did
not go to be gone a day or a year, but stayed in one place much time,
many, many years, and flew away again when the time had come to do so.

From the pass where they lived they flew to the San Fernando Mountain. This mountain they called *To to be.* From there they flew to the Cocomonga Mountain. That mountain they called *Evo quish,* meaning a stick or poker to stir the fire. From there they flew to San Gorgonio Mountain, which they called *Queri kitch,* meaning "bald" or "smooth."

From there they flew to San Jacinto Mountain. They called it *I a kitch,* meaning "smooth cliffs." There is a place near the top which has no pine trees, a place of about forty or fifty acres; right in the center of this place is a large smooth rock, about ten or fifteen feet square, not very high from the ground, about three feet. There they stayed for a long time.

From here they saw a mountain lion coming, and they said that if you saw it once, you could not see it again. But the head man of the tribe said that he could see him again. But the other said that if you see him once, you can not see him again.

The head man went and stood on the top of the rock, looking, and the people were watching from away. Then the lion leaped upon the rock before he saw the man, and they began to fight, and both died there.

Now after the head man was killed the people felt very badly, and they left that place. They did not fly, but walked down across the mountain side to Palm Canyon. Then the third head man of the tribe decided that he would not go any farther. He turned himself into a rock, and he is there in the rock yet.

The people prayed, and flew again to the end of the Santa Rosa Range. Here they found many small shells, and they called it the place of the shells. From there they flew again to the San Felipe Valley, to another open place on the plain, and here they stayed. They had lost the head men of two tribes, and so their power to go farther left them forever. They could never get it again. So they lived there and raised large families.

Juan Bautista de Anza

Juan Bautista de Anza was born in Sonora in 1736. After advancing rapidly in the army at the presidio of Fronteras, in 1772 he proposed an expedition to Alta California to the Spanish government. The request was approved, and Anza explored the area between Tubac (near present-day Tucson) and San Gabriel. Later he helped colonists settle in California to strengthen the Spanish presence there, journeying from San Gabriel to Monterey and San Francisco. He was the governor of New Mexico for ten years and died in Sonora in 1788. The route of the 1775–1776 expedition from Arizona to the San Francisco Bay Area is a National Historic Trail.

In this first excerpt from his diaries, Anza describes the San Jacinto Valley (which he calls San José). The "unfordable" Santa Ana River is described in the second excerpt; the river has changed drastically since Anza's time, now running mostly underground.

Friday, March 18, 1774

Although morning dawned with very thick clouds, we thought because it had snowed and rained so hard during the night that we should free ourselves of these elements today. With this in mind, as soon as day dawned I sent a party of six men provided with axes, to clear out, if it was necessary, the road which we must follow down the canyon which we have close by. At eight o'clock in the morning, raising our train, we all set forth on the road, which we found favorable, for only for a league was it necessary to cut here and there a tree which impeded. After this the canyon, which we followed to the north and north-northwest, kept getting wider and wider, until we reached a broad and most beautiful valley, six leagues distant from the place whence we had set out.

Through this beautiful valley, to which we gave the name of San José, runs a good-sized river, on whose banks are large, shady groves. Likewise in the mountains where the river forms there are seen pines, oaks, and various other trees. All its plain is full of flowers, fertile pastures, and other vegetation, useful for the raising of cattle, of which species as many as one might wish could be raised. And in the same way one could raise good crops, which I judge would be produced with great advantage, for although this is the cold season, from the verdure and the shadiness of the leaves there is no sign of any frost here, either now or earlier. In this place where we are today we saw some heathen women, but they did not wish to come near us, although they were coaxed in the same way [with gifts] that has been practiced at other times.

Monday, January 1, 1776

Having gone to explore this river of Santa Ana in addition to what was done yesterday, it was found to be almost unfordable for the people, not so much because of its depth as of the rapidity of its current, which upsets most of the saddle animals. For this reason it was necessary to reinforce the bridge which I made during the last journey, and also to open a road in order that our cattle might enter to cross it. These tasks could not be completed until after twelve o'clock, at which time the women were taken over first, next all the perishable things, and then the rest of the cargo and our stock, of which a horse and a cow were drowned because they did not have strength enough to withstand the force of the current....At this same time, the crossing having been completed, arrived the three soldiers whom I sent to the mission of San Gabriel on the 27th of last month for the purpose there mentioned. From the mission the father ministers sent me seventeen saddle animals. The corporal who has the mission under his command gives me the sad news that a few days ago the heathen and the reduced Indians of the mission of San Diego, together with those farther inland, attacked that mission, killed one of the missionary fathers and two servants, wounded all the few soldiers of the guard, and burned the small buildings of the pueblo.

José Romero

In an effort to bring settlers to Alta California, the Mexican government arranged an expedition in the early 1820s to examine the Cocomaricopa Trail (used for centuries by native people as a trading route) from San Gabriel to Tucson. Asked to head up the expedition, Captain José Romero successfully led his party to Tucson on his second attempt to cross the desert.

This letter, written at Palm Springs (or the "watering place of the planting fields of the Cahuillas"), illustrates Romero's difficulties on his initial attempt to traverse the trail.

Letter to Don Antonio Narbona

January 16, 1824
In an official letter of July 7, 1823, I sent you an account by special messenger via Loreto, charging that Government to forward the report I addressed to you so that it would reach your hands. In it I give you an account of all my journey, along with the Diary of the incidents of said passage. In another of the 19th of August last past, I reported to you through the same Loreto arrangement, that the Lord Governor of Alta California, Don Luis de Argüello, had called me to come to the Capital at Monterey to confer with the said Governor regarding my task.

And having discussed everything, we agreed that with forty men of this Province of Alta California in charge of the Lieutenant of the Presidio of San Diego, Don José Maria Estudillo, I would return to my province. And having departed from that capital in the month of October, I waited until the 15th of December, when, having joined the

9

forty auxiliaries I started on the José Cocomaricopa Trail, as you had advised me during my stay at your headquarters.

And having traveled a ways, guided by a Christian Indian from the Mission of San Juan Capistrano, he gave us another, opposite direction to the road we should have taken. And after traveling for three days without water for the horses, we decided to turn back, because all the horses were in no condition to travel any further, and we knew not what lay ahead of us; for not even the guide knew where he was, thus we had to turn back to a place where we arrived after three days. After having lost a number of horses for lack of water, which for drinking we did not reach for six days, although on the second day of our return it rained some, with which the animals were able to moisten their mouths a little, and got to drink some after six days, as I have related.

And finding myself at this place amid villages of friendly heathens named Cahuillas, I have availed myself of one of them to take this report to you, paying him for his trouble so that by this means and by that of the Cocomaricopas, you may be informed of our lot, for not having received any answer from you, I fear that none of my reports have reached you, much less do you know of our whereabouts.

By means of the same bearer of this, I am sending word to José Cocomaricopa to come with his people by the March moon, and I am retiring to the Mission of San Gabriel to replenish my horses and to join Captain Don Pablo de la Portilla of the Mazatlan Squadron, who is stationed with one hundred men at the Presidio of San Diego and is planning to retire next April. And I hope that you will exert your influence so that, by speeding the arrival of José Cocomaricopa, we may have some one to guide us in returning to our province. And in case he does not come I will still make my return with the said Captain, either via the lower Rio Colorado through all the Nations, which is where they robbed us, or by way of the trail of the old expeditions.

But if the said Captain has other plans, I cannot set out unless the Indian Cocomaricopa comes with his people; for these trails are very scarce of water and the horses cannot endure this, and this would mean we would perish from thirst.

The bearer of this has instructions to await an answer, which I would appreciate your sending as soon as possible. For in this land they have had three years of drought and all of the horses are dying from malnutrition. This is the cause of our having been delayed on this trip, and having had to turn back in order to rest our horses.

All of which I report to you for your superior information and final decision.

May God keep you many years,

Watering place of the planting fields of the Cahuillas, January 16, 1824,

José Romero

Horace Bell

Horace Bell (1830–1918) is alternately described as a controversial journalist, Union spy, attorney, publisher, militant political reformer, and memoirist. Leaving the Indiana of his youth for the goldfields of California, he arrived in Los Angeles in 1852 and chronicled the region's colorful life, which included fandangos, bullfights, ethnic tensions, and much violence.

This excerpt from *Reminiscences of a Ranger*, a memoir of Bell's experiences as a member of a volunteer mounted police force known as the Los Angeles Rangers, describes tensions between the Lugo family, owners of the wealthy San Bernardino rancho, and the local law. See José del Carmen Lugo's take on the events in the excerpt from his *Vida de un Ranchero*, following this selection.

from *Reminiscences of a Ranger*

November 12, 1851, late of a bright moonlight evening, standing alone at the door of his office, Main street, where now is the Oriental, Benjamin Hayes was shot at by some one within three feet, on horseback. The ball, says the *Star*, "passed through the rim of his hat and lodged in the wall on the opposite side of the room, perforating in its progress the door, which is fully an inch in thickness. The assassin (?) then instantly galloped off. A party of three, including the Sheriff, J. R. Barton, tracked him about ten miles to a house where they were received by five or six men on horseback, who charged upon them, fired several shots, and drove them from the ground. The sheriff deemed it prudent to return to the city. He did so, obtained a posse, went back to the place of encounter, and made a search that proved ineffectual. It has always been believed that this assault was intended for another individual."

So writeth the *Centennial Historian,* and hereby hangeth a tale of more than ordinary interest, of bloody import. Notwithstanding this chronicler is forced to take issue with his respected and departed friend, the lamented historian aforesaid, and maintain the truth to be that Benjamin Hayes was the very person intended to be assassinated on the occasion above referred to in quotation, and the reason thereof to be that Judge Hayes was then the legal luminary of the City and County of the Angels, and was engaged in the prosecution of two of the numerous Lugos, charged with murdering some Americans in the Cajon Pass in San Bernardino county, and it was possibly thought best by the friends of the accused to end the prosecution by ending the prosecuting attorney, hence the attempted assassination. Now the reader can easily surmise why it was that the party of gringos under the *most useful man* went to old man Lugo's and their inquisitorial intentions on that visit and the very delicate, not to say dangerous, position of Bill on that occasion, and his satisfactory definition of his position in his successful encounter with Pete Monroe, mentioned in the preceding chapter.

Sometime early in 1851, the Indians raided the San Bernardino rancho, then the property of the Lugo family, a branch of which occupied the ranch.

The successful raiders drove off a herd of gentle horses, and went out through the Cajon Pass. Two of the Lugos, with half a dozen of their dependents, followed on the fresh trail of the desert Indians, and in the Cajon they found some four or five Americans, and one half-breed Cherokee Indian. The Cherokee being the only one of the party who either spoke or understood Spanish, in response to inquiries, informed the Lugos that there were only three Indians engaged in driving off the herd, and that they (the party) never suspected that they were other than *vaqueros* legitimately engaged. The Lugo party pressed on, overtook the raiders at the Point of Rocks on the Mojave, and at once, and without counting noses, charged them, and to their intense chagrin and astonishment found the party to consist of some twenty warriors, instead of three. A fierce conflict ensued, hand to hand, in which three of the Lugo party were killed, and several Indians were made to kiss the desert sands. Fortunately the Lugos, armed with Colt revolvers, achieved a splendid victory over the Indians and recovered the entire herd. On their triumphal return with the gory scalps of their enemies dangling at their saddle-bows, they found the same small party yet in the same camp, when the chief Lugo demanded of the Cherokee why he had deceived them about the number of the Indians. The Cherokee replied that he was anxious to see them recover their stock, and was afraid to tell the truth, knowing that they would be too cowardly to follow a party of Indians respectable in numbers. This brought on words, which ended in the Lugo shooting the Cherokee dead on the spot. A short, sharp and decisive conflict then ensued, which resulted in the Americans being entirely wiped out, and hence the prosecution against the Lugos and the attempted assassination of the district attorney, Benjamin Hayes. The Lugos were finally tried and acquitted, the pioneer lawyer (Brent) who defended them receiving, as the writer has been informed, $20,000 for his fee—surely a fair legal starter in a small frontier town.

José del Carmen Lugo

José del Carmen Lugo was born in Los Angeles in 1813. He, along with his brothers and one of his cousins, was granted Rancho San Bernardino in 1842 by the Mexican governor of California after the secularization of the missions. After numerous local quarrels, in September 1851 the Lugos sold the rancho to a company of Mormon pioneers. Lugo retired to Los Angeles.

In this excerpt from his *Vida de un Ranchero*, Lugo talks about the quarrels that eventually prompted him to sell Rancho San Bernardino. For another version of the events of that year, see the excerpt from Horace Bell's *Reminiscences of a Ranger*, which precedes this excerpt.

from *Vida de un Ranchero*

In May, 1851, I received word at my ranch at San Bernardino that some Texans were coming up along the river from Jurupa, heading for my place. According to the report, they were murderers and thieves who had come from the placer mines, robbing and killing people along the way.

I learned that they had been at the home of Don Luis Rubidoux, and he had begged them to spare him because he was a poor man; that farther on they would find me, a rich man, who had received $13,000.00 at my home. They left him and proceeded toward my ranch. On this day I was conducting a stock roundup when the word came. I went to a military camp that was on my ranch in search of the captain to have him aid me in withstanding these evildoers. I found no one but his lieutenant.

15

This troop was stationed on my ranch to guard against the Indian Chaguanosos and other thieves who were entering the valley by the *Cajón*. All I could get from the lieutenant was that if I wished to remain in his camp I might do so, but that he was not authorized to take the troops away from there. As I needed help for the protection of my home and belongings, as well as my gentle horses and so on, his offer was of no value to me, so I set out to hunt assistance elsewhere.

I then ordered the Indian captain, Juan Antonio, with his men and four servants of my own to guard my house, while I and three boys went to hide the horses. I hid them in a thicket and returned home. On arriving there my people were already fighting the highwaymen who entered the house, having broken down the doors, and were looking for chests and so on. Everything that could be carried away was stolen, that is my riding saddles and such things, my ropes and so on—to the value of $1,500 or $2,000.

The evildoers had arrived and committed their outrages before Juan Antonio and his people had reached the place. These latter went in chase of the robbers, but they succeeded in escaping with their booty. However, they were overtaken and surrounded on a logging road near Yuciapa, which they mistook for the real road. There was a skirmish there in which Juan Antonio's lieutenant was killed. The Indians climbed the slopes of the cañon and from there killed with their arrows the thieves who numbered twelve or thirteen.

Shortly after they came to my house. I was there then, and they told me what had happened to those villains. Of my effects, I recovered only a pair of pantaloons I found tossed on the hillside. Everything else had been taken by the Indians who had come at the call of Juan Antonio from the three villages, to the number of a hundred or more.

Next day, Señor Estevan C. Foster arrived with a great number of Californians who were pursuing the thieves. With Sr. Foster came the commander of the troop, angry with me because I had incited the Indians against the evildoers. He even wished to arrest me, but did not dare to do so in view of the people there who were on my side. They gave him to understand that before taking matters into my own hands I had gone to his camp to seek aid and had been refused.

That same day I left for Los Angeles to give a formal account of what had occurred. A committee was named to go to the scene of the events to make a full investigation. This was done, and when it was ended I went to Los Angeles with the committee.

During my stay in the city I received word that members of the troop and other foreigners went at night to insult both the Indians and my servants for having killed those bandits. I hastened back to the ranch, and within two or three days, for this reason, the troops were withdrawn from that place.

My branding-place for cattle was near their camp. I went there with my people to work, carrying all my arms and artillery. I continued working there through May, June, and July, on account of the inconveniences the troopers had caused me. That same year I decided to sell the ranch and end the constant danger to my life. I sold it to a company of Mormons who came, and retired to Los Angeles. Since that time I have continued to live here.

Marc Reisner

Marc Reisner was born in Minnesota in 1948. After graduating from Earlham College, he worked for the Natural Resources Defense Council. An environmentalist and writer, he is best known for his 1986 book *Cadillac Desert: The American West and Its Disappearing Water*. He died in San Anselmo, California, in 2000.

This excerpt from *Cadillac Desert* is about the founding of San Bernardino by Mormons.

from *Cadillac Desert*

After fleeing Illinois for Utah, the Mormons had always been obsessed with finding escape routes to the sea. The first irrigation canals were still being dug beside the Wasatch Range when Brigham Young dispatched a party of his most loyal disciples, in 1851, to follow Jedediah Smith's old route to the coast. When they crossed the San Bernardino Mountains, they found themselves in a huge arid basin that reminded them of home and was only a day or two from the sea. The streams were less reliable than those in Utah—the southern mountains received a scantier snowpack that never lasted halfway through the summer—but the San Bernardinos got decent winter rain, and artesian wells below them flowed like geysers. With money earned by selling food and supplies at usurious prices to adventurers bound through Utah for the goldfields, the Mormons purchased a huge chunk of land from an old Spanish rancho. The soil was good, the climate was ideal, and no one was better at irrigation farming than Mormons. Before long they were supplying much of the basin with food. In 1857, the U.S. Cavalry marched on Utah and Brigham Young ordered all distant settlements abandoned, but the Mormons' achievement had left its mark. A Presbyterian colony was soon established nearby, then a Quaker colony, then an ethnic colony of Germans. In this freakish climate—semitropical but dry, ocean-cooled but lavishly sunny—you could grow almost anything. Corn and cabbages sprouted next to oranges, avocados, artichokes, and dates. The capitalists of San Francisco did not remain oblivious; the Southern Pacific ran a spur line to Los Angeles in 1867, finally linking it to the rest of the world. On this same line, huge San Bernardino Valencias found their way to the 1884 World's Fair in New Orleans, where they attracted crowds. No one could imagine *oranges* grown in the western United States. It was then and there, more or less, that the phenomenon of modern Los Angeles began.

Charles Nordhoff

Born in 1830 in Germany, Charles Nordhoff came with his parents to the United States in 1835. A New York journalist, whaler, fisher, social commentator, and travel writer, Nordhoff wrote about his travels to California in *Harper's Magazine* and the *New York Tribune*, later expanding these pieces and publishing them in *California for Health, Pleasure, and Residence*. The book was so helpful in bringing tourists to Southern California on the new railroads that Southern Pacific reprinted it in 1880. Nordhoff died in 1901.

This excerpt from *California for Health, Pleasure, and Residence* describes San Bernardino in the 1870s.

Farming in San Bernardino

San Bernardino, which is a point seldom visited by tourists, and but little known to the Eastern settler or farmer, lies sixty miles east from Los Angeles, under the mountain range from which it takes its name. It has a climate more charming and healthful in winter than Los Angeles, and no hotter in summer; but there have been cases here, in the low grounds, of a mild type of intermittent fever. This is not prevalent, however, and occurs, I was told by an intelligent physician of the place, chiefly among the class who drink the strong grape brandy of the region and live otherwise carelessly.

The San Bernardino Valley, which contains 36,000 acres, was bought many years ago by the Mormons. In 1861 Brigham Young recalled his disciples to Salt Lake, but a large number refused to go from here, and are still living here in peace. They call themselves

Josephites, I believe, and are an industrious, quiet people. The valley they bought is abundantly watered, and appears to me one of the most fruitful parts of the Southern country. All the fruits and grains which are raised in Los Angeles grow here as well, some even better. I have not seen anywhere more thrifty orange and olive trees than at one or two farms near this town.

The valley has not only abundance of running water, constant the year round, but a large number of spouting artesian wells have been bored; they get flowing water of very good quality at from one hundred and fifty to three hundred feet, and it is usual to make a seven-inch bore, which gives water enough to irrigate a large space of ground.

The country between Los Angeles and San Bernardino varies greatly in quality. Some parts are very fine. About Ruebottom's, where stage passengers stop to dine, there is first-class farming land; ten miles beyond you reach the famous Cocamungo vineyard, which produces a great deal of what seems to me a poor and very spirituous wine, and also a good deal of brandy. Beyond that you cross for ten miles a tract which was once, I believe, fertile, but has been covered by a wash of boulders, stones, and gravel from the mountains. Then you enter the valley after which San Bernardino is named, which, with the adjoining foot-hills, contains a great tact of first-class farming and orchard land—perhaps as much as half a million of acres, most of it easily watered. A part of this is in private hands, some in considerable tracts; but a large part of it is Congress land, now reserved from entry until the Southern Pacific Railroad shall have located its alternate sections, but likely to be open to entry at the double minimum rate within the year 1872.

In the mean time I noticed that farmers are ploughing (early in February) large spaces of this Congress land, and sowing it with wheat and barley, intending to get a crop off before it is open to entry, and to buy the land of Government or of the railroad company by-and-by. Unimproved farming land near the town, with water easily accessible, is sold for from three to ten dollars per acre, in tracts of from fifty to one hundred and sixty acres. Improved farms are not readily bought, as there are but a few, and they are too valuable to sell. A company of Costa Ricans have recently bought 2,600 acres near the town and intend, I believe, to raise sugar-cane as well as sub-tropical fruits; and, as they have capital, they will, no doubt, succeed.

Fencing costs one dollar and fifty cents per rod, for a proper board fence; lumber, such as is used for houses and fencing, twenty-five dollars per thousand. Common farm-horses cost from twenty-five to fifty dollars, and cows thirty dollars. One of the oldest settlers in the place, a very intelligent practical farmer, told me that irrigation was not necessary for grain crops. They sow barley here on the first of January, and, after taking off a crop of from forty to sixty bushels to the acre, plant corn on the same land, and get their second crop fully ripened, and often as much as sixty or seventy bushels per acre. On new land, one hundred bushels of corn or seventy bushels of barley is not an uncommon crop; and I was shown a large field which for seven successive years has given a crop of barley and one of corn every year. Alfalfa is cut seven times in the year, and yields from ten to fifteen tons per acre; it is fed to milch cows and to plough and hogs keep fat on it in this climate.

Where nature has done so much, you would perhaps expect to find that man had made a beautiful garden of this valley. You would be grievously disappointed. Cultivation is too often careless; men live for years on a place without planting the most valuable fruit-trees; and there is a lack of neatness in the farm surroundings, and an air of shabby thriftlessness about the houses, which disappoint an Eastern man. I supposed at first that the people were sluggish and thriftless because they lay out of the way of a market; but this is not true. San Bernardino has an important traffic with Arizona. I found a miller who has to buy wheat in San Francisco to keep his mill running; oats, which grow perfectly here, were brought from the upper country, for this place, in the same boat in which I came to San Pedro; barley brings two cents a pound here, and only one cent and a half in San Francisco; and I believe there is but one market garden near the town, though a man might make a small fortune in a year from vegetables and strawberries. "There is no market for a man who has nothing to sell" is an old adage.

Of course this unthrift is not universal. I found several well-kept farms near the town; and their owners were all doing well and making a good deal of money. In fact, wherever I found a farmer with produce to sell, he amazed me by telling me how readily he found a profitable market. Wine, from its bulky nature, is perhaps the most difficult article to sell in such a place as this; but a farmer who makes 2,500 gallons a year assured me that he sold it all, on the ground, for fifty cents per gallon; and he had not even a barrel left over a year old.

As you drive over the uncultivated part of the plain you see occasionally the white floury efflorescence of alkali. Frequently a farm would extend into the midst of this alkali land; and I was assured by the farmers that with proper handling it became, after the first crop, their best land. They plough in barley-straw, which rots quickly, and, they say, so ameliorates the soil, or decomposes the alkali, that the following winter they may put in barley, wheat, or corn.

Of course, where irrigation is practiced, the farmer is tolerably independent of droughts; but much of the farm land in this valley is not irrigated; and farmers told me that on such land they counted upon seven good seasons in ten years. The grasshopper, which did some damage last year in all this Southern country, comes, it is said, after a dry season. Some farmers thought that grasshoppers could not breed on ploughed land; I do not know how this may be, and they spoke from but a limited experience; but it seems probable, from what I was told, that the scourge is lessened when the soil is frequently and thoroughly cultivated.

The neighborhood of San Bernardino appears to me an admirable country for thrifty farmers. Land is cheaper than near Los Angeles; water is abundant; there is still much valuable Congress and railroad land; there is a good market for all products; the soil is almost universally excellent, and I do not doubt that a thrifty New England or New York farmer would here raise a large family in comfort and independence on forty or at most eighty acres of land; and if he planted ten or twelve acres in oranges and walnuts, would, in ten years, have a handsome income with trifling labor for the rest of his life. By the time the valley is settled, the Southern Pacific Railroad, whose engineers are already working this way, will run through or near it, and the Arizona trade, which it already possesses, it will not lose.

It struck me here, as elsewhere in this lower country, that the foot-hills contain the best lands for thrifty farmers. The soil is usually loose, though probably of less lasting fertility; water comes from the mountains; the views are enchanting; and the orange will certainly do better there than on the plain. The old Mission of San Bernardino, now a shapeless ruin, lies high up among the foot-hills; and 2000 feet above San Bernardino, in the San Gorgonio Pass, lies Dr. Edgar's vineyard, which produces the best light wine I have tasted in California—proving once more, what is now generally suspected by the thoughtful vine-growers of this State, that the hill and mountain sides will produce the best wine here.

Farmers in this country make two mistakes not uncommon to American farmers, but less excusable here than elsewhere. They try to own too much land, and they are content with shabby houses. Eighty acres will make an industrious farmer rich in this climate; his living ought to cost him very little money after the first year, for he may have fresh vegetables out of his garden every month in the year; of potatoes, one hundred bushels to the acre is but a moderate crop; the tomato-vine bears for two or three years in succession; every fruit-tree of the temperate zone bears here far more quickly than with us in the East; and when the pepper-tree and the acacia and eucalyptus grow from ten to twenty feet in a single season, there is no excuse for a lack of shade about the house.

As to the house itself, the family lives so much out-of-doors, and the weather is so fine all the year round, that a dwelling appears, no doubt, a secondary consideration. But it is abominable to see well-to-do farmers living, as they do hereabout, in shabby little shanties, and to find the rarest and loveliest flowers adorning what looks to an Eastern man more like a pig-pen than like a house. No doubt many of the people of whom I complain came hither poor, and have become accustomed to live as they continue to do; but half a dozen thrifty, neat, New England families would make such a change in the appearance of San Bernardino as would amaze the old settlers—unless, indeed, they too fell into the ways of their predecessors.

Fences and houses are best built by contract. Ploughing can also be done by contract. The common farm laborers are Indians. They are docile, know how to handle horses, and are used for every kind of labor. They receive from fifty cents to one dollar and twenty-five cents per day, and are a useful people; their only faults being a propensity to get drunk on Saturday night—not irregulary during the week, however—and to wander from place to place. There are but few Chinese at San Bernardino.

San Bernardino has a Methodist, Presbyterian, and a Mormon, as well as a Catholic Church. It has also, what you would hardly find in a town of its size and character outside of California, a large, well-built, and well-kept school-house. The school-houses in this State are a constant surprise to an Eastern traveler. You find them everywhere; and if you are interested in education, you will easily discover that the people take great interest and pride in their public schools. The school building at San Bernardino would be creditable to an Eastern town of 10,000 inhabitants.

Artesian wells are made here by the simple pressure of a lever upon a wrought-iron tube. The double sheet-iron tube, seven inches in diameter, costs one dollar per foot here; and for boring, in which a sand pump is used to bring up the contents of the pipe, the charge is one dollar per foot for the first hundred feet, and fifty cents per foot additional for every hundred feet lower. The water usually flows with force enough to carry it through a two-story house, and in such abundance that is used for irrigation.

Near San Bernardino lies the land of the Riverside Colony. The Company owns 8,000 acres; it has brought water down in a flume, at considerable cost, enough to irrigate not only this tract, but 15,000 acres more of a plain lying somewhat lower down. The land has been but lately open to settlement; and as it is a large, open, treeless plain, with but a few small houses scattered over it, it does not look very inviting. The company offer land for from twenty to forty dollars per acre; and the charge for water would, the agent told me, be about two dollars per annum per acre. The land is good, though I think a little less kindly than that of the valley and foot-hills of San Bernardino. I have no doubt that it is good wheat and fruit land, and it offers some advantages to persons who desire to settle in a colony. There is already a school-house, a post-office, and, of course, an abundant supply of water. But the price asked for land is high for this region, and the company propose no restrictions about liquor-selling, nor conditions for the planting of shade-trees, or the style of improvements—nor, indeed, do they stipulate that a purchaser shall improve at all.

I was not surprised to be told that several of the settlers had bought ten or twenty acres of the company lands, but were raising a crop from two or three hundred acres of the adjoining government and railroad land. The agent assured me that ten acres would support a family, and that more than twenty acres were not necessary to a farmer. But he is mistaken; no man should come out to this part of the country to make his living from the land and get less than forty, or, better yet, eighty acres. It is true that when his orange, or olive, or walnut, or almond orchard comes into bearing, he will have a handsome income from ten acres; but for this he must wait at least eight or ten years, and he must live in the mean time.

There is no doubt that Riverside has, in common with the surrounding country, uncommon advantages for consumptives and persons subject to bronchial troubles. The air is dry and bracing, and the temperature uniform and equal. One may live out-of-doors almost every day of the year in this Southern California, and I have seen, on my journey, dozens of people deeply gone in consumption when they came here, who had been restored to health by residence in some one of the southern counties, or in sheltered spots like San Rafael, north even of San Francisco.

It will, perhaps, occur to you, as it did to me, to ask what people do on such a great plain for fire-wood. They plant live fences of willow or cotton-wood, which grow so rapidly that after two years a man may cut from his cotton-wood fence not only fire-wood, but poles to support the overladen fruit-trees. This is the common custom about San Bernardino, where several thousand acres have been newly inclosed this winter— how droll it seems to call it winter, while I am writing in an open porch, and in the shade! You may see everywhere long rows of gaunt poles, from three to six inches in diameter, stuck into the ground, which will presently take root, throw out leaves, and become substantial trees; and these are at once fence and fire-wood.

George Weeks

George Weeks (1851–unknown) was among the many sufferers of tuberculosis who came to the Inland Empire for its dry climate. Traveling from New York in San Bernardino in 1876, he stayed at a sanatorium in the area for several months. He later moved to San Francisco to work for the *Chronicle* and went on to establish papers in Bakersfield and Alameda.

Weeks describes his time in the San Bernardino sanatorium in this humorous excerpt from his 1928 memoir of his journey west, *California Copy*.

from *California Copy*

The Timely Rainstorm Which Resulted in the One-Lunger Becoming a Herder of Bees and of Cattle.

The Sanitarium was a typical California farm house, two stories in height, with porch extending entirely across the front. A long extension had been constructed in the rear, the upper portion of which had a hallway leading down the center. Cubicles opened at regular intervals on either side, each roomlet being large enough to accommodate one half-size bed, one chair, one washstand, one small bureau, one set of hooks for hanging clothes, one tallow candle, one emaciated invalid of the scarecrow style, of which I was said to be a type. None of the things known as necessary modern conveniences were supplied. There was an old-fashioned zinc bathtub in a nook under a stairway, which could be used (but seldom was) by bribing an Indian to bring enough cold water from the zanja, and persuading the Chinese cook to let one have a bucket of hot water from the kitchen boiler. A bathing pool of a sort had been made in the zanja by putting logs across a narrow portion, thus backing the water up ten or fifteen feet until it was waist deep. Night was the usual time selected for using Nature's bathroom. In hot weather such a dip was most welcome and refreshing, but in cold weather—for it does get cold in California at certain seasons and certain altitudes, as will be noted *in extenso* further on—B-r-r-r-r!

The man who planned the house had apparently never heard anything about the desirability, to say nothing of the necessity, of ventilation in a human habitation, that word having to all appearances been omitted from his vocabulary as well as his house plans. This was well enough, to an extent, so far as the sleeping cubicles were concerned, for one could open his window, support the sash on a stick, and so enjoy fresh air, and on occasion rain, to the content of both heart and lungs. But it was not well enough in the sitting-room and "parlor," as also the dining-room on the first floor, especially in weather cold enough to make a fire necessary for comfort, and at this elevation—some 3500 feet—the winter and spring months were productive of much temperature of the kind, with corresponding discomfort. For many years it was a popular shibboleth with ultra-Californians, of whom I became an ardent one until I learned better, that in that so-called semitropical climate it was not necessary to make any provision for warming one's habitation. This doubtless came from the Spanish occupants of the region, since the same idea prevails in Mexico, where I was later to learn that it was regarded as highly unhealthful to live in a warm room. No provision is made for fires, beyond the one tendered me by a dear old lady who kept a *meson* for travelers in a mountain village in Durango, and who, upon my asking her for a fire one bitter cold evening, politely told me that I might build one anywhere in my room that I wished—in a corner, in the center, or wherever. Which I proceeded to do, and slept comfortably!

Morning and evening all gathered in the two rooms downstairs. Fires were built, and the patients huddled about the fireplaces with all the patience possible, and breathed the same air over and over again, poison laden as it was. If they had all been in good health, it would have been bad enough, but when nine-tenths of them were afflicted with decaying lungs, the atmosphere was merely a mass of disease germs. Draughts were rigidly excluded, and if one dared open a door for a minute or two for a breath of fresh air, a loud protest went up, and the door was quickly closed.

But the nights—oh, those nights! Those nightmare nights! How can they be described? Most of the patients retired by nine o'clock, and from then until morning there was an almost constant chorus of coughing from the sleeping-rooms. First the occupant of one cubicle, often enough myself, would have a paroxysm. It would be answered from another cubicle far down the hall. Then another in another direction would join in, and back and forth the pulmonary sphere would be tossed all night, making sound sleep impossible even for those not suffering from such attacks. In the morning all arose, unless too feeble, wearied from the fruitless attempt to secure rest, and gathered about the fires in the sitting-rooms. Each had his tale to tell of the troubles and sufferings of the night. In fact, there was no other topic of conversation, since the place was isolated and news was not only scarce but absolutely nonexistent. If it was a cloudy or rainy day, which occurred with altogether too great frequency during my own brief stay at the "*health* resort," we all sat about the fire, gloomy, despondent, and disheartened, stewing in the poisons of our own emanations, waiting for what most of us knew was coming— and *did* come in the majority of cases! The end!

When the sun shone, all who were able sought warm nooks on the porches, or went out on the plain away from the trees where they could obtain the full benefit of the life-giving rays of the sun. This plain was a mass of boulders, with scattered brush, and more or less comfortable and secluded lounging places were readily found.

Unfortunately, during the fortnight which I remained at the Sanitarium, fully half the days were rainy, foggy, or cloudy, with accompanying aggravation of one's cough and depression of spirits. I came as near losing heart during this period as at any time during all my illness. There were other contributing causes, mental ones, all of which led me one day to say to myself: "I shall surely die if I stay in this h—ospital any longer!" (No, I did not use the word I have written, but another beginning with an "h"!)

The region eastward of the Sanitarium was practically unsettled. Only two small ranches, so I was told, lay between it and the impassable mountains ten or twelve miles distant. One day, when especially blue and downhearted, I concluded to do a little exploring in the direction of the desert which lay beyond the range. Most of the region was covered with a heavy growth of chamiso, through which ran several trails. I walked and rested at short intervals, paying no attention to the sky, absorbed as I was in my gloomy thoughts, until suddenly I noticed that the light of the sun had been cut off, heavy clouds were lowering, and rain threatened. Then the threat was fulfilled, and the water began to come down. I was not far from the fringe of trees lining the zanja, and went thither to seek what shelter I might be able to find beneath them.

I struck a faint footpath which led to a log laid across the stream for the accommodation of travelers, and followed it, hoping that some habitation might be near. I crossed the zanja and passed through the fringe of trees. No sooner had I appeared in the open than a great dog came dashing toward me, in full cry. I remained motionless, talking soothingly to the animal, which made sudden rushes at me. Then I noticed a dilapidated, unpainted, crude frontier shack almost hidden in a cluster of great cottonwood trees some distance from the stream. The barking of the dog attracted attention, for a man appeared on the porch, called the dog off, and shouted: "Hullo there, stranger! Come on in out of the rain!"

I needed no second invitation, but went in without delay, as the rain was now coming down in torrents and in a few minutes I would have been soaked to the skin, as I had no protecting outer coat or umbrella. I was warmly welcomed, as is customary on the frontier, and was told to step up to the immense fireplace which occupied nearly the entire end of the room and was filled with blazing logs. It did not take me long to get well warmed, for I had been chilled through and through. I got as close to the flames as possible.

We introduced ourselves, talked awhile, and became acquainted. It appeared that we had mutual friends in the East. It developed that he was "holding down" a small cattle and bee ranch, had a wife and baby, and that his business took him away from his lonely home so much that he thought it might be well to have some one around to look after things. There were many Indians passing back and forth over the trail to the desert, and sometimes they were not very desirable company—depending upon the amount of "tiswin" they had been able to obtain.

The upshot was that I agreed to make my home with him, do what chores I might be able to manage, and receive my keep in return. The Sanitarium saw me but once again at that time. Next day I had my luggage hauled to the cattle-bee ranch, and proceeded to make myself as comfortable as possible in the three-room 18 x 20 shack.

There is a "moral" to this recital which the reader may possibly have discerned by this time. It is: Sufferers from tubercular trouble should never "herd" together. They should refrain from talking about their condition, and should as far as possible provide some mental (as also bodily) occupation which will distract their attention from themselves.

Keep away from a Sanitarium! And from other One-Lungers!

Helen Hunt Jackson

Helen Hunt Jackson was born in 1830 in Massachusetts. Her tremendous literary output included poetry, fiction, essays, travel sketches, newspaper articles, children's stories, and social commentary. After her 1881 book *A Century of Dishonor,* an indictment of the U.S. government's Indian policies, she received a federal commission to report on the Mission Indians of Southern California; her 1885 novel *Ramona* was an emotional appeal to the public about the Indians' plight—propaganda meant to have a political impact. Her continued efforts for the rights of Indians were cut short by her death in San Francisco in 1885.

Set in locations throughout the Inland Empire in the final days of the Spanish Californio aristocracy, *Ramona* tells the tragic tale of love between Ramona Ortegna, a half-Indian woman raised on a rancho by wealthy California Mexicans, and Alessandro Assis, an itinerant Indian laborer whose father is chief of the Temecula Indians. Against the wishes of Ramona's caretaker, the two decide secretly to elope; in this excerpt Ramona waits for Alessandro to come and take her away.

from *Ramona*

Alessandro passed his hand slowly over his forehead, as if trying to collect his thoughts before speaking, all the while keeping his eyes fixed on Ramona, with the same anguished look, convulsively holding both her hands in his.

"Señorita," he said, "my Señorita!" Then he stopped. His tongue seemed to refuse him utterance; and this voice,—this strange, hard, unresonant voice,—whose voice was it? Not Alessandro's.

"My Señorita," he began again, "I could not go without one sight of your face; but when I was here, I had not courage to go near the house. If you had not come, I should have gone back without seeing you."

Ramona heard these words in fast-deepening terror. What did they mean? Her look seemed to suggest a new thought to Alessandro.

"Heavens, Señorita!" he cried, "have you not heard? Do you not know what has happened?"

"I know nothing, love," answered Ramona. "I have heard nothing since you went away. For ten days I have been sure you were dead; but to-night something told me that you were near, and I came to meet you."

At the first words of Ramona's sentence, Alessandro threw his arms around her again. As she said "love," his whole frame shook with emotion.

"My Señorita!" he whispered, "my Señorita! how shall I tell you! How shall I tell you!"

"What is there to tell, Alessandro?" she said. "I am afraid of nothing, now that you are here, and not dead, as I thought."

But Alessandro did not speak. It seemed impossible. At last, straining her closer to his breast, he cried: "Dearest Señorita! I feel as if I should die when I tell you,—I have no home; my father is dead; my people are driven out of their village. I am only a beggar now, Señorita; like those you used to feed and pity in Los Angeles convent!" As he spoke the last words, he reeled, and, supporting himself against the tree, added: "I am not strong, Señorita; we have been starving."

Ramona's face did not reassure him. Even in the dusk he could see its look of incredulous horror. He misread it.

"I only came to look at you once more," he continued. "I will go now. May the saints bless you, my Señorita, always. I think the Virgin sent you to me to-night. I should never have seen your face if you had not come."

While he was speaking, Ramona had buried her face in his bosom. Lifting it now, she said, "Did you mean to leave me to think you were dead, Alessandro?"

"I thought that the news about our village must have reached you," he said, "and that you would know I had no home, and could not come, to seem to remind you of what you had said. Oh, Señorita, it was little enough I had before to give you! I don't know how I dared to believe that you could come to be with me; but I loved you so much, I had thought of many things I could do; and—" lowering his voice and speaking almost sullenly—"it is the saints, I believe, who have punished me thus for having resolved to leave my people, and take all I had for myself and you. Now they have left me nothing," and he groaned.

"Who?" cried Ramona. "Was there a battle? Was your father killed?" She was trembling with horror.

"No," answered Alessandro. "There was no battle. There would have been, if I had had my way; but my father implored me not to resist. He said it would only make it worse for us in the end. The sheriff, too, he begged me to let it all go on peaceably, and help him keep the people quiet. He felt terribly to have to do it. It was Mr. Rothsaker, from San Diego. We had often worked for him on his ranch. He knew all about us. Don't you recollect, Señorita, I told you about him,—how fair he always was, and kind too? He has the biggest wheat-ranch in Cajon; we've harvested miles and miles of wheat for him. He said he would have rather died, almost, than have had it to do; but if we resisted, he would have to order his men to shoot. He had twenty men with him. They thought there would be trouble; and well they might,—turning a whole village full of men and women and children out of their houses, and driving them off like foxes. If it had been any man but Mr. Rothsaker, I would have shot him dead, if I had hung for it; but I knew if he thought we must go, there was no help for us."

"But, Alessandro," interrupted Ramona, "I can't understand. Who was it made Mr. Rothsaker do it? Who has the land now?"

"I don't know who they are," Alessandro replied, his voice full of anger and scorn. "They're Americans—eight or ten of them. They all got together and brought a suit, they call it, up in San Francisco; and it was decided in the court that they owned all our land. That was all Mr. Rothsaker could tell about it. It was the law, he said, and nobody could go against the law."

"Oh," said Ramona, "that's the way the Americans took so much of the Señora's land away from her. It was in the court up in San Francisco; and they decided that miles and miles of her land, which the General had always had, was not hers at all. They said it belonged to the United States Government."

"They are a pack of thieves and liars, every one of them!" cried Alessandro. "They are going to steal all the land in this country; we might all just as well throw ourselves into the sea, and let them have it. My father had been telling me this for years. He saw it coming; but I did not believe him. I did not think men could be so wicked; but he was right. I am glad he is dead. That is the only thing I have to be thankful for now. One day I thought he was going to get well, and I prayed to the Virgin not to let him. I did not want him to live. He never knew anything clear after they took him out of his house. That was before I got there. I found him sitting on the ground outside. They said it was the sun that had turned him crazy; but it was not. It was his heart breaking in his bosom. He would not come out of his house, and the men lifted him up and carried him out by force, and threw him on the ground; and then they threw out all the furniture we had; and when he saw them doing that, he put his hands up to his head, and called out, 'Alessandro! Alessandro!' and I was not there! Señorita, they said it was a voice to make the dead hear, that he called with; and nobody could stop him. All that day and all the night he kept on calling. God! Señorita, I wonder I did not die when they told me! When I got there, some one had built up a little booth of tule over his head, to keep the sun off. He did not call any more, only for water, water. That was what made them think the sun had done it. They did all they could; but it was such a dreadful time, nobody could do much; the sheriff's men were in great hurry; they gave no time. They said the people must all be off in two days. Everybody was running hither and thither. Everything out of the houses in piles on the ground. The people took all the roofs off their houses too. They were made of the tule reeds; so they would do again. Oh, Señorita, don't ask me to tell you any more! It is like death. I can't!"

Ramona was crying bitterly. She did not know what to say. What was love, in face of such calamity? What had she to give to a man stricken like this?

"Don't weep, Señorita," said Alessandro, drearily. "Tears kill one, and do no good."

"How long did your father live?" asked Ramona, clasping her arms closer around his neck. They were sitting on the ground now, and Ramona, yearning over Alessandro, as if she were the strong one and he the one to be sheltered, had drawn his head to her bosom, caressing him as if he had been hers for years. Nothing could have so clearly shown his enfeebled and benumbed condition, as the manner in which he received these caresses, which once would have made him beside himself with joy. He leaned against her breast as a child might.

"He! He died only four days ago. I stayed to bury him, and then I came away. I have been three days on the way; the horse, poor beast, is almost weaker than I. The Americans took my horse," Alessandro said.

"Took your horse!" cried Ramona, aghast. "Is that the law, too?"

"So Mr. Rothsaker told me. He said the judge had said he must take enough of our cattle and horses to pay all it had cost for the suit up in San Francisco. They didn't reckon the cattle at what they were worth, I thought; but they said cattle were selling very low now. There were not enough in all the village to pay it, so we had to make it up in horses; and they took mine. I was not there the day they drove the cattle away, or I would have put a ball into Benito's head before any American should ever have had him to ride. But I was over in Pachanga with my father. He would not stir a step for anybody but me; so I led him all the way; and then after he got there he was so ill I never left him a minute. He did not know me any more, nor know anything that had happened. I built a little hut of tule, and he lay on the ground till he died. When I put him in his grave, I was glad."

"In Temecula?" asked Ramona.

"In Temecula!" exclaimed Alessandro, fiercely. "You don't seem to understand, Señorita. We have no right in Temecula, not even to our graveyard full of the dead. Mr. Rothsaker warned us all not to be hanging about there; for he said the men who were coming in were a rough set, and they would shoot any Indian at sight, if they saw him trespassing on their property."

"Their property!" ejaculated Ramona.

"Yes; it is theirs," said Alessandro, doggedly. "That is the law. They've got all the papers to show it. That is what my father always said,—if the Señor Valdez had only given him a paper! But they never did in those days. Nobody had papers. The American law is different."

"It's a law of thieves!" cried Ramona.

"Yes, and of murderers too," said Alessandro. "Don't you call my father murdered just as much as if they had shot him? I do! and, O Señorita, my Señorita, there was José! You recollect José, who went for my violin? But, my beloved one, I am killing you with these terrible things! I will speak no more."

"No, no, Alessandro. Tell me all, all. You must have no grief I do not share. Tell me about José," cried Ramona, breathlessly.

"Señorita, it will break your heart to hear. José was married a year ago. He had the best house in Temecula, next to my father's. It was the only other one that had a shingled roof. And he had a barn too, and that splendid horse he rode, and oxen, and a flock of sheep. He was at home when the sheriff came. A great many of the men were away, grape-picking. That made it worse. But José was at home; for his wife had a little baby only a few weeks old, and the child seemed sickly and not like to live, and José would not leave it. José was the first one that saw the sheriff riding into the village, and the band of armed men behind him, and José knew what it meant. He had often talked it over with me and with my father, and now he saw that it had come; and he went crazy in one minute, and fell on the ground all froth at his mouth. He had had a fit like that once before; and the doctor said if he had another, he would die. But he did not. They picked him up, and presently he was better; and Mr. Rothsaker said nobody worked so well in the moving the first day as José did. Most of the men would not lift a hand. They sat on the ground with the women, and covered up their faces, and would not see. But José worked; and, Señorita, one of the first things he did was to run with my father's violin to the store, to Mrs. Hartsel, and ask her to hide it for us; José knew it was worth money. But before noon the second day he had another fit, and died in it,—died right in his own door, carrying out some of the things; and after Carmena—that's his wife's name—saw he was dead, she never spoke, but sat rocking back and forth on the ground, with the baby in her arms. She went over to Pachanga at the same time I did with my father. It was a long procession of us."

"Where is Pachanga?" asked Ramona.

"About three miles from Temecula, a little sort of cañon. I told the people they'd better move over there; the land did not belong to anybody, and perhaps they could make a living there. There isn't any water; that's the worst of it."

"No water!" cried Ramona.

"No running water. There is one little spring, and they dug a well by it as soon as they got there; so there was water to drink, but that is all. I saw Carmena could hardly keep up, and I carried the baby for her on one arm, while I led my father with the other hand; but the baby cried, so she took it back. I thought then it wouldn't live the day out; but it did live till the morning of the day my father died. Just a few hours before he died, Carmena came along with the baby rolled up in her shawl, and sat down by me on the ground, and did not speak. When I said, 'How is the little one?' she opened her shawl and showed it to me, dead. 'Good, Carmena!' said I. 'It is good! My father is dying too. We will bury them together.' So she sat by me all that morning, and at night she helped me dig the graves. I wanted to put the baby on my father's breast; but she said, no, it must have a little grave. So she dug it herself; and we put them in; and she never spoke, except that once. She was sitting there by the grave when I came away. I made a cross of two little trees with the boughs chopped off, and set it up by the graves. So that is the way our new graveyard was begun,—my father and the little baby; it is the very young and the very old that have the blessed fortune to die. I cannot die, it seems!"

"Where did they bury José?" gasped Ramona.

"In Temecula," said Alessandro. "Mr. Rothsaker made two of his men dig a grave in our old graveyard for José. But I think Carmena will go at night and bring his body away. I would! But, my Señorita, it is very dark, I can hardly see your beloved eyes. I think you must not stay longer. Can I go as far as the brook with you, safely, without being seen? The saints bless you, beloved, for coming. I could not have lived, I think, without one more sight of your face;" and, springing to his feet, Alessandro stood waiting for Ramona to move. She remained still. She was in a sore strait. Her heart held but one impulse, one desire,—to go with Alessandro; nothing was apparently farther from his thoughts than this. Could she offer to go? Should she risk laying a burden on him greater than he could bear? If he were indeed a beggar, as he said, would his life be hindered or helped by her? She felt herself strong and able. Work had no terrors for her; privations she knew nothing of, but she felt no fear of them.

"Alessandro!" she said, in a tone which startled him.

"My Señorita!" he said tenderly.

"You have never once called me Ramona."

"I cannot, Señorita!" he replied.

"Why not?"

"I do not know. I sometimes think 'Ramona,'" he added faintly; "but not often. If I think of you by any other name than as my Señorita, it is usually by a name you never heard."

"What is it?" exclaimed Ramona, wonderingly.

"An Indian word, my dearest one, the name of the bird you are like,— the wood-dove. In the Luiseño tongue that is Majel; that was what I thought my people would have called you, if you had come to dwell among us. It is a beautiful name, Señorita, and is like you."

Alessandro was still standing. Ramona rose; coming close to him, she laid both her hands on his breast, and her head on her hands, and said: "Alessandro, I have something to tell you. I am an Indian. I belong to your people."

Alessandro's silence astonished her. "You are surprised," she said. "I thought you would be glad."

"The gladness of it came to me long ago, my Señorita," he said. "I knew it!"

"How?" cried Ramona. "And you never told me, Alessandro!"

"How could I?" he replied. "I dared not. Juan Canito, it was told me."

"Juan Canito!" said Ramona, musingly. "How could he have known?" Then in a few rapid words she told Alessandro all that the Señora had told her. "Is that what Juan Can said?" she asked.

"All except the father's name," stammered Alessandro.

"Who did he say was my father?" she asked.

Alessandro was silent.

"It matters not," said Ramona. "He was wrong. The Señora, of course, knew. He was a friend of hers, and of the Señora Ortegna, to whom he gave me. But I think, Alessandro, I have more of my mother than of my father."

"Yes, you have, my Señorita," replied Alessandro, tenderly. "After I knew it, I then saw what it was in your face had always seemed to me like the faces of my own people,"

"Are you not glad, Alessandro?"

"Yes, my Señorita."

What more should Ramona say? Suddenly her heart gave way; and without premeditation, without resolve, almost without consciousness of what she was doing, she flung herself on Alessandro's breast, and cried: "Oh, Alessandro, take me with you! take me with you! I would rather die than have you leave me again!"

Malcolm Margolin

Malcolm Margolin was born in 1940 in Boston. He is the founder and publisher of Heyday Books, specializing in books about California history, literature, and culture with special emphasis on California Indians. He is also the founder and publisher of *News from Native California,* a quarterly magazine devoted to California Indians. He lives in Berkeley, California.

"The Cupeño Expulsion of 1903" was first published in *News from Native California.* Gordon Johnson discusses modern remembrance of the expulsion in his essay "As Spirits of the Old Ones Dance, We Sing," included later in this anthology.

The Cupeño Expulsion of 1903

Before the coming of Europeans, the Cupeño were one of the smallest linguistic groups in California, numbering between 500 and 750 people and occupying a territory no more than ten miles in diameter. Like their neighbors, they hunted deer, quail, rabbits, and other small mammals, and they gathered acorns, seeds, berries, and cactus fruits.

Although they suffered severely from diseases and havoc brought by the Europeans, their desert lands were at first of little value to the newcomers. Left relatively alone, they adapted well, at least compared with many other groups. The writer and editor Charles F. Lummis visited their main village at Warner's Hot Springs (Agua Caliente) in 1902 and described them as "quiet, gentle, hard-working farmers." He continued:

The Indian village consists of some forty houses of adobe, except two or three: comfortable, substantial and neat. There is a little adobe chapel, and a new $1,200 schoolhouse....Several hundred acres are cultivated—careful little fields and orchards. There are irrigating ditches and a reservoir. Except the school, which was built by the government a couple of years ago, and a pipe-line to it from a spring, everything at the Agua Caliente is the work of the Indians. Of the American ownership, claimed to have lasted more than 58 years, there is not a stick erect nor one stone on another. ...There are 154 men, women and children living on this spot. I saw and talked with four generations in one family—all born here.

The purpose of Lummis' visit to the Warner Hot Springs village was, however, anything but social. A friend of the Cupeño and a champion of Indian causes, he had come to inform them that lawsuits on their behalf had failed, that the 30,000 acre ranch of which the village was part was up for sale, and that they would have to move from a territory that had been theirs since the creation of the world. He asked where they might like to move to. A woman who spoke English, Mrs. Celsa Apapas, answered:

We thank you for coming here and talking to us in a way we can understand. It is the first time anyone has done so. You ask us to think what place we like next best to this place where we always live. You see that graveyard out there? There are our fathers and grandfathers. You see that Eagle-nest Mountain and that Rabbit-hole Mountain? When God made them, he gave us this place. We have always been here. We do not care for any other place. It may be good, but it is not ours. We have always lived here. We would rather die here. Our fathers did. We cannot leave them. Our children were born here—how can we go away? If you give us the best place in the world, it is not so good for us as this. The Captain [chief] he say his people cannot go anywhere else; they cannot live anywhere else. Here they always live, their people, always live here. There is no other place. This is our home. We ask you to get it for us. If Harvey Downey say he own this place, that is wrong. The Indians always here. We do not go on his land. We stay here. Everybody knows this Indian land. These Hot Springs always Indian. We cannot live anywhere else. We were born here and our fathers are buried here. We do not think of any place after this. We want this place, and not any other place...

There is no other place for us. We do not want you to buy any other place. If you will not buy this place we will go into the mountains like quail and die there, the old people and the women and the children. Let the government be glad and proud. It can kill us. We do not fight. We do what it says. If we cannot live here we want to go into those mountains and die. We do not want any other home.

A short time later, the expulsion from Warner Hot Springs began. Carolina Nolasquez, in 1921, reminisced about what it was like:

We were there in our homes and all of a sudden the agent came. He said he would move us to here [Pala Reservation, where this interview was recorded]. And we said, "No." We did not want to come back here. But still he would say, "No," the agent: "Down there it's better," he would say.

Rosinda Nolasquez, speaking in 1962, recalled what happened next:

From there they moved us from our homes, from Cupa. Many carts stood there by the doors. People came from La Mesa, from Santa Ysabel, from Wilakal, from San Ignacio, they came to see their relatives. They cried a lot. And they just threw our belongings, our clothes, into the carts, chairs, cups, plates. They piled everything on the carts. First they said to them, "Go and see your relatives for the last time now. You're never going to see them again." They went to the cemetery, there they wept. Then it was time to move out. Still they did not move. They could not move outside, they still stayed there by the gate. And my great-grandmother went running away into the mountains and she said, "Here I will stay, even if I die, even if the coyotes eat me," she said, it is said. She kept on going, climbing away. And then from there the people moved out from the cemetery, they were weeping. And then from there they moved us. And there was the chapel there on a little hill. And they said to them, "Now, look behind you, see your homes for the last time." But no one turned around....They kept going on westward. They did not look back again.

Grant Wallace, in an article for *Out West* magazine, described the pain of the departure:

> Night after night, sounds of wailing came from the adobe homes of the Indians. When Tuesday [May 12, 1903] came, many of them went to the little adobe chapel to pray, and then gathered for the last time among the unpainted wooden crosses within the rude stockade of their ancient burying-ground, a pathetic and forlorn group, to wail their grief over the graves of their fathers…
>
> While I helped Lay-reader Ambrosio's mother to round up and encoop a wary brood of chickens, I observed the wife of her other son, Jesus, throwing an armful of books—pellers, arithmetics, poems—into the bonfire, along with bows and arrows, and super-annuated aboriginal bric-a-brac. In reply to a surprised query, she explained that now they hated the white people and their religion and their books. Dogged and dejected, Captain Cibermoat, with his wife Ramona and little girl, was the last to go. While I helped him hitch a bony mustang to his top buggy, a tear or two coursed down his knife-scarred face, and as the teamsters tore down his little board cabin where he had kept a restaurant, he muttered, "Let them eat sand."
>
> …Amid the shouting of the teamsters, the howling of dogs, the lowing of cattle, and the wailing of some of the women who rode on the great wagons, the caravan started.

Altogether some 98 persons were removed, and two days later the caravan arrived at Pala, in Luiseño territory. Rosinda Nolasquez described what they saw:

> All this Pala—nothing but willows, it was. There were many fleas here. And the people who came from Cupa did not know about fleas. And then there they came and they saw fleas. There were many squirrels here. The people did not know anything like this. They saw squirrels up close. At Cupa we lived well. And now, having lost our homes, we must live here at Pala today.

Carey McWilliams

Born in Steamboat Springs, Colorado, in 1905, Carey McWilliams was famous for his support of progressive causes and examination of social issues in California, especially minority rights and fair labor practices. His major works include *Factories in the Field*, an exploration of the conditions suffered by migrant farm workers; *Southern California: An Island in the Land*; and *California: The Great Exception*. He edited *The Nation* for twenty years and died in 1980.

This excerpt from *Southern California: An Island in the Land* elegantly explores the importance of Helen Hunt Jackson's novel *Ramona* in forming Southern California myth, identity, and history. See also the excerpt from *Ramona* included in this collection.

from *Southern California*

from "The Growth of a Legend"

In the spring of 1872, Mrs. Jackson had made a brief visit, as a tourist, to the northern part of California. Later she made three trips, as a tourist, to Southern California: in the winter of 1881–1882, the spring of 1883, and the winter, spring, and summer of 1884–1885. It scarcely needs to be emphasized that her knowledge of California, and of the Mission Indians, was essentially that of the tourist and casual visitor. Although she did prepare a valuable report on the Mission Indians, based on a field trip that she made with Abbot Kinney of Los Angeles, most of her material about Indians was second-hand and consisted, for the greater part, of odds and ends of gossip, folk tales, and Mission-inspired allegories of one kind or another.

She had originally been sent to Southern California by *Century* magazine to write some stories about the Missions, which, according to the illustrator who accompanied her, were to be "enveloped in the mystery and poetry of romance." In Southern California she became deliriously enamored of the Missions, then in a state of general disrepair and neglect, infested with countless swallows and pigeons, overrun by sheep and goats, and occasionally inhabited by stray dogs and wandering Indians. "In the sunny, delicious, winterless California air," these crumbling ruins, with their walled gardens and broken bells, their vast cemeteries and caved-in wells, exerted a potent romantic influence on Mrs. Jackson's highly susceptible nature. Out of these brief visits to Southern California came *Ramona,* the first novel written about the region, which became, after its publication in 1884, one of the most widely read American novels of the time. It was this novel which firmly established the Mission legend in Southern California.

When the book was first published, it provoked a storm of protest in the Southland. Egged on by various civic groups, the local critics denounced it as a tissue of falsehoods, a travesty on history, a damnable libel on Southern California. But the book was perfectly timed, providentially timed, to coincide with the great invasion of homeseekers and tourists to the region. As these hordes of winter tourists began to express a lively interest in visiting "Ramona's land," Southern California experienced an immediate change of attitude and, overnight, became passionately Ramona-conscious. Beginning about 1887, a Ramona promotion of fantastic proportions began to be organized in the region.

Picture postcards by the tens of thousands were published showing "the school attended by Ramona," "the original of Ramona," "the place where Ramona was married," and various shots of the "Ramona country." Since the local chambers of commerce could not, or would not, agree upon the locale of the novel—one school of thought insisted that the Camulos rancho was the scene of the more poignant passages, while still another school insisted that the Hacienda Guajome was the authentic locale—it was not long before the scenic postcards depicting the Ramona country had come to embrace all of Southern California. In the eighties, the Southern Pacific tourist and excursion trains regularly stopped at Camulos so that the wide-eyed Bostonians, guidebooks in hand, might detrain, visit the rancho, and bounce up and down on "the bed in which Ramona slept." Thousands of Ramona baskets, plaques, pincushions, pillows, and souvenirs of all sorts were sold in every curio shop in California. Few tourists left the region without having purchased a little replica of the "bells that rang when Ramona was married." To keep the tourist interest alive, local press agents for fifty years engaged in a synthetic controversy over the identities of the "originals" for the universally known characters in the novel. Some misguided Indian women began to take the promotion seriously and had themselves photographed—copyright reserved—as "the original Ramona." A bibliography of the newspaper stories, magazine articles, and pamphlets written about some aspect of the Ramona legend would fill a volume. Four husky volumes of Ramonana appeared in Southern California: *The Real Ramona* (1900), by D. A. Hufford; *Through Ramona's Country* (1908), the official, classic document, by George Wharton James; *Ramona's Homeland* (1914), by Margaret V. Allen; and *The True Story of Ramona* (1914), by C. C. Davis and W. A. Anderson.

From 1884 to date, the Los Angeles Public Library has purchased over 1,000 copies of *Ramona*. Thirty years after publication, the same library had a constant waiting list for 105 circulating copies of the book. The sales to date total 601,636 copies, deriving from a Regular Edition, a Monterey Edition (in two volumes), a De Luxe Edition, a Pasadena Edition, a Tourist Edition, a Holiday Art Edition, and a Gift Edition. Hundreds of unoffending Southern California babies have been named Ramona. A townsite was named Ramona. And in San Diego thousands of people make a regular pilgrimage to "Ramona's Marriage Place," where the True Vow Keepers Clubs—made up of couples who have been married fifty years or longer—hold their annual picnics. The Native Daughters of the Golden West have named one of their "parlors," or lodges, after Ramona. The name Ramona appears in the corporate title of fifty or more businesses currently operating in Los Angeles. Two of Mrs. Jackson's articles for *Century*, "Father Junipero and His Work" and "The Present Condition of the Mission Indians of Southern California," were for years required reading in the public schools of California. Reprints of Henry Sandham's illustrations for Ramona are familiar items in Southern California homes, hotels, restaurants, and places of business. In 1914 one of the Ramona historians truthfully said that "Mrs. Jackson's name is familiar to almost every human being in Southern California, from the little three-year-old tot, who has her choice juvenile stories read to him, to the aged grandmother who sheds tears of sympathy for Ramona." Two generations of Southern California children could recite from memory the stanzas from Ina Coolbrith's verses to Helen Hunt Jackson, often ornately framed on the walls of Southern California homes:

There, with her dimpled, lifted hands,
Parting the mustard's golden plumes,
The dusky maid, Ramona, stands,
Amid the sea of blooms.
And Alessandro, type of all
His broken tribe, for evermore
An exile, hears the stranger call
Within his father's door.

Translated into all known languages, *Ramona* has also been dramatized. The play based on the novel was first presented at the Mason Opera House in Los Angeles on February 27, 1905, the dramatization having been written by Miss Virginia Calhoun and General Johnstone Jones. Commenting upon Miss Calhoun's performance in the role of Ramona, the *Los Angeles Times* reported that "in the lighter parts she held a fascination that was tempered with gentleness and playfulness. Her slender figure, graceful and pliant as a willow, swayed with every light touch of feeling, and the deeper tragic climaxes she met in a way to win tears from the eyes of many." Over the years, three motion picture versions of the novel have appeared. In 1887, George Wharton James, who did much to keep the Ramona promotion moving along, "tramped every foot of the territory covered by Mrs. Jackson," interviewing the people she had interviewed, photographing the scenes she had photographed, and "sifting the evidence" she had collected. His thick tome on the Ramona country is still a standard item in all Southern California libraries. For twenty-five years, the chambers of commerce of the Southland kept this fantastic promotion alive and flourishing. When interest seemed to be lagging, new stories were concocted. Thus on March 7, 1907, the *Los Angeles Times* featured, as a major news item, a story about "Condino, the newly discovered and only child of Ramona." In 1921 the enterprising chamber of commerce of Hemet, California, commissioned Garnet Holme to write a pageant about Ramona. Each year since 1921 the pageant has been produced in late April or early May in the heart of the Ramona country, by the chamber of commerce. At the last count, two hundred thousand people had witnessed the pageant.

The legendary quality of Mrs. Jackson's famous novel came about through the amazing way in which she made elegant pre-Raphaelite characters out of Ramona and "the half-breed Alessandro." Such Indians were surely never seen upon this earth. Furthermore, the story extolled the Franciscans in the most extravagant manner and placed the entire onus of the mistreatment of the Indians upon the noisy and vulgar gringos. At the same time, the sad plight of Ramona and Alessandro got curiously mixed up, in the telling, with the plight of the "fine old Spanish families." These fine old Spanish families, who were among the most flagrant exploiters of the Indian in Southern California, appeared in the novel as only slightly less considerate of his welfare than the Franciscans. Despite its legendary aspects, however, the Ramona version of the Indians of Southern California is now firmly implanted in the mythology of the region. It is this legend which largely accounts for the "sacred" as distinguished from the "profane" history of the Indian in Southern California.

It should be said to Mrs. Jackson's credit, however, that she did arouse a momentary flurry of interest in the Mission Indians. Her report on these Indians, which appeared in all editions of *A Century of Dishonor* after 1883, is still a valuable document. As a result of her work, Charles Fletcher Lummis founded the Sequoya League in Los Angeles in 1902, "to make better Indians"; and, through the activities of the league, the three hundred Indians who were evicted from the Warner Ranch in 1901 were eventually relocated on lands purchased by the government. Aside from the relocation of these Indians, however, nothing much came of Mrs. Jackson's work in Southern California, for the region accepted the charming Ramona as a folk figure but completely rejected the Indians still living in the area. A government report of 1920 indicated that 90 percent of the residents of the sections in which Indians still live in Southern California were wholly ignorant about their Indian neighbors and that deep local prejudice against them still prevailed.[...]

Rediscovery of the Missions

With the great Anglo invasion of Southern California after 1880, the Spanish background of the region was, for a time, almost wholly forgotten. "For many years," wrote Harry Carr, "the traditions of Los Angeles were junked by the scorn of the conquering gringos. When I was a schoolboy in Los Angeles, I never heard of Ortega or Gaspar de Portolá or Juan Bautista de Anza." And then, with the publication of *Ramona*, the Spanish background began to be rediscovered, with the same false emphasis and from the same crass motives that had characterized the rediscovery of the Indian. Both rediscoveries, that of the Indian and that of the Spaniard, occurred between 1883 and 1888, at precisely the period when the great real-estate promotion of Southern California was being organized.

Insofar as the Spanish saga is concerned, it all began in 1888, when, as John A. Berger has written, "the romantic people of Southern California," under the leadership of Charles Fletcher Lummis, formed an Association for the Preservation of the Missions (which later became the Landmarks Club). With the gradual restoration of the Missions, a highly romantic conception of the Spanish period began to be culti-vated, primarily for the benefit of the incoming tides of tourists, who were routed to the Missions much as they were routed to the mythical site of Ramona's birthplace. A flood of books began to appear about the Missions, with Mrs. Jackson's *Glimpses of California and the Missions* (1883) being the volume that inspired the whole movement. It was fol-lowed, after a few years, by George Wharton James's *In and Out of the Old Missions,* which, for a quarter of a century, was the "classic" in this field. My own guess would be that not a year has passed since 1900 without the publication of some new volume about the Missions. Not only has a library of books been written about the Missions, but each individual Mission has had its historians. Books have been written about the architecture of the Missions, about the Mission bells, about the Franciscans (notably Father Junipero Serra, a popular saint in Southern California), and about the wholly synthetic Mission furniture. In fact, the Mission-Spanish background of the region has been so strongly emphasized that, as Max Miller has written, "The past is almost as scrambled as the present, and almost as indefinite...the whole thing got mixed up." With each new book about the Missions came a new set of etchings and some new paintings. In 1880, William Keith painted all of the Missions of California. He was followed by the artist [Henry Chapman] Ford of Santa Barbara, who, in 1890, completed his etchings of the Franciscan establishments. Since 1890, the Missions have been painted by Jorgenson, Edward Deakin, Alexander F. Harmer, William Sparks, Gutzon Borglum, Elmer Wachtel, Minnie Tingle, and a host of other artists.

In 1902, Frank Miller, owner of the Glenwood Cottage Inn at Riverside, with funds provided by Henry Huntington, began to con-struct the famous Mission Inn. Designed by Myron Hunt, the Mission Inn was built wing by wing around the old adobe Glenwood Cottage, until the new structure covered an entire block. Once completed, the inn gave the initial fillip to Mission architecture, so called, and soon Missionesque and Moorish structures began to dot the Southern California landscape. It was here, in the Mission Inn, that John Steven McGroarty wrote the *Mission Play*, for which he was deservedly decorated by the Pope. The play had its premiere at San Gabriel on a warm spring evening, April 29, 1912, under the sponsorship of the Princess Lazarovic-Hrebrelanovic of Serbia, with a cast of "one hundred descendants of the Old Spanish families." On the opening night, "queer chugging noises filled the air and the acrid smoke from burnt gasoline floated over the ancient Mission and the little adobes that nestled around it. It was the first big outpouring of automobiles that San Gabriel had ever had." The elite of Southern California turned out, en masse, for the premiere. The play, of course, was an enormous success. McGroarty boasted that it had been seen by 2.5 million people, a world's record. During the sixteen consecutive seasons that it played at San Gabriel Mission, over 2,600 performances were recorded. Later the play was institutionalized, under official sponsorship, and became an enormous tourist attraction. A tourist who went to California and failed to see Catalina Island, Mt. Wilson, and the *Mission Play* was considered to have something wrong with his head. In recognition of his great services to Southern California, "Singing John" [McGroarty], the songster of the green Verdugo hills, was made poet laureate of California on May 17, 1933. Needless to say, the play perpetuated the Helen Hunt Jackson version of the Indians, the Spanish dons, and the Franciscans.

Carrie Jacobs-Bond

Carrie Jacobs-Bond was born in 1862 in Wisconsin. A wildly popular songwriter, she is said to have earned more than one million dollars in royalties from her music. After the success of her first collection of sheet music, *Seven Songs: As Unpretentious as the Wild Rose*, she started her own publishing company, the Bond Shop. She moved to California for her health in 1920 and died in Hollywood in 1946.

"A Perfect Day" was one of Bond's best-known songs; more than five million copies of the sheet music for this piece were published within ten years. She wrote it in 1909 at the Mission Inn in Riverside while on a motor tour of Southern California.

A Perfect Day

When you come to the end of a perfect day,
And you sit alone with your thought,
While the chimes ring out with a carol gay
For the joy that the day has brought,
Do you think what the end of a perfect day
Can mean to a tired heart,
When the sun goes down with a flaming ray,
And the dear friends have to part?

Well, this is the end of a perfect day,
Near the end of a journey, too;
But it leaves a thought that is big and strong,

With a wish that is kind and true.
For mem'ry has painted this perfect day
With colors that never fade,
And we find at the end of a perfect day
The soul of a friend we've made.

John Jakes

Born in Chicago in 1932, John Jakes has long been one of the
nation's most popular historical fiction writers; his works include
the multivolume Kent Family Chronicles and the North and South
trilogy. Six of his novels were made into successful television
miniseries. He lives in South Carolina.

California Gold is the rags-to-riches story of Mack Chance, who
makes money in Riverside during the orange growers' heyday,
which is described in this brief excerpt.

from *California Gold*

The orange was blessed with a rich and mystical heritage long before
it came to California. Somewhere in the cradle of civilization, legend
said, it flourished in a lush garden. Someone named it the golden apple
of the Hesperides: the golden apple of the sun.

Bedouin princes savored the orange, imperial Romans sucked its
juice at their banquets, and medieval Spaniards planted and cultivated
the trees. Columbus carried the fruit to the New World on his second
voyage, and the conquistadors spread it and propagated it. By 1750,
most of the Jesuit fathers in California grew oranges on Church lands.

In this early period, the California orange was thick-skinned, generally sour, and full of seeds. Its enormous value would not be perceived
until it had caught the eye of venturesome newcomers. The fruit itself
had to change as well.

In 1841, a former trapper from Kentucky, William Wolfskill, set out
two acres of Mediterranean Sweet oranges on some land at Central

Avenue and East Fifth Street, Los Angeles. Though his neighbors ridiculed his agricultural adventure, Wolfskill steadily expanded his grove to seventy acres, and by the 1870s the old trapper began to boast of profits of $1,000 an acre. That was enough to attract other farmers. New groves started to appear, and then new varieties, more suited to popular taste.

But the true watershed was 1873. That year, cuttings from sweet seedless oranges from Brazil arrived in California via the U.S. Department of Agriculture. A Riverside couple, Luther and Eliza Tibbets, planted and nurtured the cuttings. Like so many Californians, the Tibbetses had started out elsewhere, but they found their home, and their life's reward, on the Pacific slope. Before long, everyone wanted "Washington navel" cuttings. Luther Tibbets could ask $5 for every bud and get it. In 1876, America's centennial year, Valencia oranges came to the state from Spain. Valencias ripened in the summer, navels in winter, so citrus could become a year-round industry.

All that was needed was a year-round market, and old Wolfskill helped create it. In 1877, he loaded an entire freight car with his oranges and dispatched it to St. Louis. The car was a month in transit, but when it arrived, mid-westerners rolled back the doors and stood in awe before the bounty it contained: fruit as bright as sunshine, from trees ever green, in a land where snow never fell. Even after a month, the fruit was still edible and flavorsome.

Older sour varieties were improved, and the groves multiplied. The Riverside-Redlands area proved the ideal location for navels, while Valencias grew best in parts of the new Orange County. But Southern California was equally hospitable to bright yellow lemons from Sicily and Spain, which did especially well in sections of Santa Barbara, Ventura, and San Diego counties.

In 1887, the first California oranges reached New York City, arriving in ventilated boxcars, and by 1889, refrigerated cars were being developed. The railroad, cursed by so many, quickly transformed a local industry into a national one. By 1890, there were more than a million orange trees in Southern California; five years later there were at least three or four million, and tourists were taking special excursion trains to Riverside, Redlands, and the other new citrus towns just to admire and photograph the groves.

Gentlemen who never would have dreamed of owning pigs or potato fields found the cultivation of oranges an entirely suitable occupation.

They established great tracts and great homes and a tradition summed up by the slogan "Oranges for health—California for wealth."

Thus, once again, the golden apples of the Hesperides grew in a magical garden in the West.

Kate Sanborn

Kate Sanborn was born in 1839 in New Hampshire. She taught English at Smith College and traveled extensively, lecturing on literary topics. In addition to *A Truthful Woman in Southern California*, she authored *The Wit of Women*, a collection of anecdotes and commentary that examines women's humor in a social context. She died in 1917 in Massachusetts.

Sanborn offers amusing and anecdotal advice for tourists to Southern California in her 1893 *A Truthful Woman in Southern California*. This excerpt specifically deals with Riverside, which she compares to Pasadena.

from *A Truthful Woman in Southern California*

"Knowest thou the land where the lemon trees bloom,
Where the golden orange grows in the deep thickets' gloom,
Where a wind ever soft from the blue heavens blows,
And the groves are of laurel and myrtle and rose?"

Yes, that describes Riverside, and reads like a prophecy. If Pasadena is a big garden with pretty homes scattered all through its shade and flowers, then Riverside is an immense orange grove, having one city-like street, with substantial business blocks and excellent stores, two banks, one in the Evans block, especially fine in all its architecture and arrangements, and the rest is devoted by the land-owners to raising oranges and making them pay. You will see flowers enough to overwhelm a Broadway florist, every sort of cereal, every fruit that grows, in prime condition for the table ten months out of the twelve. Three hundred sunny days are claimed here out of the three hundred and sixty-five. They are once in a while bothered by a frost, but that is "unusual." Before 1870 this was a dusty desert of decomposed granite. What has caused the change? Scientific irrigation and plenty of it. Or, as Grant Allen puts it, "mud." He says: "Mud is the most valuable material in the world. It is by mud we live; without it we should die. Mud is filling up the lakes. Mud created Egypt, and mud created Lombardy."

Yes, one can get rich here by turning dust into mud. It is said to be the richest town "per capita" in all California of the same size, $1,100 being the average allowance for each person. This is solemnly vouched for by reliable citizens. And they have no destitute poor—a remarkable record. The city and district are said to enjoy an annual income of $1,500,000 from the fruit alone, and there is a million of unused money in the two banks.

Irrigation is better than rain, for the orange growers can turn on a shower or a stream whenever and wherever needed. It requires courage and faith to go straight into a desert with frowning mountains, big, little, and middle-sized, all about, and not an available drop of water, and say, "I'm going to settle right here and turn this desert into a beautiful home, and start a prosperous, wealthy city. All that this rocky, barren plain needs is water and careful cultivation, and I will give it both." That was Judge Brown's decision, and the result shows his wisdom. No one agreed with him; it was declared that colonists could not be induced to try it. But he could not relinquish the idea. He was charmed by the dry, balmy air, so different from Los Angeles. He saw the smooth plain was well adapted for irrigation, and Santa Ana could be made to furnish all the water needed. So that it is really to him we owe the pleasure of seeing these orchards, vineyards, avenues, and homes. Where once the coyote and jack-rabbit had full sway, land now sells at prices from $400 to $3,000 per acre. There are no fences—at least, there is but one in all Riverside. You see everywhere fine, well-trimmed cypress hedges with trees occasionally cut in fantastic, elaborate designs. There are many century plants about the grounds; they blossom in this climate after twelve years, and die after the tall homely flower has come to maturity. The roadsides have pretty flowers planted all along, giving a gay look, and the very weeds just now are covered with blossoms. Irrigation is carried on most scientifically, the water coming from a creek and the "cienaga," which I will explain later. There are several handsome avenues shaded with peppers, and hedges twenty feet high, through which are obtained peeps at enchanting homes; but the celebrated drive which all tourists are expected to take is that to and fro through Magnolia Avenue, twelve miles long. The name now seems illy chosen, as only a few magnolia trees were originally planted at each corner, and these have mostly died, so that the whole effect is more eucalyptical, palmy, and pepperaneous than it is magnolious. People come here "by chance the usual way," and buy because they see the chance to make money. You are told pretty big stories of successes; the failures are not alluded to.

I saw a large and prosperous place belonging to a woman of business ability, who came out all alone, took up a government grant, ploughed and planted and irrigated, sent for a sister to help her, sold land at great prices, and is now a wealthy woman. If I had not passed through such depressing and enthusiasm-subduing experiences as an agriculturist in the East I might be tempted here. I did look with interest at the ostrich farms, and had visions of great profits from feathers, eggs, and eggshells. But it takes a small fortune to get started in that business, as eggs are twenty dollars each, and the birds are sometimes five hundred dollars apiece. And they are subject to rheumatism and a dozen other diseases, and a blow from a kicking bird will kill one. I concluded to let that dream be unrealized. Did you ever hear of the nervous invalid who was told by his physician to buy a Barbary ostrich and imitate him exactly for three months? It was a capital story. The lazy dyspeptic was completely cured. As a hen woman I will remark *en passant* that it is hard to raise poultry in this part of California. The climate is too exhilarating, and if the head of each chicken does not get a drop of oil at once it dies of brain disease.

Corn does not thrive. Mr. Brown at first put down ten acres to corn. It looked promising, but grew all to stalk. These stalks were over twelve feet high, but corn was of no value, so he sold the stalks for eighty dollars, and started his oranges.

The English are largely interested here, and have invested two or three millions, which will pay large interest to their grandchildren. Their long avenue is loyally named "Victoria." A thrifty Canadian crazed by the "boom," the queerest mental epidemic or delusion that ever took hold of sensible people, bought some stony land just under Rubidoux Mountain for $4,000. It was possibly worth $100, but in those delirious days many did much worse. It is amusing to see what hard work and water and good taste will do for such a place. He has blasted the rocks, made fountains and cisterns, planted several acres of strawberries, set out hundreds of orange trees, has a beautiful garden, two pretty cottages, and some day he will get back his original price for a building site, for the view is grand.

Riverside, while leading the orange-producing section of Southern California, is not exactly the location which would have been selected by the original settlers had they possessed the experience of the producers of today. The oranges do not have to be washed, as in some other places; they are not injured by smut or scale; the groves are faultless in size of trees, shape, and taste of fruit. One orange presented to me weighed thirty-one ounces. But the growers, having lost $1,000,000 by Jack Frost several years ago, are obliged now to resort to the use of lighted tar-pots on cold nights to make a dense smudge to keep the temperature above the danger line. One man uses petroleum in hundred-gallon casks, one for each acre, from which two pipes run along between the rows of trees, with half a dozen elbows twenty feet apart, over which are flat sheet-iron pans, into which the oil spatters as it vaporizes. An intensely hot flame keeps off the frost. This I do not hear spoken of at Riverside; you must go to a rival for any disagreeable information. At Pasadena their severe winds are called "Riversiders"; at Anaheim they are "Santa Anas"; and friends write me from damp Los Angeles to the dry air of Riverside, "How can you stay in that 'damp' place?" The inhabitants of Riverside do not concede that Pasadena is a place for orange growers. At Redlands, luckily above frost terrors, the terrible losses at Riverside from that trouble are profusely narrated. San Diego gets its share of humorous belittlement from all. You hear the story quoted of the shrewd Chinese who went to that city to look for business, where one hears much of future developments, but did not settle, saying, "It has too muchee bymbye." Friends, and especially hotel proprietors, exclaim in disgusted astonishment, "What! going to Riverside? Why, there's nothing there but oranges."

I find more: fine and charming drives, scenery that differs from that of Pasadena, "that poem of nature set to music beneath the swaying rhythm of the pine forests of the lofty Sierra Madres," but is equally enjoyable and admirable.

Still, above all, and permeating every other interest, is the *orange*. As to dampness, a physician threatened with consumption, and naturally desirous of finding the driest air, began while at Coronado Beach a simple but sure test for comparative degrees of "humidity" by just hanging a woolen stocking out of his window at night. At that place it was wet all through, quite moist at Los Angeles, very much less so at Pasadena, dry as a bone or red herring or an old-fashioned sermon at Riverside. Stockings will tell! (From April to September is really the best time to visit Coronado.) I experienced a very sudden change from a warm, delightful morning to an afternoon so penetrating by cold that I really suffered during a drive, although encased in the heaviest of Jaeger flannels, a woolen dress, and a heavy wrap. I thought of the rough buffalo coat my uncle, a doctor, used to put on when called out on a winter night in New Hampshire, and wished I was enveloped in something like it, with a heated freestone for feet and a hot potato for each hand. If I can make my readers understand that these sudden changes make flannels necessary, and that one needs to be as careful here as in Canada as regards catching cold from night air and these unexpected rigors, I shall feel, as the old writers used to say, "that I have not written entirely in vain."

In one day you can sit under the trees in a thin dress and be too warm if the sun is at its best, and then be half frozen two hours later if the wind is in earnest and the sun has retired. In the sun, Paradise; in shade, protect yourself!

Harry Lawton

Harry Lawton was born in Long Beach in 1927. Educated at the University of California, Riverside, he went on to become an award-winning journalist at the *Riverside Press-Enterprise* before returning to the university to work in the Department of Creative Writing. He founded the university's Writers Week, which annually brings famous writers to Riverside. A self-taught historian with strong ties to the local American Indian community and interest in the history of the Chinese in the area, he helped found the Malki Museum on the Morongo Indian Reservation and the nonprofit Malki Museum Press. His novel *Willie Boy: A Desert Manhunt*, based on historical events that took place in 1909, was made into a movie starring Robert Redford. He died in 2005.

Lawton meditates on the history of Riverside in this excerpt from his unpublished manuscript "Orange Groves and Rice Bowls: A Narrative History of the Chinese Pioneers of Riverside, California, 1869–1974."

from "Orange Groves and Rice Bowls"

The Sandlot in the Garden

Orange groves and rice bowls! Concrete nouns evoking images unlikely to differ too greatly in my mind or yours. We are nearing the end of what has been called the "sunny seventies"—that decade of prehistory, starting with the Riverside Colony, which foreshadows the emergence of the great interior citrus belt, those millions of orange trees sprawling over thousands of acres that dominated the Southern California landscape for almost a century. Maybe you have a rice bowl in mind—shaped like an upside down Cantonese hat, but with a tiny rimmed base. Glazed white chinaware with pastel blue designs running around the bowl. It doesn't quite matter what you imagine for your design: we both visualize the approximate rice bowl.

Orange groves too can be imagined with some clarity. They may be neatly pruned or luxuriantly unpruned and run amok like a jungle, but they are still orange groves. Having grown up as the son of an orange rancher along the banks of the Gage Canal, I have my own particular grove in mind, still lingering firmly in time and space, although I watched the subdividers a few years ago rip those trees from the earth and burn them in piles into white ash. Our grove was always neatly pruned, limbs bent with the weight of golden fruit—the Washington navel. The enameled leaves of the orange trees sparkled against sunlight or turned intensely green beneath cloudy skies after winter rains. In April, the leaves gave forth white blossoms, and their smell lay across the land at dusk. The trees ran west in orderly rows from the canal bank, separated by six or more feet of plowed reddish earth with straight irrigation furrows running beside the trees. Beyond our grove lay the lower orange groves of other ranchers, descending westward down the plain to the outskirts of the city of Riverside. Here were orange groves!

Although I have delineated them in swift strokes of prose, you should by now also have some sense of those early orange growers, those eastern and midwestern emigrants, ignorant of citriculture, who despite the snickerings of their neighbors first dared to plant orange trees on an unwatered plain: the pragmatic, Utopian visionary, Judge John W. North; dashing, resourceful Tom Cover; a lively, cultivated minister, Rev. J. W. Atherton; over-eager K. B. Shugart; eccentric Luther Tibbets and his plain wife, Eliza, whose stolid face, resembling that of Queen Victoria, will soon adorn thousands of citrus box labels. These were the orange growers of the first decade of Riverside—these and many other men and women whose names may be found on the yellowing pages of old packinghouse ledgers.

Rice bowls may be imagined concretely, but the men who ate from them—our earliest Chinese pioneers in the Riverside Colony—can only be seen as in a glass darkly. They left no known record of their thoughts, and only Anglo reports tell us of their daily lives in an alien land. Those first Chinese sojourners and settlers present themselves through western eyes as quaint, exotic figures in Celestial dress—amiable, industrious, stoic, even, yes, inscrutable—perhaps you too know the stereotypes. They remain shadowy men with hidden thoughts who press raisins in packing sheds, trot along dusty streets with baskets of laundry hanging from long poles bent across their backs, get up at dawn to load their vegetable wagons, and sleep in the cramped tiered bunks of washhouses in the Chinese Quarter that some Riversiders refer to as "rookeries." Each year they arrive in San Francisco in large numbers: more than 22,000 in 1876; moving toward a peak of 39,579 by 1882. More and more of them turn south toward the young orange groves of Southern California—now the new center of railroad building activity. Soon they will essay to master that remarkable new invention, the bicycle, and be seen—queues flying in the wind, pedalling along the unpaved streets of Riverside and out into the countryside.

Do they dream in their tiered bunks at night? Among orange growers there is Edward North, son of the colony's founder, who masters Cantonese and sees his Chinese workers as diverse men and not stereotypes. Perhaps North knew something of their dreams or overheard them at times talking to each other of their loneliness and their distant families. Near the end of the decade, a few Chinese are already guiding irrigation water down furrows with sturdy hoes that have large curved blades.

Mary Paik Lee

Mary Paik Lee was born in 1900 in North Korea. Escaping Japanese political oppression in their homeland, her family came to California in 1906 by way of Hawaii. Her 1990 memoir, *Quiet Odyssey: A Pioneer Korean Woman in America,* chronicles her life in California from childhood, through marriage and adulthood, and into advanced age. One of the few published memoirs by a Korean American woman, it describes her family's struggle to survive on their earnings from the backbreaking work available to immigrants. She died in San Francisco in 1995.

Paik Lee describes her family's time in Riverside in this excerpt from *Quiet Odyssey.*

from *Quiet Odyssey*

We landed in San Francisco on December 3, 1906. As we walked down the gangplank, a group of young white men were standing around, waiting to see what kind of creatures were disembarking. We must have been a very queer-looking group. They laughed at us and spit in our faces; one man kicked up Mother's skirt and called us names we couldn't understand. Of course, their actions and attitudes left no doubt about their feelings toward us. I was so upset. I asked Father why we had come to a place where we were not wanted. He replied that we deserved what we got because that was the same kind of treatment that Koreans had given to the first American missionaries in Korea: the children had thrown rocks at them, calling them "white devils" because of their blue eyes and yellow or red hair. He explained that anything new and strange causes some fear at first, so ridicule and violence often result. He said the missionaries just lowered their heads and paid no attention to their tormentors. They showed by their action and good works that they were just as good as or even better than those who laughed at them. He said that is exactly what we must try to do here in America—study hard and learn to show Americans that we are just as good as they are. That was my first lesson in living, and I have never forgotten it.

Many old friends came with us from Hawaii. Some stayed in San Francisco, others went to Dinuba, near Fresno, but most headed for Los Angeles. We ourselves went straight to the railroad depot nearby and boarded a train for Riverside, where friends would be waiting for us. It was our first experience on a train. We were excited, but we felt lost in such a huge country. When we reached Riverside, we found friends from our village in Korea waiting to greet us.

In those days, Orientals and others were not allowed to live in town with the white people. The Japanese, Chinese, and Mexicans each had their own little settlement outside of town. My first glimpse of what was to be our camp was rows of one-room shacks, with a few water pumps here and there and little sheds for outhouses. We learned later that the shacks had been constructed for the Chinese men who had built the Southern Pacific Railroad in the 1880s.

We had reached Riverside without any plans and with very little money, not knowing what we could do for a living. After much discussion with friends, it was decided that Mother should cook for about thirty single men who worked in the citrus groves. Father did not like her to work, but it seemed to be the only way we could make a living for ourselves. She would make their breakfast at 5 a.m., pack their lunches, and cook them supper at 7 p.m. But my parents did not have the cooking utensils we needed, so Father went to the Chinese settlement and told them of our situation. He could not speak Chinese but he wrote *hanmun*, the character writing that is the same in Korean and Chinese. He asked for credit, promising to make regular payments from time to time. They trusted him and agreed to give us everything we needed to get started: big iron pots and pans, dishes, tin lunch pails, chopsticks, and so forth. They also gave us rice and groceries.

The Korean men went to the dumpyard nearby and found the materials to build a shack large enough for our dining area. They made one long table and two long benches to seat thirty men. Father made a large stove and oven with mud and straw, and he found several large wine barrels to hold the water for drinking and cooking. That was the start of our business. Mother had long, thick black hair that touched the ground. It became a nuisance in her work, so Father cut it short, leaving just enough to coil in a bun on the back of her head. It must have caused her much grief to lose her beautiful hair, but she never complained. We had already lost everything else that meant anything to us.

We lived in a small one-room shack built in the 1880s. The passing of time had made the lumber shrink, so the wind blew through the cracks in the walls. There was no pretense of making it livable—just four walls, one window, and one door—nothing else. We put mud in the cracks to keep the wind out. The water pump served several shacks. We had to heat our bath water in a bucket over an open fire outside, then pour it into a tin tub inside. There was no gas or electricity. We used kerosene lamps, and one of my chores was to trim the wicks, clean the glass tops, and keep the bowls filled with kerosene.

The Chinese men who had lived there in the 1880s must have slept on the floor. Father solved the problem of where we were going to sleep by building shelves along the four walls of our shack. Then he found some hay to put on each shelf. He put a blanket over the hay, rolled up some old clothes for a pillow—and that was a bed for a child. I used a block of wood for my pillow. It became such a habit with me that even to this day I do not like a soft pillow. My parents themselves slept on the floor.

After our shelter was taken care of, I looked around and found that all our immediate neighbors were old friends from Korea. Philip Ahn, who became a movie actor many years later, lived across from us. His father was Mr. Ahn Chang-ho. Mr. Ahn and my father, who had been boyhood friends in Korea, felt like brothers to each other and kept in touch through the years. It was good to see so many familiar faces again, and we felt happy to be there together.

Every day after school and on weekends, my older brother and I had to pile enough firewood up against the kitchen shack to last until the next day. Father found some wheels and boards at the dumpyard to make a long flatbed for carrying the wood, but we had to make several trips each day. An acre of trees grew some distance from us, where we found plenty of broken branches to gather up.

Meung's job was to keep the wine barrels filled with water so Mother could do her work. I cleaned the oil lamps, kept our shack in order, looked after my baby brother, and heated the bath water for the men at 6 p.m. so they could bathe before supper. The workers' bathhouse had just one large tub inside; I heated the water by building a fire under the floor. The men washed themselves with a hose before entering the tub.

Every Saturday Meung and I went to a slaughterhouse some distance away to get the animal organs that the butchers threw out—pork and beef livers, hearts, kidneys, entrails, tripe—all the things they considered unfit for human consumption. We were not alone—Mexican children came there also. They needed those things to survive just as we did. The butchers stood around laughing at us as we scrambled for the choice pieces. When I told Father I didn't want to go there anymore because they were making fun of us, he said we should thank God that they did not know the value of what they threw out; otherwise, we would go hungry.

Meung started school at the Washington Irving School, not far from our settlement. When I was ready to go, Father asked a friend who spoke a little English—a Mr. Song—to take me. My first day at school was a very frightening experience. As we entered the schoolyard, several girls formed a ring around us, singing a song and dancing in a circle. When they stopped, each one came over to me and hit me in the neck, hurting and frightening me. They ran away when a tall woman came towards us. Her bright yellow hair and big blue eyes looking down at me were a fearful sight; it was my first close look at such a person. She was welcoming me to her school, but I was frightened. When she addressed me, I answered in Korean, "I don't understand you." I turned around, ran all the way home, and hid in our shack. Father laughed when he heard about my behavior. He told me there was nothing to be afraid of; now that we were living here in America, where everything is different from Korea, we would have to learn to get along with everyone.

The next day when I went to school with my brother, the girls did not dance around us; I guess the teacher must have told them not to do it. I learned later that the song they sang was:

> Ching Chong, Chinaman,
> Sitting on a wall.
> Along came a white man,
> And chopped his head off.

The last line was the signal for each girl to "chop my head off" by giving me a blow on the neck. That must have been the greeting they gave to all the Oriental kids who came to school the first day.

Because our Korean names were too difficult for them to remember, the children at school always said "Hey you!" when they wanted our attention. I told Meung that it was too late to change our names, but we should give American names to our siblings. So we started with Paik Daw Sun, who had been born in Hawaii, by calling him Ernest. When another brother was born in Riverside on August 8, 1908, we named him Stanford.

Meung was only three years older than I, but he was extremely observant and considerate for his age. He told me to stop playing around and to notice how much work our mother had to do. He said that to help her, every day before school he would wash the baby's diapers, and I was to hang them on the line. After school, before going for firewood, I was to take them in, fold them, and put them away. Meanwhile he would fill the wine barrels with water from the pump. We followed this routine from then on. I was always taking care of the babies, bathing them every night, changing their diapers, and feeding them midnight bottles. He heated their bath water in a bucket outside so I could give them baths in the tin tub inside our shack.

There was one large building for community meetings in Riverside, where religious services were held on Sundays. We didn't have a minister, but several persons read the Bible and discussed it. Father preached there whenever he had time. An American lady named Mrs. Stewart, who lived in Upland, used to come to our church on Sundays. She was interested in the Korean people and brought presents for everyone at Christmastime. She gave me the first and only doll I ever had.

Meung and I had a special "gang" consisting of six members about the same age. We ran to school together, ran home for lunch, back to school, and home again. On the way to school there was a large mulberry bush growing in the front lawn of one house. Whenever we passed, we noticed the big black berries that had fallen on the lawn. They looked so tempting that we just had to stop and see what they tasted like. They were so delicious we couldn't stop eating them. After that, every time we passed that house we helped ourselves, but we had an uneasy feeling about whether it was right or wrong to take the fruit. We childishly decided that it was all right because the berries were on the ground and weren't picked off the bush. We had a big argument about it one day. When Meung said it was wrong to take something that belonged to someone else, my girlfriend got so angry she picked up a piece of firewood and hit him on the head. When we told Father about it, he said that the berries belonged to the owner of the bush, whether they were on the bush or on the ground. That settled our arguments. From then on we looked the other way every time we passed that house.

An old Chinese peddler used to come to our place once a week with fruits and vegetables on his wagon. I told Philip Ahn to climb up the front of his wagon and talk to him while I climbed up the back and filled my apron with small potatoes, lima beans, and corn, which we roasted in hot ashes. It was our first taste of such vegetables, and they were so good. But the old man got wise to us after a while, so whenever we approached his wagon, he used the horsewhip on us.

One evening, as I was helping Mother wash the lunch pails the men brought back, I asked her what kind of work the men were doing. She told me they were picking oranges, which gave me an idea, but I didn't dare to tell her about it. After breakfast the next day, as I passed out the lunch pails, I asked some of the men why they never brought me an orange. I said I had never seen or tasted one. That evening as I took in the lunch pails, they felt a bit heavy; when I opened one I saw a beautiful orange for the first time. I was so excited I told Father about it. He must have talked to the men, because there were only a few oranges after that. It helped make the work of washing the lunch pails seem less tiring to find a few. One night some time later, when I took in the lunch pails every single one felt heavy. I got really excited, but to my surprise, each pail had a rock in it. When I asked why, the men said they were afraid I would scold them if they didn't bring something, but there were no more oranges to be picked. Everybody had a good laugh about it.

After the orange season was over, the men picked lemons and grapefruit. In the fall there was work in the walnut groves. The men would shake the walnuts from the trees with long poles, then the women and children would gather them up in sacks, take them to a clearing, and peel off the outer shells [hulls]. They got paid by the sack for their labor. Between the walnut harvest and the time to prune the orange trees, the men got a short rest. When there was no work in the citrus groves, Father worked at the Riverside Cement Company on the edge of town.

Two incidents happened in Riverside that will always remain in my memory. The first was when I told Father I needed a coat to wear to school. He said that he would see what he could do about it. He rode to town on his bicycle to buy some material, and he made a coat for me. Since we did not have a sewing machine, he had to sew it by hand one evening. It was a beautiful red coat; I was so happy to wear it. All the girls at school wanted to know where I had purchased it. They couldn't believe my father had made it himself. When I asked Mother how

Father could do such a wonderful thing, she smiled and said that, among other things, Father had been an expert tailor in Korea. He had studied to be a minister and had taught the Korean language to missionaries, but tailoring was how he made a living.

My second memory is equally wondrous. One evening Father woke us up in the middle of the night and said a wonderful thing was happening in the sky. Looking out the window, we saw a big star with a very long sparkling tail that seemed to stretch across the whole sky. The tail was full of small sparkling stars. It was a spectacular, awesome sight, a bit frightening to us children. We didn't understand what was going on and couldn't sleep the rest of the night, wondering what it meant and if everything would be all right the next day.

R. S. Malloch

In the 1980s, San Diego's Great Basin Foundation led a major project that excavated the remaining portion of Riverside's Chinatown and researched its history. Findings from the project, including R. S. Malloch's letters describing his memories of Chinatown, are published in a two-volume monograph, *Wong Ho Leun: An American Chinatown*. Malloch's letters are housed at the Special Collections Library of the University of California, Riverside, and one of them is included here.

Founded in 1879 and relocated in 1885, Riverside's Chinatown at its height housed about five hundred residents. The population dwindled significantly as a result of restrictive immigration policies in the 1920s; by the 1930s there was only one property owner in Chinatown, George Wong, who stayed until his death in 1974. Most of the old Chinatown site has been paved over and replaced by a county building and parking lot.

When asked to put it on paper...

Dear B. J.,

When asked to put it on paper I am surprised at how little I knew of Chinatown in Riverside. The evidence of China was all about us. A blue Mandarin's coat with gold and red embroidery used to lie on the piano and near it a brass plate enameled in blue with a white bird hung on the wall. There were Chinese boxes, Chinese fans, and in the front hall a Chinese gong sat on its red lacquer stand to call us to the meals our

Chinaman prepared. But all these things came from Chinatown in San Francisco—or later, Gumps.

I think none of us must have ever thought of visiting Chinatown in Riverside, and I was never told that any of our elders had done so. In a way Chinatown was like a freeport or diplomatic enclave where the Chinamen could retire for a night to rest, untroubled by our Western law, religion, or morality. What we knew of Chinatown was what came out of it to us.

John and I occasionally had a pack of firecrackers from Chinatown which we carefully unbraided so as not to set them all off at once. On the veranda rails of most of the old houses were the green pottery jars strapped with wicker, with their clay tops, which had been filled with the Chinese ginger which sometimes substituted for chutney with our rice and curry, and might turn up as a sort of surprise in Western dishes like trifle. These jars must have come from Chinatown, were valueless and ubiquitous, and, so far as I remember, ended holding only cigarette ashes and an occasional sprig of geranium.

There may have been venturesome people who visited Chinatown. These would be boys going and coming from Grant School or living on Fourteenth Street. It is probable that Bill Evans, Chesnaye Woodill, or Louie Allebaster would have tales to tell of excursions to the wrong side of Brockton. There were tales of mystery and horror, of gambling and opium, of tong wars, but looking back I believe these must have been mainly tales of imagination. The Chinese I knew were men of dignity and propriety, thoughtful and generous, patient and kind, and if, occasionally, one fell in a fit of hysteria and went after some youth with a meat cleaver, it is little wonder, considering the spareness of their lives and how little they were understood except by those who depended on them and benefited from their faithfulness.

We depended on Chinatown for two things. On a certain day of the week a great bundle of laundry, tied in a sheet, would roll down the back stairs and lie, a mountain to negotiate to get to the back door. After school this bundle would be gone by some mysterious hand of which no one bothered to inquire. A few days later packages neatly tied in paper and string would be on the side porch railing and, an hour or two later, again by a mysterious levitation, would lie open in the upstairs hall by the door of the linen closet. This laundry from Chinatown had a fresh smell not matched in the automatic washers of today; the beauty of the ironing of Irish linen tablecloths and napkins is gone with the cloth they were made of; and the laundrymen should have had a copyright on the words "stiff shirt" for the perfection in their use of starch. The economist might well follow the historian through old Chinatown to discover the means by which this great volume of work was carried with such perfect result.

The other product of Chinatown we enjoyed was brought to our backyard by Wong with his vegetable cart. In our childish imagination we thought that Wong had no other customer but our Grandmother. He would show up in the yard on perhaps two mornings a week, ring his hand bell and, without waiting, fill his basket with what he thought we would need. He would bring this basket into the kitchen porch where, unloading and displaying it to our Jim Ah, there would be much chatter, business and gossip no doubt, in Cantonese. No one seemed to worry what he gave us and I never saw him paid. Jim's vegetables were always so good that no one ever questioned his choice. No one ever asked where the vegetables were grown, or how Wong got them. It is probable that the entire process from field to dinner table was a Chinese enterprise in which Wong and Jim were both agents and shareowners.

My slight knowledge of Chinatown came through Jim's visits to it. He had "a day off" once a week. This day began, however, after lunch and ended when everyone expected breakfast as usual next day. After washing the lunch dishes, Jim would go to "the Chinaman's house." These houses can be found on many California ranches today, still called by that name, but acting as toolsheds, shops, or storerooms. They were seldom more than 10 or 12 feet square, with one door and two small windows. They were lit and heated in winter by coal oil lamps or stoves but sweltered in summer. They had no water supply, and the watercloset provided was usually in the stable, shared by teamsters and stable boys. The Chinese cooks we knew not only kept their kitchens and dishrags clean, even in the camps like Victoria, Windsor, and Mockingbird, they themselves gave the impression of being meticulously clean not only in their white jackets and aprons but from the skin out. Their hands were as dry and pleasant to touch as parchment. This is remarkable in Jim because he had nowhere to wash himself or his clothes beside a washtub or the horse trough and he was never seen to use these. Arrangements must have existed in Chinatown as one of the luxuries of the Chinaman's day off.

After lunch on Thursdays Jim would go to the Chinaman's house which stood half way between the kitchen and the stable, a matter of 50 yards, and change from his coat and apron. He would put on a black

Chinese silk coat with a buttoned collar with frogged buttonholes. With this he wore cotton trowsers of fine pale blue and white stripes; black Chinese slippers with the sewing in their soles, and a straw hat or "boater" with a bright ribbon, probably in the colors of Cornell, which he had adopted from the selection in the back hall closet. He would then mount his bicycle with the high seat and handlebars such as are seen today in newsreels of Peking streets. He wore his hat formally, straight and level, and did not lean to pedal but sat straight and presumably rode in that dignified way the four miles to Chinatown. Just what conditions he found there or how he spent his time does not appear but, years later, I discovered he had a 32 caliber Ivor-Johnson pistol, hammerless and stylishly nickel plated, which he admitted carrying for his protection, probably returning from games of FanTan in the dawn.

Jim Ah must have been with us for nearly 20 years and died on the ranch. He is buried at Olivewood next the grave of Ah Yum, his dear friend and for many years the Bettner's cook. Their graves are to the right as you go in the main gate and are in the plot nearest Arlington Avenue. Jim had cooked for Mrs. Mylne when my grandmother stayed at Greystones and it was she who suggested the epitaph which is carved on his stone: "He remedied in silence what the foolish rail against."

Sometime after Jim's death I took his few things to Old Wong. It was a great surprise then to hear that, although Wong said Jim had left China at 16, he had a wife and son there. I suggested that she should have what Jim had left but Old Wong seemed very reluctant to send his things, and it was only with great difficulty that I got him to explain. Finally he burst out with, "Me tellum he dead seven years." Jim had got Wong to write to China of his death seven years before. Jim had got tired of sending money after all those years.

Perhaps two years after Jim's death, one day at Raeburn, three young Chinamen came to the door. They were well dressed and obviously not farmers or cooks, probably shop owners from Los Angeles. They had asked about Jim, where he was buried, and seemed hesitant to come to their point. Finally it appeared that they proposed to send him back to China to sleep with his ancestors. When I asked how this was to be done they said simply, "We send him suitcase." I rejected this idea and I am sure Jim still rests next to Ah Yum in Olivewood. His Chinese name was Quon Ock.

Several years after Jim's death George Wong, who was Old Wong's son, began to come to the house occasionally, apparently just to talk. It was after the Japanese invasion of Manchuria and George made it understood that he was an agent, a secret agent, of the Chinese government buying and shipping arms to China, and in this role in touch with sources of power and money which could not be disclosed. His talk, however, was of the old days, of his father, and of Jim and Ah Yum, but always in reference to the old families of the town for whom the Chinamen had worked.

One day, in 1932 or '33, after my marriage, George Wong told me that through his diplomatic relations he had got a Thousand Year Old Egg and that he wanted to share it with me. It was finally decided to make a ceremony of it and for this our friend and contemporary, Evelyn Griffith, was to be invited, together with our consorts. A few nights later my wife and I went in the evening with Evelyn and Peter Traphagen to George's room in Chinatown, where George gave us cups of a rice drink like the Chinese Tequila of Ensenada, followed by a Chinese dinner and finally, with some trepidation, the Thousand Year Old Egg. It turned out to be a dusky black, both white and yoke, and to taste like a rare and delicate cheese.

After dinner, in the warmth of friendship and wine, George got expansive, referred to his work for the Chinese government, but went on to describe in a very genial way his sources of knowledge and influence in the local scene. In the summer of 1927 my mother had made a trip to England and during her absence, with Jim Ah at Greystones where my grandmother was staying with Mrs. Mylne, had written him postcards and several letters to keep him in mind of his first loyalty to Raeburn. It now appeared that George Wong had all these letters—and I might be curious as to what was in them. I laughed at this and made so little of it that George was driven to go farther. He told us that, when he was taken to the jail, he never spent more than an hour because he had always one telephone call.

This he would make to Bill Evans followed by his immediate release. When Peter and I made light of this possibility, George said he would show us and took us to a neighboring room with a locked door to the street. This room was stacked and packed with bundles of paper from floor to ceiling, leaving only a passage the width of the door from front to back. Here, he said, were the papers accumulated for Old Wong through the year by the Chinamen who worked for the old families.

This room may hold the greatest store of ancient history to be found in Riverside.

Polingaysi Qoyawayma

Polingaysi Qoyawayma, whose first name roughly translates to "butterfly sitting among flowers in the breeze" in Hopi, was born in 1892 in Old Oraibi on the Hopi Reservation in Arizona. In a time when Hopi mothers would frantically hide their children from the authorities who would send them away to school, Qoyawayma deliberately chose to get a white education despite the protests of her parents. For a time she turned her back on Hopi customs, but she eventually devoted her successful career as a teacher to educating Hopi children while encouraging them to value their heritage. She died in 1990.

No Turning Back: A Hopi Woman's Struggle to Live in Both Worlds is an account of Qoyawayma's life. This excerpt describes her decision to go to the Sherman Institute, an Indian boarding school, and the confusion she experienced when her Hopi customs and the expectations of her teachers clashed on her arrival.

from *No Turning Back*

Tawaquaptewa was right. Polingaysi had wanted to be a white man. The white man had abundant supplies of food, good clothing, and opportunities to travel. She had a desire to share the good things of the white way of living.

It was soon after the Oraibi split, and before the Qoyawayma family moved into the New Oraibi home, that Polingaysi heard of plans for sending a group of Hopi young people to Riverside for training at Sherman Institute. She began to daydream of going with them. She envied the chosen ones. Why, she asked herself, shouldn't she be asked to go along? Hadn't she been a good scholar? Hadn't she learned to spell words, and write them, and speak them, at least after a fashion? She was ready for a taste of life beyond the mesas.

She was old enough to be included in the group that was going to that far-off place beyond the Snowy Peaks. Although she was so small that she might well be mistaken for a ten-year-old, she was in reality in her early teens, perhaps fourteen. But, as far as worldliness was concerned, she was completely ignorant.

One clear day in that September of 1906, she saw a covered wagon on the hill road that led down from Second Mesa. A vast excitement ran through her. Perhaps this wagon had in it the children from Keams Canyon School, the children who were bound for the outside world of the white man.

Stationing herself at a vantage point, she waited for the wagon's arrival in the village. It could be that the wagon contained relatives or friends, though no ceremonial dances were being held at that time. Relatives were always received with fitting honors. One of the uncles would take them in tow and go with them from house to house, introducing them to other relatives. At each place they would eat a little *piki*, some sweet corn cakes, or other food given to them in welcome.

But these people in the wagon that rolled steadily nearer, drawn by a lazy team of horses, were not relatives. Boys scrambled from the canvas-covered enclosure and came running ahead, racing each other in Hopi fashion. These, Polingaysi felt certain, were children from the government school at the Agency, embarking on their great adventure. Then and there she made her decision to go with them.

As soon as the driver pulled the horses to a halt near the trading post, Polingaysi ran to the wagon and climbed up to have a look inside. There was an Oraibi girl in the wagon, and to that familiar, friendly face Polingaysi appealed for information.

"Are you coming home to stay, or are you going on somewhere in this wagon?" she asked.

"We're going to the land of oranges," the schoolgirl told her. "Far away. In California."

Polingaysi's face took on a rapt expression. Land of oranges! She visualized ground covered with great, golden oranges, sweet to the taste, pungent to the nostrils. How wonderful it would be to live in such a land! Still, perhaps there was a trick in this. Would those children ever be allowed to return to the mesas?

She plied the other girl with questions and was somewhat reassured. They were going to a school. They would ride from Winslow on a train which would go very fast. What was a train? The girl didn't know, exactly. Someone had told her it was a string of long houses on wheels, drawn by an iron house that screamed with ear-splitting loudness. They would come home someday, but not soon.

Polingaysi eyed the girl suspiciously. Was she telling the truth? Was there such a place as she described? And how did she know about the thing that screamed, since she had never seen it?

Another of the girls, a few years older, took the doubt from Polingaysi's eyes. Their teacher had shown them pictures of trains. She had also shown them pictures of orange trees, heavy with fruit, this girl said, like peaches on the Hopi peach trees, only much larger.

Polingaysi relinquished her picture of oranges golden on the ground, accepted a picture of orange trees.

"There are so many the schoolchildren play ball with them," one of the boys said. "Anyone may eat as many as he wishes. There are piles of them."

Polingaysi abruptly jumped to the ground and sped homeward. Arriving breathless and windblown, she asked her mother to teach her to make a plaque.

Astonished, her mother asked why she was suddenly in such a hurry to learn an art she had never before been willing to consider. Hopi girls from time immemorial had learned to make reed and yucca plaques as a matter of course. One of the duties of a Hopi mother is to teach her daughters plaque-making, for many plaques are needed in a Hopi household. Anna had been an apt and willing student. Polingaysi had been too restless, too filled with projects of another nature to learn such sedentary work.

"I want to buy an orange," Polingaysi answered truthfully. "The trader will give me oranges for the plaque. I tasted an orange once, but I don't remember very well how it tasted. I think it tasted very good. If oranges taste good, I'm going to the land of oranges where the other schoolchildren are going." She had already picked up a plaque her mother had nearly completed. "I will finish this one. I am in a hurry," she told her mother.

"Always you must be doing something different," her mother sighed. "How is it that you are not content to be a true Hopi, but must learn more and more of the ways of the *Bahana?* Where is this land? Who is going, and why?"

Bent over her work, Polingaysi told about the wagon and the children from Keams Canyon School.

"I have heard of this school in the west," Sevenka said. "Your father told me. Children from many Indian tribes go there. Even Foreheads."

For an instant Polingaysi's hands were still. Foreheads. Would it be safe? But then, there would be teachers to protect her from the Navajos.

Her mother sat down beside her and began instructing her in plaque-making.

"I am glad to see that you are interested in this work," she said, "but as for going away with anyone, that you cannot do. You are too young to be away from home. You belong here, with me and your father."

Polingaysi did not argue. She finished the plaque, not too skillfully, and took it to the store. The oranges she received for it tasted sweet and tangy. She decided to eat many of them in California. Going to the home of her California-bound friend, she asked when the group expected to begin the journey.

The student gave her bad news. There would be no traveling until the parents had signed a paper stating their willingness to allow their children to go away to school. Some of the parents were too conservative to want their children to leave them. The sparkle of excitement died from Polingaysi's eyes. Would her parents sign for her? She doubted it. Should she try to find a way to go, or should she stay at home and become the true Hopi maiden her parents wished her to be?

She had to think this over. Down the path there was a huge boulder that had broken from the dill and fallen against another rock in such a manner as to provide a hiding place. In this sheltered nook Polingaysi sat down to think. A broken bit of pottery lay at her feet, and from long habit she picked it up and began digging in the sand with it.

She thought of the wagon leaving Oraibi without her. She thought of the other girls and boys waving goodbye. She visualized their happy time in the land of oranges while she languished here at home. Tossing the pot shard aside she returned home to ask permission to go with the others to Riverside. Her parents flatly refused to allow her to go.

Polingaysi brooded and waited, keeping in touch with her more fortunate friend. The night before the travelers were to begin their journey by covered wagon to the railroad town of Winslow, about seventy miles south of Oraibi, Polingaysi made a bundle of her few belongings and hid it beside the house. Before daylight she crept out, snatched up her bundle, and fled.

No one was near the covered wagon. She climbed into it and crouched beneath the wagon seat, hoping no one would discover her until it was too late to force her return to the village. She had slept fitfully the night before, and it was chilly in the pre-dawn. She pulled her blanket around her and fell asleep, to be awakened by the driver, a white man.

"Well, now! What's this? You a stowaway?" he laughed.

"No." Polingaysi shook her head, not knowing what the word meant. "I'm going to the land of oranges. I came early to keep you from waiting for me."

Then he asked her for "the paper" and she had no paper. He told her he couldn't take her without her parents' consent and asked her to get out of the wagon. Her hopes were dwindling, but she sat there stubbornly. She would not surrender to circumstance, though she did not know what to do next.

The driver summoned a Hopi girl who was acting as overseer of the girl students, and this girl told Polingaysi she must get out of the wagon.

"You're too young," she said. "You'd be lonesome. You'd be crying for your parents before we got to Winslow."

"I am old enough not to cry," Polingaysi insisted, her eyes flashing proudly. "I will not get out of the wagon. I am going along."

The girl went away and returned with Polingaysi's parents. Sevenka, large and stern always, seemed even more imposing to the defiant girl in the wagon box, but Polingaysi's slender little father wore a look of understanding on his expressive face.

"I think we should allow her to go," he told his wife. "She will be well taken care of. She will learn more of the writing marks that are in books. I think we should sign the paper."

Sevenka gave in. "It shall be as you say," she said turning away to hide the tears in her eyes.

Thus Polingaysi won her weaponless battle for another sample of white man's education.

Before the wagon left the village her father came to tell her goodbye and to place in her hand three silver dollars, his wage for six days of hard labor for the missionary. Polingaysi had never before seen so much money at one time. Awed, she knotted the silver pieces into a corner of her shawl and held the knot tightly in one hand, fearful of losing her fortune.

How wealthy she felt! As the wagon rolled away from her home, from parents, brothers, sisters, and grandparents, her mind teemed with plans for spending the money. What a lot of things she could buy with it!

The long trip across the desert that day was like a party. The children got out now and then and walked to stretch their legs. They played games whenever the horses rested. But that night, in camp on the bank of the Little Colorado, the world seemed cold and unfriendly.

Coyotes howled, sending shivers of apprehension over Polingaysi. She rolled up in a blanket, as did the others, but could not go to sleep at once. Instead, she thought of her patient mother, her adoring and adorable brothers, Anna and her new baby boy. In spite of her determination, tears oozed beneath her eyelids, but she smothered her loneliness and no one knew she wept. Once it flashed into her mind to slip away and return to the village, following the wagon tracks. She could make the trip in two days, or at most three. Then she thought of her mother. She could almost see the accusing black eyes and hear the stern words: "Finish what you begin. Those who leave things half done get boils on their heads. Do you want boils on your head?"

In the quiet dark, Polingaysi's fingers crept up to her scalp. Her exploring fingers found no evidence of boils forming there. It was best not to take a chance of getting them. Her mother would scorn her, if she went back weeping and sniveling, a coward running away from her own decision.

Again, there was no turning back.

It was the first time Polingaysi had ever slept away from home. She had once more willfully departed from the Hopi frame of action. Whatever happened to her was her own fault; it would be up to her to take the consequences without complaint.

The realization that they were indeed leaving their desert home seemed to strike the older students the next morning. They were tired, silent, awed by the change, even before they reached Winslow.

After their pueblo villages, crowded together on the mesas' rocky points, the small town of Winslow seemed to them a noisy and huge place. Trains rumbled and screeched along the rails that bisected the town, accompanied by a clickety-clacking sound, unfamiliar yet interesting. The streets seemed alive with men and women; freight wagons, buggies, buckboards formed a traffic pattern along the main street. Cowboys and Navajos on horseback turned to stare at the wild-looking little band from the mesas.

For the first time, Polingaysi entered a store where quantities of food, dress goods, and other supplies were displayed. Why they went inside, she could never remember. Perhaps the white matron in charge of the girls merely wanted them to see the interior of a normal place of business in the white man's world. Certainly they were not a clean group of young people. Wearing their worn ticking dresses, cheap shoes, Hopi shoulder blankets, and trading-post shawls, the girls were less than charming. The boys were just as unkempt in their homemade floursack shirts and denim pants, and just as shy and frightened as the girls.

That night they slept in a warehouse, with the government matron in charge. Next day they were herded onto a passenger train to begin their journey by rail to Riverside, California. Never had Polingaysi heard such a confusing din. Never had she imagined so much movement and clanking of machinery as followed. Then the train pulled out of the station, wheezing and whistling and clickety-clacking up the grade.

Polingaysi sat stiffly on the red plush cushion beside another girl and stared at the changing scenery. The desert growth changed from rabbit brush to low junipers and pinyons and, as the train carried its passengers into higher elevations, ponderosa pines appeared, rosy-boled and green of foliage. One of the boys was the first to spy the snowy heights of the San Francisco Peaks that tower above the town of Flagstaff.

"Look!" he whispered, indicating the direction by pursing his lips and pointing with his chin. "Nu-va-da-ka-o-vi!"

Polingaysi went with the others to the north side of the car and stared at the beautiful peaks. She had known them all her life, but this was her first close look at them. On those jagged peaks, according to Hopi legend, lived the Kachina people, ancestors of her father.

"Remember, you are a child of the Kachinas," her paternal grandmother had always told her. Hopis must not boast, they must not show pride, but they could feel inner pride in ancestry. Her father was of Kachina Clan, therefore she was a child of the Kachinas, as a daughter of a Bow Clan man would be a child of the Bow people. To Polingaysi, identification with the august, revered, legendary Kachinas was a mark of distinction.

While the children stared, a man came through the coach selling fruit. Polingaysi forgot the mountains. Should she spend a portion of her fortune for food? There were apples and oranges in the basket. With those she was familiar, but what were those long, yellow things that grew in a bunch like so many fat fingers?

A married couple had been assigned to the coach with the younger children. Both were very young and eager to go to school in California. Polingaysi asked the young wife about the fruit. She giggled, hiding her face as she admitted her own ignorance, but her husband knew.

"Bananas," he said. "Good to eat, but very sweet. I do not like them very much."

Polingaysi, the adventurous, decided to try one. She also bought an apple and an orange, then was horrified to see how much of her silver dollar she had spent. Her chagrin increased when, after peeling the banana as the young man instructed, she was repelled by the strange taste and texture of the fruit. She gave the rest of it away, smarting under the knowledge that she had acted foolishly and without due consideration.

"I'll not spend any more of my money until I get to the land of oranges," she vowed silently, and kept her vow. When tempted to break it, she remembered her mother's remedy for hunger and drank a cup of water to "weigh her down."

Arriving in Riverside in a stupor of weariness, the nervous and frightened strangers were taken to dormitories. Polingaysi, the youngest and smallest, was assigned to a place in one of the dormitories for girls and told to remove her clothing and take a shower. Now this was terror, genuine terror, from the viewpoint of a Hopi maiden. Who could tell from what spring this gushing water came? Who knew, positively, that Water Serpent was not peering from that faucet?

The fear of snakes had been instilled in Polingaysi at a very early age. Her first awareness of the dreaded water serpent came when she was little more than a baby. Toddling after her mother, her own little water jar on her back, she had gone to the village spring. At that time it was like a huge cone, narrowing at the bottom where there was a pool of water that reflected the blue sky and brightly colored cliffs. The steep sides were terraced, and the women often spent hours there, gossiping while they awaited their turn to fill their jars.

As children will, Polingaysi absorbed everything and asked many questions. At the spring's edge, Polingaysi's mother caught her handwoven woolen blanket dress closely about her legs as she bent to dip water into her *wigoro*. Across from them, where the water seeped from the mossy rocks, there was an earthen pot. In that light it looked very pretty to the little girl. Above it something moved. It was a feather, affixed to a prayer stick which was thrust into a little niche above the water and the submerged pot.

"Look, Mother," Polingaysi said. "Someone has lost a pretty little pot."

Her mother almost fell into the water, so violent was her reaction.

"Don't look back in there, and don't talk," she hissed. "Do you want to be charmed by Water Serpent?"

Her mother's stern and fearful face, and the haste with which she filled her water jar and hurried out of the funnel of the spring, was enough to impress the episode upon the child. Later she learned that the reason women held their skirts about them at the spring was to guard against molestation by the snake, which might make a girl or woman become pregnant, just by breathing on her. Also, that the little pot she had admired was a "transplanter" buried there by some priest of the rainmakers, and therefore sacred. To have removed it would have been dangerous.

And here, in this strange room, she was being asked to bare her body and stand beneath that stream of water, to be seen and perhaps breathed upon by Water Serpent.

The matron in charge was unaware of Polingaysi's fears. She might have been more tolerant had she known why the girl cowered in a corner, her eyes wide with fright. As it was, she made it clear that Polingaysi was to take her shower...at once!

That night for the first time, Polingaysi slept in a real bed. She climbed up onto it giddy with fear and nervousness, feeling the softness of the mattress and the resilience of the springs beneath the tautly drawn sheets. Her bed was one of many, ranged the length of the room. In each bed there was a girl, a stranger, not one of them a Hopi from Polingaysi's homeland. Eyes watched her get into bed and lay her freshly washed head on the white pillow, but no one spoke a word of welcome and no one smiled. They were strangers, not knowing nor caring how this new girl felt. For all the comfort they offered, the Oraibian might as well have been alone.

She had no sooner pulled up the covers than helpless tears began to flow. She tried to blink them back, but they kept coming, gushing like a spring from beneath her closed eyelids. Finally she dived beneath the pillow and wept, all but suffocating before her tears were spent.

For weeks, each night was a repetition of the first. With the coming of darkness, all the confusions of the day welled up in her and had to be released.

Villiana Hyde and Eric Elliott

Villiana Calac Hyde was born in 1903, a member of the Rincon band of the Luiseño tribe of Southern California; she attended the Sherman Institute, at that time a government-run Indian boarding school, during the First World War. She was the last native speaker of the Luiseño language, and her efforts to keep her language alive led to her 1971 book *An Introduction to the Luiseño Language*. She died in 1994.

Eric Elliott is a Southern California native with a Ph.D. in linguistics from the University of California, San Diego. From 1988 to 1994, Elliott transcribed Hyde's stories, told in Luiseño, a project that culminated in the fourteen-hundred-page bilingual compilation *Yumáyk Yumáyk: Long Ago*. "Going to Sherman" is one of these narratives, excerpted below. Elliott also worked with native Serrano speaker Dorothy Ramon; see those selections later in this anthology.

The dollar sign ($) represents a non-English sound (retroflex s) formed by making an "s" sound while keeping the tip of your tongue curled back, touching the alveolar ridge.

from "Going to Sherman"

Ngééngi cháám escuela-yk.
We left for school.

'ayániy-m kíí-ngay cháám-i.
They took us from home.

Cham-kíí-ngay 'ayániy-m cháám-i. Cháám ngééngi.
They took us from our home. We left.

Pí' lóóvi-qu$ chóó'on híí-cha.
But everything was alright.

No-$úún lóóvi-qu$ 'amáy-m-i 'awóó-m-i tííwi-nik.
I was happy to see other children.

Pom-kí' 'awóng míí-qu$.
They had different types of buildings (i.e., 'houses').

Pí'-sunpoku nóó kiháá-t míí-qu$.
So, I was pretty small.

Qáy nóó chaqwííl-ya.
I was not sad.

'awó-m qál-qu$ 'amááy-um póplov-um.
There were some good kids there.

Yí'yi-k chóó'on-um cháám.
We all played.

Pí' hikáhka-qu$ po-pilách i-pi.
But learning was difficult.

Po-marchar-pi hikáhka-qu$.
Marching was difficult.

Pá' pilách-ax, pilách-ax nóó, 'ííxmaqanik.
But still I did learn, finally.

'ahúyaxi tó$ngu-vuk-t-um qál-qu$.
There were very strict directors.

Qál-qu$ tó$ngu-vuk-t-um.
There were directors.

Chóó'on-ngay híí-ngay cháám-i kwavíchu-qu$.
They watched us closely in everything we did.

Tóów-qu$ wunáá-l-um cháám-i.
They looked after us.

Tááki-k cháám-i 'aláxwi-ch-i
And they would punish us if we did

hí-sh cham-loví'i-qala.
something wrong.

Pí' cháám-i tááki-k. Téétil-uk cháám-ik.
And they would punish us. They would tell us.

Húú'uni-qu$ cháám-ik michá' 'axáninik
They would teach

kíí-sh cham-limpiar-pi-y 'ayáálinik.
us how to clean house correctly.

Pí' cháám pilách-ax poné-y pó' 'axáninik.
And we learned how to do it, like that.

Míí-qu$ páchxamla-sh 'amááy-um pom-kwáán.
There was a laundry room for the children.

Chóó'on-um 'amááy-um pomóm qál-qat-um wuná'
All the children who lived there used this

pom-míx míí-qu$, páchxamla-sh.
laundry room.

Pí' qál-qu$ cham-nóó'u-m.
And we had directors.

Cháám-ik húú'uni-qu$ michá' 'axáninik
They taught us how

po-híqwi-pi-y máquina.
to run the machines.

Mómka-t purúy-qu$ po-$ún-nga páchxamla-nga.
Big ones (machines) stood there in the laundry room.

Pí' 'awó-m 'amááy-um $óti-qu$.
Some children ironed.

'amááy-um pom-mííxan-i $óti-qu$.
The children ironed their clothes.

Pí' qáy cháám humáhma-ch-i.
And we had to be careful. (i.e., 'We could not [do] nonsense.')

$óti-nik qáy wuní-yk cham-wa$áána-pi míí-qu$.
We weren't supposed to stretch things when we ironed.

Cháám $óti-k poné-y 'ayáálinik.
We ironed them properly.

Pá' cháám huní'i-k tó$ngu-ka-t pó-yk hamúúla.
We'd have to show it to the director first.

Pí' tó$ngu-ka-t poné-y tííwi-k 'ayáálinik.
And the director would look at it carefully.

Pí' pá' lóóvi-k.
And then it was all right.

Pa' cháám taváni-k wuní-yk.
Then we would put it away.

Téé qáy cháám 'ayáálinik loví'i-k:
If we didn't do it right,

pí' cháám yú'pan loví'i-k.
then we'd do it again.

Pí' cháám poné-y loví'i-k.
We would do it (again).

Hikáhka-qu$ pomlééyu 'angááyi. Pí' cháám pilách-ax.
It was pretty difficult at first. But we learned.

Cháám 'ó'na-qu$ hí-sh cham-loví'i-pi-y.
We knew what to do.

Pí' 'ayáálinik ló'xa-qu$.
And we did it right.

William S. Hart

Born in New York in 1864, William S. Hart was first a ranch hand and then a successful Shakespearean actor on Broadway before he came to California and started his memorable career filming and starring in Westerns. He made more than sixty-five silent films, including *Tumbleweeds*, and died in 1946 in Newhall, California.

Searching for a ready-made western location to shoot his movies, Hart "discovered" Victorville in 1914. The town became the backdrop for more than two hundred films; it was, for example, transformed into Dodge City, Kansas, for Hart's *Wild Bill Hickok*. In this excerpt from his autobiography, *My Life East and West*, Hart describes a raucous party in Victorville that starts when people on a film set there discover a train car filled with wine.

from *My Life East and West*

Cowboys are children—from eight to eighty, age makes no difference. They are boys just the same. Idleness is bad for children.

A heavy Santa Fe freight was sidetracked to allow a passenger train to go through. One of the cars of the heavy freight was to all outward appearance an oil-tank car. But it wasn't an oil-tank car! Appearance was all wrong. It was a camouflage. I never knew who put it there, nor who was responsible for it, but ninety-seven million gallons of the finest Mexican wine ever made from grapes was in that car. Where it was going, I do not know. I only know it never arrived there, and that through the medium of several short pieces of garden hose, enough wine was siphoned out of that oil car to irrigate the Mojave Desert.

Only it was not used for such purpose. At the end of every piece of hose was an endless line of cowboys, each with a receptacle that would hold liquid—wooden buckets, tin buckets, milk pans, garbage pails, horses' canvas nose bags, washtubs—every repository available within two miles of Victorville was on that line. The heavy freight and the sadly depleted oil-tank car passed on.

For two whole days and nights the carnival lasted. The streets of the town became a public dance hall. Innocent and harmless—yes! But to those who knew not the way of the cowboy—menacing. The more timid citizens telephoned to San Bernardino, forty miles away, for help. The sheriff and twenty deputies, all armed to the teeth, arrived on a special train. They did not need guns. They needed husky men and stretchers. The merrymaking had ended. Every foot of available space outside or inside at Victorville was occupied by a sleeping cowboy. The courthouse was full—the jail was full. Nothing was sacred to those bacchanalian inebriates.

There were no "goody-goods." They were all alike, from the manager and the director down. I was ill in bed, but I can make an affidavit that it was good wine, and said affidavit can be supported by a reliable witness—the sheriff was in the room at the time. The sheriff was a real sheriff; no one had been harmed, no damage had been done. He returned with his deputies to San Bernardino.

I often wonder what some of those old desert rat prospectors think when they uncover some of those covered buckets that were cached during those two days of revelry and the location forgotten. I'll bet they don't try the contents on the burro first!

Celeste DeBlasis

Born in 1946, Celeste DeBlasis was a lifelong resident of Victorville, home of the well-known Kemper Campbell Ranch established by her grandparents. A graduate of Pomona College, she is best known for her historical romances—in particular the Swan trilogy, published in the 1980s. She died in 2001.

This excerpt, about both the history of the Kemper Campbell Ranch and DeBlasis's early childhood there, is from her book *Graveyard Peaches: A California Memoir*.

from *Graveyard Peaches*

A hundred miles northeast of Los Angeles, and one mile south of the town of Victorville, the ranch [Kemper Campbell Ranch] is in the "high" Mojave Desert; the altitude marker near my front porch says 2700 feet. The Mojave River runs through it.

Its history as a cattle ranch began in the second half of the nineteenth century. It was the major spread for a large area because other ranches used it as a shipping point for their cattle. Its brand, the "hashknife," was well-known. The cattle business was still in operation in 1924 when my maternal grandparents and their law partner, Andy Sorenson, purchased the 4000 acres from a client. The man had hoped his son-in-law would make a success of the land, but he hadn't. My grandparents and Andy immediately divided the place, the grandparents drawing the new boundaries and Andy in turn having first choice. The Verde Ranch became the North Verde and the South Verde. Andy chose the 2200 acres of the South Verde because the grazing was better for livestock; my grandparents were pleased to get the 1800 acres of the North Verde because the land was more varied, more beautiful.

First purchased as an investment, the ranch quickly appealed to my grandparents as a country home, a place to bring their children away from Los Angeles, where the grandparents practiced law. There were old buildings on the ranch, but the central part of the Main House was begun in 1927 and finished in 1929. The world changed for almost everyone in 1929 with the crash of the stock market, and by 1931, my mother and her two brothers were living here full-time, though their parents still practiced law in the city. By 1932, those Californians who'd had money to travel in luxury to exotic, faraway places now needed a closer—and more affordable—retreat. The first paying guests appeared then, which turned out to be the beginning of the guest ranch, a business that would continue until 1975 and would host people from all over the United States and from Europe.

During much of this time, the ranch continued to be a working ranch. The beef-cattle business went on until 1955; Arabian and Palomino horses were bred and raised commercially from the 1930s to 1951; there was a dairy until 1970. Field crops were planted and harvested, and poultry was fattened to be served for Sunday dinners at the guest ranch. I and my brother David were raised here, as were our cousins, Kemper, Craig, and Scott.

Most of the ranch buildings are against the hills and fit so well that they appear to have grown from the landscape. The Main House looks as if has been in place for 150 years. It was designed by John Byers, an architect who specialized in the Monterey style, an imaginative interpretation of the wedding of the Anglo influence and Spanish Colonial houses, a union that occurred mostly in Northern California in the 1800s when New Englanders arrived and added their own shapes, such as pitched roofs and second-story balconies, to adobe buildings. But John Byers did his best known work in the 1920s.

The adobe bricks for the Main House were made on the ranch, and the tiles for the roof were hand-shaped, molded over the thigh, in Mexico. Great timbers support the roof and the porch, and the floors are mahogany or tile. The primary living room is two stories high with an inside balcony running along the back wall, giving access to a little suite of rooms and to the attic. The balcony is reached by an inside, open-step stairway on the south wall and from the outside by a parallel staircase.

A labyrinth of dining rooms and living quarters was added over the years and wanders west, north, and south from the main living room, yet the house remains so harmonious, it seems to have been built all at once.

The Main House is one of the few places I knew as a child that has not seemed to shrink now that I am grown.

Innumerable meals have been shared in the Main House. There have been countless hours of discussion and debate. There have been weddings, funerals, birthday parties, poetry readings, concerts, dances, political rallies, and charity drives. New Year's Eve, Easter, the Fourth of July, Thanksgiving, and Christmas Eve have been celebrated for decades there. Generations of families and thousands of people have come and gone. Far more than the cemetery, the ranch has become my sacred ground, holding the traces of all that has been celebrated and mourned in it. Once shaped by human hands, it has since then shaped in one way or another the humans that have been sheltered by it.

When I was a small child with an insular view, I thought everyone lived as we did; I didn't realize how eccentric the place and the people were until my experience broadened. I remember going to stay overnight with a school friend. I came home in shock.

"They don't say anything at the table except 'Pass the salt' or 'Pass the ketchup,'" I reported. "And they don't say much away from the table either."

My mother tried to explain that a lot of people were like that, that the ranch just happened to be a place where people liked table conversation. That made sense, but nonetheless, it was the beginning of my recognition that ranch life was different.

The natural configuration of the ranch has long kept it hidden. I used to imagine that there was a magic wall around it that made it invisible. Because we are so close to town, the main road is really just an extension of Victorville's "C" Street, but it gives no warning of where it is going. Past the cemetery, the hill is steep going up along the western flank of the Narrows, a high jumble of rocks that channels the Mojave River from both sides as it flows north, not south, until it disappears into the desert. The Mojave is a quixotic river that flows underground along some of its course, though the portion that travels through the ranch has always been aboveground, forced upwards by the Narrows. And when you crest the Narrows, the surprise of the ranch is there, an oasis cradled on the western side by hills. Looking east from the Main House, the view is spectacular. Desert quickly gives way to green country: meadows, ponds, sloughs, and forest until the horizon stretches to desert again where the old boundary of the ranch used to be. From there, you can see across the desert to distant hills that change color all day as the earth travels, sometimes soft gray, sometimes bright pink to deep purple and blue. Even the most accurate paintings of this landscape look false, as if the pieces fit only through the eye and brain and heart, not through someone else's brush.

The green land is rich with wildlife. Hawks hunt the long days, and owls the nights. Skunks bustle homeward at dawn after nocturnal feeding. Beavers build dams wherever they can find sufficient water. Coyotes trot the meadows even when the sun is high, and cottontails and jackrabbits burst from cover. The bobcats, kit foxes, and weasels were always elusive, and their numbers are much diminished now, but with patience and luck one can still see them occasionally. Sightings of mountain lions used to cause great excitement, but now the wild land is so surrounded by development that there is no way for the lions to get here.

The ranch lies in the path of one of the major flyways for migrating birds. More than two hundred and fifty species have been identified here, and it is not unusual to see forty or fifty in a single fall or spring morning.

Many species stay here the year around. The red-tailed hawks and the great blue herons are my favorites, the hawks for their slow sailing watch over all, and the herons for looking prehistoric. They can stand four feet tall; and with their blue-gray, color-of-twilight plumage and their huge wingspan, with their necks pulled in as they fly and their croaking cries, they create the illusion that the earth is forever newly born.

The view from the hills is open and vast, as it is from the shore of a sea, but here, there are spaces of silence. Just at dawn and just at dusk, everything stills; even the wind usually stops its singing, a stately pause to mark the passage from darkness to light, from light to darkness.

As the crow flies, this place is about seventy miles from the Pacific Ocean; as a man walks or rides or drives a wagon, it is much, much farther than that, separated by mountains and by areas that were once inaccessible. These conditions have kept the human history of the region prior to the twentieth century to a minimum, but even so, various peoples did pass through. In addition to the vanished tribes, Native Americans of the past few centuries are known to have frequented the area, including some who escaped control of the mission fathers over the mountains and killed some Spanish soldiers in their bid for freedom. Utes captured wild horses to sell, as well as to "liberate" some that weren't so wild. Even Willie Boy was here early in the century. He was a Paiute Indian who lived for a while in Victorville and worked on the ranch. He made history in 1909 when he led lawmen on a five-hundred-mile chase across the desert, this despite the fact that he was on foot and they were on horseback. Robert Redford played a good sheriff in the movie *Tell Them Willie Boy Is Here*, which was sympathetic to Willie Boy, played by Robert Blake. Local history is not so kind. According to that version, Willie Boy, after being refused permission to marry Lolita, the Indian girl of his choice, murdered her father, kidnapped her, and, in the process of fleeing from the posses, shot the girl, leaving her body behind. He also severely wounded a deputy Sheriff, albeit in self-defense. In both versions of the story, the posses eventually caught up with him only to discover he had committed suicide.

The Spanish expeditions that passed through during the eighteenth century were followed in the nineteenth by trappers and scouts such as Jedediah Smith, John C. Frémont, and Kit Carson, and then by more organized bands of settlers, including some Mormons who felt God had intended them to travel beyond Utah. Most of these were headed for California's inland valleys, rather than the desert itself, but river land meant fodder and water for livestock. One of the buildings on the ranch, the Red House, was a hotel for travelers, and the man who built it, Mr. Brown, had the toll rights to the Cajon Pass, which leads through the mountains toward San Bernardino. In exchange for collecting the tolls, Mr. Brown was obliged to keep the road as passable as possible.

And as noted before, toward the latter part of the last century, the land was a cattle ranch with attendant rights to water holes across the desert that enabled the driving of the cattle without having them die of thirst. The old bunkhouse where the cowboys slept and the thick-walled creamery still remain.

The discovery of gold, silver, and copper in the region also influenced the community, enough to make it worthwhile for a rail line to be built. This in turn fostered the growth of Victorville and other small towns, a process that was responsible for the settlement of much of the nation beyond the eastern seaboard. Victorville's original name was Victor, for Jacob N. Victor, the construction superintendent of the Santa Fe railroad's push through the Cajon Pass. As more people arrived, vast cattle grazing lands became smaller farms, orchards, and turkey farms. Soft mining—cement and lime—took the place of hard mining when the metals ran out.

Not far from here is an archaeological site. It was uncovered and explored several years ago and then it was carefully reburied so that more could be learned from it at a later date when knowledge and technology will have advanced enough to make preservation more certain than it is today.

The estimated age of the artifacts is from four hundred to eleven hundred years old, but the prints uncovered in the lower stratum are judged to be six thousand years old. The site is not far from the river and was marshland all those years ago. The tracks of the animals that gathered there to drink, feed, and hunt were embedded in the mud. They hardened and lasted like plaster molds and were covered over by layers of protective earth. I saw the ones that the archaeologists had uncovered. There were paw prints of various small mammals, and there were prints of larger mammals, a human family, the footprints of a man and of a woman, and those of the child who had walked between them.

No human bones were found, but ornaments and tools from later ages were, and among those were a crystal drill and dainty carved beads decorated with a floral pattern. The drill was made to be functional, probably to make holes in plant materials and animal hides, but it was also fashioned to be beautiful. It was carved from quartz, and it catches and refracts the light as if it were a jewel. Nothing has ever made me feel the continuity of the best in humankind as keenly as I did when I held that crystal drill in my hand—small, exquisite, shaped equally for beauty and for use.

Closer to home, only a ten-minute walk away from my doorstep, the rocks of the Narrows hold their own mysteries. There are petroglyphs carved there, records of maturation rites and of belief in the power of the sun. There are metates where grain was ground into meal. There are dark shadows from ancient fires.

Some places are sacred ground. The part of me that wants scientific proof for everything shies away from this, but the part of me that saw those footprints, held the carved crystal, and has wandered the Narrows and this river valley believes.

I know that all things change with time. Civilizations once rich in life often leave no more than faint traces, which can be translated into only imperfect accounts of what was. Even stone is finally worn away.

I know about change, but I do not accept all of it gracefully. In the mid-fifties, 400 acres of the ranch that lay across the river were sold. The 1800 acres of my grandparents' original holding became 1400. Then in 1968, 800 acres were sold to the state to become a regional park. This was all of the land across the tracks, most of the fields, and all of the forest. I was heartbroken even though the sale was the only way to preserve the land. At the same time, the South Verde was plowed under and resurrected as a jumble of houses around an artificial lake. Every day that I am home, I walk on the park land, but it is not the same. A shortage of funds and staff prevents the park from being cared for as it deserves to be.

In the eighties, the remaining 600 acres were reduced to 172 as the back hills and the southern desert space were sold. This sale is far worse than the park. Someday there will be buildings all along the hills behind us and out on the desert. But there is no way around it. For all of its beauty, this is marginal land for farming and ranching, much of it totally unfit for cultivation; it could not generate enough profit to offset the taxes and maintenance costs.

We are doing everything we can to save what is left, but I have no doubt that the cemetery and those peach trees will be here long after traces of the ranch as it used to be are gone.

Harry Lawton

Harry Lawton was born in Long Beach in 1927. For more biographical information, see the selection from "Orange Groves and Rice Bowls" included earlier in this anthology.

The following excerpt is from his novel *Willie Boy: A Desert Manhunt*. In this controversial version of the actual 1909 events, Willie Boy, a Chemehuevi\Paiute Indian, kidnaps Carlota (called Lolita in Lawton's version), another Chemehuevi in the area, and when her father intervenes, kills him. A posse intent on justice chases them, and Carlota's dead body is found several days later. The saga ends only when Willie Boy takes his own life. An alternate version of the story—which differs dramatically from the conclusions drawn by the media and echoed in Lawton's novel—can be found in Larry E. Burgess and James A. Sandos's *The Hunt for Willie Boy*, an excerpt of which follows this selection.

from *Willie Boy*

The Walk to One Horse Spring

Willie Boy got a good start that night, walking from the Gilman Ranch along the furrow rows of the almond orchards south to the Southern Pacific tracks. The girl followed, trailing along in the darkness so subdued, so quiet, he was almost unaware of her presence.

Once Willie Boy imagined a sob and glanced back at Lolita. His shot had awakened her. She had cried out on seeing her father's body under the eucalyptus. Now there was no show of emotion, fear or hatred, on her face. That was good in a Chemehuevi girl. He halted to shift the Winchester 30-30 under an armpit, while he cinched the buckle tighter on the cartridge belt he had taken from young Gilman's bunkroom. There were fifteen shells—enough to cross the desert wastes and reach his people at Twentynine Palms.

His head still hurt. It was luck the bottle had not been full. He recalled that other time in Victorville after payday at Verde Ranch when he drank too much and foolishly lost his senses. A sheriff's deputy had arrested and taken him before the judge. The judge had locked him up for twenty days in San Bernardino Jail.

This time was far worse. Willie Boy didn't intend to be caught. He was Swift Fox. As a child that Paiute name had always given him a sense of confidence. His people had come from miles around to watch an Indian youth who could pitch a baseball better than the Victorville white boys.

Willie Boy and the girl skirted several homes on the village edge. A kerosene lamp glowed in a window, framing a yellow square across a yard. They crossed the railroad tracks and turned east. He shook his head to clear the dizziness. The black felt hat, bought with last week's pay, tilted back on his head. He righted it.

The bright moon—old woman with a hatchet—slid from behind a cloud. It rode between banks of clouds and the heavens seemed to spin. He shook his head again. The girl's mother, Maria, didn't worry him. She had seized his gun after the shooting, struggled to take it away, and begged him to leave. Her will had crumbled when he threatened to kill the children. She made a choice quickly.

"Go with him, Lolita," she said. "You are his."

She had made the decision and in making it her bond was understood. Willie Boy knew that woman. He had affection in his heart for her, remembering how in his boyhood, when he shot his first quail and brought it back to his aunts in their *ramada,* she had been present, and found praise for him.

Willie Boy could not be sure of the brothers. They had fled quickly with their mother, when Maria picked up the baby and turned toward the hills. They were greatly frightened. But John Mike would be ashamed. Even now the boy might be returning to the ranch to tell Jim Gilman.

He knew what to expect from the *haiko-yam,* the whites. They would follow swiftly when alarm was given, but they might also soon abandon the chase. Indian quarrels were rarely given the same attention whites gave to disputes between their own people. There would be delays.

Constable de Crevecouer would probably first see Miss True, the Indian agent woman at Morongo Reservation. The Indian Police would be called. He was not afraid of Indian Police: they were children with silver badges. But he did not like that de Crevecouer. The man talked and smiled too much.

Probably de Crevecouer would get his friend Joe Toutain. He would not like to shoot Toutain. He had ridden with the man, eaten red beans from the same kettle and slept with him under the wagon that summer when they fenced waterholes on the Mohave range. Toutain was much like an Indian. He would not like to shoot him.

There was a dry rattle of rocks behind Willie Boy. He spun about. Lolita had stumbled along the railroad ties, dislodging a stream of pebbles. They stopped and he listened. They were within fifty yards of the Banning railroad station. A light was on in the office. He could see the agent, Gates, hunched over some papers. There was no movement from the bent body. They moved on again, passing the station. The stars hung above them, green specks pasted across the night sky.

They walked. The station light faded to a golden glimmer. The long corridor of the Pass between the two mountain peaks stretched ahead. He felt better now and the mist was clearing from his skull. On both sides of the railroad track clumps of creosote and spiny stands of Spanish-bayonet marched off to the dark foothills.

The night had been cool, but now the Pass floor slanted downward and a hot breeze rushed upon them from the oven of the Colorado Desert. He took off his coat and handed it to the girl. She received it with a slight grimace. He laughed and swung forward in a loping stride. The Bear Shaman song flowed through his head.

Una Ki'ta aya' haidu flu patci do kwo vina kwai du.
(There is much danger as I go. You see my tracks.)

He must begin to think about tricks to throw off pursuit. They would expect him to strike north along the lower slopes of Mount San Gorgonio. Instead he would turn south near Cabazon and climb the Cahuilla trails up over the triangular spurs of foothill that arched down from the flanks of Mount San Jacinto. There would be water at One Horse Spring. They could rest there before beginning the climb into the granites.

A meteoric ball of fire crossed the east, burst above the horizon and melted down the sky in trickling ribbons of flame. Lolita gasped. He knew she was thinking of the Chemehuevi superstition, the meteor as a portent of death. He had lived with white men and no longer believed the old superstitions. Then he smiled grimly, for this was a true omen. Someone had died.

He jerked with alarm at the ascending roar of thunder in their rear. The rails thrummed suddenly. A train!

They mustn't be seen. He grabbed the girl by an arm and darted down the embankment. He threw her down behind a curtain of brush and lay by her side. The eastward bound El Paso Passenger steamed past, dropping sparks. Its whistle mourned long and low as it rumbled through Cabazon in the distance.

The lanky Paiute stared at the girl beside him. Her black hair, parted in the middle of the head, fell behind her ears and was wrapped at the base of the neck. She was slender as arrow weed and tall for an Indian girl. He recalled her voice, cool and softspoken, and her impassive eyes when he stopped to talk with her two days before. She was sitting in the shed behind the ranch, hulling almonds.

"My father has said not to speak with you," she said. She dropped her eyes and continued working. They were both silent, and he felt she was thinking—as he was—of that morning in June when they had left Twentynine Palms Oasis together. Her father had come after them, eyes blazing, and leveling his gun at Willie Boy, had taken her away. His hatred for Old Mike had grown then, a hot stone in the basket of his ribs.

But she had spoken once more, looking up from the almonds.

"I'm going to school."

It was a strange desire for a desert girl. She was telling him it was ended. He knew then how different she was and that he must have her.

He grunted and rose, shaking sand from his clothing. The girl's eyes were fixed gravely upon him. Then she also rose and they went on. They hid again when the next train roared upward from the desert floor shortly after three o'clock.

They stopped in a vineyard near Cabazon and stripped clusters of grapes from the vines. The girl ate indifferently, but he was hungry. A band of pale light extended above the hollow bowl of desert below. While they ate, it spread rapidly, sweeping the stars from the sky, expanding into a new dawn.

Ahead lay the Bailiff Ranch and he decided it was time to cut south through the brush. They walked on for several hours. They circled the chocolate spur beyond Cabazon and walked toward the knife-point splash of green creasing the head of One Horse Point, defining the spring below.

The sun was well up in the sky when they reached the spring and sprawled out under the cottonwoods. They could rest a few hours and from the ridge above he could watch for pursuers. He turned to look at the girl and her eyes faltered.

Larry E. Burgess and James A. Sandos

Larry E. Burgess is director of the A. K. Smiley Public Library in Redlands. A prominent local historian, he lectures extensively on the history of Southern California and the West, in addition to Abraham Lincoln and the Civil War. His publications include *The Smileys: A Biography*; *The Hunt for Willie Boy: Indian-Hating and Popular Culture*; and *Images in America: Redlands*. James A. Sandos is a history professor at the University of Redlands and is the author of *Converting California*, a reinterpretation of mission history, and coauthor of *The Hunt for Willie Boy*. Both live in Redlands.

Published in 1994, *The Hunt for Willie Boy* reinterprets evidence surrounding the 1909 deaths of Willie Boy, Carlota, and her father. The conclusions of Burgess and Sandos contrast sharply with the tale told in Harry Lawton's *Willie Boy* (see the previous selection in this anthology) and other media depictions, which they ultimately criticize as sensational and racist. In this excerpt, the authors reconstruct the story using the Chemehuevi pattern of storytelling.

from *The Hunt for Willie Boy*

Whenever my mother would tell this story, she always began by saying, "Love is hard."

Willie Boy lived with his mother in the desert. She was a wonderful basket maker, and her sign was the rattlesnake. She made her baskets without fear that the snake would strike her. Willie Boy was a very good hunter because he could run faster than many animals. He needed a wife, but there were no young women nearby. He was young and strong, so he went across the desert looking for a wife. One day he saw his cousin, Carlota, and he wanted her. She looked back at him openly, and they both ran away together. Family [members] followed and found them. Willie Boy and Carlota were separated. He was not to look at her again. Both their hearts were still restless. He wanted Carlota, but her father was a man of power. One night Willie Boy got a rifle and came to see her father. They argued, and Willie Boy got mad. Willie Boy killed her father, then he and Carlota ran away again.

This time the whites chased them, along with some of The People. Willie Boy hid his wife in a wash, gave her his coat and waterskin, and went for food. He ran in the old way, for he was like the wind, and no one could catch him then. He came back with food but could not find his wife. He searched everywhere, but she had died. He found the men chasing him and shot their horses with his rifle so that they would have to run like he did. They could not. He was so much faster that he quickly ran off.

In his running he came again to his mother, but she now turned away. He ran farther, far out into the desert, away from all his family. None of The People saw him again, and we later heard that he had died.

J. Smeaton Chase

J. Smeaton Chase was born in 1864 in London. At the age of twenty-five he moved to California, and his love of travel inspired him to take lengthy horseback trips around the state; one time he went all the way from Mexico to Oregon. He wrote about these adventures in *Yosemite Trails*, *California Coast Trails*, and *California Desert Trails*. He died in Banning in 1923 after having lived in Palm Springs for many years.

This excerpt, about trying to find the small town of Twentynine Palms with his guide Kaweah, is taken from *California Desert Trails*.

from *California Desert Trails*

I came to a standstill in doubt. I had made careful inquiries at Indio and Coachella, and of Emmons, as to forks, crossroads, and land-marks, and had been duly warned as to the roads I had already passed; but this new turn-off had not been spoken of by any one. However, I knew that my direction for Twentynine Palms was northerly, and the trail in that direction seemed a trifle the better marked, so I resolved on that and started.

In a cactus bush I chanced to notice a scrap of board, loosely stuck as if it had been tossed there. Going over to investigate, there seemed to be faint scratches on it, apparently made with a nail. I turned it this way and that, but for some time could not make even a guess at what was written. At last, by patching possibilities together, the scratches took on vague coherence, a questionable "2," a hazardous "9," and a conceivable "P." The fragment as found pointed toward the easterly trail, but from the casual way it hung there it might have been twisted hither and thither by the wind, so it seemed a matter of chance which direction it was meant to indicate. It was one of those puzzles that may bring one into serious trouble in this country where distances are so great, water and food so far between, and travel so scanty that it was probably a month, possibly three times as long, since the last person had passed or until the next one would appear.

I resolved to trust the dubious sign and take the eastward track. There was difficulty in following it, for it was often so faint as to be mere guesswork. It is this sort of thing that takes the pleasure out of desert travel. The county of Riverside, in which I now was, has lately done useful work in the placing of metal guide-posts at the main desert road crossings, but a good deal more needs to be done, while other counties quite ignore this need of their desert populations. Unfortunately, the maps of the Geological Survey do not cover the greater part of this troublesome region: and such as are to be had, cheap "county" or "miners" maps, are little better than none at all.

Persistently eastward ran my elusive trail. It was nearing a mountain range, the Pintos, and must soon turn either north or south, so I kept on, though in considerable doubt. At last, when close to the hills, it ran into a better traveled track, and with relief I found a sign-post with Twenty-nine Palms on its northern arm and Cottonwood Springs thirty miles to the southeast.

At this junction, as marked on my map, there are supposed to be, near together, two more waterholes, Stirrup Tanks and White Tanks. I searched for signs of them (the usual signs being the trails made by animals going to drink) but failed to discover either. I learned afterwards that one of them is half-a-mile away in the Cottonwood Springs direction; of the other, nobody that I have met has any knowledge at all. Fortunately, I had an ample supply of water, but Kaweah had to be satisfied with a promise payable fifteen miles farther on. He is an intelligent fellow, and quickly grasps the bearing of any indecision that may arise on the matter of trails. On such occasions he watches every movement of mine with almost human anxiety, and plainly reflects my own doubtful frame of mind. He had been as pessimistic as I ever saw since we left the forks, but brightened up when we found the road, and made the best of a dry tussock of galleta while I ate my lunch: and when we were ready he moved off with alacrity and surprised me by offering to canter.

We were now on a gradual descent, the southern rim of the Mojave Desert. From time to time there opened vistas of volcanic-looking ranges, with glimpses of shimmering gray level or splashes of pure white where dry lake-beds glistened with alkali. For hundreds of miles this strange dead land extends to north and east, known only to venturous prospectors, a scientific man or two, a few surveyors, a handful of miners; to the rest of the world as foreign and unimaginable as if it were some territory of Mars. Yet what wealth lies locked in that great desolation, for it is, as indeed it looks, a veritable treasure house of mineral. Looking out over it one easily imagines "goblin or swart fairy of the mine" at work on veins of wondrous ore under those gaunt hills, ashy gray, livid purple, or dull red as if they had been roasted.

At last, five miles down the slope of a narrow valley I saw a speck that might be a building, perhaps a ranch-house, though no trace of greenness was in view as far as eye could see. I pushed on towards it, indulging thoughts of eggs, "stove" bread, milk, perchance a lettuce. But these hopes faded when the supposed farm-house turned into the grouped shanties of a small mine. However, I was welcomed heartily by the three men on the place, and Kaweah was entertained with barley and water—the latter no trifling gift, for their supply must be replenished at Twentynine Palms, four miles away. I was eagerly questioned for news, for my items were only five days old, while their last "news" had passed into history two weeks before. The six men who were concerned in developing the mine had formed themselves into two shifts of three a side, taking alternate spells at the works and "inside" (the term used by desert men to signify the cities and the coast country). The other shift was some days overdue, ensnared by the charms of Los Angeles, and these poor fellows were continually scanning the horizon, like marooned sailors, for signs of the relieving party. Evening was coming on, so I soon took the road. Tracks led off to other small mines, reminders of the lively days of the seventies, when this Twentynine Palms district was a "camp" of renown. Before long the palms came in sight, and we ended a long day's march soon after sunset. I off-saddled under a cottonwood that stood near a deserted house, and found pasturage for Kaweah in a little *ciénaga*, or marshy spot, formerly the site of a village of Chemehuevi Indians from the Colorado River. I do not know who now owns the land, and, what is of more account, the water; but when I come on these abandoned settlements of the Indians, at places where they would no doubt have wished to remain, I take them for links in an old but still lengthening chain of wrong.

The population of Twentynine Palms at the time of my visit numbered two, so that my arrival, on the eve of the Fourth of July, seemed to cast an air of festivity over the scene. The two, one a prospector and old haunter of the locality, the other a consumptive from "inside" who was sacrificing every comfort of life for the sake of the dry air of this lonely spot, received me cordially enough, but remained convinced, I think, in spite of my plain story, that I was "lookin' up mineral, ain't you now?" They felt it an insult to their intelligence to be asked to believe that any one would come to Twentynine Palms in July for the sake of seeing the country and "them old pa'ms." "Country?" said the sick man, waving toward a sunset landscape that would have thrown Turner into a frenzy—"Country? Th' ain't no country round here to 'mount to nuthin'. You ever see any, Mac?" And Mac sententiously replied, "Durned if I ain't forgot what real country looks like, anyways."

Nevertheless, the country was satisfactory to me. To lie at dawn and watch the growing glory in the east, the pure, dark light stealing up from below the horizon, the brightening to holy silver, the first flush of amber, then of rose, then a hot stain of crimson, and then the flash and glitter, the intolerable splendor, of the monarch, Phœbus Superbus, tyrant of the desert—and of me: I jump up hastily and hurry through my morning cookery, but not before he has taken toll of my day's store of energy.

Our Fourth was celebrated with make-believe shower-baths. At intervals we resorted to the *ciénaga* and ladled water over ourselves from a tepid pool, and I may say that with a temperature of 112° I found it more exhilarating than some displays of gunpowder and rhetoric that I remember. Between times we talked "lodes" and "pockets," or my friends would grind up some bit of "float" and pan it out at the spring, with brief excitement over "grades" and "colors." Toward evening I walked a mile up the slope to the west and enjoyed a memorable sunset. By some peculiarity of the light, the landscape had much the quality of a wash drawing in black and white, seen through a thin purplish haze. The line of palms made a charming foreground, each one a study of airy grace; beyond rose the Bullion Mountains, dark dull gray with splashes of white where sand had lodged far up, as if it were snow; farther to the east another range, the Sheepholes, of the dead hue of volcanic ash; and over all the luminous arch, infinitely remote, with flecks of snowy cloud like sheep straying in the blue pastures of the sky. Spaciousness and solitude were the elements of the scene, and reacted with trance-like spell upon the mind.

As the sun went down a blood-red light suddenly came over all the view. I never saw anything more startling and instantaneous in its coming, or more theatric in its intensity of hue. For the few seconds that it lasted I held my breath. The mountains burned as if they were incandescent: Bullion? no, the lava of rubies. Then in a moment it had paled and like an expiration was gone.

As I walked back to camp I noticed a small enclosure, almost hidden among arrowweed. It marked the grave of a young girl, most likely one who had been brought here in hope of a cure for consumption. There is something inhuman in choosing such a place of burial for a girl. Nature sets a difference even in death, and it seemed a brutal thing to leave a girl's young body here.

Some tokens of old inhabitation at Twentynine Palms may be seen in remains of shacks and dugouts. One of these had been the den—it is the only word—of one Wilson, the former *habitué* of the place, who held on here in more than pagan squalor until he was lately forcibly removed by the county authorities. The hut of old Jim Pine, the last of the Twentynine Palms Indians, stands open to sky and gaze, and shows a litter of "rock" specimens (for Jim was something of a miner in his day). But mining camps are in their nature evanescent: why build a house, when to-morrow the rush will move on to a newer "strike"? But Twentynine Palms is still a base for prospectors in the desert ranges, on account of its water, which is plentiful and good, and by reason of being on one of the roads to the still important mining settlement of Dale.

Dorothy Ramon and Eric Elliott

Dorothy Ramon was born in 1909 on the Morongo Indian Reservation in Riverside County, and Eric Elliott is a Southern California native who received his Ph.D. in linguistics from the University of California, San Diego. He is passionately committed to recording and preserving the indigenous languages of Southern California. Ramon passed away in 2002.

In 1991, Elliott started transcribing stories told by Ramon in her native language of Serrano, and the project culminated in the nine-hundred-page bilingual series of texts *Wayta' Yawa': "Always Believe,"* which includes the excerpts that follow. Material from Elliott's collaboration with Villiana Calac Hyde, a native Luiseño speaker, appears earlier in this anthology.

Railroad Tracks over Great-Grandfather's Grave

'Uvihtvu' nenya', nekak 'ana', kwenevu' qatt, heermc wehtivec.
Long ago lived my relative, my grandfather's father, his father, the old man shaman.

'Ani' kwenevu' 'aheermi' 'ivi' xhiit *electricity*. Kwenevu' 'aheermi'.
His power came from electricity. That was his power.

'Ama' kwenevu' 'ama' 'aheermi'. 'Anivu' qatte'. Kwenevu' wehtivec.
That was his power. He lived. He was an old man.

'Ani' 'apyu' Maarra'nu' kwenemu' hunuk 'im Maarrênga'yam 'ingkwa'.

At that time the Serrano people were moving from Twentynine Palms over here.

'Aam kwenemu' qatt xhayp *Crafton*, keym 'amay'.
They were going to live in "Crafton," as they now call it.

Taaqtam 'uviht 'im tewa'nkin 'amay *yaavika*', keym.
Long ago the Indians used to call the place *Yaavi*'.

'Ami' huwatt qatt chevêk 'atewan. 'Ap mit hiit peenyu' kwan weney waat 'ahuurrki'.
It certainly has another name. This is where the *waat* tree (oak species) grew.

'Amay kwana' qwa'i' 'ap.
They apparently used to eat it (*waat* acorns, 'gray colored species of oak') there.

'Aam 'aame' 'angkwa' pichuucu' Taaqtam 'ipyu' tum haypyu'.
The Indians from all over went there.

Waat hiit hami': 'ama' ma' tewa'nkin 'amay terva'tti'. *Waat* keym.
It was *waat* or something: that's what they called that territory. *Waat* they called it.

'Amay' 'ama' waat *Crafton* keym xhinyim yarra'nkam.
Nowadays white people refer to *Waat* as "Crafton."

'Ani' 'ap kwenemu' qatt mit hinyiki' 'atahtamerav. 'Uvihanu' kwenemu' 'ap qatt.
I don't know how long they stayed there. They lived there their whole lives.

'Animu' 'uvya' hakup niniihtavem weftti'yam hamin 'ivin.
They were probably already very old people.

'Ama nenya' kwenevu' meme', 'ap 'ama' nekak 'ana'.
And then my relative apparently died, my grandfather's father.

'Amay 'anim pukay, nevehkin. 'Ap peenyu' muukich qatte'ka'.

Then they buried him. That was supposed to be their grayeyard there.

Peenyu'...Taaqtavim key *muukich*. Taaqtam peenyu' kwan qatt muukich.
Theirs...in Indian it is called *muukich*. It was the Indians' graveyard.

'Ana' 'amay' kwan petkw 'ap nevehek 'ama' nekak 'ana' 'ap *railroad track*
    petkw kwan 'ama' nevehek.
And to this very day my grandfather's father is buried under the railroad
    tracks.

Kwan 'ap nevehek 'ama' 'amay'. Pe'wi' kwan pehpa' penehek *railroad*
    track.
He is still buried there today. The railroad tracks run right over him.

Nekak 'ana', 'ani' kwan 'ap petkw nevehek. Keym ki' pana'. Pana'nu'
    maac.
My grandfather's father is buried under it. That's what they say. That is
    what I heard.

Taaqtam pana' 'aav 'uviht. 'Uviht kwana' pana' kwenemu' nyihay, keym.
That is what people used to say long ago. That's what they did long ago,
    they say.

'Ama' 'ayee'.
That's all.

Indians Building the Railroad

'Uviht 'ip taaqtam kiikam 'ip Morongo keym 'amay.
The old-timers from the Morongo reservation talked about this long ago.

'Ivin haami' tewa'nkinich tervac...mutu' 'ap qac 'amay' 'ervrayt.
That's what they called the place...and they're still there to this very day.

Mutu'ch 'ap qac kiti'ik.
We're still here, barely.

'Ama' ni'…aaa…'uviht taaqtam 'ip kiikam kwenemu' 'ayay pam xhinyim
  'ama' xhiit…aaa…'ichamc tewa'nkin 'amay kwana', *kut 'aper'* keych
  'amay, 'ama' xhiit 'ater'ac xhinyip ya'i' 'ama' kut 'aperp.
Then…long ago they came and took people…what do we call it now,
  "fire road" we call it, that big thing that runs around on tracks.

'Aper' qaci'.
There is that (rail) road.

'Im 'ani' Amêrrikaanu'yam xhinyim yarra'nkam 'aam tewa'nkin *railroad*
  tracks, keym.
The Americans, white people, refer to it as "railroad tracks," as they say.

Taaqtam qay' enan hamya'qac peetewa'nkiniktti' pana' nyaawnk.
The Serrano had no word for it.

'Ama' ni' kwenemu' 'ayay taaqtam. Kwenemu' tehteyanin.
So they came and took people by force. They forced them to work.

Kwenemu' 'amay puuyu' 'ichu'kin 'amay *kut 'aper'* keych 'icham.
They (the Indians) made the entire "fire road" as we call it.

Kwana' 'ichu'kin payika': mit haynkwa' nikcu' 'ama', 'ama' Herqarniv 'ani'
  qac payika' mit hayp kwenevu' nikttu' pee-, 'ipyu' pee'ichu'k Taaqtam.
They build it up to I don't know where, it passed through Palm Springs
  and somewhere over there ends the part which…which was built by
  the Indians.

'Awee' qay' kwenemu' haypa'n nemer'.
And they were never paid.

'Ayee' xhiit cheenyu' cheme'puchca'i'ac wowyêêrrnu' peehaka' 'ama'.
So much for the word of our government, the one who was supposed to
  take care of us.

Qayvu' nemer'kin Taaqtam, keymu' ki' 'uviht Taaqtam 'atuchinim.
It (the government) never recognized the Indians' contribution, as the
  old-timers said.

Pepya'mu' tehtey kut 'aper'ci 'ichu'kinaym. 'Ama' ni' pana' 'ama' mutu' qac.
They build the railroad. And it's still there.

Qayu' haypa'n nermer': 'aam puuyu' 'uviht qer'qer' chevêk. 'Ama' 'ayee'.
They never paid them, and they all died long ago at any rate. That's all.

Coyote Crying

'Aya' Qaynu'…wahi' kwenevu' 'uviht qatte'.
From San Gorgonio…long ago there was a coyote from there.

Kwenevu' mit 'anya', 'anyu' *friend* hiit hami' naasht, 'ahintu'.
He apparently had a friend, a girlfriend, a wife.

Qayn 'enan nehaktti' *friend*ti' Taaqtav. Wahit 'apuuyu' kwenevu' naasht.
I don't know how to say 'friend' in Indian. (Remembering:) It was the
    coyote's girlfriend.

'Ama' ni kwenevu' peyika' yaam wahi'ti'. Kwenevu' penu' mih wahi'ti'.
She apparently got angry with the coyote. She left the coyote.

Wahi' 'ama' 'ani' kwenevu' yahyuu'. 'Anim taaqtam hihii wahi'ti' yuhyuu'ow.
And then the coyote apparently began to cry. People saw the coyote crying.

"Haminat nyihay 'anim yuhyuu'?" wahi'tim maaya' kwana'.
"What happened to you? Why are you crying?" they asked the coyote.

"'Oo, pata' pa'pa'yu' mrat cherrupk nowp 'Aya Qaynu'," key kwan.
"Oh, smoke from San Gorgonio has just gotten into my eyes," he said.
    (San Gorgonio used to be a volcano.)

"'Amatunga'…ne' qayn yuhyuu'. Ne'ushp wangakt 'ayee'," key kwan.
"And so…I'm not crying. My eyes are just watering," he said.

Mary Austin

Mary Austin, born in Illinois in 1868, arrived in California in 1888. Her first and most popular published work, *The Land of Little Rain*, vividly captured the landscape of the Mojave Desert in a series of meditations. Having studied Indian life in the region for seventeen years, she also published widely on that subject. She died in Santa Fe, New Mexico, in 1934. (Heyday Books will publish *Essential Mary Austin*, a collection her best works, in late 2006.)

This excerpt, describing the San Gorgonio Pass, is taken from *The Lands of the Sun*, originally published as *California, Land of the Sun* in 1914 and revised in 1927.

from *The Lands of the Sun*

The desert winds along the eastern bases of the range in deep, indented bays, white-rimmed with the wave marks of its ancient sea. Out a very little way beyond the pilae of the broken mountains, where the shuddering heat waves trick the imagination, the land seems about to be retaken by the ghost of tumbling billows. Nothing else moves in it, nothing sounds.

Plantations of growing things near the Pass lean all a little toward it, edging, peering. The wild, spiny, thorny things of the desert struggling to enter the rain-fed paradise, the full-leaved offspring of the sea wind plotting to take the unfriended, sandy spaces. They creep a little forward or back as the years run wet or dry. The green things stand up, they march along the cliffs, they balance on the edge of precipices, but desperation is in every contorted stem of mesquite and palo verde. And with all this struggle, so still! East, on the desert rim, the Colorado ramps like a stallion between its walls, westward the Pacific rings the low foreshore with thunder; but the land never cries out. Quartz mountains disintegrate, but they do not murmur.

It is odd here, in a land rife with the naked struggle of great pagan forces, to find the promontories so lend themselves to the gentle names of saints. Perhaps the Padres were not so far from nature as one thinks. In the southerly range, which, with San Bernardino on the north, shores up the Pass, they rendered for once the pagan touch. San Jacinto—Saint Hyacinth—was he ever anything but a Christianized memory of a Grecian myth, or does it matter at all so long as there are men to see, in the deep purple light that dies along the heights, the color of blood that is shed for love? Perhaps the best thing beauty can say to Greek or Christian is that there are still things worth dying for. No doubt the veins of Padre Jayme Bravo were as rich in martyr passion as the stained air of the mountain is in purples, paling to rose at morning, thinning at noon to pure aërial blues.

Seen from the coast, the range has a finny contour as of some huge creature risen from the sea, low hills about it like dolphins playing. But the prevailing note of the landscape is always blue, repeating the tints of the wild hyacinth that may be found on the lomas early in April, sending up its clustered heads between two slender, curving spears.

Near at hand the masking growth is seen to be green, the dark secretive green of the chamisal. Nowhere does one get the force of the Spanish termination al—the place where—as in that word. The chamisal is the place of the chamiso: miles and miles of it, with scarcely another shrub allowed, spread over the mesa and well up into laps and bays of the hills. It grows breast-high, man-high in the favored regions, but even where, under the influence of drought and altitude, it creeps to the knees, it abates nothing of its social character. Its evergreen foliage has a dull shining from the resinous coating which protects it from evaporation, and a slight sticky feel, characteristics that no doubt won it the name of "greasewood" from the emigrants who valued it chiefly because it could be burned green. The spring winds blowing up from the bay whip all its fretted surface to a froth of panicled white bloom, that, stirring a little as the wind shifts, full of bee-murmur, touches the imagination with the continual reminder of the sea. Higher up the thick, lacy chaparral flecks and riffles, showing the light underside of leaves, and tosses up great fountain sprays of ceanothus, sea-blue and lilac-scented.

Harold Bell Wright

Harold Bell Wright was born in New York in 1872. A best-selling writer of fiction, essays, and nonfiction, he is said to have been the first American writer to sell a million copies of a novel. When he was a minister in Redlands, Wright's parishioners persuaded him to publish a story he had written; soon afterward he left the ministry to devote his time to writing. Major novels include *The Winning of Barbara Worth* and *The Shepherd of the Hills*, both made into movies in his lifetime. He died in 1944 in La Jolla.

The Eyes of the World is the story of a painter who moves to Fairlands (a thinly disguised Redlands) and is faced with two options: compromise his art to please his wealthy benefactors or develop his talents fully at the expense of material comfort. In this excerpt he meets with a best-selling author who took the first route.

from *Eyes of the World*

All the next day, Aaron King—in the hotel dining-room, the lobby, and on the veranda—watched for the famous novelist. Even on the streets of the little city, he found himself hoping to catch a glimpse of the uncouth figure and the homely, world-worn face of the man whose unusual personality had so attracted him. The day was nearly gone when Conrad Lagrange again appeared. As on the evening before, the young man was smoking his after-dinner cigar on the veranda, when the Irish Setter and a whiff of pipe smoke announced the strange character's presence.

Without taking a seat, the novelist said, "I always have a look at the mountains, at this time of the day, Mr. King—would you care to come? These mountains are the real thing, you know, and well worth seeing—particularly at this hour." There was a gentle softness in his deep voice, now—as unlike his usual speech as his physical appearance was unlike that of his younger companion.

Aaron King arose quickly. "Thank you, Mr. Lagrange; I will go with pleasure."

Accompanied by the dog, they followed the avenue, under the giant pepper trees that shut out the sky with their gnarled limbs and gracefully drooping branches, to the edge of the little city; where the view to the north and northeast was unobstructed by houses. Just where the street became a road, Conrad Lagrange—putting his hand upon his companion's arm—said in a low voice, "This is the place."

Behind them, beautiful Fairlands lay, half lost, in its wilderness of trees and flowers. Immediately in the foreground, a large tract of unimproved land brought the wild grasses and plants to their very feet. Beyond these acres—upon which there were no trees—the orange groves were massed in dark green blocks and squares; with, here and there, thin rows of palms; clumps of peppers; or tall, plume-like eucalyptus; to mark the roads and the ranch homes. Beyond this—and rising, seemingly, out of the groves—the San Bernardinos heaved their mighty masses into the sky. It was almost dark. The city's lamps were lighted. The outlines of grove and garden were fast being lost in the deepening dusk. The foothills, with the lower spurs and ridges of the mountains, were softly modeled in dark blue against the deeper purple of the canyons and gorges. Upon the cloudless sky that was lighted with clearest saffron, the lines of the higher crests were sharply drawn; while the lonely, snow-capped peaks,—ten thousand feet above the darkening valley below,—catching the last rays of the sun, glowed rose-pink—changing to salmon—deepening into mauve—as the light failed.

Aaron King broke the silence by drawing a long breath—as one who could find no words to express his emotions.

Conrad Lagrange spoke sadly; "And to think that there are,—in this city of ten thousand,—probably, nine thousand nine hundred and ninety people who never see it."

With a short laugh, the young man said, "It makes my fingers fairly itch for my palette and brushes—though it's not at all my sort of thing."

The other turned toward him quickly. "You are an artist?"

"I had just completed my three years study abroad when mother's illness brought me home. I was fortunate enough to get one on the line, and they say—over there—that I had a good chance. I don't know how it will go here at home." There was a note of anxiety in his voice.

"What do you do?"

"Portraits."

With his face again toward the mountains, the novelist said thoughtfully, "This West country will produce some mighty artists, Mr. King. By far the greater part of this land must remain, always, in its primitive naturalness. It will always be easier, here, than in the city crowded East, for a man to be himself. There is less of that spirit which is born of clubs and cliques and clans and schools—with their fine-spun theorizing, and their impudent assumption that they are divinely commissioned to sit in judgment. There is less of artistic tea-drinking, esthetic posing, and soulful talk; and more opportunity for that loneliness out of which great art comes. The atmosphere of these mountains and deserts and seas inspires to a self-assertion, rather than to a clinging fast to the traditions and culture of others—and what, after all, is a great artist, but one who greatly asserts himself?"

The younger man answered in a like vein; "Mr. Lagrange, your words recall to my mind a thought in one of mother's favorite books. She quoted from the volume so often that, as a youngster, I almost knew it by heart, and, in turn, it became my favorite. Indeed, I think that, with mother's aid as an interpreter, it has had more influence upon my life than any other one book. This is the thought: 'To understand the message of the mountains; to love them for what they are; and, in terms of every-day life, to give expression to that understanding and love—is a mark of true greatness of soul.' I do not know the author. The book is anonymous."

"I am the author of that book, sir," the strange man answered with simple dignity, "—or, rather, I should say,—I *was* the author," he added, with a burst of his bitter, sarcastic humor. "For God's sake don't betray me. I am, *now*, the *famous* Conrad Lagrange, you understand. I have a *name* to protect." His deep voice was shaken with feeling. His worn and rugged features twitched and worked with emotion.

Aaron King listened in amazement to the words that were spoken by the famous novelist with such pathetic regret and stinging self-accusation. Not knowing how to reply, be said casually, "You are working here, Mr. Lagrange?"

"Working! Me? I don't *work* anywhere. I am a literary scavenger. I haunt the intellectual slaughter pens, and live by the putrid offal that self-respecting writers reject. I glean the stinking materials for my stories from the sewers and cesspools of life. For the dollars they pay, I furnish my readers with those thrills that public decency forbids them to experience at first hand. I am a procurer for the purposes of mental prostitution. My books breed moral pestilence and spiritual disease. The unholy filth I write fouls the minds and pollutes the imaginations of my readers. I am an instigator of degrading immorality and unmentionable crimes. *Work!* No, young than, I don't work. Just now, I'm doing penance in this damned town. My rotten imaginings have proven too much—even for me—and the doctors sent me West to recuperate."

The artist could find no words that would answer. In silence, the two men turned away from the mountains, and started back along the avenue by which they had come.

When they had walked some little distance, the young man said, "This is your first visit to Fairlands, Mr. Lagrange?"

"I was here last year"—answered the other—"here and in the hills yonder. Have *you* been much in the mountains?"

"Not in California. This is my first trip to the West. I have seen something of the mountains, though, at tourist resorts—abroad."

"Which means," commented the other, "that you have never seen them at all."

Aaron King laughed. "I dare say you are right."

"And you—?" asked the novelist, abruptly, eyeing his companion. "What brought you to this community that thinks so much more of its millionaires than it does of its mountains? Have *you* come to Fairlands to work?"

"I hope to," answered the artist. "There are—there are reasons why I do not care to work, for the present, in the East. I confess it was because I understood that Fairlands offered exceptional opportunities for a portrait painter that I came here. To succeed in my work, you know, one must come in touch with people of influence. It is sometimes easier to interest them when they are away from their homes—in some place like this—where their social duties and business cares are not so pressing."

"There is no question of the material that Fairlands has to offer, Mr. King," returned the novelist, in his grim, sarcastic humor. "God! how I envy you!" he added, with a flash of earnest passion. "You are young— You are beginning your life work —You are looking forward to success— You—"

"I *must* succeed"—the painter interrupted impetuously—"I must."

"Succeed in *what*? What do you mean by success?"

"Surely, *you* should understand what I mean by success," the younger man retorted. "You who have gained—"

"Oh, yes; I forgot"—came the quick interruption—"I am the *famous* Conrad Lagrange. Of course, you, too, must succeed. You must become the *famous* Aaron King. But perhaps you will tell me why you must, as you call it, succeed?"

The artist hesitated before answering; then said with anxious earnestness, "I don't think I can explain, Mr. Lagrange. My mother—" he paused.

The older man stopped short, and, turning, stood for a little with his face towards the mountains where San Bernardino's pyramid-like peak was thrust among the stars. When he spoke, every bit of that bitter humor was gone from his deep voice. "I beg your pardon, Mr. King"—he said slowly—"I am as ugly and misshapen in spirit as in body."

But when they had walked some way—again in silence and were drawing near the hotel, the momentary change in his mood passed. In a tone of stinging sarcasm he said, "You are on the right road, Mr. King. You did well to come to Fairlands. It is quite evident that you have mastered the modern technic of your art. To acquire fame, you have only to paint pictures of fast women who have no morals at all—making them appear as innocent maidens, because they have the price to pay, and, in the eyes of the world, are of social importance. Put upon your canvases what the world will call portraits of distinguished citizens—making low-browed money-thugs to look like noble patriots, and bloody butcher of humanity like benevolent saints. You need give yourself no uneasiness about your success. It is easy. Get in with the right people; use your family name and your distinguished ancestors; pull a few judicious advertising wires; do a few artistic stunts; get yourself into the papers long and often, no matter how; make yourself a fad; become a pet of the social autocrats—and your fame is assured. And—you will be what I am."

The young man, quietly ignoring the humor of the novelist's words, said protestingly, "But, surely, to portray human nature is legitimate art, Mr. Lagrange. Your great artists that the West is to produce will not necessarily be landscape painters or write essays upon nature, will they?"

"To portray human nature is legitimate work for an artist, yes"—agreed the novelist—"but he must portray human nature *plus*. The forces that *shape* human nature are the forces that must be felt in the picture and in the story. That these determining forces are so seldom seen by the eyes of the world, is the reason *for* pictures and stories. The artist who fails to realize for his world the character-creating elements in the life which he essays to paint or write, fails, to just that degree, in being an artist; or self-branded by his work as criminally careless, a charlatan or a liar. That one who, for a price, presents a picture or a story without regard for the influence of his production upon the characters of those who receive it, commits a crime for which human law provides no adequate punishment. Being the famous Conrad Lagrange, you understand, I have the right to say this. You will probably believe it, some day—if you do not now. That is, you will believe it if you have the soul and the intelligence of an artist—if you have not—it will not matter—and you will be happy in your success."

Laura Kalpakian

Born in 1945 in Long Beach, Laura Kalpakian grew up in Southern
California and holds degrees from the University of California,
Riverside, the University of Delaware, and the University of
California, San Diego. She has taught English at several universi-
ties, including the University of Redlands and Western Washington
University, and has received a National Endowment for the Arts
fellowship and a Pushcart Prize. Her novels include *Steps and Exes*,
Graced Land, *Caveat*, and *These Latter Days*. *Fair Augusto*, one of her
collections of short stories, won the PEN/West Award for Best
Short Fiction. *American Cookery*, a novel set in Southern
California, will be published in the fall of 2006. She lives in
Washington.

This excerpt is from Kalpakian's 1998 novel *Caveat*, set in 1916
in a fictional town in San Bernardino County.

from *Caveat*

The St. Elmo train station, a huge, clay-colored Moorish monstrosity,
had four squat towers, and each wore a toupee of ivy, all askew. The
windows were fancifully grilled with wrought-iron lyres, suggesting a
theatrical past, and out front, iron spears resting on ornate posts served
to tether horses. Four men, clearly official, corpulent and soberly clad,
alighted from a gleaming Locomobile and hastened along the station
arcades. Their footsteps grated audibly, even within the cool vaulted
waiting room. Noting that the westbound from Arizona had not yet
arrived, they hurried through the station to the crowded platform,

where a slightly fetid breeze from the nearby stockyards disturbed the hovering flies. The four men restlessly checked their gold pocket watches, nodding agreeably to their fellow citizens who were meeting this same train for other, less pressing reasons.

They were sleek men, girded with flesh, years, and contentment. Their hands were white and soft as bread dough, their hair clipped, shoes shined. The four represented the civic union of commerce and politics, each routinely elected to one public office or another while they plunged their hands into private tills as well. Sid Ferris, owner of the New Town Hotel and other properties, was currently mayor. Art Whickham represented the city's oldest bank and one of its oldest families. Otis McGahey, a lawyer, represented Art's bank and Sid's hotel and his own interests. Judge Lew Cannon represented the judiciary, if not justice. But at this moment, they all wore the same expression of collective anxiety.

"I still say it's risky," said Sid Ferris, tucking his watch back in his waistcoat.

"Everything's risky," Art Whickham replied gruffly. Art was the shortest of the quartet, trim, dapper, mustachioed, and bristling.

"We all but promised the voters rain. I just hope Hank Beecham can deliver."

"Look what he did up north last year," remarked Otis McGahey. Otis had a lawyer's love of precedent. "They brought in Hank Beecham and he brought in five inches of rain. Saved the whole town. Saved their crops. You read the testimonials. They was dying like flies in Santa Rosita."

"Where are all these flies coming from anyway?" asked Art, batting at them with his hat.

Otis nodded in the direction of the stockyards. "Cattle can't stand it. They drop where they stand. Three hundred and one straight days without rain."

"Three hundred and two," Judge Lew Cannon corrected him. "It's God's curse on us. God's cursed St. Elmo with drought before. We ought to wait for God. He delivered us in 1911." Lew Cannon wore a gray patriarch's beard and had the heavy-lidded, thick-limbed bearing of a deliberate man. He spoke slowly and with practiced Almighty inflections.

"Yes," said Sid Ferris, a shudder rattling his fleshy upholstered frame. "He delivered and He ruined. That flood swept my whole hotel away."

"Near swept everything away," McGahey observed. A pale man with red hair receding rapidly over his freckled pate, Otis wheezed and flushed under duress.

"We been over this before," Art reminded them curtly, just as he and the others were required to execute short respectful bows to a delegation from the Ladies' Culture League, a group of matrons—including their own wives—who moved in a silken mass, rather like a herd of jellyfish.

"Yes," added Lew Cannon in a dour voice after the ladies had passed, "but that flood was only a few years ago and we ought to remember the damage done then."

Art turned to him savagely. "You want to remind the voters, Lew?"

Judge Cannon sulked. "I still say we're interfering with God's plan if we hire someone to reverse His will."

"Save it for Sunday," Art snapped.

Like the others, Art was a devout church member. St. Elmo, California, boasted a Baptist chapel and the African Redeemed Church of the Lamb, which didn't actually have a church, but its believers gathered under the Reverend Eli Washington's spellbinding voice every Sunday in a warehouse, and their music and hosannas echoed in the empty streets. The Catholic Church of the Assumption served the needs of the Mexican and Irish populations. At one time, there had been a Chinese temple, but it had burned in 1909, and now the Chinese implored their gods privately. Despite this display of religious tolerance and plurality, the city's elite remained—as it had always been—solidly Methodist and Mormon. Of these four, Sid was Methodist, Art and Lew and Otis were Mormons.

The men busied themselves looking downright Augustan, greeting voters till the train came in at last, billowing smoke and steam, splashing cinders and ash, screeching like a beast brought down in defeat. People on the platform pressed forward as the doors opened, and passengers disembarked amid a bevy of greetings and reunions. The four men watched expectantly as the westbound disgorged dusty women with drooping feathers on their hats, fussy children, bland-faced workingmen, natty commercial travelers, and even an opera impresario from Chicago, who was met by the ladies from the Culture League. The four men again doffed their hats as the ladies passed by with their impresario in tow. The impresario wore a carnation in his buttonhole; a garland of gleaming mustache luxuriated across his face, and he had a dark complexion and long-lashed, liquid brown eyes.

"He looks like a Mex to me," said Art under his breath.

"Signor Federicci," said Otis. "My wife says he's Italian."

Art's features did a swift dance of derision around his nose, and he muttered a few choice observations on Signor Federicci's ancestral origins.

As the platform throng thinned and their rainmaker did not appear, Sid Ferris asked if anyone could remember what Hank Beecham looked like. No one could till Lew Cannon, older than the others, remarked succinctly, "Like his old man." He nodded as the last passenger stepped down. "Remember?"

Having pinned their hopes on Hank Beecham, the four were disappointed. He had none of the jaunty confidence expected of a miracle worker. His lanky body appeared pinned together hastily, and his limbs refused to work in unison. Collarless, carrying his coat and hat and a single battered satchel, he wore crumpled pants and shirt, the seams frayed, his clothes pocked with cinder holes, his boots gray with dust. His hair was sparse, lusterless, and long, his face weathered as the west wall of a desert barn. He walked right up to them.

"Well, if it ain't Hank Beecham!" Sid Ferris, with a hotel owner's bonhomie, clapped him on the back. A puff of dust or powder wafted from the rainmaker's clothes. "Hank Beecham, our native son. What's it been? Twenty years? More? I'd know you anywhere, Hank. Welcome home!"

Without smiling, Hank Beecham shook hands with the four, who were reluctant to put their white hands into his. Beecham's hands were quilted with scars, hairless, and hard. His eyes were pale, vacant, and blue and the eyelashes, eyebrows, and mustache singed so many times they appeared to be mere sketches upon his face, as though the Creator had planned to include them but forgot the final execution. From his body came the faint unmistakable odor of gunpowder. "You need rain, all right." That was the first thing Hank Beecham said, as he rolled himself a cigarette and lit it, striking the wooden lucifer on the buckle of his suspenders.

The four steered him through the station and out to Art's Locomobile. A horse tied nearby whinnied in protest at their approach and unceremoniously relieved itself all too near Art's shoes, obliging him to dance an unexpected jig as he opened the door. "We've made arrangements for you at the New Town Hotel. You're Sid's guest."

"Don't even think of paying, Hank," said Sid, taking the satchel, which was unexpectedly heavy.

"New Town?"

"Didn't you hear? We had quite the flood in 1911, and it wiped out most of the old town—of what you'd remember, anyway. Even wiped out Sid's old hotel," Otis informed him. Otis was a puffy man who perspired easily.

"But I rebuilt in New Town," Sid added proudly. "Bigger and better than ever. Electric light. Two baths on every floor. Why, this whole town is different! Improved! We built up from the ashes."

"I thought you said it was a flood," Hank remarked dryly.

"God's cursed us again with drought," Lew Cannon began.

"Just step right in here," said Art, interrupting the judge. Hank took the front seat. The other three men were obliged to squeeze all too intimately in the backseat. "Yes, Hank, we're taking you to the New Town Hotel. We didn't think you'd want to stay all the way out at your family's old place. Your brother Horace and his boy, Earl, haven't had much luck there."

"Nobody had much luck there," said Hank.

Nobody contested this. Indeed, as president of the St. Elmo National Bank and Trust, Art Whickham had been prevailed upon by the other three not to foreclose on Hank's brother and nephew—at least not until St. Elmo had its rain.

Art had reminded them that Hank Beecham hadn't seen or spoken to his brother in more than twenty years. "I don't care," Sid Ferris had replied. "Blood is thicker than water. Blood is thicker than rain." To this, Art had merely observed that no Beecham's blood was any thicker than cheap whiskey, but he held off foreclosing just the same.

Of all the Beechams, Hank was the only one graced with so much as a morsel of luck. His father's luck had begun and ended with the Civil War, which is to say he lived through it. Jeremiah Beecham had fought with the Confederacy, the Third Army Corps, forty thousand strong, at Shiloh, one of the Yell Rifles under Brigadier General Patrick Cleburne of Arkansas. General Cleburne's troops led the Confederate attack at Shiloh that bloody Sunday morning in April 1862, surprising the Union army at breakfast. Beecham fought in the thick of it, the Hornet's Nest, the peach orchard, the fighting so terrible that when it was over, corpses covered the ground for acres. Though Cleburne's men were decimated— a third of their number dead, dying, wounded—Jeremiah Beecham lived to fight again the second day of Shiloh, when the Confederates were defeated. At Shiloh, he took a bullet in the cheek that exited through his mouth, which was open at the time. He took a bullet in the thigh at Missionary Ridge in 1863. He carried a couple of spent cartridges in his body from other engagements and powder burns along his neck and hands all his life, but he survived. His luck alone would have got him promoted, but he couldn't read or write, and he remained a private in Cleburne's division.

Jeremiah could get teary on the subject of the immortal General Cleburne, the fightin'est Irishman who ever drew breath and the bravest and smartest general in the whole Confederate States of America. *If Old Pat hadda been commander, he woulda saved the Confederacy, by God, and there'd be slavery right now in the South.* Moreover, Jeremiah would whup any scoundrel—*You jes' name yer weapons, name 'em! Fists, knives*—who suggested that Grant was a greater general than Cleburne. Jeremiah spit on Grant. Sherman too. They never should have won at Shiloh. Why, that first day—to hear Jeremiah tell it—Sherman's men were so surprised they were bayoneted sleeping in their tents. And Grant? Grant had his back to the Tennessee River that first night and nowhere to go. *Grant shoulda drowned in the Tennessee River. Woulda drowned too, 'cept for...*

For forty years, Jeremiah told these tales to men enthralled and men indifferent, to men who remembered the conflict and men born long after the War. His battle experience was vast, and his accounts were long, detailed, and grisly. Jeremiah maundered on drunkenly: lost opportunities, blunders, brutal weather, inaccurate intelligence, high-command bickering that condemned the Confederacy and Jeremiah Beecham to defeat.

But of all Jeremiah's battles, it was Shiloh—that bloody and contested piece of Tennessee ground—that he returned to again and again, as though perhaps in repetition lay understanding or redress. That first day of battle, Rebel commanders believed they had broken the Union army in the West. That Sunday night, Rebel commanders slept in Sherman's tent and Rebel troops looted the Union camps. But at the end of the second day, cruelly defeated, the Confederate army—including the ragged remnants of the Yell Rifles—retreated south. In the mud and rain, they straggled, stumbled, staggered, leaving Tennessee. From Shiloh, Jeremiah carried a queerly collapsed right cheek, the result of the bullet. From Shiloh, he took a sword, an Enfield rifle, a pair of epaulettes and brass buttons he'd cut from the uniform of a dead Union general.

Even the St. Elmo pawnbroker had granted these articles were genuine Union, if not genuine Union general, and they so often graced his shop that the sword had its own place of pride, hanging high above the counter. Eventually, these tokens were not redeemed, but they had been so often spoken of that the words themselves—*Enfield rifle, sword, epaulettes, buttons*—came to have solidity, girth, and weight of their own, came to have significance, to resonate with the honor of the Beechams.

In the ruinous aftermath of the War, Jeremiah Beecham had left the land of cotton and fetched up eventually in the St. Elmo Valley, bringing with him his tired, sun-strained wife and three little sons. (A girl and Hank were born in California.) He homesteaded a hundred and sixty acres of land that would have daunted even a sober, hardworking, productive man, which Jeremiah was not. He had the mouth, the mind, eventually the palsied rattle of a man cursed with drink, and as the ranching went downhill, the curse accelerated, as though obeying the laws of physics. When the curse was on him, Jeremiah Beecham would have sold his own mother into slavery for a drink.

He was eloquent and brutal on the topic of slavery, and he regarded all black people as little better than runaway chattels without rights or honor. For their part, St. Elmo's black population avoided Beecham—drunk or sober—crossing any street he happened to be on. Jeremiah accepted this as a mark of respect, instead of seeing its implicit contempt. He could not have borne their contempt, especially since—he would wax on—it was galling and against the laws of nature to see a black man prospering when a white man could not, to see black families comfortable while white children had no shoes.

This anomaly was all the more bitter given the Beechams' glorious past. Given drink and a listener, indeed, given just drink, Jeremiah would augment his vivid accounts of Shiloh, Chickamauga, Missionary Ridge, all the rest of them—the smoke, the shot and shell, the bloody bayonets, the mud, the muskets, the buttons and sword, the epaulettes and Enfield rifle—with a sonorous lament for the things defeat had stolen from him: land, crops, slaves, an opulent home, prize stock, a stable of racehorses, a carriage (several carriages as the years passed), a pianny, and silver spoons. In truth, from the time Beechams had first crawled out of the alluvial Arkansas mud, they had clung by their fingernails to whatever scrap of land they'd tenanted, without even owning so much as a divot of sod. They could not even hope to inherit the earth, since they were not meek. If it wasn't for the dirty Yanks, Jeremiah would often hiccough in closing his soliloquy, he would yet be sitting on some well-swept veranda tended by dusky deferential servants.

It was in this vein—an ill-omened moment, a sentimental nod toward the Confederacy, the Lost Cause, the Bonnie Blue Flag, the Yell Rifles, and Patrick Cleburne—that Jeremiah Beecham named his St. Elmo ranch Shiloh. He was defeated there as surely as he had been at the original. His daughter ran off one night, taking with her the family's last horse and every cent Mrs. Eulalie Beecham had managed to scrape, hoard, and hide from her husband. Eulalie pleaded with Jeremiah that the daughter's defection meant one less mouth to feed. Enraged about the horse (he did not know about the money), Jeremiah went to the sheriff and drunkenly swore out a complaint for her arrest. The sheriff took it all down, although, alas, he could not act on it, as it had not been notarized. St. Elmo's civic servants never relax their sense of duty.

The eldest son inherited his fathers taste for drink and died in a brawl before he was twenty. Another son was sent to prison for assault with a knife. He died there. Jeremiah himself, the old soldier, unaccountably lived on till 1906, succumbing finally to alcoholic convulsions. His third son, Horace, found him one day, dead, sprawled in the yard at Shiloh between the clapboard house and the splintering barn, the chickens cheerily picking him clean, louse by louse.

Horace, his frail wife, and his little son, Earl, saw Jeremiah decently into a grave (and one far distant from the grave of Mrs. Eulalie Beecham). And then Horace got drunk and tried to storm the pawnshop to redeem the sword, the Enfield, the epaulettes and brass buttons, his family's honor. Failing in this, he spent the night in jail and went home the next day.

Most of Shiloh had been sold off long before, the ranch reduced to a few acres, which Horace mortgaged to Art Whickham's bank. He drank for months on this money, happy as the proverbial pig in shit. Horace neither sowed nor reaped, but scraped by, enough to keep little Earl in shoes and make some of the mortgage payments. As the years passed, and certainly after his wife died, Horace gave up all pretense of ranching, and he and Earl, now a young man, kept no more livestock than the chickens, which, aside from the occasional coyote foray, required very little of them, scarcely even vigilance.

Hank Beecham did not drink. He may have looked like Jeremiah, but he was his mother's son. He had Eulalie Beecham's knack for study and invention, her sure steady hand, her long delicate fingers. His actual education was haphazard and incomplete—due mainly to a lack of shoes—but he put his time to good use. Before he was fifteen, he was doing a tidy business fixing things for people for miles around. His reputation spread, and sewing machines were his specialty. Hank Beecham could take a sewing machine that had been rusted shut since the Red Sea parted and make it hum again.

Before he was seventeen, Hank scraped together his fix-it earnings and left Shiloh for good. He took his mother with him. Without a tear or parting word, Eulalie left her husband and Horace to the bottle and the glories of the Confederacy. She and Henry moved into town, lived in two rooms above a little rented shop where Henry fixed things, his practice not limited to sewing machines. Eulalie kept the books for the shop and kept house for her son. Henry Beecham worked six days a week and on the seventh he rested not. He rested not ever.

Upon moving to town, he presented himself to the fledgling public library with inquiries after science and military history. The librarian showed him where he might best look, and he took his first two books, Thorpe's *Dictionary of Applied Chemistry* and Hardee's *Rifle and Light Infantry Tactics*, to a table near the works of Sir Walter Scott. On that shelf, he saw *Life of Napoleon Bonaparte* by Sir Walter, and he took that too.

Sitting across from him was Miss Emmons, teacher of the elementary grades at Pioneer School and a graduate of Spartana Normal School. Brown as a she-sparrow, Miss Emmons was tiny and birdlike, old enough to have a pinch to her lips and a bristle in her walk. She elicited from her students neither affection nor fear, nor anything really, save perhaps their easygoing contempt, so casual as to be scarcely deserving of the word. Winter and summer, Miss Emmons wore white, high-collared shirtwaists and black wool skirts, her clothes so oft-washed that the white darkened and the black faded, both to a dull off-brown matching the coat she donned for her daily walk from Sister Whitworth's boardinghouse to Pioneer School.

Miss Emmons was a regular patron of the struggling public library and took her work always to the table near Sir Walter Scott, out of loyalty to that prolific poet and author. Hank, on the other hand, was a creature of habit, and having once sat near Sir Walter, he returned as though obeying the dictates of cams and cranks on a sewing machine. For a while, Miss Emmons watched him struggle through his heavy tomes of science and history, using his index finger along the page and forming the words with difficulty on his lips. It was more than she could bear.

Eventually, Hank Beecham could be found several evenings a week in the empty classroom at Pioneer School, his ungainly frame tucked uncomfortably into a diminutive desk while Miss Emmons broadened his literacy skills and ciphering abilities. Once he caught on, Hank burned through books, though his interests were narrow, limited finally to military history and science, chemistry especially.

About this time, Hank Beecham began hiring a wagon on Saturday nights, though it was more visibly in use on Sunday mornings. When the godly gathered in churches and the godless tossed on crapulent beds, Hank drove his rented horse and wagon up into the foothills, occasionally accompanied by Miss Emmons. The sight of them together gave

St. Elmo a communal guffaw, especially as Hank admitted he was conducting "chemical experiments." However, if the wind blew the right way, sometimes an acrid plume of smoke blew with it. A year or so later, the wagon was destroyed and the horse killed—blown to bits, actually— when it took a notion to run off and the chemicals and gunpowder in the wagon ignited in an unforeseen explosion. The godly came pouring from the churches and the godless came stumbling from their inebriate beds to look eastward. Hank was some distance from the blast. Miss Emmons was not with him.

Following this incident, the city council quickly added a statute to the books prohibiting chemical experiments without a permit, which they were not about to grant. Hank didn't care. Eulalie Beecham was dying of a long terrible illness, and for the final months of her life, Hank gave up everything to care for her till she died. She was buried in the city cemetery. For the words of farewell, Hank prevailed on a good-natured Baptist (and made a donation), though no Beecham had ever set foot in his church. At the funeral, Hank nodded to the doctor who had attended Eulalie's last illness, but he was otherwise silent, not so much as a nod or word to Jeremiah or Horace, both of whom were sloshed. These four were the only mourners.

From the cemetery, Hank went directly to the repair shop and picked up the bag he had already packed. Thence to the printer, where he collected cards he had ordered. Five hundred of them.

HENRY C. BEECHAM

RAIN MADE TO ORDER
SUCCESS GUARANTEED

He left St. Elmo without a single goodbye, not even to Miss Emmons, and he never came back.

News of his rainmaking success all over the West drifted back to town, as everything drifts back to a railroad town, and people who had known him and his family were continually astonished to hear of his achievements. Not because they didn't believe that rain could be made to order or success guaranteed, but because Hank was a Beecham, and they were luckless, shiftless, worthless, violent, and drunken and always would be.

So it was something of a comedown for the august city fathers to greet Hank at the station, to take him in one of their fine cars to the city's best hotel and put him up as the city's guest. They might not have invited him at all, except that their hour of need had stretched from days into months, month after month without rain, though from every pulpit—Mormon, Methodist, Catholic, Baptist, the African Redeemed Church of the Lamb, the private pulpits of the Chinese—the Almighty was beseeched to send rain to the St. Elmo Valley. Persistently, He declined. St. Elmo wilted. Forage crops that could usually endure the dryness withered, the infant citrus industry puckered up, collapsed; sheep too dumb to seek water dropped beside dried-up troughs; even hogs searching for a bit of forbidden wallow in the city streets (there were ordinances against this) couldn't find three square inches of mud and died where they fell. Every two-bit grass fire aided and abetted by a stiff wind threatened to become an inferno. Prices rose, tempers flared, and the desert sun seared into the flesh and burnt the eyes of everyone in the St. Elmo Valley.

All this in an election year.

Edmund Jaeger

Born in 1887 in Nebraska, Edmund Jaeger was a world-renowned naturalist and botanist whose published works—including *Desert Wildflowers*, *The North American Deserts*, and *Desert Wildlife*—are a testament to his passion to protect the deserts of the Southwest. His 1946 discovery of a hibernating poorwill in the Chuckwalla Mountains proved that there are birds that hibernate. Jaeger taught for thirty years at Riverside Community College. He died in 1983.

This excerpt from *Desert Wildlife* describes a common but haunting scene: turkey vultures gathering in spring in the Mojave (here Mohave) Desert.

from *Desert Wildlife*

Every autumn and every spring there takes place on the Mohave Desert one of the most remarkable phenomena of bird life—the spectacular gathering of thousands of turkey vultures. These two assemblages have probably taken place for centuries with no cessation or variance.

The autumn gathering of the birds usually takes place in early October, the spring assemblage in middle and late March. The larger of the two gatherings occurs in autumn. Then, from hundreds of miles around, the birds come in, and soon we see their great communal roosts in the cottonwood trees, especially dead ones, along the Mohave River bottoms from near Hesperia, California, to the site of old Camp Cady. In the morning before sunup the vultures are so crowded on the dead branches of the trees that their black-feathered bodies are plainly visible from a distance of half a mile. There may be hundreds of them in a single roost. Sometimes one large tree may hold as many as thirty or forty birds—six to eight lined up close together on a single horizontal limb. As the sun comes up, they turn about, fluffing their feathers and stretching their wings, one at a time. It reminds one of the similar action of the California road runner. This goes on for an hour or so. After that the birds exchange positions on the trees. Then, one after another, they sluggishly take off, joining others in that slow, cyclic flight that continues without interruption all through the day.

By nine o'clock every bird is in the air in that eternal gliding that carries them around and around like autumn leaves in a slow-moving whirlwind. We see them move in ever changing circles tip to heights almost beyond human sight and gradually down again. Sometimes twenty or thirty of these formations, each composed of about sixty to one hundred birds, are to be seen at one time along the Mohave River's course and over the hills or low plains to the east, even as far as the Ord Mountains and the vicinity of Twentynine Palms. In any one formation, some of the birds circle clockwise, others move counterclockwise, the whole group slowly drifting now in one direction, now in another.

From all I can observe, little or no food is taken during this period. There is little enough carrion for the few that are permanent summer residents of the area in normal seasons.

Then one day, driven perhaps by hunger, the turkey vultures begin their migration flight. Lee Smith, who lives at the site of old Camp Cady on the Mohave River east of Daggett, tells of seeing in late October of 1945 such a flight of 417 turkey vultures, "all flying at low altitude dead east along the river's course as if toward the Colorado River." I myself have witnessed such migrations, but with fewer birds, headed directly south over and along the crest of the Little San Bernardino Mountains. In a few days the whole sky is cleared of birds, and except for a few stragglers not another vulture is seen until the return flight the following spring. Middle and southern Mexico apparently is their wintering place.

Erle Stanley Gardner

Erle Stanley Gardner was born in Massachusetts in 1889 and moved with his family to the West Coast in 1909. He worked as a lawyer and eventually established his own law firm but quickly got bored with the legal profession. He turned to writing Western and mystery stories for pulp magazines in the early 1920s, creating such memorable characters as Perry Mason and Bob Zane. The author of at least 120 novels and numerous short stories, he died in 1970 in his home at Rancho del Paisano.

Chapter three from his 1930 novelette *Blood-Red Gold* appears below.

from *Blood-Red Gold*

Now desert whispers are funny things. Maybe you've got to believe in the desert before you believe in desert whispers. At any rate, you've got to know what it's like to spend the long desert nights bedded down in the drifting sand before you'll know much about the desert, or the whispers, either.

The desert is peculiar. It's something that can't be described. You either feel the spell of the desert or you don't. You either hate it or you love it. In either event you'll fear it.

There it lies, miles on miles of it, dry lake beds, twisted mountains of volcanic rock, sloping sage-covered hills, clumps of Joshua trees, thickets of mesquite, bunches of giant cactus. It has the moods of a woman, and the treachery of a big cat.

And always it's vaguely restive. During the daytime the heat makes it do a devil's dance. The horizons shimmer and shake. Mirages chase one another across the dry lake beds. The winds blow like the devil from one direction, and then they turn and blow like the devil from the other direction.

Sand marches on an endless journey, coming from Lord knows where, and going across the desert in a slithering procession of whispering noise that's as dry as the sound made by a sidewinder when he crawls past your blankets.

It's at night when the desert's still and calm and the steady stars blaze down like torches that you can hear the whispers best. Then you'll lie in your blankets with your head pillowed right on the surface of the desert, and you'll hear the dry sagebrush swish in the wind. It sounds as though the leaves are whispering. Then you'll hear the sand rattling against the cactus, and it'll sound like a different kind of a whisper, a finer, more stealthy whisper.

And then, usually just before you're getting to sleep, you'll hear that finest whisper of all, the sand whispering to the sand. Of course, if you'd wake up and snap out of it, you'd know that it was just the sound made by windblown sand drifting across the sandy face of the desert.

But you don't wake up like that. You just drift off to sleep, lulled by the sound of the sand whispering to the sand.

I've never really figured it out, but I guess that's why the desert is so full of whispers. Strange stories seep through the desert just the way the sounds of the drifting sand seep into your ears. Take a man who has lived a long time in the desert, and his voice gets a dry, husking whisper in it that's like the sound of a lizard's feet scratching along the surface of a sun-baked rock.

Everything whispers in the desert, and some of the whispers would sound reasonable anywhere. Some of 'em only sound reasonable when you're half asleep in the middle of the desert.

Edith Eason first came to me as a whisper.

I was camped up north of Shoshone when I heard of her. And I swear I can't tell who it was that first told me. It was just a whisper, a casual, seeping whisper. You'd probably laugh if I said so, but, somehow or other, I have an idea it was a sand whisper that first told me about her.

At any rate the name didn't sound strange to my ears when Humpy Crane gave me the low-down on her. It's the sort of a name that lends itself to a whisper. Sand drifting over sand or rustling against cactus would give forth a sound like that: "Eason-Eeeeason-Eeeassssssssssson - Edith Eassssson!"

Humpy came in to my camp fire up north of Shoshone. I was camped on a slope of the Funeral Range, and it was a typical desert night. Humpy saw my supper fire, and came on over. I could hear him and his burro long before I could see them. Their feet shuffled through the dry sand with a sort of whispering noise that muffled the steps.

"Hello, Humpy," I said, when the fire lit on his lined face and white hair. "Had anything to eat?"

"Nope. I'm short o' grub, an' I saw your fire. Didn't know it was you, Bob Zane. Got any tea, or tomatoes?"

I opened the pack.

"I got a little of everything here, old-timer. Sit down while I get her ready."

We ate under the stars. The burros moved around through the dwarf sage.

"Wasn't you one of the fellows that went in after the lunger that got bumped off in the desert?"

"You mean Sid Grahame, the one that went out with Ortley?"

"Yeah."

"Uh-huh, I was; why?"

"Nothin' much. There's a red-headed girl come out from Denver. Her name's Eason. Edith Eason. She's hanging around Randsburg, lookin' for you, or for Stringy Martin, either one."

"What's she want?"

"Don't know. It's got something to do with this lunger that got croaked. She grubstaked him or something, and she thinks he found some quartz stuff and was taking Ortley in to show it to him."

I sipped a graniteware cup of tea.

"That," I told him, "is different."

Even then, I began to put two and two together, the weight of the bag when Ortley had lifted it off the burro, the eager way he'd cut the pack ropes to get it loose.

"Eason, Edith Eason—I've heard the name somewhere."

"Maybe. It's a name that's easy on the ears. You goin' in to Randsburg?"

I hadn't been headed that way, but I didn't hesitate any when Humpy asked the question.

"I'm goin' back," I told him.

Edith Eason had bright red hair and eyes that were a calm gray. She looked like a woman who could manage her own way in the world.

"Sid was working in the office with me when he developed the sickness," she told me. "The doctors said sunshine and fresh air would cure him, but he was cooped up in a stuffy office, and he wouldn't quit because he didn't have anything saved up and he didn't want to be a burden on any one.

"So I pretended to get awfully interested in mining, and then I told him I didn't want to be working for wages all of my life, and I was going out in the desert and prospect, or else grubstake some old desert rat. He warned me I'd get stung, and finally I worked the situation around so it seemed logical for me to offer to grubstake him in the desert and let him prospect.

"He was out six months in all, and he started to get well almost from the first. He wrote to me and mailed the letters whenever he came to a post office. Sometimes I'd get three or four of them in one mail. The last batch of letters said he had something that looked awfully good, that he had a capitalist coming in to look it over and that he'd let me know. Then the next I heard was when I read of his death. So I wrote to the sheriff for details, and he told me stuff that brought me out here."

She let her calm gray eyes bore right into mine, and read my mind.

"You think I'm a fool for giving up my job and trying to come out here, don't you?"

Out in the desert you get so you shoot straight from the shoulder on most things, or else you get crooked all over.

"Yes," I told her.

She nodded.

"That's the way I like men. You and I are going to get along."

"You talk as though you were considering adopting me," I said.

"I am," she said, and her eyes didn't even twinkle. "You and I are going into the desert together."

"Huh?"

"Yes. I want to see where Sid's buried, and I want to try and trail where they went on their expedition."

"It's a cold trail."

"I know it. But I've heard a lot about you, Bob Zane. They say you can make the desert talk to you, that there's nothing in the Mojave you can't find out."

I told her straight from the shoulder.

"Yes, ma'am, the desert talks all right. It talks in sand whispers that are easy to believe—in the desert. They don't sound probable anywhere else. I'm afraid you've been listening to sand whispers."

She shook her head and reached her hand inside the blouse of her suit. When it came out there was a little tissue paper parcel in the palm. She unfolded the paper parcel.

"Look," she said.

I looked, and then I looked again, and then I rubbed my eyes and looked some more.

They were little nuggets of red metal. They were almost blood-red, but I knew what they were even before I scratched under the red with the point of my knife.

"Gold," I told her. "It's a gold that's alluvial, and it's been through some chemical or other that's given it a red coating. You get all sorts of gold here in the desert. They even have a black gold, that's dead black on the surface."

She nodded.

"The garage man found these. When Ortley drove off, something spilled from his pockets when he took out the money to pay his bill. The garage man found these on the dirt floor."

I shook my head.

"No. This couldn't be what Sid discovered. This is a placer deposit. If he found something that needed capital, it would have been quartz. A deposit of this sort of gold could be washed out without requiring enough capital to bother about. A man all by himself could make the claim pay its way."

She stamped her foot.

"I tell you I *know*. I don't know what the explanation is. That's what I'm going in to find out. But I know that this is from Sid's mine. And Ortley insisted on taking his clothes, his shaving things, and his tooth brush and paste in a leather hand bag."

I nodded.

"Yeah. I saw that. I saw him bring the hand bag out, too, and put it in the car. That don't prove anything."

"The dickens it doesn't!" she snapped. "When they unpacked the burros, they found all of his personal things wrapped in a canvas. So what was in that bag when he brought it out?"

I did some fast thinking and remembered how he'd cut that bag loose from the pack and put it in the car before he did any talking, and I remembered how heavy the bag seemed.

"You win," I told the red-head. "Can you be ready to leave by tomorrow morning?"

The smile that twisted her lips was a funny one.

"Want to get drunk, Bob Zane?" she asked.

"No; why?"

"I wondered why you wanted to stay in town tonight."

"Lord, I don't want to stay. But we've got to get a couple more burros and some grub and some water cans."

"I've got them all. How long will it take for you to put the packs on?"

"About forty-five minutes, for the first packing."

"Then we can leave in an hour."

It was settled, just like that. We left in exactly fifty-seven minutes. And I did something I haven't done in the desert for a long time—I strapped my old forty-five onto my waist and got a box of fresh shells.

You get acquainted with people quick in the desert. They can't fool themselves and they can't fool you, out where there's nothing but eternity and silence. I never found out why it is, but it's so. Take a two-day trip in the desert with some one and you'll know him like a book, no matter if he doesn't say a thing.

We traveled late the first night, and we rolled our blankets under the stars. I made the girl as comfortable as I could, and then I went up the ridge a hundred yards or so, so she wouldn't feel I was intruding. I've acted as guide, off and on, for lots of women parties, and the first night they usually sleep with a gun clenched in their fist.

Funny thing about people. They'll sleep in a Pullman car with nothing between them and a lot of strangers but a little green cloth with some numbers on it; but when you get 'em out in God's outdoors they're likely to get self-conscious.

Not this girl.

She was one of the kind that was sure of herself, and of every move she made. She had the poise of a thoroughbred, and she took to the desert like a duck to water.

People are like that. They either take to the desert or they don't. They either love it or they hate it, and if they hate it, the hatred is born of fear.

That night a faint breeze sprang up out of nowhere. The stars blazed steadily. The sage leaves commenced to rustle against each other, and then the sand began to whisper. I went to sleep with the sand making little whispering noises that sounded more and more like words.

In the morning she was up, waiting for me, which I hadn't expected. It was early. The desert was cold with a dry cold that penetrated. There was just the faintest streak of dawn in the east. The stars hadn't commenced to pinpoint out before the day. They were still blazing steadily.

She threw some sage branches on the fire and the red flared up over the desert.

"Go get the burros," she said. "I can get the breakfast." She was like a great shadow, moving between me and the fire.

"No fancy stuff," I warned. "Coffee and something we can handle quick. We've got to get started before it gets too hot."

She clattered the pans about and I could hear the gurgle of water from a canteen. I rounded up the burros, put on the saddles, and heard the beat of a spoon against a pan.

It was a good breakfast, and it came up on the dot.

"One cup of water for dishwater," I told her.

"No more than that?"

"No. You've got to get accustomed to the desert, and you might as well begin."

She didn't argue. She just measured out a cup of water and poured it in the frying pan. Fifteen minutes later we were throwing the last rope on the pack, and she knew a lot about the squaw hitch.

The east was a red gold now, the color of the gold that had fallen from Ortley's pocket, the color of bloodstained gold. She watched it as the burros shuffled their way through the sage and greasewood clumps.

"I heard whispers last night," she said.

"Sand," I told her.

She said nothing.

John Steinbeck

John Steinbeck, born in Salinas, California, in 1902, is one of America's most celebrated writers, winner of the Pulitzer Prize in 1940 for *The Grapes of Wrath* and recipient of the Nobel Prize in literature in 1962. Other major works include *Of Mice and Men*, *East of Eden*, and *Cannery Row*—all set in California. Seventeen of his novels have been made into major Hollywood films. Steinbeck died in 1968.

This excerpt from *The Grapes of Wrath*, the powerful story of an Oklahoma family traveling to California to escape Dust Bowl poverty, describes U.S. Route 66 ("the mother road") from Oklahoma to California, a major migratory path west at the time. The highway first entered California at Needles and continued through Barstow and San Bernardino on its way to Santa Monica. It was decommissioned in 1985.

from *The Grapes of Wrath*

Highway 66 is the main migrant road. 66—the long concrete path across the country, waving gently up and down on the map, from Mississippi to Bakersfield—over the red lands and the gray lands, twisting up into the mountains, crossing the Divide and down into the bright and terrible desert, and across the desert to the mountains again, and into the rich California valleys.

66 is the path of a people in flight, refugees from dust and shrinking land, from the thunder of tractors and shrinking ownership, from the desert's slow northward invasion, from the twisting winds that howl up

out of Texas, from the floods that bring no richness to the land and steal what little richness is there. From all of these the people are in flight, and they come into 66 from the tributary side roads, from the wagon tracks and the rutted country roads. 66 is the mother road, the road of flight.

Clarksville and Ozark and Van Buren and Fort Smith on 64, and there's an end of Arkansas. And all the roads into Oklahoma City, 66 down from Tulsa, 270 up from McAlester. 81 from Wichita Falls south, from Enid north. Edmond, McLoud, Purcell. 66 out of Oklahoma City; El Reno and Clinton, going west on 66. Hydro, Elk City and Texola; and there's an end to Oklahoma. 66 across the Panhandle of Texas. Shamrock and McLean, Conway and Amarillo, the yellow. Wildorado and Vega and Boise, and there's an end of Texas. Tucumcari and Santa Rosa and into the New Mexican mountains to Albuquerque, where the road comes down from Santa Fe. Then down the gorged Rio Grande to Los Lunas and west again on 66 to Gallup, and there's the border of New Mexico.

And now the high mountains. Holbrook and Winslow and Flagstaff in the high mountains of Arizona. Then the great plateau rolling like a ground swell. Ashfork and Kingman and stone mountains again, where water must be hauled and sold. Then out of the broken sun-rotted mountains of Arizona to the Colorado, with green reeds on its banks, and that's the end of Arizona. There's California just over the river, and a pretty town to start it. Needles, on the river. But the river is a stranger in this place. Up from Needles and over a burned range, and there's the desert. And 66 goes on over the terrible desert, where the distance shimmers and the black center mountains hang unbearably in the distance. At last there's Barstow, and more desert until at last the mountains rise up again, the good mountains, and 66 winds through them. Then suddenly a pass, and below the beautiful valley, below orchards and vineyards and little houses, and in the distance a city. And, oh, my God, it's over.

The people in flight streamed out on 66, sometimes a single car, sometimes a little caravan. All day they rolled slowly along the road, and at night they stopped near water. In the day ancient leaky radiators sent up columns of steam, loose connecting rods hammered and pounded. And the men driving the trucks and the overloaded cars listened apprehensively. How far between towns? It is a terror between towns. If something breaks—well, if something breaks we camp right here while Jim walks to town and gets a part and walks back and—how much food we got?

Listen to the motor. Listen to the wheels. Listen with your ears and with your hands on the steering wheel; listen with the palm of your hand on the gear-shift lever; listen with your feet on the floor boards. Listen to the pounding old jalopy with all your senses; for a change of tone, a variation of rhythm may mean—a week here? That rattle—that's tappets. Don't hurt a bit. Tappets can rattle till Jesus comes again without no harm. But that thudding as the car moves along—can't hear that—just kind of feel it. Maybe oil isn't gettin' someplace. Maybe a bearing's startin' to go. Jesus, if it's a bearing, what'll we do? Money's goin' fast.

And why's the son-of-a-bitch heat up so hot today? This ain't no climb. Le's look. God Almighty, the fan belt's gone! Here, make a belt outa this little piece a rope. Le's see how long—there. I'll splice the ends. Now take her slow—slow, till we can get to a town. That rope belt won't last long.

'F we can on'y get to California where the oranges grow before this here ol' jug blows up. 'F we on'y can.

And the tires—two layers of fabric worn through. On'y a four-ply tire. Might get a hunderd miles more outa her if we don't hit a rock an' blow her. Which'll we take—a hunderd, maybe, miles, or maybe spoil the tube? Which? A hunderd miles. Well, that's somepin you got to think about. We got tube patches. Maybe when she goes she'll only spring a leak. How about makin' a boot? Might get five hunderd more miles. Le's go on till she blows.

We got to get a tire, but, Jesus, they want a lot for a ol' tire. They look a fella over. They know he got to go on. They know he can't wait. And the price goes up.

Take it or leave it. I ain't in business for my health. I'm here a-sellin' tires. I ain't givin' 'em away. I can't help what happens to you. I got to think what happens to me.

How far's the nex' town?

I seen forty-two cars a you fellas go by yesterday. Where you all come from? Where all of you goin'?

Well, California's a big State.

It ain't that big. The whole United States ain't that big. It ain't that big. It ain't big enough. There ain't room enough for you an' me, for your kind an' my kind, for rich and poor together all in one country, for thieves and honest men. For hunger and fat. Whyn't you go back where you come from?

This is a free country. Fella can go where he wants.

That's what *you* think! Ever hear of the border patrol on the California line? Police from Los Angeles—stopped you bastards, turned you back. Says, if you can't buy no real estate we don't want you. Says, got a driver's license? Le's see it. Tore it up. Says you can't come in without no driver's license.

It's a free country.

Well, try to get some freedom to do. Fella says you're jus' as free as you got jack to pay for it.

In California they got high wages. I got a han'bill here tells about it.

Baloney! I seen folks comin' back. Somebody's kiddin' you. You want that tire or don't ya?

Got to take it, but, Jesus, mister, it cuts into our money! We ain't got much left.

Well, I ain't no charity. Take her along.

Got to, I guess. Let's look her over. Open her up, look a' the casing—you son-of-a-bitch, you said the casing was good. She's broke damn near through.

The hell she is. Well—by George! How come I didn' see that?

You did see it, you son-of-a-bitch. You wanta charge us four bucks for a busted casing. I'd like to take a sock at you.

Now keep your shirt on. I didn' see it, I tell you. Here—tell ya what I'll do. I'll give ya this one for three-fifty.

You'll take a flying jump at the moon! We'll try to make the nex' town.

Think we can make it on that tire?

Got to. I'll go on the rim before I'd give that son-of-a-bitch a dime.

What do ya think a guy in business is? Like he says, he ain't in it for his health. That's what business is. What'd you think it was? Fella's got—See that sign 'longside the road there? Service Club. Luncheon Tuesday, Colmado Hotel? Welcome, brother. That's a Service Club. Fella had a story. Went to one of them meetings an' told the story to all them business men. Says, when I was a kid my ol' man give me a haltered heifer an' says take her down an' git her serviced. An' the fella says, I done it, an' ever' time since then when I hear a business man talkin' about service, I wonder who's gettin' screwed. Fella in business got to lie an' cheat, but he calls it somepin else. That's what's important. You go steal that tire an' you're a thief, but he tried to steal your four dollars for a busted tire. They call that sound business.

Danny in the back seat wants a cup a water. Have to wait. Got no water here.

Listen—that the rear end? Can't tell.

Sound telegraphs through the frame. There goes a gasket. Got to go on. Listen to her whistle. Find a nice place to camp an' I'll jerk the head off. But, God Almighty, the food's gettin' low, the money's gettin' low. When we can't buy no more gas—what then?

Danny in the back seat wants a cup a water. Little fella's thirsty.

Listen to that gasket whistle.

Chee-rist! There she went. Blowed tube an' casing all to hell. Have to fix her. Save that casing to make boots; cut 'em out an' stick 'em inside a weak place.

Cars pulled up beside the road, engine heads off, tires mended. Cars limping along 66 like wounded things, panting and struggling. Too hot, loose connections, loose bearings, rattling bodies.

Danny wants a cup of water.

People in flight along 66. And the concrete road shone like a mirror under the sun, and in the distance the heat made it seem that there were pools of water in the road.

Danny wants a cup a water.

He'll have to wait, poor little fella. He's hot. Nex' service station. *Service* station, like the fella says.

Two hundred and fifty thousand people over the road. Fifty thousand old cars—wounded, steaming. Wrecks along the road, abandoned. Well, what happened to them? What happened to the folks in that car? Did they walk? Where are they? Where does the courage come from? Where does the terrible faith come from?

And here's a story you can hardly believe, but it's true, and it's funny and it's beautiful. There was a family of twelve and they were forced off the land. They had no car. They built a trailer out of junk and loaded it with their possessions. They pulled it to the side of 66 and waited. And pretty soon a sedan picked them up. Five of them rode in the sedan and seven on the trailer, and a dog on the trailer. They got to California in two jumps. The man who pulled them fed them. And that's true. But how can such courage be, and such faith in their own species? Very few things would teach such faith.

The people in flight from the terror behind—strange things happen to them, some bitterly cruel and some so beautiful that the faith is refired forever.

Norman Mailer

Born in 1923 in New Jersey, Norman Mailer has published prolifically, gaining attention early in his career with the world-famous novel *The Naked and the Dead*, based on his experiences in the army in World War II. A screenwriter, biographer, novelist, and essayist, he has often written on political themes, and his stances have often been controversial. He won Pulitzer Prizes in 1968 and 1979 for *Armies of the Night* and *The Executioner's Song*, respectively, and for the former he also won a National Book Award. He lives in Massachusetts.

This excerpt from *The Deer Park* describes the fictional desert town of Desert D'Or, a thinly disguised Palm Springs.

from *The Deer Park*

In the cactus wild of Southern California a distance of two hundred miles from the capital of cinema, as I choose to call it, is the town of Desert D'Or. There I went from the Air Force to look for a good time. Some time ago.

Almost everybody I knew in Desert D'Or had had an unusual career, and it was the same for me. I grew up in a home for orphans. Still intact at the age of twenty-three, wearing my flying wings and a first lieutenant's uniform, I arrived at the resort with fourteen thousand dollars, a sum I picked up via a poker game in a Tokyo hotel room while waiting with other fliers for our plane home. The curiosity is that I was never a gambler, I did not even like the game, but I had nothing to lose that night, and maybe for such a reason I accepted the luck of my cards. Let me leave it at that. I came out of the Air Force with no place to go, no family to visit, and I wandered down to Desert D'Or.

Built since the Second World War, it is the only place I know which is all new. A long time ago, Desert D'Or was called Desert Door by the prospectors who put up their shanties at the edge of its oasis and went into the mountains above the desert to look for gold. But there is nothing left of those men; when the site of Desert D'Or was chosen, none of the old shacks remained.

No, everything is in the present tense, and during the months I stayed at the resort, I came to know it in a way we can know few places. It was a town built out of no other obvious motive than commercial profit and so no sign of commerce was allowed to appear. Desert D'Or was without a main street, and its stores looked like anything but stores. In those places which sold clothing, no clothing was laid out, and you waited in a modern living room while salesmen opened panels in the wall to exhibit summer suits, or held between their hands the blooms and sprays of a tropical scarf. There was a jewelry store built like a cabin cruiser: from the street one peeped through a porthole to see a thirty-thousand-dollar necklace hung on the silver antlers of a piece of driftwood. None of the hotels—not the Yacht Club, nor the Debonair, not the Yucca Plaza, the Sandpiper, the Creedmor, nor the Desert D'Or Arms—could even be seen from outside. Put behind cement-brick fences or wooden palings, one hardly came across a building which was not green, yellow, rose, orange, or pink, and the approach was hidden by a shrubbery of bright flowers. You passed through the gate to the Yacht Club, the biggest and therefore the most exclusive hotel in the resort, and followed its private road which twisted through the grounds for several hundred yards, expecting a mansion at the end, but came instead to no more than a carport, a swimming pool in the shape of a free-form coffee table with curved-wall cabañas and canasta tables, and a set of lawn-tennis courts, the only lawn in all that part of Southern California. At night, along yellow sidewalks which crossed a winding artificial creek, lit up with Japanese lanterns strung to the tropical trees, you could wander by the guest bungalows scattered along the route, their flush pastel-colored doors another part of the maze of the arrangement.

I blew a piece of my fourteen-thousand-dollar fortune and stayed at the Yacht Club until I picked the house I was to rent for the rest of my stay in Desert D'Or. I could describe that house in detail, but what would be the use? It was like most of the houses in the resort; it was modern, ranch-style, of course, with light furniture and rugs which felt like poodle wool, and it had a garden and a wall which went around the garden, the standard fault of Desert D'Or architecture; along the desert table, the walls were made of glass to have a view of mesa-colored sand and violet mountains, but the houses were so close to each other that the builders had to fence them in, and the result was like living in a room whose walls are mirrors. In fact, my house had a twenty-foot mirror which faced the wall of plate-glass window. No matter where I stood in the living room, I could never miss the sight of my rented garden with its desert flowers and the lone yucca tree.

During the dry season, which lasted for nine months of the year, the resort was parched by the sun. Every twilight the spray from a thousand sprinklers washed dust and sand from the gray foliage; morning and afternoon the sun scorched the sap from the plants and the desert circled the resort, its cacti standing on the horizon while croppings of dusty rock gathered like scavengers in the distance. The blue sky burnt on the pale desert. It would come on me at times that Desert D'Or was a place where no trees bear leaves. The palms and the yuccas lifted a foliage of tufts and fans and fronds and shoots but never leaves, and on some of the roads where tall palms lined the way, their dead fronds hung from the trunk like an ostrich's muff.

During the off-season, most of the activity took place in the bars. The bars were a village in the town, or at least a kind of main street in the absence of any other, yet they were as different from the warm front of Desert D'Or as the inside of one's body is separate from the surface of one's skin. Like so many other places in Southern California, the bars, cocktail lounges, and nightclubs were made to look like a jungle, an underwater grotto, or the lounge of a modern movie theater. The Cerulean Room, to take an example, had an irregular space of rose-orange walls and booths of yellow leatherette under the influence of a dark blue ceiling. Above the serving bar with its bank of bottles, its pyramids of citrus fruit, a smoky-yellow false ceiling reflected into the mirror behind the bar and colored the etching of a half-nude girl which had been cut into the glass. Drinking in that atmosphere, I never knew whether it was night or day, and I think that kind of uncertainty got into everybody's conversation. Men lacquered with liquor talked to other men who were sober, stories were started and never finished. On a typical afternoon in the air-cooled midnight of the bar, you could see a fat old man in a Palm Beach suit talking to a young girl with orange lipstick and the deep suntan of Desert D'Or, the girl more interested in the old gent than the gentleman in her. Promoters and tourists, middle-aged women with new-colored hair, and high school kids who had competed in running hot-rods across the desert, were jammed together. The talk was made up of horses, stories of parties the night before, and systems for roulette. Running along the heavy beat of a third-rate promoter trying to raise money, there would come the solo shriek of one hysterical blond or another, who seemed to be laughing in that tune which goes, "I'm dumb, I'm dumb, but you're a scream."

In such a way, afternoon was always passing into night, and drunken nights into the dawn of a desert morning. One seemed to leave the theatrical darkness of afternoon for the illumination of night, and the sun of Desert D'Or became like the stranger who the drunk imagines to be following him. So I spent my first few weeks doing little more than pick up the bar checks of all those small sharp prospectors for pleasure from the capital, and in the capsule biography by which most of the people knew one another, I was understood to be an Air Force pilot whose family was wealthy and lived in the East, and I even added the detail that I had a broken marriage and drank to get over it. As a story it was reasonable enough to pass, and I sometimes believed what I said and tried to take the cure in the very real sun of Desert D'Or with its cactus, its mountain, and the bright green foliage of its love and its money.

Mary Jo Churchwell

Born in 1942 in Santa Barbara, Mary Jo Churchwell grew up in
Palm Springs. After a career in banking, she began writing maga-
zine articles that focused on her back-to-the-land lifestyle in the
Salmon River Mountains of central Idaho. Her nonfiction books
include *The Cabin on Sawmill Creek: A Western Walden*; *Palm
Springs: The Landscape, the History, the Lore*; and *Arizona: No
Ordinary Journey*. She lives in Borrego Springs, California.

This amusing excerpt about taking a tour of celebrity houses in
Palm Springs is from *Palm Springs: The Landscape, the History, the
Lore*.

from *Palm Springs*

Ah, Palm Springs: the glitz, the glamour, the energy, the fun. *You're
from Palm Springs?* I heard this throughout my teens, tone saying
all. Back then, I had enormous gratitude for all those famous people
who poured excitement into our lives. So wonderful to see them in the
flesh, to stand for a moment in their spotlight. As I write this I see them
once again: Red Skelton, Kirk Douglas, Cary Grant, Bobby Darin, Tab
Hunter, John F. Kennedy, Gerald Ford, Timothy "turn on, tune in, drop
out" Leary, Walt Disney, Bob Hope…so many. It mattered little whether
the face represented a movie, a political office, an art, a science, or a
scandal, the thrill of recognition provided conversation at school for an
otherwise lost weekend.

You would be hard put to name a celebrity who didn't live in Palm
Springs at one time or other. "Here was little Frank [Sinatra] when he

first came out here, and he made his first million," recalls Prickly Pear architect Roger Williams. "And his idea—and he was a grocery clerk, and the son of a grocery store owner. And his idea was that if he ever had money he was going to build a big, beautiful Georgian mansion with columns and stone balustrades on it." In other words, architecture with a capital A, as Sinatra understood it, an extravagant landmark that would make the neighbors feel impoverished and small. Everyone would have hated it, and Sinatra's architects came to see it as a calamity to their careers. "We'd have been ruined right then and there." With as much tact as they could muster, they persuaded Old Blue Eyes to stick with the standard fat-cat design. Architecture, in other words, as a metaphor for the good life as it is locally understood. Into such a scheme, Sinatra's swimming pool, shaped like an amoeba, fit perfectly.

The current fashion among celebrities is to fix your villa, at fabulous expense, to the side of a mountain. It appears that for the sake of a view, some people are willing to gamble the whole investment, and perhaps life itself, on the slim hope that our segment of the San Andreas Fault will not move in a big way. On a mountainside called Southridge, the homes of Arnold Schwarzenegger and Sylvester Stallone overlook the vast gridded flatland—and thereby dominate it. Bob and Dolores Hope's multi-million-dollar dream house stands even higher. It's an altogether curious structure, a clear visual and social statement that has never been a neutral topic in town. Some people say it looks like the Anaheim Convention Center. Some say it looks like an extra-terrestrial invasion of the mountain. Hope's Folly they call it. The Volcano. The Mushroom. The Turtle-Top. Everyone agrees a thing like that takes over the mountain, and it takes the Georgian mansion metaphor several steps further.

Hope's house is 25,000 square feet of steel and glass, capped by a roof of ostentatiously gleaming copper. The scale is indicated by the living room; it seats three hundred guests. Hope's swimming pool, it is said, is shaped like Hope's profile. The person who says so is Shirley, and she ought to know because she works for the company that recently brought me up to date on celebrity homes.

Sometimes we locals miss things; think of the New Yorker who has never taken the ferry out to the Statue of Liberty. Well, it was about time for me to complete the Palm Springs experience. Although, to be honest, I have little interest in celebrity homes and even less interest in tours, which are, after all, more suited to tourists. Tour companies like large groups. They like herding them, lecturing them, counting them, scheduling their day, which always has something of an air of ritual to it, the timetable posted in the hotel rooms:

5:00 a.m. Wake-Up Call
5:45 a.m. Breakfast
7:00 a.m. Meet in Lobby

Armed with box lunches, cameras, and sunscreen, they're off to the celebrity homes today, the Indian canyons tomorrow, the Living Desert (check out the Meerkat Cafe their guidebook suggests), the Palapas Gardens (which they will entirely take over), the air museum, the wind farms, a half hour here, an hour there, a forced march of sight-seeing, with a perky tour guide expounding, interpreting, hustling them back aboard their air conditioned coach so they can get on to the next place, and the next, until finally, blessedly, exhausted beyond caring *what* Palm Springs has to offer, they head back to the hotel without really seeing Palm Springs at all. There wasn't time.

Twenty of us boarded Shirley's bus that day, retired couples mostly, in dreamy wintertime retreat; we had exchanged basic information in the hotel lobby. Behind me sat two young wives sprung from their hotel rooms for an afternoon's outing while their husbands were at a house-wares convention, discussing closet organizers and hide-away hampers. At the helm was Shirley, retired realtor and grandmother of six. She was heavy-set, the shoulders were square, the arms thick with the unar-guable strength of a prison matron. Her one meaty hand gripped the steering wheel, her other, the microphone. Her voice, husky from ciga-rettes and overuse, had kept the tone of her New York roots, but you could tell it had been places. "The first thing people want to know when they come to Palm Springs is, Where are the movie stars? Do we ever get to see any? Well, I do not guarantee a celebrity today, but I'll do my best to find one. Yesterday I found Barry Manilow in his driveway. He was backing out, and he smiled and waved." Shirley gave us all this while avoiding a collision with a white Cadillac that had rushed at her suddenly from the left. It soon became apparent that Shirley did not leave a lot of time during her running commentary for scrupulous atten-tion to traffic. Several times she had to drown out her own voice with indignant blasts of the horn.

After managing a remarkably deft turn off the highway, Shirley plied the quiet streets of the Old Movie Colony, a deeply romantic enclave of "our very best homes," many of which were considered mansions in the

1920s. The homes looked owned but not lived-in, as if their absentee owners had brought the decor to a high pitch then wandered away, bored.

On we rolled to the proud old-money neighborhood of Las Palmas, a stratosphere of Spanish-style homes, some of which take up entire blocks with their swimming pools, tennis courts, and clusters of guest-houses. Hurling her elderly bulk from side to side, Shirley pointed out the estates as if they were national shrines. "*That's* where Dean Martin lived before his divorce. *That's* where Kenny Rogers lived before he moved. *That's* where Dinah Shore lived before she died. *That's* the home of Barbara Hutton, the poor little rich girl who went wherever Cary Grant went. The shop-keepers tagged them Cash and Carry. Funny, huh?" Only one thing was indisputable: it was hard for Shirley to tell a joke a hundred times.

I cannot tell you how pleased we were to learn that the unsinkable Debbie Reynolds is still living here. At the twelfth or twentieth stop, I forget which, we were directed to lift our eyes to a hillside buried in scarlet bougainvillea. But what can you say about another stucco villa; it's another stucco villa and that is that. After squelching a sudden hope that Ms. Reynolds would suddenly walk out her gate and invite the whole bunch of us in for iced tea, the lady from Cleveland slumped in her seat. "Debbie's very nice, you know." She could tell because she had seen her on the stage at Las Vegas.

Reciting movie titles and song titles and book titles, Shirley talked us happily up and down the narrow streets, summarizing lives at break-neck speed, making them sound all the more reckless and exotic. "Here's where Vicki Carr stayed when she was in town. Here's where Spiro Agnew stayed when he was in town and did not stay with Frank Sinatra. Here's where the Prince of Wales booked a room but did not stay when he stayed at the Walter Annenberg estate." With the pride of an owner, with sweeping waves of her microphone, she drew our atten-tion to the house where Debbie Reynolds and Eddie Fisher spent their honeymoon, to the house where Eddie Fisher and Liz Taylor spent *their* honeymoon, to the house where Liz Taylor and Mike Todd spent *their* honeymoon, to the house where Liz Taylor and Mike Wilding spent *their* honeymoon. Obediently we followed her every gesture, took her star stories as gospel, these endless anecdotes culled from the soci-ety pages of our local press. After all, this is what we had come for. We wanted the marriages, the separations, the divorces of all of Hollywood's perfect couples.

The bus swung from curb to curb. Our mass swayed, tilted, and slid. Our heads rolled right, then left, then right. Out the delicately tinted windows we stared at the suggestion of roof lines behind miles of walls that the rich and famous had thrown around themselves to keep us from trespassing even visually. What secrets were they hiding? A marijuana patch? A movie great sunbathing in the raw? Oh, occasionally, when someone left a gate open, we got a glimpse of a deep, green courtyard with rare potted palms in the wall niches, a vignette so brief it was only tempting. "Beautiful home," said the man from Seattle, a comment he repeated at five-minute intervals all afternoon.

Beautiful indeed, but with a self-important showing of seclusion, a seclusion that suggested conflict rather than neighborly love, the iron fences cast in a pattern of spears, the walls posted with warnings of armed response, hidden mikes, and closed circuit cameras. The guard dogs not only warned of intruders but dealt with them. I pictured savage rottweilers bursting from their sheet-metal doghouses and lunging at the gates. Or in one case, a pair of fat, slothful Great Danes guided by a wildly yapping poodle.

To judge from the speed at which we progressed through the rest of the tour, Shirley had already transferred her interest to the next group on her schedule. Nevertheless, we kept our heads covertly aswivel for Barry Manilow, Tammy Fay Bakker, Trini Lopez—I could go on, except that Shirley hung up her microphone and zoomed us back to the hotel, the traffic once again making way for our hooting-tooting grandmother. Presently, and quite remarkably, we came to a grinding halt in the parking lot, without a collision. By this time, I felt as if I had known Shirley—Shirl—all my life. In the last hour or so we had been through a lot together. Now that she had gone quiet, I could tell she was upset, that she had very badly wanted to show us a celebrity, so we wouldn't think she had made everything up. I sympathized with her disappointment but I did not share it. Indeed, most of us enjoyed the tour. For a few of us it was "okay" or "not bad." Only one of us found it far from what the "Where to go in Palm Springs" advertisement made it out to be. That settled, I dutifully purchased a picture postcard of Jean Harlow's gate and another of Elvis Presley's wall, planning to donate them both to the next starstruck tourist I met.

Raymond Chandler

Raymond Chandler was born in Chicago in 1888. Educated in England, he eventually returned to the United States and settled in La Jolla. He was a professional writer from his college years until his death in 1959, but he was most famous for his detective novels, which were written in his trademark hardboiled style and vividly evoked the Southern California of the 1940s. He was honored with the Edgar Award from the Mystery Writers of America in both 1946 and 1954.

In this excerpt from *The Lady in the Lake* (1943), private investigator Philip Marlowe is working on a case that takes him to the San Bernardino Mountains.

from *The Lady in the Lake*

San Bernardino baked and shimmered in the afternoon heat. The air was hot enough to blister my tongue. I drove through it gasping, stopped long enough to buy a pint of liquor in case I fainted before I got to the mountains, and started up the long grade to Crestline. In fifteen miles the road climbed five thousand feet, but even then it was far from cool. Thirty miles of mountain driving brought me to the tall pines and a place called Bubbling Springs. It had a clapboard store and a gas pump, but it felt like paradise. From there on it was cool all the way.

The Puma Lake dam had an armed sentry at each end and one in the middle. The first one I came to had me close all the windows of the car before crossing over the dam. About a hundred yards from the dam a rope with cork floats barred the pleasure boats from coming any closer.

Beyond these details the war did not seem to have done anything much to Puma Lake.

Canoes paddled about on the blue water and rowboats with outboard motors put-putted and speed boats showing off like fresh kids made wide swathes of foam and turned on a dime and girls in them shrieked and dragged their hands in the water. Jounced around in the wake of the speedboats, people who had paid two dollars for a fishing license were trying to get a dime of it back in tired-tasting fish.

The road skimmed along a high granite outcrop and dropped to meadows of coarse grass in which grew what was left of the wild irises and white and purple lupine and bugle flowers and columbine and penny-royal and desert paint brush. Tall yellow pines probed at the clear blue sky. The road dropped again to lake level and the landscape began to be full of girls in gaudy slacks and snoods and peasant handkerchiefs and rat rolls and fatsoled sandals and fat white thighs. People on bicycles wobbled cautiously over the highway and now and then an anxious-looking bird thumped past on a power-scooter.

A mile from the village the highway was joined by another lesser road which curved back into the mountains. A rough wooden sign under the highway sign said: *Little Fawn Lake 1¾ miles.* I took it. Scattered cabins were perched along the slopes for the first mile and then nothing. Presently another very narrow road debouched from this one and another rough wood sign said: *Little Fawn Lake. Private Road. No Trespassing.*

I turned the Chrysler into this and crawled carefully around huge bare granite rocks and past a little waterfall and through a maze of black oak trees and ironwood and manzanita and silence. A bluejay squawked on a branch and a squirrel scolded at me and beat one paw angrily on the pine cone it was holding. A scarlet-topped woodpecker stopped probing in the bark long enough to look at me with one beady eye and then dodge behind the tree trunk to look at me with the other one. I came to a five-barred gate and another sign.

Beyond the gate the road wound for a couple of hundred yards through trees and then suddenly below me was a small oval lake deep in trees and rocks and wild grass, like a drop of dew caught in a curled leaf. At the near end of it was a rough concrete dam with a rope hand-rail across the top and an old millwheel at the side. Near that stood a small cabin of native pine with the bark on it.

Across the lake the long way by the road and the short way by the top of the dam a large redwood cabin overhung the water and farther along, each well separated from the others, were two other cabins. All three were shut up and quiet, with drawn curtains. The big one had orange-yellow venetian blinds and a twelve-paned window facing on the lake.

At the far end of the lake from the dam was what looked like a small pier and a band pavilion. A warped wooden sign on it was painted in large white letters: *Camp Kilkare*. I couldn't see any sense in that in these surroundings, so I got out of the ear and started down towards the nearest cabin. Somewhere behind it an axe thudded.

I pounded on the cabin door. The axe stopped. A man's voice yelled from somewhere. I sat down on a rock and lit a cigarette. Steps came around the corner of the cabin, uneven steps. A man with a harsh face and a swarthy skin came into view carrying a double-bitted axe.

He was heavily-built and not very tall and he limped as he walked, giving his right leg a little kick out with each step and swinging the foot in a shallow arc. He had a dark unshaven chin and steady blue eyes and grizzled hair that curled over his ears and needed cutting badly. He wore blue denim pants and a blue shirt open on a brown muscular neck. A cigarette hung from the corner of his mouth. He spoke in a tight tough city voice.

"Yeah?"

"Mr. Bill Chess?"

"That's me."

I stood up and got Kingsley's note of introduction out of my pocket and handed it to him. He squinted at the note, then clumped into the cabin and came back with glasses perched on his nose. He read the note carefully and then again. He put it in his shirt pocket, buttoned the flap of the pocket, and put his hand out.

"Pleased to meet you, Mr. Marlowe."

We shook hands. He had a hand like a wood rasp.

"You want to see Kingsley's cabin, huh? Glad to show you. He ain't selling for Chrissake?" He eyed me steadily and jerked a thumb across the lake.

"He might," I said. "Everything's for sale in California."

"Ain't that the truth? That's his—the redwood job. Lined with knotty pine, composition roof, stone foundations and porches, full bath and shower, venetian blinds all around, big fireplace, oil stove in the big bedroom—and brother, you need it in the spring and fall—Pilgrim combination gas and wood range, everything first class. Cost about eight thousand and that's money for a mountain cabin. And private reservoir in the hills for water."

"How about electric light and telephone?" I asked, just to be friendly.

"Electric light, sure. No phone. You couldn't get one now. If you could, it would cost plenty to string the lines out here."

He looked at me with steady blue eyes and I looked at him. In spite of his weathered appearance he looked like a drinker. He had the thickened and glossy skin, the too noticeable veins, the bright glitter in the eyes.

I said: "Anybody living there now?"

"Nope. Mrs. Kingsley was here a few weeks back. She went down the hill. Back any day, I guess. Didn't he say?"

I looked surprised. "Why? Does she go with the cabin?"

He scowled and then put his head back and burst out laughing. The roar of his laughter was like a tractor backfiring. It blasted the woodland silence to shreds.

"Jesus, if that ain't a kick in the pants!" he gasped. "Does she go with the—" He put out another bellow and then his mouth shut tight as a trap.

"Yeah, it's a swell cabin," he said, eyeing me carefully.

"The beds comfortable?" I asked.

He leaned forward and smiled. "Maybe you'd like a face full of knuckles," he said.

I stared at him with my mouth open. "That one went by me too fast," I said. "I never laid an eye on it."

"How would I know if the beds are comfortable?" he snarled, bending down a little so that he could reach me with a hard right, if it worked out that way.

"I don't know why you wouldn't know," I said. "I won't press the point. I can find out for myself."

"Yah," he said bitterly, "think I can't smell a dick when I meet one? I played hit and run with them in every state in the Union. Nuts to you, pal. And nuts to Kingsley. So he hires himself a dick to come up here and see am I wearing his pajamas, huh? Listen, Jack, I might have a stiff leg and all, but the women I could get—"

I put a hand out, hoping he wouldn't pull it off and throw it in the lake.

"You're slipping your clutch," I told him. "I didn't come up here to enquire into your love life. I never saw Mrs. Kingsley. I never saw Mr. Kingsley until this morning. What the hell's the matter with you?"

He dropped his eyes and rubbed the back of his hand viciously across his mouth, as if he wanted to hurt himself. Then he held the hand in front of his eyes and squeezed it into a hard fist and opened it again and stared at the fingers. They were shaking a little.

"Sorry, Mr. Marlowe," he said slowly. "I was out on the roof last night and I've got a hangover like seven Swedes. I've been up here alone for a month and it's got me talking to myself. A thing happened to me."

"Anything a drink would help?"

His eyes focused sharply on me and glinted. "You got one?"

I pulled the pint of rye out of my pocket and held it so that he could see the green label over the cap.

"I don't deserve it," he said. "God damn it, I don't. Wait till I get a couple of glasses or would you come into the cabin?"

"I like it out here. I'm enjoying the view."

He swung his stiff leg and went into his cabin and came back carrying a couple of small cheese glasses. He sat down on the rock beside me smelling of dried perspiration.

I tore the metal cap off the bottle and poured him a stiff drink and a light one for myself. We touched glasses and drank. He rolled the liquor on his tongue and a bleak smile put a little sunshine into his face.

"Man, that's from the right bottle," he said. "I wonder what made me sound off like that. I guess a guy gets the blues up here all alone. No company, no real friends, no wife." He paused and added with a sidewise look. "Especially no wife."

I kept my eyes on the blue water of the tiny lake. Under an overhanging rock a fish surfaced in a lance of light and a circle of widening ripples. A light breeze moved the tops of the pines with a noise like a gentle surf.

"She left me," he said slowly. "She left me a month ago. Friday the 12th of June. A day I'll remember."

I stiffened, but not too much to pour more whiskey into his empty glass. Friday the 12th of June was the day Mrs. Crystal Kingsley was supposed to have come into town for a party.

"But you don't want to hear about that," he said. And in his faded blue eyes was the deep yearning to talk about it, as plain as anything could possibly be.

"It's none of my business," I said. "But if it would make you feel any better—"

He nodded sharply. "Two guys will meet on a park bench," he said, "and start talking about God. Did you ever notice that? Guys that wouldn't talk about God to their best friend."

"I know that," I said.

He drank and looked across the lake. "She was one swell kid," he said softly. "A little sharp in the tongue sometimes, but one swell kid. It was love at first sight with me and Muriel. I met her in a joint in Riverside, a year and three months ago. Not the kind of joint where a guy would expect to meet a girl like Muriel, but that's how it happened. We got married. I loved her. I knew I was well off. And I was too much of a skunk to play ball with her."

I moved a little to show him I was still there, but I didn't say anything for fear of breaking the spell. I sat with my drink untouched in my hand. I like to drink, but not when people are using me for a diary.

He went on sadly: "But you know how it is with marriage—any marriage. After a while a guy like me, a common no-good guy like me, he wants to feel a leg. Some other leg. Maybe it's lousy, but that's the way it is."

He looked at me and I said I had heard the idea expressed.

He tossed his second drink off. I passed him the bottle. A bluejay went up a pine tree hopping from branch to branch without moving his wings or even pausing to balance.

"Yeah," Bill Chess said. "All these hillbillies are half crazy and I'm getting that way too. Here I am sitting pretty, no rent to pay, a good pension check every month, half my bonus money in war bonds, I'm married to as neat a little blonde as ever you clapped an eye on and all the time I'm nuts and I don't know it. I go for *that*." He pointed hard at the redwood cabin across the lake. It was turning the color of oxblood in the late afternoon light. "Right in the front yard," he said, "right under the windows, and a showy little tart that means no more to me than a blade of grass. Jesus, what a sap a guy can be."

He drank his third drink and steadied the bottle on a rock. He fished a cigarette out of his shirt, fired a match on his thumbnail and puffed rapidly. I breathed with my mouth open, as silent as a burglar behind a curtain.

"Hell," he said at last, "you'd think if I had to jump off the dock, I'd go a little ways from home and pick me a change in types at least. But little roundheels over there ain't even that. She's a blonde like Muriel, same size and weight, same type, almost the same color eyes. But, brother, how different from then on in. Pretty, sure, but no prettier to anybody and not half so pretty to me. Well, I'm over there burning trash that morning and minding my own business, as much as I ever mind it. And she comes to the back door of the cabin in peekaboo pajamas so thin you can see the pink of her nipples against the cloth. And she says in her lazy, no-good voice: 'Have a drink, Bill. Don't work so hard on such a beautiful morning.' And me, I like a drink too well and I go to the kitchen door and take it. And then I take another and then I take another and then I'm in the house. And the closer I get to her the more bedroom her eyes are."

He paused and swept me with a hard level look.

"You asked me if the beds over there were comfortable and I got sore. You didn't mean a thing. I was just too full of remembering. Yeah—the bed I was in was comfortable."

He stopped talking and I let his words hang in the air. They fell slowly and after them was silence. He leaned to pick the bottle off the rock and stare at it. He seemed to fight with it in his mind. The whiskey won the fight, as it always does. He took a long savage drink out of the bottle and then screwed the cap on tightly, as if that meant something. He picked up a stone and flicked it into the water.

"I came back across the dam," he said slowly, in a voice already thick with alcohol. "I'm as smooth as a new piston head. I'm getting away with something. Us boys can be so wrong about those little things, can't we? I'm not getting away with anything at all. Not anything at all. I listen to Muriel telling me and she don't even raise her voice. But she tells me things about myself I didn't even imagine. Oh yeah, I'm getting away with it lovely."

"So she left you," I said, when he fell silent.

"That night. I wasn't even here. I felt too mean to stay even half sober. I hopped into my Ford and went over to the north side of the lake and holed up with a couple of no-goods like myself and got good and stinking. Not that it did me any good. Along about 4 a.m. I got back home and Muriel is gone, packed up and gone, nothing left but a note on the bureau and some cold cream on the pillow."

He pulled a dog-eared piece of paper out of a shabby old wallet and passed it over. It was written in pencil on blue-lined paper from a note book. It read:

"I'm sorry, Bill, but I'd rather be dead than live with you any longer. Muriel."

I handed it back. "What about over there?" I asked, pointing across the lake with a glance.

Bill Chess picked up a flat stone and tried to skip it across the water, but it refused to skip.

"Nothing over there," he said. "She packed up and went down the same night. I didn't see her again. I don't want to see her again. I haven't heard a word from Muriel in the whole month, not a single word. I don't have any idea at all where she's at. With some other guy, maybe. I hope he treats her better than I did."

He stood up and took keys out of his pocket and shook them. "So if you want to go across and look at Kingsley's cabin, there isn't a thing to stop you. And thanks for listening to the soap opera. And thanks for the liquor. Here." He picked the bottle up and handed me what was left of the pint.

We went down the slope to the bank of the lake and the narrow top of the dam. Bill Chess swung his stiff leg in front of me, holding on to the rope handrail set in iron stanchions. At one point water washed over the concrete in a lazy swirl.

"I'll let some out through the wheel in the morning," he said over his shoulder. "That's all the darn thing is good for. Some movie outfit put it up three years ago. They made a picture up here. That little pier down at the other end is some more of their work. Most of what they built is torn down and hauled away, but Kingsley had them leave the pier and the millwheel. Kind of gives the place a touch of color."

I followed him up a flight of heavy wooden steps to the porch of the Kingsley cabin. He unlocked the door and we went into hushed warmth. The closed-up room was almost hot. The light filtering through the slatted blinds made narrow bars across the floor. The living room was long and cheerful and had Indian rugs, padded mountain furniture with metal-strapped joints, chintz curtains, a plain hardwood floor, plenty of lamps and a little built-in bar with round stools in one corner. The room was neat and clean and had no look of having been left at short notice.

We went into the bedrooms. Two of them had twin beds and one a large double bed with a cream-colored spread having a design in plum-colored wool stitched over it. This was the master bedroom, Bill Chess said. On a dresser of varnished wood there were toilet articles and accessories in jade green enamel and stainless steel, and an assortment of cosmetic oddments. A couple of cold cream jars had the wavy gold brand of the Gillerlain Company on them. One whole side of the room consisted of closets with sliding doors. I slid one open and peeked inside. It seemed to be full of women's clothes of the sort they wear at resorts. Bill Chess watched me sourly while I pawed them over. I slid the door shut and pulled open a deep shoe drawer underneath. It contained at least half a dozen pairs of new-looking shoes. I heaved the drawer shut and straightened up.

Bill Chess was planted squarely in front of me, with his chin pushed out and his hard hands in knots on his hips.

"So what did you want to look at the lady's clothes for?" he asked in an angry voice.

"Reasons," I said. "For instance Mrs. Kingsley didn't go home when she left here. Her husband hasn't seen her since. He doesn't know where she is."

He dropped his fists and twisted them slowly at his sides. "Dick it is," he snarled. "The first guess is always right. I had myself about talked out of it. Boy, did I open up to you. Nellie with her hair in her lap. Boy, am I a smart little egg!"

"I can respect a confidence as well as the next fellow," I said, and walked around him into the kitchen.

There was a big green and white combination range, a sink of lacquered yellow pine, an automatic water heater in the service porch, and opening off the other side of the kitchen a cheerful breakfast room with many windows and an expansive plastic breakfast set. The shelves were gay with colored dishes and glasses and a set of pewter serving dishes.

Everything was in apple-pie order. There were no dirty cups or plates on the drain board, no smeared glasses or empty liquor bottles hanging around. There were no ants and no flies. Whatever loose living Mrs. Derace Kingsley indulged in she managed without leaving the usual Greenwich Village slop behind her.

I went back to the living room and out on the front porch again and waited for Bill Chess to lock up. When he had done that and turned to me with his scowl well in place I said:

"I didn't ask you to take your heart out and squeeze it for me, but I didn't try to stop you either. Kingsley doesn't have to know his wife made a pass at you, unless there's a lot more behind all this than I can see now."

"The hell with you," he said, and the scowl stayed right where it was.

"All right, the hell with me. Would there be any chance your wife and Kingsley's wife went away together?"

"I don't get it," he said.

"After you went to drown your troubles they could have had a fight and made up and cried down each other's necks. Then Mrs. Kingsley might have taken your wife down the hill. She had to have something to ride in, didn't she?"

It sounded silly, but he took it seriously enough.

"Nope. Muriel didn't cry down anybody's neck. They left the weeps out of Muriel. And if she did want to cry on a shoulder, she wouldn't have picked little roundheels. And as for transportation she has a Ford of her own. She couldn't drive mine easily on account of the way the controls are switched over for my stiff leg."

"It was just a passing thought," I said.

"If any more like it pass you, let them go right on," he said.

"For a guy that takes his long wavy hair down in front of complete strangers, you're pretty damn touchy," I said.

He took a step towards me. "Want to make something of it?"

"Look, pal," I said, "I'm working hard to think you are a fundamentally good egg. Help me out a little, can't you?"

He breathed hard for a moment and then dropped his hands and spread them helplessly.

"Boy, can I brighten up anybody's afternoon," he sighed. "Want to walk back around the lake?"

"Sure, if your leg will stand it."

"Stood it plenty of times before."

We started off side by side, as friendly as puppies again. It would probably last all of fifty yards. The roadway, barely wide enough to pass a car, hung above the level of the lake and dodged between high rocks. About halfway to the far end another smaller cabin was built on a rock foundation. The third was well beyond the end of the lake, on a patch of almost level ground. Both were closed up and had that long-empty look.

Bill Chess said after a minute or two: "That straight goods little roundheels lammed off?"

"So it seems."

"You a real dick or just a shamus?"

"Just a shamus."

"She go with some guy?"

"I should think it likely."

"Sure she did. It's a cinch. Kingsley ought to be able to guess that. She had plenty of friends."

"Up here?"

He didn't answer me.

"Was one of them named Lavery?"

"I wouldn't know," he said.

"There's no secret about this one," I said. "She sent a wire from El Paso saying she and Lavery were going to Mexico." I dug the wire out of my pocket and held it out. He fumbled his glasses loose from his shirt and stopped to read it. He handed the paper back and put his glasses away again and stared out over the blue water.

"That's a little confidence for you to hold against some of what you gave me," I said.

"Lavery was up here once," he said slowly.

"He admits he saw her a couple of months ago, probably up here. He claims he hasn't seen her since. We don't know whether to believe him. There's no reason why we should and no reason why we shouldn't."

"She isn't with him now, then?"

"He says not."

"I wouldn't think she would fuss with little details like getting married," he said soberly. "A Florida honeymoon would be more in her line."

"But you can't give me any positive information? You didn't see her go or hear anything that sounded authentic?"

"Nope," he said. "And if I did, I doubt if I would tell. I'm dirty, but not that kind of dirty."

"Well, thanks for trying," I said.

"I don't owe you any favors," he said. "The hell with you and every other God damn snooper."

"Here we go again," I said.

We had come to the end of the lake now. I left him standing there and walked out on the little pier. I leaned on the wooden railing at the end of it and saw that what had looked like a band pavilion was nothing but two pieces of propped-up will meeting at a flat angle towards the dam. About two feet deep of overhanging roof was stuck on the wall, like a coping. Bill Chess came up behind me and leaned on the railing at my side.

"Not that I don't thank you for the liquor," he said.

"Yeah. Any fish in the lake?"

"Some smart old bastards of trout. No fresh stock. I don't go for fish much myself. I don't bother with them. Sorry I got tough again."

I grinned and leaned on the railing and stared down into the deep still water. It was green when you looked down into it. There was a swirl of movement down there and a swift greenish form moved in the water.

"There's Granpa," Bill Chess said. "Look at the size of that old bastard, he ought to be ashamed of himself getting so fat."

Down below the water there was what looked like an underwater flooring. I couldn't see the sense of that. I asked him.

"Used to be a boat landing before the dam was raised. That lifted the water level so far the old landing was six feet under."

A flat-bottomed boat dangled on a frayed rope tied to a post of the pier. It lay in the water almost without motion, but not quite. The air was peaceful and calm and sunny and held a quiet you don't get in cities. I could have stayed there for hours doing nothing but forgetting all about Derace Kingsley and his wife and her boy friends.

There was a hard movement at my side and Bill Chess said, "Look there!" in a voice that growled like mountain thunder.

His hard fingers dug into the flesh of my arm until I started to get mad. He was bending far out over the railing, staring down like a loon, his face as white as the weather tan would let it get. I looked down with him into the water at the edge of the submerged staging.

Languidly at the edge of this green and sunken shelf of wood something waved out from the darkness, hesitated, waved back again out of sight under the flooring.

The something had looked far too much like a human arm.

Bill Chess straightened his body rigidly. He turned without a sound and clumped back along the pier. He bent to a loose pile of stones and heaved. His panting breath reached me. He got a big one free and lifted it breast-high and started back out on the pier with it. It must have weighed a hundred pounds. His neck muscles stood out like ropes under canvas under his taut brown skin. His teeth were clamped tight and his breath hissed between them.

He reached the end of the pier and steadied himself and lifted the rock high. He held it a moment poised, his eyes staring down now, measuring. His mouth made a vague distressful sound and his body lurched forward hard against the quivering rail and the heavy stone smashed down into the water.

The splash it made went over both of us. The rock fell straight and true and struck on the edge of the submerged planking, almost exactly where we had seen the thing wave in and out.

For a moment the water was a confused boiling, then the ripples widened off into the distance, coming smaller and smaller with a trace of froth at the middle, and there was a dim sound as of wood breaking under water, a sound that seemed to come to us a long time after it should have been audible. An ancient rotted plank popped suddenly through the surface, stuck out a full foot of its jagged end, and fell back with a flat slap and floated off.

The depths cleared again. Something moved in them that was not a board. It rose slowly, with an infinitely careless languor, a long dark twisted something that rolled lazily in the water as it rose. It broke surface casually, lightly, without haste. I saw wool, sodden and black, a leather jerkin blacker than ink, a pair of slacks. I saw shoes and something that bulged nastily between the shoes and the cuffs of the slacks. I saw a wave of dark blond hair straighten out in the water and hold still for a brief instant as if with a calculated effect, and then swirl into a tangle again.

The thing rolled over once more and an arm flapped up barely above the skin of the water and the arm ended in a bloated hand that was the hand of a freak. Then the face came. A swollen pulpy gray white mass without features, without eyes, without mouth. A blotch of gray dough, a nightmare with human hair on it.

A heavy necklace of green stones showed on what had been a neck, half imbedded, large rough green stones with something that glittered joining them together.

Bill Chess held the handrail and his knuckles were polished bones.

"Muriel!" his voice said croakingly. "Sweet Christ, it's Muriel!"

His voice seemed to come to me from a long way off, over a hill, through a thick silent growth of trees.

M. F. K. Fisher

M. F. K. Fisher was born in Michigan in 1908 and grew up in Whittier, California. Author of more than twenty books, she wrote mostly on the topic of food—the pleasure of it, its effects on people, and the culture and philosophy surrounding it. She also lived for extended periods in France and wrote about the cuisine and culture there. She died in 1992.

"Spirits of the Valley," from her 1993 *Stay Me, Oh Comfort Me: Journals and Stories, 1933–1941*, describes her life near Hemet.

Spirits of the Valley

Some people believe that it is a fortunate thing if a person can live in a real valley instead of on flat open land, and they may well be right. For some sixteen years, from 1940 on, I lived most of the time on ninety acres of worthless land southeast of the little town of Hemet in southern California, and they were fine magical ones, important in the shaping of many people besides me, perhaps because Hemet Valley was a true one in every sense. At its far eastern end rose the high mountains that separated coastal land from desert, and our little town lay almost as near their base as Palm Springs did on their other side. Mount San Jacinto loomed on the north; to the south, high rocky hills rolled toward the Mexican border, and westward the valley opened gently, as any proper valley should, toward broad coastal flats and the far Pacific Ocean.

My husband, Dillwyn Parrish, and I bought our land for almost nothing: it was haunted, for one thing, and completely untillable. And we lived there intensely until he died three years later, according to medical schedule, of Buerger's disease. Then I stayed on, through another marriage and two little daughters, who spent their first years there with me after I divorced their father. When the oldest was going on six, we moved to my family ranch near Whittier to live with Father after Mother died. I worked half-time on his newspaper and ran the household, and as often as possible (weekends, vacations) we went back to Hemet to the little ranch house in the wild rocky hills.

It became clear that I could not raise two growing females there alone, where I had decided to remain. Now and then I found someone to repair storm damage and so on, but finally it seemed wise to sell the place. I felt thankful for everything I had learned there, and when I said it was no longer mine, I withdrew forever from it, even though ashes of my love and my mother may still blow from under some of its great rocks. I know the wind still sings over the Rim of the World and always will.

Tim (my husband was always called that by people who loved him, which meant everyone) named our ranch Bareacres, after a character in *Vanity Fair* who had several marriageable daughters and countless acres of barren land. He managed to sell the land, bought a string of pearls and a husband for each girl, and he and Lady Bareacres lived penniless but happy ever after, as I remember.

Certainly our land was bare! It rose in rough steep hills, with one deep canyon that split it down from the Rim of the World, its horizon, to the wide dead riverbed that was its northern boundary. A thin little road track went up from the valley floor, past our house and on up past the trickle of our only spring, to a deserted old ranch on the Rim of the World. There was a big sturdy redwood tank at the spring and a handful of stubby cottonwoods, and down nearer our house in the canyon, dry except for an occasional mud puddle from the underground trickle, stood a few tall eucalyptus trees. The rest of the place was covered with great harsh boulders, some of them bigger than a house. On the flat top of an enormous rock above the spring, two oblong tubs had been chipped out centuries ago, and we were told that sick Indians were brought there to lie in the hot sun while soothing water was poured over them, water that we found was heavy with lithium.

In front of the house, which stood about a thousand feet up off the wide dry riverbed that separated us from Hemet Valley, the land was steep but with fewer big rocks, almost like a meadow, covered with sage and mesquite and low cactus. Across the riverbed, northward, between us and Mount San Jacinto, lay the flat valley land, rich with apricot orchards. It was neatly laid out with roads and little houses here and there, but we could see only a general kind of lush carpet, flowery in spring, then green, and then winter-silver. Hemet was westward, invisible.

Our narrow dirt road went straight across the riverbed and up to the valley floor to meet Crest Drive, which curved the whole length of the valley. Directly opposite us, a small grove of eucalyptus trees grew down the slope where Fredrika van Benschoten had a little orange orchard along Crest, and in that grove the Squawman, who had left his land for us to find, had a correct Navaho house built for his bride. It was of adobe, one room and wide closet and a corner hearth, and it was so heavily plastered that there were no hard corners or lines but a softness to everything under the thick whitewash, as if it were a robe to be worn, firm and protecting but with no part of it to cut or hurt or rub against. The floor was of dark crude tile. The beams across the low ceiling were slender eucalyptus trunks. There was a kind of kitchen in the closet whose wall came up only to eye height, and Freda had piped cold water to a small sink. There was no toilet, and since the Squawman had not made an outhouse, I decided the grove was answer enough.

I spent much time in the squaw house, mostly after Tim died. I wrote a couple of books there. I never slept there, strange to say, but would go down from Bareacres in the mornings. I always took a thermos of broth or a cool drink, and about 11:00 I'd go out and look up across the riverbed and see my home there, sometimes with my two little girls waving from the west terrace, with a neighbor to watch them until I got back. The trees Tim and I had planted back of the house and down into the canyon were thriving: sycamores, eucalyptus, tough cottonwoods.

When Tim and I bought the place, with a veteran's bonus of $2,000 plus $225 we borrowed (we were dead broke after his illness made us leave Switzerland in 1938 when World War II got under way), it was flatly undesirable, even according to the realtor who showed it to us. It had been owned by a shady fellow said to be a degraded government Indian trader, an army officer, whose Navaho woman followed him to Hemet Valley. He bought what we called Bareacres twenty years later, but she, of course, did not live there, so her relatives unwillingly came from New Mexico and built her a decent house across the riverbed from Freda's grove.

Because of strict caste laws, the Navaho was not only called a lost member of her own tribe but could not have anything to do with the local Indians, the Sobobans, who were beneath her social level. It must have been very lonely for her. The Squawman, as he was always scorn-fully called, had a lot or some or a few valuable Indian artifacts, depending on who was talking about him to us, and most of them were gone when his body was found in the house and a clean bullet hole showed in the south window. Perhaps it was robbery? Navaho are good shots, we were told. The little house in Freda's grove was empty, with not even a blanket or cup left. Nobody knew "anything." Up on the hill across the dead riverbed the air blew through the unlocked door of the Squawman's house. Everything in it was stolen, gradually and without real harm…no vandalism, no ugly dirt, no mischievous fires. It was haunted, for sure.

It looked empty and welcoming when Tim and I first saw it in the kind January sunlight, and we stepped into it past the bullet hole as if it had been waiting. We rented an airy little house near Moreno, toward Riverside, and came every day over the Jack Rabbit Trail around the base of the mountain with two old carpenters Tim found. We shifted a few walls around and screened the long front porch that was held up by six trunks of cedar trees that Indians had brought from Mexico, it was said, for the Squawman.

His rock foundations were good. The porch floors across the north and east sides of the little U-shaped house were of well-poured smooth cement, and there was a big fireplace of rough brownish stone in the living room. We made one room and its porch into a fine studio, and put in another little toilet and lavatory there, and slept on the porch outside, looking east. The kitchen spread out to the east, too, over the old cement porch. Down in the canyon we built a big doghouse, with a fenced yard to fool the coyotes and the occasional lynx. On the west side of the U was an entry and office for me and a bedroom and bath for anybody we liked enough. (Hemet had no motels then, but there was a small adobe hotel behind a half circle of fine palm trees in town.) And in the hollow of the U was the patio, the most delightful one I have ever known—indeed, the heart of the place. French doors opened onto it on all three sides. We paved it with flat stones from the canyon. Tim devised a series of strips of bright canvas on slanted wires that pulled across it at will, so the air and light would stay filtered. We pulled them back and forth according to wind, weather, the time of day.

There were low tables and chairs, all-weather stuff, and two chaise lounges that could be beds. A wide Dutch door opened into the kitchen. The south side of the patio was a stone wall perhaps four feet high, and on the terrace above it were cottonwood trees and some sycamores, so that always there was the sound of leaves growing, blowing, falling. The Squawman had started the wall, and we carried it on past the house to make a fine terrace of sandy earth. Tim and I kept native succulents and cacti growing in the wall crevices, and when my girls were small, they played out there in the warm dry winter days, and now and then we put out a croquet set for the long hot summer twilights. And often we pulled the chairbeds out to the terrace in the brilliant August nights and lay naked in the silky air, watching the meteors shoot and tumble in the pure black sky.

Bareacres bordered the Ramona Bowl on the west, where the pageant based on Helen Hunt Jackson's book about Indians was given every year in a lovely little open-air theater. Tim helped rewrite some of the new script, and we maintained an aloof cordiality with the cast every year. The Indian hero was played by a skilled actor from Hollywood, much as summer theater on Long Island is now held together by stage stars who need fresh air and a nice piece of pocket money, and we knew a few visitors like Victor Jory who came to Hemet. Ramona the Beautiful Indian Maiden was always played by a local girl. And the finale of the long afternoon performance was when a posse of thirty or forty of the valley's best horsemen thundered through the amphitheater and up over the eastern horizon and down onto our land! We always had bottles of cold ale, open and ready, for the excited riders on their panting prancing horses. It was fun….We waited to hear the guns sound to the west and then opened bottles as fast as we could. And they would come pouring over, a thunder of hooves, wild yahoo yells. We forgot that they were hunting the Indian Alessandro, poor devil, every afternoon at precisely 4:54 for three weekends. (He, or some reasonable facsimile, was safely panting in a hidden bunker up the theater hill.)

We stayed aloof from active life in Hemet while Tim was there, because we knew his time was short and he had a lot of painting to do. We made fine firm friends, though, and some of them still live. And later I made many more, when my little girls were starting there. Of course, they don't remember much about people, but they still know how to walk away smoothly and quickly when they meet a rattlesnake and how to listen to what the wild quail mothers say.

Freda stayed my dear friend until she died, a very old woman, the last of all her group of strange witty people who seemed to take Tim and me for granted as a part of their own very private lives. And there was Spittin Stringer, who lived in the cottage at our turn off Crest Drive down into the riverbed and on up homeward. Spittin was called that, of course, because he spat a lot. He was the only man we ever met who had gone to France in World War I and then back to Oklahoma without setting foot off dry land. He knew this was a fact because he had just gone with his buddies into a big dark room that had bumped along the road a long time and then they had gotten off and started lighting. There was no arguing about a fact like that. What's more, nobody in his whole family could rightly remember how many kids there were. He said around thirteen. His wife couldn't rightly recall either, and if she had ever counted she would not admit it in front of Spittin. But the oldest boy, J. B., said flatly it was fourteen.

J. B. used to pose for Tim, once he and his mother had walked up the hot hill together so that she could see if we were decent. When I met her at the door, she had on a store-bought dress and shoes, but she took off the killers when she saw I was barefoot and went back with them in her hand, satisfied that J. B. would be all right. Though I never saw her smile, the next time I passed she called out, "Hi ya! Still got mah bar' feet!" and stuck one big muddy toe out from behind the washtub by the door.

When J. B. enlisted, Spittin could not think of what the initials might be for. J. B. was simply his oldest boy's name. And on second thought, maybe his, too. So Tim suggested putting Joseph Benjamin on his papers to satisfy the army, and perhaps he is still alive to remember that J. B. might as well stand for that as anything else. Tim painted one unforgettable picture of him, a thick young boy sitting dully, vacantly, with one hand on his knee holding a green Coke bottle. Tim called it *Kola High*.

On the other side of our turnoff, up on a knoll in a grove of trees, was the Lee house. It was something of a palace, at least compared with Spittin's place or Bareacres or even Freda's prim little white house behind the orange trees on Crest Drive. The younger son of its owners lived there with his wife and a burgeoning family, and they raised turkeys and a few noisy beautiful peacocks and stayed pretty much to themselves, the way we did. Later, though, my girls and theirs were peers, and their mother Isabel became a quietly true-forever person in my life.

And over all of us rose proud San Jacinto Mountain, sacred to many Indians of its own and other tribes. The Jack Rabbit Trail snaked around its west side, between Hemet and Moreno, and it seemed to hold the raw steep slopes up almost like an invisible wall. The Indians called it a hot mountain, and steaming water burst out of it, more or less controlled for human bathing, in places like Gilman Springs and Soboba Springs and even downtown in the little town of San Jacinto just outside the Indian reservation. Once when I was about ten, relatives came from the Midwest to spend the winter at the Vosburg Inn so that an uncle could "take the baths," and I was embarrassed to have my aunt tell us how Mrs. Vosburg cut up her very fat husband's worn trousers to make clothes for all her small children. Years later one of the Vosburgs was a very beautiful Ramona in the pageant, and I helped with her makeup and never told her what I knew about her father's pants.

A man named Leonardo came often to help us. He was a Pala Indian from the agrarian tribe farther south, but had lost caste by taking up with a Soboban girl. He was cut off from his tribe, and gradually I watched him turn heavy and morose. He was always courteous to me but did not really see me, the way one does not see every leaf on a tree. He loved Tim but would not pose for him. Now and then he drove his girl and their little son Cowboy over to see us in his shabby truck. Cowboy was a dimpled brown nugget, but we only smiled at each other. The girl was silent, unsmiling but not hostile. Leonardo and Tim talked in his studio. Then they would go away, without any words to me but a quick wave and a smile between the two men.

After Tim died, Leonardo returned a few times and cut back some branches in the cottonwoods and made the little tool shed outside the kitchen very tidy. But he grew heavier, and I knew that he was drinking much of the time instead of only for the few religious retreats that the Sobobans were allowed to mix in with their Catholic celebrations at Saint Hyacinth's Chapel on the reservation. And, of course, every year it was almost as ritualistic to round up him and a few other gifted braves for fire fighting. They were sold or perhaps given spiked gallons of sweet muscatel wine, fixed with a half pint of straight alcohol to fill the drained tops. A friend who ran the local bar showed us how this was done.

The men got drunk very fast, and the one cop and the judge who was also the bartender knew when to move in. I felt as shocked as I ever have in my life, and as disgusted. But it was considered fair play there in those days, when good fire fighters were as much a need as water itself and the best ones could be had for a gallon of spiked wine and a couple of nights in jail to make their indenture legal. The awful thing was that every time it happened, it got easier for the men to stay drunk, of course, so that after several seasons Leonardo was half lit most of the time, with a fat body and a bitter dull face, no more the lithe man who ran up our road with a flashing smile when he saw Tim wave from the big studio window.

Another fine friend was Arnold. He was always thin, although I am sure he had drunk his fair share of rotgut all over the world. He had been a desert rat for many years, the kind of shadowy drifting loner who becomes almost dust colored—protective coloration, it is called in toads and mice and serpents, and the few real desert rats I have met were the same. By the time he came to be our friend and protector, he had married a little round brown girl named Lena and they had two little round brown daughters, but he still wore dust-colored cotton clothes, and his eyes were as hard and colorless as stone, except when they smiled at Tim and now and then toward me.

Arnold knew more about native desert plants than anyone I ever heard of, and while he was the caretaker up at the Ramona Bowl it was a kind of secret paradise for botanists and crackpot gardeners who came to watch him plant the unplantables and whom he in turn watched like a hawk, because they almost always tried to steal some of his cuttings. It was a game they all played, and Arnold reported every sneaky trick, every artful dodge, of this unending tournament of trickery among the famous people who came to watch him. He turned weeds into jewels, for sure.

After Tim died, Arnold buried the little tin box of clinkers [Tim's ashes] under an enormous hanging rock. I said, "Let's go up to the Rim of the World and let the winds catch them," but he said, "Nope," and simply walked off. I knew it was all right, and went back to Bareacres and waited, and when he came back, we had a good nip of whiskey.

That is the way Bareacres is, of course. I am told that the fine pure air that first drew us there, half mountain and half desert, is now foul with smog and that the rich carpet of fruit trees we looked down on is solid with RVs and trailer parks. One block on Main Street is now in the *Guinness Book of World Records*, or maybe it is *Ripley's Believe It or Not*: something like 182 banks and savings-and-loan offices on that sleepy little stretch of sidewalk! And there are almost a hundred doctors, most of them connected with "convalescent homes" of varying status and opulence. And Crest Drive is lined with million-dollar villas, with the subdivision where Bareacres was (a "ninety-acre hell of red-hot rocks and rattlesnakes," as one New Yorker described it to us after a lost weekend there) the most snobbish and stylish area between Palm Springs and Los Angeles.

That is the way it is, I say, and I do not grieve or even care, any more than I did when Arnold went up the hill with the little box. I have taken and been given more than can ever be known that is heartwarming and fulfilling forever from that piece of wild haunted untillable land we named Bareacres for a time. No doubt roads have been cut into it and rocks have been blasted away, but I know that the contours cannot change much in a few hundred years in that country. And meanwhile the ghosts are there, even of the sick sad Indians who went to lie in the magic lithium waters of the spring, and even of the poor Squawman with a bullet in his heart, and of my own mother who loved the place…they are all there to cleanse and watch over it. They, and many more of us, keep an eye on things so that time itself can stay largely unheeded, as anyone will know who spends more than a few minutes in country like Bareacres.

There are many pockets of comfort and healing on this planet, and I have touched a few of them, but only once have I been able to stay as long and learn and be told as much as there on the southeast edge of Hemet Valley.

Charles Tomlinson

Charles Tomlinson was born in 1927 in Stoke-on-Trent, in
England. A poet, translator, editor, teacher, and artist, his pub-
lished works include *Collected Poems*; *Selected Poems: 1955–1997*;
Skywriting; and *In Black and White: The Graphics of Charles
Tomlinson*. He lives near Wotton-under-Edge, in England.

   "At Barstow" (1966) is from Tomlinson's *Collected Poems* and
was reprinted in the second edition of the *Norton Anthology of
Modern Poetry*. Dick Barnes's response to Tomlinson's poem follows
this selection.

At Barstow

Nervy with neons, the main drag
was all there was. A placeless place.
A faint flavour of Mexico in the tacos
tasting of gasoline. Trucks refuelled
before taking off through space. Someone lived
in the houses with their houseyards wired
like tiny Belsens. The Gotterdammerung
would be like this. No funeral pyres, no choirs
of lost trombones. An Untergang
without a clang, without
a glimmer of gone glory
however dimmed. At the motel desk
was a photograph of Roy Rogers
signed. It was here

he made a stay. He did not
ride away on Trigger
through the high night, the tilted
Pleiades overhead, the polestar low, no
going off until
the eyes of beer-cans
had ceased to glint at him
and the desert darknesses
had quenched the neons. He was spent.
He was content. Down he lay.
The passing trucks patrolled his sleep,
the shifted gears contrived
a muffled fugue against the fading of his day
and his dustless, undishonoured stetson rode
beside the bed,
glowed in the pulsating, never-final twilight
there, at that execrable conjunction
of gasoline and desert air.

Dick Barnes

Dick Barnes was born in San Bernardino in 1932. He taught medieval literature and creative writing at Pomona College for many years while also working as a musician, dramatist, translator, editor, and filmmaker. His published works include *A Lake on the Earth* (1982) and *Few and Far Between* (1994), in addition to *A World Like Fire* (2005), which collects poems from his entire career. He died in 2000.

All three of these poems are from *A World Like Fire*. "'At Barstow'" responds to poet Charles Tomlinson's bleak view of Barstow in his poem of the same name, also included in this collection. "Willie Boy" is a sympathetic treatment of events also explored earlier in this collection, in the excerpts from *Willie Boy* and *The Hunt for Willie Boy*.

"At Barstow"

Midway through the Sixties the English poet,
Charles Tomlinson, was benighted in Barstow,
California, that used to be my home town.
He had his car refuelled, he took a quick walk and
a look around: he had a taco at a taco stand;
then being a rather tired poet
stayed overnight at a motel.

He remembered the air, how he could smell
the gasoline; he heard big trucks throb in the night;

he remembered how neon looks from afar,
yet to him it seemed a placeless place,
not European and at the same time
not English; to him the North Star
seemed lower than it ought to be;
he didn't speak with someone, and though
he read reports of his four senses
he didn't notice much. Memory and fancy
eked out with irony, he composed
a poem for his fans: "At Barstow."

In the morning
up rose the sun, and up rose Tomlinson,
and on he went.

Tomorrow the world.

Few and Far Between

If only we could forgive ourselves, and didn't
have to have somebody else forgive us—

Where I came from everybody could see anyone coming,
even storms: and out there the etiquette

was not to say right off what you came for when you did
or ask anybody why, if they came where you were

in all space, and time; it made for a kind
of trust, or—well, it was like trust.

I remember some of those storms, how the dust
would kick up before them in the wild wind, and behind it

the blueblack cloud piled high white on top
with lightning flaring inside, and maybe only a few miles wide,

coming over the desert sort of slow and grand:
you could have got out of the way if you wanted to

but nobody did; as I said, seldom enough is welcome.
Didn't I say that? One night when mother was away

my dad and I followed a storm clear down
to Needles in the state car. His job

was to take care of the highway, so it was work, sort of,
for us to ride along behind that cloud we could see by its own light

through the wild fragrance the desert has after a rain
in the lone car on the road that night, to keep track

of the damage it did. He showed me a place near Essex
where a flash flood had ripped out three hundred feet of roadbed

two years before, where it hadn't rained
in fifty years before that. The foreman said so,

Billy Nielson, and he'd been there fifty years
without seeing the ground wet.

My dad and I stopped on the grade below Goffs
and watched the storm go on out of his territory

across the river into Arizona
where the sky was getting gray,

and turned for home as the sun rose behind us
back across the clean desert in slant light

that lit the smoke trees in washes that were churned smooth
where the water went, and sharpened along the edges

through Essex and Cadiz Summit, great tamarisked Chambless,
Ludlow for breakfast with the humorous Chinaman, Lee,

Newberry Springs, Daggett and Elephant Butte, Nebo hidden by wire,
on home over the hill to Barstow on the good road.

Willie Boy

If you were a young Paiute in 1905, and got arrested
for drunken disturbance of the Anglo peace
and the sheriff took your picture in the county jail,
you'd look okay—you'd look about the way Willie Boy did,
inward during adversity, solitary, brave enough;
but if I were a young Paiute in 1909, and wished somehow
to alleviate solitude, and tried to become intelligible,
got a white shirt with sleeve garters, a necktie
with polkadots, a pretty good hat, and even a fountain pen,
then went to a photographer in Banning and paid him
to take my picture, I'd have that blank mad hopeless look,
an expression you see now and then on an outlaw horse,
fierce but drawn back, my eyes the wrong side out.
It's the look of a man who knows nobody sees things his way,
whatever wavering way that might be—knows, and can't say.
Come down the dry side of the mountain, you get into juniper and
     piñon pine
then at a certain elevation you see a lone greasewood or Joshua
among the granite boulders—what is there to say about that.
Maybe it was a woman made him feel that way—not that she willed it
but it was his reaction. Let him go, then, let him kill to get her
then kill her too when she can't keep pace in flight over the desert;
hounded down let him shoot three horses from under the posse
but hit one of the men, a white man, in dismay—
that won't make him intelligible. Back in town
the reporters interpreted him to their own community,
"the Beau Brummel of the Indian colony," a suitor
"whose ardor fanned by opposition always disappeared
when conquest was complete" —smug ignorance
to which everything is equally falsely intelligible—
when the blowflies had beat them to it and got it right.
Let the fire have the last word, smoke, stink and light.

Let the metal parts of his suspenders mark the place
fifty years with their name, SHIPLEY or is it SHIRLEY PRESIDENT.
Let the granite boulders keep quiet, as if it didn't make any difference.

W. Storrs Lee

Born in 1907 in Connecticut, W. Storrs Lee was an English instructor and a dean at Middlebury College for nearly two decades. After his retirement in 1956 he pursued regional history projects, including two books about California: *The Great California Deserts* and *The Sierra*. He also edited *California: A Literary Chronicle*. He died in Maine in 2004.

In this excerpt from *The Great California Deserts*, Lee traces the history of military presence in areas near Barstow and Twentynine Palms.

from "What Did I Do to Deserve This, Sergeant"

If worst came to worst and the desert had to be defended against a paratroop invasion from Mars or Muscovy, the Mojave could put up some very stiff resistance. The Army is there. The Air Force is there. The Marines are there. The Navy is there. No other desolate area in the world shelters such a concentration of military might.

Over the course of a century and a quarter the desert has seen some weird and wonderful defenders marching across the sands: leatherstockings scouting a passage for overlanders, armies of occupation patrolling the Mexican border, vengeance-seeking posses on the trail of outlaws, veterans campaigning against the Piutes and Yumas, even an Army camel brigade plodding West to subdue unidentified foes of the Republic.

But none of these parades of militia was half as weird, wonderful and sinister as the forces that began assembling in the desert when

World War II was shaping up. And the encampments have been swelling ever since.

Down near Twentynine Palms, tubas and trumpets blare across the parade grounds of the Marine Corps Base and echo against the bleak, hot hillsides. Field-dressed troops of the Fleet Marine Force are on parade. In precise formation, units clomp past the reviewing dignitaries, responding like robots to the barked orders. They click, stomp, swivel, shoulder arms, by the right flank march, halt, present, parade rest. Overhead the colors flutter against a dry, cloudless sky. Leatherneck musicians ump and clarion their martial harmony, casting the reverberations far out into the once-silent wastelands.

In the broad expanse between the Bullion Mountains and Joshua Tree National Monument the Marines have broken that silence alarmingly. Out of earshot of the band is heard the rumble of distant guns, and the earth trembles underfoot. The thunder and rumble come at any hour of the day or night, and at night the far-off flashes are like heat lightning. Somewhere out in the desert, gunners of the First Field Artillery Group are ramming projectiles home, hard at work in their war games.

Then there are three Light Antiaircraft Missile battalions, whose pet plaything is the devastating guided missile Hawk, designed especially to lambast low-flying targets, traveling close to the speed of sound. The blasts come from fixed positions or from tactical points far afield, where carriages and equipment were dropped by whirlibirds only minutes before.

And supporting the attack units is "D" Company, Seventh Engineer Battalion, with giant vehicles and massive machinery, ready to tackle any kind of construction job, whether it is bridging a canyon on a new road to a firing area or paving another runway for a landing field. All belong to Force Troops, Fleet Marine Force, Pacific.

The vast military complex at Twentynine Palms is the largest Marine Corps Base under the United States flag. The combined areas of better-known Quantico, Camp Pendleton and Lejeune could be multiplied by two and fitted inside the base boundaries. Sprawling Los Angeles and a like-sized twin could be chucked into place there, with space left over for a few more moderate-sized cities.

Actual military installations, gun parks, warehouses, motor pools and quarters occupy a mere 20 square miles, while the undeveloped land used for unrestricted training and impact areas stretches out over more than 900 additional square miles—a total of more than 500,000 acres.

The Marine Corps dates back to 1775, and Quantico to 1917, but the biggest home of the corps was not staked out until 1953. For a few years prior to that the site had been used by an Army glider and training school, and by General Patton for training his famed tank corps. The Navy also shared it briefly as an aerial gunnery range.

Among Marines of the fifties, Twentynine Palms is still remembered as a tent city pitched alongside a dry lake bed in the middle of the Mojave. There was no air conditioning to temper the 120° flights of the thermometer. Billowing canvas and dilapidated buildings leftover from the days of Army control were the only shield against rip-roaring sand-storms and chill winter nights. Comforts and conveniences were unknown, and so was the usual gung-ho spirit. In hollow commendation, the early tenants of Twentynine Palms Base were known as "pioneers," and orders to the desert outpost were welcomed with the same kind of enthusiasm as assignment to the outer Aleutians or Tierra del Fuego.

But the pioneer period was of short duration. Within two or three years the base was as perky as a gate sentry's salute. Neat concrete build-ings took the place of the tents. Fourteen miles of surfaced road linked a half-dozen identical semi-independent units—each complete with air-conditioned barracks, mess hall and administration building, ware-houses, vehicle and equipment parks. Life was pretty tolerable, even when sixty-mile-an-hour winds whipped up the sandstorms, when sum-mer temperatures climbed to 110°, 115° and 120°, or when the ther-mometer dipped 10° or 15° below freezing in January.

Along with Honest John, the Hawk, the Terrier, the latest in flame throwers, Howitzers and 155mms., Twentynine Palms got the refine-ments of a deluxe family summer camp—officer housing that would bespeak status in suburban Palm Springs, clubs, theatre, gymnasium and swimming pools.

"The Theatre is on distribution for the very latest film releases," boasted a slick, four-color brochure advertising the attractions of the camp. "Admission is ten cents for all Marines and their dependents… The Enlisted Club is one of the finest service clubs at any military instal-lation in Southern California. Facilities of the club include game room, dining room, snack bar where beer and ale are dispensed, and a patio.

"The dining room serves outstanding meals, and a sandwich grill and short-order counter prepares many tasty and inexpensive sandwiches. Special activities, dances, parties, movies, etc. are conducted on a con-tinuing basis for the pleasure of all… The Base Beauty Shop is located on the service road to the old area… It is operated by fully trained and qualified beauticians, and prices are quite reasonable. For appointment call 7392…."

Nor were intellectually inclined leathernecks shortchanged. At the education center they could sign up for courses in anything from philosophy to flute playing, and at the library browse through a display of books that would be the envy of many a small college. Plugged the corps circulars: "A large selection of well over 10,000 volumes in all categories, plus magazines and newspapers, is available for your reading pleasure. There is a good stock of reference material and space for letter writing and studying. In addition the library has a special room for artists where they may work on current projects."

Churches? Tailor shop? Bank? Western Union service? Radio station? Nursery school? Dental clinic? Bowling alleys? Golf? Hobby shop? The Marines had them. The intramural athletic program of thirteen major sports was as "well rounded" as that of any institution of higher learning. Extracurricular dramatics? "To appeal to the fancy of would-be Thespians, there is an amateur theatrical group…If you would like to gain some interesting experience in make-up, costuming, set construction, property, stage management, lights, publicity, acting and directing, keep this in mind when you report aboard."

And as far as general entertainment was concerned, all the enticements of the Southwest were within an easy day's drag. "Twentynine Palms is centrally located in the Southern California recreation area," advised the publicists, "and playtime pursuits of almost any variety may be satisfied. Two and a half hours' drive to the east is the Colorado River, Lake Havasu and Lake Mojave, where boating, fishing, waterskiing and camping can be enjoyed.

"Two hours to the northwest you can climb into the mountains around Big Bear and Arrowhead for all types of winter sports and summer fun. Twenty minutes to the south is the Joshua Tree National Monument, a wonderful area for hiking, camping and picnicking. Farther to the west is Los Angeles, Long Beach, Oceanside, San Diego, the beaches, Disneyland, the Angels and the Rams. Four hours' drive to the northeast is the glamour and glittering night life of Las Vegas. Recreation unlimited is available for the pursuit of your hobby or pleasure."

Join the Marines! See the desert! Why pay $35 a day for lodgings and entertainment at Desert Palms when they come free under the auspices of the United States Marine Corps?

The brochure writers could make the desert sound mighty alluring, but most of the enlistees responding to the appeal were well aware that holiday maneuvers took a remote second place to harsh military maneuvers. Nevertheless, after release from service that had included a hitch at

Twentynine Palms, it was amazing the way ex-Marines in civies drifted back to the area to talk business with local realtors and architects. In large measure they and their friends were responsible for the boom all through the high desert of Morongo Basin—at Joshua Tree, Yucca Valley, at Palm Wells, Morongo Valley and Twentynine Palms itself.

Inadvertently the Marines were developing into some of the best publicists the desert had. But the Army? Its spokesmen were perhaps more reserved. Compared to the array of niceties advertised for the corps at Twentynine Palms, Fort Irwin—150 miles to the northwest— was rather Spartan. The Army made no attempt to play it up as a resort or vacation center.

Fort Irwin had its library and educational opportunities, its crafts shop, gymnasium, theatre, swimming pool, beer bars, bank and beauty shop, but the barrens, thirty-seven miles north of Barstow, were not portrayed as a recreational retreat. The command did not try to decorate the truth.

"Fort Irwin is located in the Mojave Desert in San Bernardino County, the largest county in the United States," buck privates were bluntly informed. "It is thirty-seven miles northeast of Barstow (road distance) and thirty-seven miles south of Death Valley (crow distance).... The road to Irwin is a stretch of black top known as Barstow Road at Fort Irwin and Fort Irwin Road at Barstow. You'll get used to it.

"A word of caution: the last service station between Barstow and Irwin is located at the corner of Route 91 and Fort Irwin Road. The road runs through country that is best described as barren wasteland. In case something should go wrong while you are on Irwin Road, four emergency telephones are available to summon aid from the post. They are mounted on telephone poles along the route, and their locations are well-marked by yellow arrow-shaped signs."

Then, in one of those rare outbursts of official Army humor, the soldier was warned: "Your first sight of Fort Irwin will come at the top of the hill four miles from the post. The first appearance of military life is a sign nine miles from the post proper, which marks the southern boundary of the reservation. Your reaction on this first sight may be, 'What did I do to deserve this?'"

"It isn't really that bad, and most of us really like it," comforted the Fort informant. "It is our proud boast that Fort Irwin is probably the friendliest post at which you will ever be stationed. This is the result of remoteness..."

Getting down to the dry facts, the military exile learned: "There is little grass on post, and none off it....The desert itself is made up of small pieces of eroded rock, washed down from the five mountain ranges that border the desert. Except for Joshua and greasewood trees, most of the vegetation grows no more than two feet high. The Mojave is characterized by bright sun, low humidity, infrequent rain and occasional high winds. It is recognized by its many dry stream beds, canyons, arroyos, hills and ranges, but few sand dunes. The desert is full of peculiar and seldom-seen wild life, including jackrabbits, coyotes, wildcats, snakes, lizards, spiders, field mice, owls, large crows, hawks and eagles.

"Yes, the weather is hot and cold, to an extreme in either case. During the summer months the days are hot. In winter from about 0900 to 1600, it is a warm spring day; from 1600 on, in a matter of minutes, you may be in the arctic, and you'd better have a coat ready.

"The sand and wind can do considerable damage to your private vehicle, particularly on paint and glass. It is advisable to consult your insurance agent in this respect prior to reporting for duty. There are no garages available at Fort Irwin. One of the nicest features of the post is the year-round sunshine. It is unfortunate that this can also cause sunburn, heat stroke and heat exhaustion....The other threats to your welfare include spiders, snakes and scorpions. The obvious solution is to studiously avoid spiders, snakes and scorpions."

Fort Irwin is the United States Army Armor and Desert Training Center—larger even than the Twentynine Palms Marine Base, so big that a 90mm. tank gun can be fired at maximum elevation in any direction near its center without overshooting the bounds of the 1,000-square-mile reservation. Isolation is what the Army required for that kind of target practice, and the Mojave was one of the few spots left on the continent that offered enough of it.

According to Irwin legend, the desolate 1,000 square miles first made Army news back in 1857. That was the year when Secretary of War Jefferson Davis talked Congress into appropriating $30,000 for importing a herd of dromedaries to form the Army Camel Corps. The beasts arrived from the Middle East, reluctantly padded down the gangways at the little port of Indianola, Texas, and set out, caravan fashion, on a five months' march to the West Coast.

In charge of the camels was a heterogeneous squad of Syrian, Turkish, Arab, Greek, Mexican and Pennsylvanian mercenaries, under the command of veteran desert trailbreaker Lieutenant Edward F. Beale. As scribe, Beale took on a young adventurer named May Stacey, who jotted in his diary at the end of the first day, "It is my decided opinion that these camels will prove a failure." Stacey's opinion proved to be prophetic.

Fort Irwin historians hint that the expedition paused in the Barstow area long enough to investigate the virtues of the site as an Army post, before proceeding to Los Angeles. Once they had reached their destination, however, neither Lieutenant Beale nor the Secretary of War seemed to have any definite plan of action for the Camel Corps, least of all setting up headquarters near Barstow.

The foreign mercenaries gradually deserted. There were few unemployed camel drivers in California to take their places, and the bewildered dromedaries sooner or later found their way into circuses, zoos, private barnyards and Western folklore. The episode was never regarded as one of the more glorious triumphs of the United States Army. Nevertheless, Irwin proudly boasts that it is "the only army post that can trace its history from camels to tanks."

The modern history of the fort dates from August 8, 1940, when President Roosevelt, by executive order, created Mojave Antiaircraft Range. For five years during World War II, planes with targets in tow shuttled back and forth over the range. Guns sputtered during the day; tracers lit up the night skies; and bursts of ack-ack were heard overhead at any hour of the day or night. As a name, Mojave Antiaircraft Range lacked distinction commensurate with the high order of training provided there, so in 1942 the place was redubbed Camp Irwin, in honor of the distinguished World War I field artillery commander, Major General LeRoy Irwin.

By late 1944 the camp had served its purpose and was inactivated. For seven years the desert winds and sandstorms did their best to wipe it off the map. But there was enough left to patch up in 1951 when the Korean trouble broke out. Camp Irwin came back to life with military emphasis switched from antiaircraft to armor. It proved its worth as a training center, continued to grow, and ten years later was designated as a permanent installation and accorded the added nominal dignity of "Fort" rather than "Camp."

The most vicious-looking vehicles in the Army's cavalcade of armor have been groaning across the sands ever since, walloping shells into the void, scaring the hide off the jack rabbits, the coyotes and human intruders imprudent enough to disregard the CLOSED TO THE PUBLIC signs.

Fort Irwin means business—very serious business; as deadly a business as there is in the United States of America. "The mission of the U.S. Army Armor and Desert Training Center," recites the post commander in grim earnestness, "is to provide the command, operation, training, administration, service and supply to (a) complete the individual and unit training of tank units involving firing of the main armament which cannot ordinarily be carried out at home stations, (b) familiarize tank units with the operation and employment of special armor equipment; (c) familiarize tank units with the operation and employment of the latest types of tanks and related equipment; and (d) conduct combat firing and tactical exercises as time and facilities permit."

In effect, Fort Irwin offers a postgraduate as well as undergraduate curriculum in heavy armor. Indoctrination comes in big doses, highly concentrated. It is not the "remoteness" alone that keeps morale at a high pitch and life on the rugged side. The desert-club recreation refinements are there, but in the interests of national defense they sometimes get neglected.

America's Armageddon is as likely to be fought on a desert as anywhere else, so there was military foresight in selecting the Mojave as a training ground for soldiery. But ordinary civilian logic would have to exclude the Navy. The desert is no place for sailors. Davy Jones in the sand hills would be as incongruous as a burro and prospector on the thwarts of a rowboat in mid-Pacific. Yet there the fleet arm is, and not merely a token force. Including Marine contingents, the Navy representation in the Mojave and Colorado deserts is larger than Army and Air Force combined, and the biggest establishment rubs shoulders with Fort Irwin, plumb in the middle of the northwest Mojave.

The only Navy-commanded metropolis in the continental United States is not where one would expect it to be—say, on the north or south shore of Boston, on the Virginia coast, on the outskirts of San Diego or Bremerton. It is 150 miles inland, stranded in the desert—a city of 12,000 where everything from kindergarten to commissary is Navy owned and Navy operated.

China Lake is the place, but no cruiser, PT boat or captain's gig will ever be launched on the lake. The city is incongruously named for a borax colony of Chinese coolies who decamped three quarters of a century ago, and for a lake that is not there. The lakesite is bone dry, and has been within the memory of man.

Nudging Fort Irwin on the east is a vast naval estate of 2,000 square miles, 1,250,000 acres, one of the most complex and vital defense installations in the country—the Naval Ordnance Test Station, NOTS for short. In fact, there is not a United States submarine, destroyer or carrier afloat that does not owe a debt in armaments to the laboratories and firing ranges of NOTS.

The details of what goes on at China Lake are "classified." None of the 12,000 residents and employees may enter or leave the city without presenting authentic credentials to the Marine guards at the municipal gates, and ordinary rubberneck tourists are looked upon askance, except during the exciting Armed Forces Day celebration and the annual open-house Wild Flower Show which the station puts on. Roads and trails which once crossed the station proper are "permanently closed," and on adjoining Randsburg Wash Test Range they might as well be, though the parlance used is "restricted travel."

The reservation boundaries fence in a lot of history, as well as naval confidences. Across these grounds trudged early trailblazers like Joseph Reddeford Walker, overlanders like the jayhawkers, and a host of gold prospectors heading into the Coso, Argus and Panamint ranges. Only with a Navy pass can one hope ever again to retrace the old twenty-mule-team road between Death Valley and Mojave.

The vast quadrangle of the main station sprawls halfway between the Sierra Nevada and Death Valley, and Randsburg Wash stretches from a few miles north of Barstow to the Panamints. All this unlovely country is out of bounds to ordinary civilians, and few of them begrudge the Navy's appropriation of it. No land anywhere could suffer less from the scars of gunnery demolition.

George Fujimoto, Jr.

George Fujimoto, Jr., was born in Riverside in 1921. His diaries from 1942 to 1948, housed at the Special Collections Library of the University of California, Riverside, describe the evacuation and internment of Riverside-area Japanese American families—including his own—during World War II. After his internment in Arizona, Fujimoto returned to school, earned a degree in poultry management, and formed a farming partnership with his father. Now retired, he lives in Washington.

The following is an excerpt from Fujimoto's diaries. Deborah Wong, a music professor at the University of California, Riverside, is working with Fujimoto on a book that will include selected entries from these diaries, *From Riverside to Poston: The Fujimoto Diaries*.

from "Diary from 1942"

Wednesday, March 11

Went to school as usual. Shok at work in packing house. Came home about 5 pm and was shocked to learn that pop was taken into custody by federal officials today. 28 Riverside Japanese aliens were rounded up in today's raid; Mr. Sanematsu and pop included. Fortunately, pop was partially prepared.

Thursday, March 12

Stayed out of school today to assume pop's duties and responsibilities. Went to bank first thing after feeding hens wet mash to change pop's,

Cha's, and my check account to mine and Cha's. Successful. Mr. and Mrs. Hiroto paid visit. Offered assistance.

Friday, March 13
  Took eggs to S.B. and had good day—sold all 9 1\2 cases.
  Cha stayed out of school to help in the emergency. Cha took mom, Shok, Betty to see pop at county jail, but refused admittance. At same time Cha went to get the approved tire application that pop had applied for. Pop's signature was needed before and after buying the tire. Cha got first signature in pop's cell, but when he returned afterwards for the second, pop was gone—left by bus for undisclosed destination. After much, debate, Cha was able to get tire by signing himself by counter-signatures of rationing board members.

Sunday, March 15
  Cha, Mek, Shok, and Betty off to church as usual. Harrie took Cha and me out riding. Went through Pigeon Pass after much goose-chasing. Mr. and Mrs. Horikawa paying respects this afternoon. Mr. and Mrs. Sugi, Chihiro, Tumiko, Mrs. Kobayashi, and Byron also offering their "don't worries" this afternoon. Ben and Mother came to notify us that pop was temporarily stationed in Tujunga Canyon but that Mr. Sanematon was evidently taken directly to Santa Fe, N.M.

Wednesday, March 25
  ...Another round-up of Japanese aliens. 9 from Riverside (Cr.). Nishimoto, Yoshida. Aoki, Kajiyama, Ogawa, and Horikawa. Raid took place yesterday afternoon. Checked out of school today.

Thursday, March 26
  Curfew of all enemy aliens and Japanese Americans starts tomorrow. Curfew hours— 8 pm-6 am incl. Final Bible class at Mrs. Beck's tonight instead of usual uncle Filo's.

Friday, March 27
  All my Japanese egg customers have or are going to sell out in near future in San Bernardino and Colton.
  Visited Mr. Gibson at his place to talk about lease and paid disc bill. Favors monthly rent plus 25% of walnut crop.
  Mr. and Mrs. Ohno came this evening to say good-bye. Are leaving tomorrow for L.A., then Owen's Valley. Have sold land, cars, furniture,

and everything.

Sunday, May 3
L.A. city well under way evacuating Japs.

Thursday, May 7
Both sides claim heavy enemy losses in greatest naval battle of all time. Sacramento and Stockton areas got exclusion orders.

Friday, May 8
Ben helped with berries.
Far east as Pomona got orders to evacuate by next Thursday. Los Angeles about through. Lil' Tokyo—a ghost town. Looks like Riverside next.
Sea battle off Australian Coast slackened temporarily (?).
Japs advancing up Burma Road—China's back door.

Saturday, May 16
Mrs. Hiroto telephoned saying we had to evacuate by next Wednesday. Mr. and Mrs. Sugi and Fomiko scared home by the report.
Cha bought a thousand dollar war bond today at the bank.

Wednesday, May 20
Let Gibson feed chickens himself. Went to register for evacuation this morn. At 8 o'clock for family. To leave Sat. 7am by Santa Fe limited. Ben, Harrie, Mr. Hiroto, and I registered consecutively.
Ontario, Upland, S.B., Redlands, and Riverside county west of Mt. San Jacinto registered in Riverside…

Saturday, May 23
Got up at 5 o'clock and finished getting luggage tied up and prepared. Cha and I took one load of luggage to Santa Fe depot at 6:30. When we got back Mrs. Hugan was here ready to take family over.
Mr. Gibson helped load dodge again. When we got to the depot, hardly anyone there; time 7:10, 10 minutes too late, we thought M.P. ordered us to 5th and Main.
Found big crowd there. Boarded 8 Santa Fe Buses. Left 8:30 am. Made numerous stops. Banning, Indio, Desert center (passed out lunch boxes). Arrived in Poston Camp about 3:30pm.
Registered, assigned to barracks.

Another load from Delano arrived about 6pm. Baggage trucks came 8pm. Helped unload. Art, Ben, Cha sick from bad tap water.

Monday, June 22

Radio in office blaring that Oregon coast shelled by Jap submarine; likewise Vancouver coast.

Power went off shortly after 1am this morning with consequent failing of water because of electric pumpers.

Had to take own cups and plates to mess [hall] because lunch dishes couldn't be washed. Took shower under a trickle. Toilets full—unable to flush.

Sunday, November 22

Coordinating council passed resolution prohibiting anything remotely resembling or symbolic of a Japanese flag. Brought down our banner. We can have unity without involving loyalty, or disloyalty. Jeopardizes Nisei's chances here in U.S.

Sumi Harada

Sumi Harada was born in Riverside in 1909. Her parents, Jukichi and Ken Harada, bought a house in Riverside in the early 1900s, placing it in the names of their American-born children; Asian Americans could not buy property under the Alien Land Law of 1913. Her family was sued and the case went to the California Supreme Court in 1918, where judges ruled in favor of the Haradas. Sumi Harada helped her parents run their restaurant until her entire family was sent to internment camps during World War II. After the war, she moved back to Riverside, to the family's original house, and lived there until shortly before her death in 2000.

"My Mother, March 17, 1943" was written after the author's mother died in an internment camp. It includes references to her family's neighborhood in Riverside, and is from the extensive Harada House archives at the Riverside Municipal Museum. The museum is working to restore the Harada House, with plans to turn it into a museum that tells the story of the Harada family. More information on the history of the Haradas can be found in Mark Rawitsch's *No Other Place*.

My Mother, March 17, 1943

Today, more than ever I am
thinking of her.

Her sharp, bright eyes, full
of memories of the past that

would light up when you
caught her attention. Her wavy
hair brushes back to produce a
clean cut face. Her hands soft
and gentle. I remember them
so often, when in sickness and
in pain.
O, thy loving hands.
The memories are so hard
to bear.
Your loving gracious presence,
To me will never be forgotten.
O, thou were so willing to forgive
Which made thee more gracious
In my sight.
I can only ask forgiveness
When it is too late.
O kindly spirit who
Guided me,
Your goodness shall never
Leave my mind.
I see you everywhere. I
can see you at the old Eighth
Street restaurant. I can re-
member you at Ninth Street. I
can remember at Eighth
Street, and there at the Lemon
Street house. The rides on Sunday
you were so alive.

Joan Baez

Joan Baez, born in New York in 1941, is a highly influential folk singer and songwriter known for her dedication to outspoken political activism. Emulated in this arena by artists from Joni Mitchell and Bonnie Raitt to the Indigo Girls, and responsible for introducing her audiences to a young Bob Dylan, she has recorded more than fifty albums. Baez has won many awards for both her music and her public service. She currently lives in Woodside, California.

This excerpt from her memoir *And a Voice to Sing With* recalls her adolescence in Redlands with her sisters, Pauline and Mimi.

from *And a Voice to Sing With*

One of the first problems I had to confront in junior high school was my ethnic background. Redlands is in southern California and had a large Mexican population, consisting mainly of immigrants and illegal aliens who came up from Mexico to pick fruit. At school they banded together, speaking Spanish—the girls with mountains of black hair, fizzed from sleeping all night long on masses of pin curls, wearing gobs of violet lipstick, tight skirts and nylons, and blouses with the collars turned up in back. The boys were *pachucos*, tough guys, who slicked back their gorgeous hair with Three Roses Vaseline tonic and wore their pegged pants so low on the hip that walking without losing them had become an art. Few Mexicans were interested in school and they were ostracized by the whites. So there I was, with a Mexican name, skin, and hair: the Anglos couldn't accept me because of all three, and the Mexicans couldn't accept me because I didn't speak Spanish.

My "race" wasn't the only factor that kept me isolated. The 1950s were the heart of the Cold War, and if anyone at Redlands High School talked about anything other than football and the choice of pom-pom girls, it was about the Russians. I had heard that the Communists had rioted at the University of Baghdad when my father taught there, and that some of them always warned him to keep away when there was going to be trouble. But in America during the overheated McCarthy years, *communism* was a dirty word and the arms race a jingoistic crusade. In my ninth-grade class I was almost alone in my fear of and opposition to armaments (to me they made the world seem even more fragile) and was already considered an expert on anything political.

It wasn't that I knew so much but rather that I was involved, largely because of the discussions taking place in my own home. And the family attended Quaker work camps, where I heard about alternatives to violence on personal, political, national, and international levels. Many of my fellow classmates held me in great disdain, and some had been warned by their frightened parents not to talk to me.

I don't know how Pauline felt about politics in those days. She was an excellent student but suffered terribly from shyness. I idolized her because she got good grades, never carried a wrinkled lunch bag, wore a ponytail which didn't make her ears stick out, and smelled of violets. Also because she was white. She never said a word about social issues. And Mimi—well, my own pacifism did not yet extend to Mimi, who was avoiding me in public because I was brown.

It was the sense of isolation, of being "different," that initially led me to develop my voice. I was in the school choir and sang alto, second soprano, soprano, and even tenor, depending on what was most needed. Mine was a plain, little girl's voice, sweet and true, but stringy as cheap cotton thread, and as thin and straight as the blue line on a piece of binder paper. There was a pair of twins in my class who had vibratos in their voices and sang in every talent show, standing side by side, each with an arm around the other, angora sweaters outlining their developing bosoms, crinoline slips flaring. They swayed to and fro and snapped their fingers, "Oh, we ain't got a barrel of money..." I heard a teacher comment that their voices were very "mature." I tried out for the girls' glee club, and when I wasn't accepted, figured it was because (1) I was not a member of the in crowd and (2) I had no vibrato so my voice wasn't mature. Powerless to change my social standing, I decided to change my voice. I dropped tightrope walking to work full time on a vibrato.

First I tried, while standing in the shower, to stay on one note and force my voice up and down slowly. It was tedious and unrewarding work. My natural voice came out straight as an arrow. Then, I tried bobbing my finger up and down on my Adam's apple and, to my delight, found I could create the sound I wanted. For a few brief seconds, I would imitate the sound without using my hand, achieving a few "mature"-sounding notes. This was terrific! This is how I would train!

The time it took to form a shaky but honest vibrato was surprisingly short. By the end of the summer I was a singer.

At the same time I was giving myself a new voice, I was also under the tutelage of my father's much loved physics professor, Paul Kirkpatric, P.K. for short, conquering the ukulele. I knew the four basic chords used in ninety percent of the country-and-western and rhythm-and-blues songs then dominating the record market, and I was learning a few extra chords to use if I needed to sing in a key other than G. Some of my favorites were "You're in the Jailhouse Now," "Your Cheatin' Heart," "Earth Angel," "Pledging My Love," "Never Let Me Go," and the Annie series—"Annie Had a Baby," "Work with Me, Annie," "Annie's Aunt Fanny" (I was disgusted with the watered-down "white version," "Roll with Me, Henry")—as well as "Over the Mountain," and "Young Blood." These songs all could be played with five chords, most only with four. All were either melodic and sweet, upbeat and slightly dirty, or comic. I even did a vile racist version of "Yes Sir, That's My Baby" called "Yes Sir, Zat-a My Baby," and Liberace's inane "Cement Mixer, Putty Putty." And this list is only a bare beginning of what I listened to on my little gray plastic bedside radio. I cannot describe the satisfaction I got from memorizing tunes by ear and scribbling down words anytime, day or night; finding the right key (the choices were C or G); and making the song my own.[...]

Before long an exhibitionist impulse overcame me. I took my ukulele to school. At noontime I hung around the area where the popular kids ate lunch and waited for them to ask me to play, which they did soon enough. I sang "Suddenly There's a Valley" and when they applauded and asked for more, I sang the current hits of the day: "Earth Angel," "Pledging My Love," and "Honey Love." I was a big hit and came back the next day for a command performance. This time I did imitations of Elvis Presley, Della Reese, Eartha Kitt, and Johnny Ace. Before the week was out I had gone from being a gawky, self-conscious outsider to being something of a jesterlike star.

Someone suggested that I try out for the school talent show. At the tryouts, while standing at the microphone, I rested my foot on the rung of a stool to feign calm, and discovered that my knee was shaking. Afraid I would rattle the stool, with seeming nonchalance I raised my foot off the rung and held my knee suspended in the air, foot dangling, my entire leg trembling. The rest of my body was impressively composed, and sang "Earth Angel" all the way from start to finish with a "mature" vibrato. Nobody noticed my shaky knee, and I discovered that I had an innate poise and a talent for bluffing. Clearly I would "make" the talent show. I hoped to win the prize.

For my first stage performance I wore my favorite black jumper, polished my white flats, and even dabbed on some lipstick. I was terrified, but was told later that I had been "cool as a cucumber." As the crowd clapped and cheered I grew so nervous and thrilled I thought I would faint. They wanted me back for an encore, so, knees watery, I went back out and sang "Honey Love."

There had been nothing showy about my performance. I had walked out and sung exactly the way I would in my room or on the back porch. The actual time in front of an audience was both frightening and exhilarating, and afterwards I was euphoric.

I did not win the prize. It went to David Bullard, the only black in the show. The judges had picked the only horse darker than me. David had befriended and defended me in the fifth grade and I loved him. He was tall and smoky black, had perfect teeth, and may have been the only person in that school who smiled as readily as I did. He also had a good voice. The fact that I didn't win the prize I'd been expecting dampened that day only a little. For all the anxiety, I knew I'd been really good and that, in some strange way, my peers loved me and were proudly claiming me as one of their own, as someone who truly belonged to Redlands High School. My sense of having arrived was almost as heady as my satisfaction with the performance.

Michael Jaime-Becerra

Michael Jaime-Becerra was born and raised in El Monte, California. Educated at the University of California in both Irvine and Riverside, he is currently an assistant professor in the latter's Department of Creative Writing. His collection of short stories *Every Night Is Ladies' Night* was published in 2001. He lives in El Monte.

"Georgie and Wanda" is from *Every Night Is Ladies' Night*.

Georgie and Wanda

Georgie winces as he walks into Walt's Barber Shop. He steps toward the short row of red folding chairs facing the sink and mirrors, a deep sigh escaping his chest when he sits down. The bruise is spread across his ribs, but other, smaller pains shoot through his arms and legs, nagging him with stinging bursts when he moves. Walt looks up from the gray-haired old-timer he's working on to say good morning, and Georgie only manages to grunt a response. He tries to sit still and wonders if this is what his body will feel like when he gets old. He closes his eyes and listens to the quiet sounds of Saturday morning, the snipping of Walt's shears, and the country music coming from the Motorola. The old man hums along with the radio. There's only one part in the song that he seems to know, the chorus which he sings softly, "Go cry your heart out, don't come cryin' to me."

Georgie's own heart is beating in odd places. His head pumps and the foot in his right boot pulses. In the ring and pinkie fingers on his right hand, his heart throbs as if last night's crack-up had shattered it, sending its pieces to the most remote parts of his body. Underneath his blue T-shirt, a black arc curves across his chest. The bruise is deep and it marks the place where he was rammed into the roadster's steering wheel. Georgie wonders if he's fractured anything, if any of his ribs are cracked, if something broken keeps the little bones in his right hand from making a complete fist. Last night, his roadster's restraints held loosely and Georgie was flung forward fast and hard. Somewhere in the fogginess, he told Link he'd have been better off strapping himself down with rubber bands.

He hasn't slept or showered. He smells of smoke, and his T-shirt and jeans are stiff, marked in places with chalky blotches of dried sweat. After the crack-up, Georgie spent much of last night with the roadster, watching Link and some people from the other crews douse it with water, only to have the flames flare up from the engine a few minutes later. Georgie watched from the infield as his '32 Ford burned and died, fire truck sirens approaching, the other roadsters rumbling on the dirt track around him.

When Walt finishes with the old-timer, he slaps the red barber chair with a rag. Since Georgie was a child, his hair's been cut every two weeks on a Saturday morning. Georgie's father is a barber in Joliet, Illinois, a pincher of cheeks and a giver of lollipops, who always told Georgie that there's no greater shame than a handsome man who lets a good haircut grow out.

The old man hands Walt a few dollars and nods as he shuffles past. Walt tells Georgie, "Okay champ! You're next." In the five years that Walt has cut Georgie's hair, he's always called him "champ," and this morning more than ever, the nickname makes him uneasy. He shifts in his seat and takes a deep breath. Even though he's done well enough with racing, moving from the amateur ranks to A Class in just a few years, Georgie has yet to prove himself a true champion of anything.

Last night was only his third time in Gardena, but he was sure his tires would hold if he went into turn three with the throttle open, sure that the dirt of Carrell Speedway wouldn't betray him. Georgie saw this track as he saw all tracks, the same simple ring with the promise of wide open space for the man brave enough to trade the most paint with his opponents. Everyone racing in A Class had one of four engines under their hoods, and sure the engine made you fast, but it was the driver who won the race. Georgie started this racing season by placing fifth at the Highway 99 in Modesto. In Bakersfield he took third, and just last week, at the Orange Bowl in San Bernardino, he finally walked away with a kiss on the cheek from Etiwanda Andrade, the Mexican-American beauty queen who appears at each race in a bathing suit and sunglasses to hand out the day's only trophy.

That kiss turned into a conversation, which turned into a phone number. Last Wednesday night, Georgie made plans with Etiwanda over the telephone. He promised her a win, and besides a second kiss on the grandstand, she agreed to have dinner somewhere afterwards. Georgie can't decide which is worse, wrecking his car or missing out on his date with Etiwanda, and he quickly arrives at the conclusion that both are nothing but bad, bad news.

Walt ties the apron around Georgie's neck and starts to spray his hair. He asks Georgie if he's been keeping cool, for it's been an unseasonable September. Smog has hazed the city, and the normally hot temperatures have soared into the hundreds and have stayed parked. As Walt begins cutting Georgie's hair, the mercury is close to ninety. In four hours, it's expected to peak in the San Gabriel Valley at 108 degrees.

Walt asks Georgie about last night's race and Georgie tells him it isn't worth talking about. "It was going good," he says. "My only competition was a guest entry from Tucson who was holding a shaky lead going into lap ninety-five." Walt sprays Georgie's hair with more water. When he cocks Georgie's head to catch the right light, Georgie winces and stops talking.

Last night, behind the wheel of the roadster, Georgie told himself there was no reason why he couldn't push a hundred going into turn three. Out of fear, no one else was breaking ninety miles an hour in Gardena's third turn. With four laps to go in the race, Georgie saw himself whipping ahead of the pack, emerging from turn three with nothing ahead of him but empty space and that second kiss from Etiwanda. As the pack of roadsters reverberated with downshifting, Georgie pictured his leg made of steel, his foot carved from stone. The gas pedal remained flat against the floorboard, and Georgie was certain, from his head to his gear box, that he couldn't be stopped by physics.

Señorita Etiwanda Andrade, Reina de Churubusco, Queen of the Black and White Ball. For the duration of this summer's racing season, Georgie kept a picture of Etiwanda Scotch-taped between the fuel and speed gauges on his dashboard. The picture came from a newspaper clipping cut from Section II of the *Times*, one day after her coronation in mid-May. In the photo, the tiara on Etiwanda's head is tilted at an angle, her hands holding her trophy by its heavy wooden base. There have been nights, long nights spent alone in the shop, when Georgie has sat in his roadster and has done nothing more than smile back at Etiwanda, pretending that their eyes are locked, her gaze fixed on him. Once at a timing meet in Russetta, dehydrated from racing and dizzy from the vibrations of the crankshaft under his seat, Georgie swore that she nodded to him as the roadster flew across the hard desert floor. However, he has kept all of this to himself.

The accompanying article is taped to the lamp on Georgie's night-stand. Beginning in May, and all through June, he spent his nights memorizing the small gray square of text, running the four sentences through his mind until they replaced the heat and the smell of motor oil to send Georgie off to sleep:

QUEEN PRESENTED WITH TROPHY
A stately 22-year-old El Monte señorita is the proper and fitting queen of Southern California's bevy of Latin-American beauties. Señorita Etiwanda Andrade, of 11335 Medina Court, reigned at the 16th annual Black and White Ball at the Los Angeles Breakfast Club, sponsored by Stoltz Lincoln. Her selection was based on beauty, personality, education, and personal appearance from a field of eight candidates by a board of judges, which included the Cuban consul, four Los Angeles newspapermen, one of Mexico's movie queens, and Bill Stoltz, owner of three Southern California Lincoln dealerships. As queen, Señorita Andrade's primary responsibility will be to represent Stoltz Lincoln at regional California Racing Association events.

It's the beginning of the second sentence that Georgie has studied clos-est. He's turned the numbers of Etiwanda's address and the name of her street over and over in his mind, but he's too afraid to actually go and see the place. Each time that he's considered visiting Medina Court, a series of new and childish fears envelopes him: What if she's already seeing someone? A girl like that's gotta be seeing someone. What if she sees me and recognizes me? What if she doesn't? What do I do then? The questions spring open like a set of trapdoors, and Georgie falls through one after another after another.

Much of this spring was spent sitting on his lumpy mattress, eyes closed, content to imagine Etiwanda's address in three huge dimensions, to study it from different angles and pretend as though Etiwanda would be hiding in the curves and crevices of the type if only he looked closely enough. Since his win in July, Georgie has raced all over the state with her in his mind. Thoughts of Etiwanda rode with him at Huntington Beach Speedway, Gilmore Stadium, Bonnelli Stadium in Saugus, and the S.C.T.A. time trials at El Mirage. Georgie sees himself standing on the winner's podium again, close enough to catch the shine on her lips, to simply smell her. Once at Sears, Georgie went through the women's department and sniffed all the perfumes, fruitlessly looking for the one he remembered as hers.

In the races before winning the Orange Bowl, Georgie did well with the exception of Huntington, where his radiator blew a hose, and he was forced to drop out early in a mad gush of steam. Even with oven mitts on, Link couldn't replace the torn hose because of the hot engine, and Georgie spent the rest of the afternoon on the tailgate of Link's truck, looking out into the parking lot for the blue Lincoln that brings Etiwanda to each event. In the other two races, Georgie came in second. He was beat by thirty-two hundredths of a second at Saugus, and by twenty-six hundredths at Bonnelli. Before San Bernardino, Georgie's guts had turned to sauerkraut in these moments. He made his way to the winner's podium, and looked at his boots when Etiwanda passed him to plant one on the cheek of Bill Paterson or Larry Soto or whoever happened to be this week's lucky man.

After Walt's, Georgie stops by the Woolworth's to buy some aspirin. He opens the jar while waiting in line, and he starts chewing a handful of the bitter pills as the cashier hands him his change. He takes a long drink from the water fountain to help him swallow the pasty mixture. From there, Georgie walks down Atlantic Boulevard, back toward Link's Speed Shop, the place he's lived the last four years.

Link Kelly has been Georgie's mechanic since Georgie left his brothers in an Illinois storm window factory to race professionally in California where the weather was warm and the prize money was big. Link's father was a Baptist who started preaching in the Texas badlands after the first World War and didn't stop until he talked his way clear out to Los Angeles. The way Link tells it, Old Man Kelly thought his son was a connection between the divine hands of Jesus and the wretched people here on Earth, and that's how he was named. Link has also told

Georgie that sitting in church and listening to all the holy songs and sermons was like having someone throw pennies at his head for an hour.

In the Army, Link not only learned how a motor works, but he figured out different ways to improve its operation. Link owns five patents and no Bibles. Georgie's been working for him for six years, but it wasn't until two seasons ago that Link started turning the wrenches on Georgie's roadster. Right away, Georgie noticed the way it performed. Among other things, Link machined custom gears and piston rings. The differences with the new parts were small, but they were important. That first race with Link in the pits was the first time Georgie's roadster truly sounded the way the other cars sounded, and Georgie felt for the first time that he was competing on a level field.

Today the ten-minute walk back to the shop takes Georgie twenty, the sun beating down all the way. Georgie steps into the office, and, despite the heat, Link is behind the counter pouring what, most likely, isn't the morning's first mug of coffee. "There you are," he says. Link is tall and thin, with arms and legs that seem to be made of pipe cleaners, and a blond flattop that looks like he's trying to grow a broom. Some of the coffee spills out of his mug as he talks, and he steps back to avoid it. "The way you disappeared this morning, I thought you got hit by a car or captured by a flyin' saucer." Link sits on his stool and slaps the counter like he just told a joke. "How'd you like that for luck? You survive a crack-up and then, *pow!*, you get kidnapped by little green Martians."

"I just been out walking," Georgie says, "walking and thinking."

"For three hours?" Link asks. "That musta been some walk."

The phone rings and Link answers. He takes a pencil and licks the tip and starts quoting prices and writing things down. He holds his hand up so Georgie will wait, but Georgie ignores him. He grabs one of the waiting room chairs and drags it into the warehouse through the doorway on his right, stopping a foot from the charred roadster. Even with three industrial fans blowing and the doors wide open, the warehouse is steaming and still smells of burned rubber and metal. It seems to Georgie as if his car is still burning, as if some part of it, some chamber inside the engine's core, is still on fire. Georgie sits and stares and takes a long, hard look. Because of the stink, he covers his mouth with his hand.

Georgie's been racing since he was fourteen, piloting midgets up and down the streets of suburban Chicago. He's been in a few crack-ups before, but this is the first car he's ever totaled. Halfway through the turn, Georgie could feel his tires slipping, the roadster sliding up the embankment toward the retaining wall as if someone on the other side was reeling him in. The rear of the car was put to the wall first, the force of the collision nearly tearing the rear axle away from the frame. Georgie vaguely remembers spinning light and a large flash as the roadster ricocheted, the other axle cracking when the front end hit the wall. This second impact lifted the car sideways and sent it rolling into the infield on two wheels. The other cars swerved, and, in the moment before Georgie reached the grass, he was inches away from striking the roadster running in second place.

Here in Link's garage, the roadster rests on four sad, misshapen rubber stumps. The tires' tread was torn away in the collision, the sidewalls collapsing in the fire, the steel belts now exposed in dull silver patches. Both the roadster's grille and nerfing bar are missing, along with the body panels on the right side. The left side of the body is crumpled. Fortunately for Georgie, the gas tank riding in the seat next to him was thrown clear, and the doors that took Link two days to weld shut had come loose in the impact. Georgie unbuckled himself and fell from the car when it stopped rolling. As someone pulled him away, the air he had just been breathing fed a burst of flame. Now, the steering wheel droops toward the ground and there is nothing left of the seat except the charred springs. The wooden floorboard is burnt away. The glass in all the gauges is cracked, the numbers blackened with soot, each exposed needle curled like an eyelash. Etiwanda's photo is gone.

The fans hum heavily, Link to Georgie's right, both men staring. A passing car honks emphatically, but they don't bother to look away.

"This came for you a little while ago," Link says.

Georgie takes the yellow telegram from Link's hand, sees the return address of the C.R.A. offices downtown, and shoves the envelope in his back pocket without bothering to open it. Whatever's inside can't be good.

"The car's gotta go out back until we can figure out if we can keep anything from it," Link says.

There are customized pieces in this hulk that Georgie still owes money on, pieces that probably welded together in the fire, forming a fused chunk of intricately carved steel. Georgie will be working until Christmas just to pay this chunk off. He watches Link roll the engine hoist over, and passes the thick three-quarter-ton chain back after Link slides it under the roadster and turns the hydraulic crank. Both men are quiet as the roadster slowly comes off the ground.

"Goddamn," Link mutters, his voice somber as if he's somehow seeing the roadster for the first time. "When they come apart on you, they really come apart."

"Yup," Georgie says.

He has given the last six years of his life to this car. He bought it from a widow in Pomona for thirty-five dollars. It belonged to her husband, but he died somewhere in Europe during the war, and she felt more comfortable riding the bus. The roadster wobbles slightly as they push it toward the lot of old hulks and broken parts that Link has out back.

The muscles ache in Georgie's back and shoulders, and with each step he hopes the aspirin he chewed earlier will kick in.

Most of the '54 season was spent running around with a girl named Ruthie Lee. Georgie was still banging around with the weekend racers in "C" class when he met her. Ruthie Lee was from Pasadena, and hung around the pit area of the Glendale Fairgrounds like they were handing out twenty-dollar bills. A looker with big black hair and a purse full of French cigarettes, Ruthie Lee liked to drink. Don't get Georgie wrong, he's been shit-faced and wall-eyed plenty of times, but Ruthie Lee really liked to drink. When Georgie thought back, he couldn't remember a time when her lips didn't taste like some kind of booze.

Ruthie Lee also liked to smoke reefers and sometimes she shared her occasional funny cigarette with Georgie. He already had a tendency to worry, but Ruthie Lee's reefers made him downright paranoid. There were races at Glendale where Georgie suspected that every last nut and bolt on his roadster was loose, that the engine would somehow drop from the chassis as Link pushed the car off the starting line. Pit stops turned into full-blown tune-ups. One time Georgie got out of the car, took off his driving gloves, and overtightened the carburetor manifold, stripping half the nuts. Link had to yank the wrenches from his hands, and shove him into the car to get it back in the race. His knuckles had been seared by the engine. He could barely hold the wheel, and eventually pulled out of the race, blowing a thin lead, but a lead nonetheless.

The ride back to the shop that afternoon was a quiet one, no radio. Link drove and Georgie alternated his hands in a small bucket of ice water. When they pulled in the Speed Shop's driveway, Link cut the engine and sat for a moment with his large ring of keys in his lap.

"Pull another bonehead stunt like that, and you'll be on your own." He didn't look at Georgie as he said this, but his tone was cold and clear, and for Georgie that flagged the end of things with Ruthie Lee.

Georgie doesn't have much besides the knife in his boot and the twenty-three dollars in his wallet. Link doesn't have a second car he might race, and even if he did, the C.R.A. has suspended Georgie's racing license for the remaining five weeks of the season. The telegram that arrived earlier termed Georgie "a reckless hazard and a menace to the good name of stock car racing." He's also a couple hundred dollars in the hole to Link, and for all Georgie knows he might end up in the hospital with internal bleeding. Georgie's heard of guys getting into crack-ups, and two or three days later keeling over right on the street. Still, twenty-three dollars can buy dinner for two, and maybe a movie, or maybe a rock 'n' roll show at the Legion Stadium. Georgie knows that if he loses track of Etiwanda now, if he doesn't get on the phone and call her, he'll probably never have a reason to see her up close again.

He's got the number memorized—KLondike 9-8216. Georgie decides to use the phone in the office, because he can't hear anything in the garage over the droning of the fans. Georgie dials. The phone buzzes once and it buzzes again and as it buzzes a third time, Georgie can feel himself starting to sink inside. Someone picks up on the fourth buzz, and Georgie holds his breath and says, "Hello."

The girl on the line's other end says "Yeah," instead of "Hello." She sounds clearly annoyed, sounds as if Georgie had spoken another language where "Hello" meant "Fuck you." Georgie asks for Etiwanda and the girl asks, "Who's this?"

"It's Georgie. Georgie Kuluzni. I'm a friend of hers from the race-track."

"Hold on." Georgie hears the girl put the phone down. He flips on a small desk fan that blows warm air in his face. Georgie closes his eyes and rubs a spot of soreness in his neck.

"Yes." Etiwanda's voice is the complete, comforting opposite of the first one, soft and cool as melting ice cream. In a perfect world, it would be a capsule for Georgie's aches and pains.

"Etiwanda? It's Georgie."

"Georgie? Oh Georgie, how are you?"

"I'm fine." Georgie winces as he switches the telephone to his other ear. "Just some bumps and bruises."

"My God, you're lucky to be alive. I saw the whole thing. It was awful. They didn't stop the race, and the other cars didn't even slow up, and when I tried to get down to the track to see you, the guards wouldn't let me through."

"I don't remember seeing you come down," Georgie says. "In fact, I don't remember too much of the whole thing."

Georgie tells Etiwanda some of what he's pieced together from last night. He was out cold for almost an hour, and when he woke up, the race was long over. Most of the people were gone, except for the gawkers who gathered around the smoldering roadster. Link borrowed a winch from one of the other crews and pulled the hulk onto the trailer and drove it back to the shop. Georgie tells Etiwanda that he couldn't sleep, but he doesn't tell her about sitting up the rest of the night with a fifth of Dixie Belle and a fire extinguisher in case the car should flare back up, about jabbing his knife into the soft rubber of the deformed tires, and kicking the body panels until he collapsed. Georgie was never prone to weeping, but last night he came close.

Georgie asks Etiwanda who won, and she says she doesn't remember the guy's name. "He was the guest entry from Tucson. Number 229, I think."

Georgie nods and swallows, his ability to make conversation, good and interesting conversation, slipping from him. "Yeah. Well listen, I was wondering if you still wanted to get together. Maybe tonight, if you don't already have plans." Georgie stares at the silver blur of the fan blade, and though it hurts, he wraps the phone cord around his fingers.

"I'm sorry Georgie, but I already have an engagement." Georgie wants to bang his head on the counter as Etiwanda tells him she's busy with Crawford's Supermarket's Fall Festival. "I'm supposed to pull the curtain on something called The Big Cheese. They tell me it's a two-ton block of cheddar."

Georgie recovers a bit, and asks if she'd like to go to dinner before that. "I'll pick you up," he says.

"Should you even be driving right now?"

"I'm fine," Georgie says. "I could pick you up at six or seven o'clock. Whenever you're ready."

"I don't know, Georgie. You wouldn't have much fun just sitting there, watching me smile and sign autographs for people. And what about the car? Having the Lincoln with me at events is part of my contract, and it's not like either one of us is on the list of approved drivers. Maybe we could get dinner some other time. Right now, the whole thing sounds too complicated."

"I'd really like to see you tonight," Georgie says. "It doesn't have to be complicated."

Things get quiet. There's the oppressive droning of the fans, and Link hosing the black smudges left on the warehouse floor by the road-ster. The distant sound of a rooster crowing comes through the receiver in Georgie's hand, but there's nothing else, nothing important, until Etiwanda says, "Let me check on something, and I'll call you back in five minutes."

Georgie gives her the number to the shop, and he doesn't hang up the phone until he hears the click on the other end.

Not long after Ruthie Lee, Georgie met a woman named Claudette. Claudette was a typist in the advertising department of the *San Gabriel Tribune*. Link ran an ad for the Speed Shop in their sports section, and Georgie met Claudette when he dropped in to pay for the month's advertisements. He told her a joke and made her laugh, and they met for dinner that night. They made plans for Saturday and that turned into six months of lunch dates. When it was sunny they'd go to Almanzor Park, or they'd stop by The Hat for pastramis and soggy French fries, or sometimes they'd stay and brown-bag it, eating Claudette's homemade tuna salad sandwiches on the benches in front of the *Tribune's* office.

Against Link's advice, Georgie was still driving the roadster around town, risking the impound for breaking the vehicle code. Whenever Georgie took Claudette anyplace, she would tie bright scarves over her hair that matched her skirt and her shoes. Georgie would tap the gas pedal, and the engine would rumble, and Claudette would recoil as though a wild animal was clawing its way through the firewall. Georgie couldn't go over forty-five miles an hour with her in the car. Claudette would watch his speedometer as he drove, following the needle and gripping the seat so firmly with her bare hands that her nails left marks. When Georgie told Link about this, Link laughed and told Georgie to make her wear mittens so she wouldn't ruin the leather.

Georgie couldn't get very far with Claudette. She was saving herself, and each time things managed to get interesting, they were quelled by Claudette's talk of rings and wedding dresses and honeymoon suites in Hawaii. Claudette was fond of reading the society section of the newspaper on Mondays and sighing at the pictures of the brides who were married over the weekend.

All of Claudette's pent-up energy went into the one thing she enjoyed most: dancing. Claudette knew the bunnyhop and the mambo, the stroll and the walk, the jitterbug and the cha cha cha. Her favorite song was something called "The Woodpecker Rock," and on Friday nights she'd bug Georgie for nickels to call KFWB so that the disk jockey would get it on the radio. Georgie never really went for music in a big way. Whenever music was playing—if there was a radio around, if something she liked came on the jukebox, or a car went by blaring—Claudette's foot would start tapping and Georgie would get nervous.

Link is drying his hands on his shirt when he comes into the office. Georgie waits until he's refilled his coffee mug before asking if he can borrow his car that night. Link drives an emerald-green '48 Chevy, a two-door with shaved handles, a bull-nosed hood and custom black-and-white leather upholstery. Link takes a sip of his coffee, and gives Georgie a quizzical look. "Why?"

Even though Link knows what Georgie had planned for last night, Georgie explains the current situation with Etiwanda in careful detail. Link listens and shakes his head. "I'm sorry, Georgie, but after last night, you could have a date with Lana Turner, and I still wouldn't loan you my car."

The telephone rings as Link steps out of the office. Georgie says hello and he listens for a few moments and says that six sounds great, that he'll pick her up, no problem, that he's got a great restaurant in mind for dinner. He copies down some directions and smiles as he hangs up the phone.

Link is watching from the doorway. "Okay," he says, "you can take the truck." He takes a long sip of his coffee, then nods toward the pickup parked out front, the '46 Ford with its faded and flaking yellow paint, the old machine smudged with hundreds of greasy handprints. The hinges on its driver door are rusted shut, the cab steeped in sweat and gasoline, but its engine is as sturdy as a Clydesdale. "It won't be towing anything in the near future."

After Claudette came Miss Pearl. Miss Pearl was older, Italian and widowed. She owned a hair salon over on Las Tunas, and the rumor was that Miss Pearl had poisoned her husband with the same chemicals she used to make curly hair straight and straight hair curly. Georgie met Miss Pearl at the bar during a fellow racer's wedding reception. She insisted that he call her "Miss," and she dangled her fingers in front of him and said, "See, no rings."

After Georgie bought her a few Greyhounds, they went back to her apartment in Alhambra. Miss Pearl had pillows stuffed with down and a mattress that cupped Georgie like a nest. She kept a large picture on the dresser across from the bed, a portrait of her late husband, Harold, wearing an expression so serious that it appeared carved from fine wood. Midway through the act, Georgie opened his eyes and saw Miss Pearl's gaze fixed on Harold. Afterwards Miss Pearl and Georgie slept, and Georgie dreamt that there were ducks squawking in Miss Pearl's living room, that her mattress was indeed filled with feathers, that Miss Pearl sat with a bird at the foot of the bed, and yanked them out one by one.

In the daytime, Miss Pearl wore a green uniform with her name embroidered in white stitching; and no matter how much she scrubbed, her hands still smelled like chemicals. Georgie told her about the regularity of his haircuts, and she insisted on trimming his hair from that point forward. When he wouldn't let her, they squabbled over Georgie's greasy, curly crown. The fight escalated, Miss Pearl first hurling her half-finished highball at Georgie's head. Then came a glass ashtray. If it was ever in Georgie to hit a woman, Miss Pearl would have been the one. She accused him of not trusting her, and, rather than give her the honest answer, he left.

He stopped at a diner where he ordered an early breakfast, scrambled eggs and sausage with sourdough toast, orange juice with extra ice. He flipped through a rumpled newspaper while he waited, and ran into the article with Etiwanda. It was the photo that immediately struck Georgie. He studied Etiwanda carefully, the substantial bouquet and her heavy-looking trophy, the way her smile eclipsed the twinkling crown on her head. Something in the plain and simple joy of the moment displaced all thoughts of Miss Pearl, of Claudette and Ruthie Lee and all the other women Georgie had known in between.

Georgie tore out the article, and, sitting there at the diner counter, after reading and rereading the caption and knowing Etiwanda Andrade would be there this Saturday and every Saturday for the next twenty-two weeks, Georgie found his purpose in racing renewed. The season's starting race was in two weeks at the Speed Bowl in Porterville. The prospect of winning it consumed Georgie so immediately that his hunger subsided and he left his eggs and sausages untouched. He took the toast and the paper with him, and when Link came to work the next morning and raised the warehouse doors, he found Georgie tinkering with the roadster to secure every last fraction of speed.

Georgie can't tell if the heat or his nerves are making him sweat. The fifteen-minute drive from Link's Speed Shop in San Gabriel to Etiwanda's house in El Monte has taken him half an hour because he couldn't stay on the expressway. Georgie's running late, ten minutes late at this point, and though he's worried about the time, his chest was seized with a choking fear when he checked his mirror and saw the traffic thrusting toward him. It was as if God had placed Georgie in His hand and squeezed like King Kong. As the cars zoomed past, horns blaring, the truck running out of on-ramp, Georgie felt like the engineer of an antique locomotive, the equipment in his hands and at his feet suddenly unfamiliar, their operations confusing and foreign. Georgie exited quickly, and even though he's complained about the truck's poor performance every time he's driven it, even though Etiwanda's probably tapping her toe and checking the clock, Georgie doesn't mind going slow tonight.

Georgie doesn't have any change on him to call Etiwanda. It wouldn't look good to call her collect, and even if there was a nickel in his pocket, Georgie's not about to tell her about this new phobia. To make up some time, Georgie decides to go down Valley Boulevard instead of taking Garvey into El Monte. The banks and movie theaters and department stores with shiny display windows give way to thrift stores and feed shops with gold pyramids made of hay, the buildings progressively dilapidated as Georgie nears Medina Court.

Georgie's done his best to improve the truck. Though he was too sore to give it a decent cleaning, he covered the bench seat's stains and splotches with a clean bedsheet. He also swiped a few air fresheners from the shop. Somewhere along the way, Georgie pulls over to change into his maroon, short-sleeve shirt that's been dangling behind him on a hanger to keep it clean and crisp. Multiple flashes of pain ignite, especially in his shoulders, his left side shuddering as he straightens his collar in the rearview mirror. He puts the truck into gear and adjusts his hair with a comb, waiting for the traffic to dissipate. Georgie's fingers become tacky from his pomade, and he wipes them on the bedsheet as the truck eases onto the street.

Medina Court is a narrow road, some houses more ramshackle than others, with dead brown lawns and the occasional thin, sickly tree. There are no curbs and no sidewalks. Georgie spots Etiwanda's blue Lincoln in a driveway, and he drives past it, turning the truck around. He parks across the street. A tough bunch of Mexican kids a few houses down stop smoking their cigarettes and guarding their mailbox, and Georgie can feel their gaze evaluating him as he walks up to Etiwanda's house. 11335 Medina Court is a small blue house, light blue that's chipped away in spots to show the white plaster underneath.

Georgie presses the doorbell, but it doesn't ring. He knocks once, then he knocks again. He can hear something going on behind the door, and, when it finally opens, the young Mexican woman standing before him is so small that it takes Georgie a second to discern that she's not a child. It takes him two more seconds to figure out that the black patch over the woman's right eye is real.

"Hi," Georgie says. "I'm here for Etiwanda."

The woman looks up at him and uses her hand to shield her good eye. "Yeah," she says. "Of course you are."

Georgie steps inside. The woman shuts the door and goes back to a couch that sits in the center of the living room. On the coffee table, along with some scissors, envelopes, and a sheet of stamps, is a stack of newspapers. The woman ignores Georgie and picks up a paper, resuming the project he apparently interrupted. She casts the first section aside, and Georgie recognizes its headline from the day following Etiwanda's coronation—9 "PACHUCOS" HELD IN BIZARRE MURDER CASE. The woman turns to Section II and begins cutting.

Had Georgie been welcomed, he might've asked her for a copy, a replacement for the one he lost last night, but he wasn't, and so he just stands there, forcing a smile. Earlier he thought about buying flowers, but in recalling the oversized bundle of roses Etiwanda had held in the newspaper photo, Georgie's pride convinced him that any bouquet he might scratch together on his thin twenty-three-dollar budget would be pointless, practically an insult. Now he wishes he'd stopped for a simple rose of his own to keep him from feeling so purposeless. Georgie stretches the ache in his left shoulder. He jams his hands in his pockets, and stares at the pile of newspapers as longingly as a man possibly can.

"They're for the family in Mexico."

Georgie looks up and there she is.

"Those newspapers have been sitting there for five months and we're just getting around to sending them to the little fan club my tías have started down there." Etiwanda's wearing a red blouse, a charcoal skirt, and matching red heels. Her curly hair is pinned up, piled atop her head like an assortment of dark exotic seashells. Georgie apologizes for being late and Etiwanda squeezes his arm and tells him it's all right. "It's really good to see you," she says. Along with her purse, she takes a white sash hanging from a hat rack, its words printed in black letters: SEÑORITA DE LAS AMERICAS.

She tells the woman that she might be home late. "I'll bring you a piece of cheese," Etiwanda says, and, without looking up from the envelope she's addressing, the woman tells her, "Don't do me any favors."

Georgie steps aside to let Etiwanda shut the door. "Would you believe that she's my sister?" she says. "I have to pay her to do this."

They walk out to the truck, Etiwanda's heels clicking on the concrete as they pass the blue Lincoln. Georgie asks how she got out of the obligation with the car dealership, and Etiwanda points to the tires and tells Georgie that she let the air out. "You can't drive a car with four flats," she says with a smile. "And it's not my fault if Mister Stoltz can't get someone out here to change them in time. Besides, Jorge will be grateful for the night off." Etiwanda explains that her cousin Jorge usually drives the Lincoln for her. "Jorge's seventeen and he's barely learned how to drive, but I lied and told Mister Stoltz that he's twenty-two. He's a good kid. Sometimes, I'll bring my case of 45s and Jorge will play them. He'll drive slow so the record won't skip, and I'll sit in the back and pretend that I'm a starlet." Etiwanda laughs and puts her hand over her mouth, looking around after she says this.

They get to the truck and Georgie explains about the driver door not opening. He slides across the seat and Etiwanda looks at the sheet skeptically before getting in. When she does, Georgie starts up the truck. The motor catches and Georgie puts both hands on the wheel. Before pulling away from the curb, he takes a deep breath that jabs a needle into his chest. He looks at Etiwanda, smiling and hoping she didn't notice. They drive past the tough guys on the corner, and one of them whistles. Another says something in Spanish that Georgie can't understand. Etiwanda blushes.

It's still hot when Etiwanda and Georgie arrive at a dimly lit restaurant on Rosemead Boulevard. The place is called The Chuck Wagon, and the hostess seats them in back, in a brown leather booth with a glass table laid over a wooden wagon wheel. A waitress arrives with menus, and

Georgie orders a Pabst. Etiwanda gets ice water. A few minutes later, Georgie gets winter food despite the heat, meat loaf with mashed potatoes and green beans on the side. Etiwanda decides on a Coke and a salad and the chicken-fried steak.

Alone, they sit silently in the racket of clanking dishes and other people's chatter. Etiwanda looks around. She shifts, apparently uncomfortable in her seat.

"What's wrong?" Georgie asks.

"I just noticed something," Etiwanda says. "Take a look at this place."

Georgie glances around The Chuck Wagon and doesn't see anything unusual. Their waitress is wiping the table two booths down. Across from them, a baby girl in a high chair throws a biscuit, striking the mural of smiling cowboys that runs the length of the restaurant. The baby claps with delight, oblivious to her scolding parents. The other waitress is busy behind the counter, filling the glass case with slices of cherry pie, and joking with the hostess who's changing the roll of paper in the cash register.

"What is it?"

It didn't occur to Georgie that everyone in the restaurant would be white, that there might be places in this world where you might not take a Mexican, even if she is a beauty queen.

"Never mind," Etiwanda says. "It's just me." She takes a sip of her water, and uses her napkin to carefully wipe away the lipstick print left on the glass. "I'm a little tired of all these official events." Etiwanda tells Georgie about her other obligations besides the Big Cheese and C.R.A. races. "The worst are the appearances at supermarkets and department stores," she says. "Every time I go to one of these functions, there will be some—" Etiwanda looks at Georgie and pauses to find the right word, "some person, some housewife or a group of teenage boys, someone who talks to me like I shouldn't understand English. When I answer them, they're always surprised. Last week, this old woman actually congratulated me on spelling her name right." Etiwanda laughs a little. "I guess I'm happy this whole 'Señorita' thing is only temporary."

Georgie asks what she plans on doing when it's all over. Etiwanda smiles and cocks her head as though a photo of her future is framed on the wall. "I think going to school would be nice."

"To study what?" Georgie asks.

"I'm not sure. I've always been good with numbers. Maybe business? Maybe accounting? All I know," she says, giving Georgie a quick glimpse of the tiara in her purse, "is that this won't last forever."

Georgie nods, and, in doing so, notices that Etiwanda is wearing the same silver necklace that she had in her newspaper photo. The necklace catches the light and he offers Etiwanda a drink of his beer, but she declines.

"I want you to call me Wanda," she says. "See, when we were kids, my family moved all around Riverside, and my dad named us for the different streets in the city because he was so happy to be in the States. Maggie's whole name is Magnolia, and we had a younger sister, God rest her soul, whose name was Madison."

Wanda makes the sign of the cross when she finishes. "Maggie's really jealous of all this beauty queen stuff," she says. "Maggie wanted to be the beauty queen in the Andrade family. She had won a title—Miss Teenage Casablanca—when she was sixteen. The year after, though, Maggie fooled around with this guy and his fiancée came after her with a bicycle chain. That's how she lost her eye."

Georgie says, "Ouch," and, in trying to make a joke, he manages to remind himself of his own pain. He takes two of the six aspirin in his shirt pocket and follows them with a swallow of beer. Wanda asks if he's all right and Georgie says, "Yeah, it's just the bruises from the crack-up. I'll be okay."

Wanda smirks.

"What?" Georgie asks.

"You and your 'crack-ups.' You're just like all the other guys."

Georgie can't recall the moment when the term entered his vocabulary, who exactly he learned it from. All he knows is that for as long as he's been behind the wheel, he's never used the word "accident" for any scrape he's been involved with.

"One of the first things you learn," Georgie says, "is that if anything bad happens, it's always the car's fault. Calling something an 'accident' says that things are out of your hands. It says that whatever happened wasn't what the driver intended to do. But drivers can't be wrong. You can't say you made a wrong decision on the track, because you'll start second-guessing yourself. It'll make you think too much, make you think about traveling that fast, make you think about how soft your body really is compared to everything else around it." Georgie goes quiet. He stares at the napkin dispenser and taps it with his fingernail. When he speaks, his mood is tainted, indignant. "You let that happen and you'll be too afraid to stick the key in the ignition."

"So the car always breaks down? Never the driver?" Wanda looks around the table as if the cowboys in the murals are eavesdropping. She leans in close to Georgie and moves the napkin dispenser aside, lowering her voice to a whisper. "Was it the car that drove into the wall last night? The car that was trying so hard for first place?"

Georgie slides back to his side of the booth and fights the urge to crawl under the table. Wanda takes his hands in hers. She rubs the rough calluses, the scars and burn marks on Georgie's hands. "Just between the two of us, is that what really happened?"

Georgie looks up. He shakes his head sheepishly.

"You ask me, I think you did the right thing," Wanda says. "The whole time I was up in the grandstands, I was hoping the winner would be you."

When the waitress brings the bill for dinner, Wanda asks her the time. It's a quarter to eight. Wanda gathers her things and Georgie pays, not bothering to wait for any change. Outside, the sun has almost finished setting. They get in the truck and Georgie fumbles with the names and directions of different surface streets until Wanda declares that the fastest way from The Chuck Wagon to Crawford's Market is on the expressway.

Down the street there's an entrance, and what little glare is left from the sundown finds its way into Georgie's eyes as the truck curves up the on-ramp. He presses the gas pedal hard and pumps the clutch to move the truck through its first few successive gears. The truck shudders, lurching forward as if someone yanked on the grille, and Georgie apologizes. Wanda simply smiles. Georgie checks his mirrors as the expressway approaches. He hangs his arm out the window to signal, and he sticks out his head to judge the space behind him.

Georgie merges into the first lane while Wanda removes her lipstick and compact from her purse. She holds the round mirror in her palm and works her lipstick with a calm and steady hand. She kisses a tissue and crumples it into a tiny ball, and she shows no signs of tension, no nervousness, no wringing fingers, nothing. In fact, Wanda's only annoyance seems to be the temperature. She rolls down her window, then turns the knob on the smaller one in the corner, pushing the small triangle of glass outward so that cool evening air begins to fill the cab.

The needle on the speedometer rises as the truck moves among the other automobiles. Sixty-five. Seventy-five. Eighty-five miles per hour. The engine is laboring under Georgie's foot and the steering wheel shudders in his hands. He closes both sets of fingers and ignores the pain by telling himself to hold on. Georgie had a crazy-son-of-a-bitch uncle named Leonard, a marine who returned from the South Pacific with a piston tattooed on the length of each forearm. Leonard taught Georgie to drive in the narrow and bumpy roads that separated the nearby fields. His chief advice to young Georgie was basic. "You let go of that wheel, and all hell will break loose. You hold on and you can beat anybody." Georgie recalls the fragrant tomatoes and the short trees filled with apples, recalls how it felt to have command over the machine slicing the green blur of the outside world in two. These are Georgie's earliest recollections of speed, of the tremendous burst of pleasure that surges through him when he knows he's faster than anyone else.

The Valley Boulevard exit approaches, less than a quarter mile away. Wanda takes her carefully folded sash from her purse and holds the band of white silk in her lap. Georgie changes lanes without looking, cutting left around a moving van, cutting right to avoid a slow-moving station wagon. He can tell exactly where the other cars are, remembers their positions around him, how fast they're going, and how much faster he needs to be, the calculations immediate and natural. Georgie can feel the engine working, the compression in each cylinder, the pistons rising and falling, falling and rising. He can feel the valves' delicate pitter-patter, the intake closing, the exhaust opening, each instantaneous and explosive stroke happening over and over and over again. Georgie's secured the truck's toil in his grip. He's not reckless. He's driving, and he's certain Wanda won't be late.

Eric Schlosser

Eric Schlosser was born in 1959 in New York. A journalist and author educated at Princeton and Oxford, he began his career working for *The Atlantic Monthly*. In addition to the popular *Fast Food Nation*, Schlosser wrote *Reefer Madness: Sex, Drugs, and Cheap Labor in the American Black Market* and the play *Americans*. He lives in Manhattan.

    Fast Food Nation: The Dark Side of the All-American Meal is an exposé of the fast food industry, which, according to Schlosser, has used political influence to increase profits at the expense of human health and fair labor practices. This excerpt discusses the first McDonald's restaurant, in San Bernardino.

from *Fast Food Nation*

Speedee Service

By the end of 1944, Carl Karcher owned four hot dog carts in Los Angeles. In addition to running the carts, he still worked full-time for the Armstrong Bakery. When a restaurant across the street from the Heinz farm went on sale, Carl decided to buy it. He quit the bakery, bought the restaurant, fixed it up, and spent a few weeks learning how to cook. On January 16, 1945, his twenty-eighth birthday, Carl's Drive-In Barbeque opened its doors. The restaurant was small, rectangular, and unexceptional, with red tiles on the roof. Its only hint of flamboyance was a five-pointed star atop the neon sign in the parking lot. During business hours, Carl did the cooking, Margaret worked behind the cash register, and carhops served most of the food. After closing time, Carl stayed late into the night, cleaning the bathrooms and mopping the floors. Once a week, he prepared the "special sauce" for his hamburgers, making it in huge kettles on the back porch of his house, stirring it with a stick and then pouring it into one-gallon jugs.

After World War II, business soared at Carl's Drive-In Barbeque, along with the economy of southern California. The oil business and the film business had thrived in Los Angeles during the 1920s and 1930s. But it was World War II that transformed southern California into the most important economic region in the West. The war's effect on the state, in the words of historian Carey McWilliams, was a "fabulous boom." Between 1940 and 1945, the federal government spent nearly $20 billion in California, mainly in and around Los Angeles, building airplane factories and steel mills, military bases and port facilities. During those six years, federal spending was responsible for nearly half of the personal income in southern California. By the end of World War II, Los Angeles was the second-largest manufacturing center in America, with an industrial output surpassed only by that of Detroit. While Hollywood garnered most of the headlines, defense spending remained the focus of the local economy for the next two decades, providing about one-third of its jobs.

The new prosperity enabled Carl and Margaret to buy a house five blocks away from their restaurant. They added more rooms as the family grew to include twelve children: nine girls and three boys. In the early 1950s Anaheim began to feel much less rural and remote. Walt Disney bought 160 acres of orange groves just a few miles from Carl's Drive-In Barbeque, chopped down the trees, and started to build Disneyland. In the neighboring town of Garden Grove, the Reverend Robert Schuller founded the nation's first Drive-in Church, preaching on Sunday mornings at a drive-in movie theater, spreading the Gospel through the little speakers at each parking space, attracting large crowds with the slogan "Worship as you are…in the family car." The city of Anaheim started to recruit defense contractors, eventually persuading Northrop, Boeing, and North American Aviation to build factories there. Anaheim soon became the fastest-growing city in the nation's fastest-growing state. Carl's Drive-In Barbeque thrived, and Carl thought its future was secure. And then he heard about a restaurant in the "Inland Empire," sixty miles east of Los Angeles, that was selling high-quality hamburgers for 15 cents each—20 cents less than what Carl charged. He drove to E Street in San Bernardino and saw the shape of things to come. Dozens of people were standing in line to buy bags of "McDonald's Famous Hamburgers."

Richard and Maurice McDonald had left New Hampshire for southern California at the start of the Depression, hoping to find jobs in Hollywood. They worked as set builders on the Columbia Film Studios back lot, saved their money, and bought a movie theater in Glendale. The theater was not a success. In 1937 they opened a drive-in restaurant in Pasadena, trying to cash in on the new craze, hiring three carhops and selling mainly hot dogs. A few years later they moved to a larger building on E Street in San Bernardino and opened the McDonald Brothers Burger Bar Drive-In. The new restaurant was located near a high school, employed twenty carhops, and promptly made the brothers rich. Richard and "Mac" McDonald bought one of the largest houses in San Bernardino, a hillside mansion with a tennis court and a pool.

By the end of the 1940s the McDonald brothers had grown dissatisfied with the drive-in business. They were tired of constantly looking for new carhops and short-order cooks—who were in great demand—as the old ones left for higher-paying jobs elsewhere. They were tired of replacing the dishes, glassware, and silverware their teenage customers constantly broke or ripped off. And they were tired of their teenage customers. The brothers thought about selling the restaurant. Instead, they tried something new.

The McDonalds fired all their carhops in 1948, closed their restaurant, installed larger grills, and reopened three months later with a radically new method of preparing food. It was designed to increase the speed, lower prices, and raise the volume of sales. The brothers eliminated almost two-thirds of the items on their old menu. They got rid of everything that had to be eaten with a knife, spoon, or fork. The only sandwiches now sold were hamburgers or cheeseburgers. The brothers got rid of their dishes and glassware, replacing them with paper cups, paper bags, and paper plates. They divided the food preparation into separate tasks performed by different workers. To fill a typical order, one person grilled the hamburger; another "dressed" and wrapped it; another prepared the milk shake; another made the fries; and another worked the counter. For the first time, the guiding principles of a factory assembly line were applied to a commercial kitchen. The new division of labor meant that a worker only had to be taught how to perform one task. Skilled and expensive short-order cooks were no longer necessary. All of the burgers were sold with the same condiments: ketchup, onions, mustard, and two pickles. No substitutions were allowed. The

McDonald brothers' Speedee Service System revolutionized the restaurant business. An ad of theirs seeking franchisees later spelled out the benefits of the system: "Imagine—No Carhops—No Waitresses—No Dishwashers—No Bus Boys—The McDonald's System is Self-Service!"

Richard McDonald designed a new building for the restaurant, hoping to make it easy to spot from the road. Though untrained as an architect, he came up with a design that was simple, memorable, and archetypal. On two sides of the roof he put golden arches, lit by neon at night, that from a distance formed the letter M. The building effortlessly fused advertising with architecture and spawned one of the most famous corporate logos in the world.

The Speedee Service System, however, got off to a rocky start. Customers pulled up to the restaurant and honked their horns, wondering what had happened to the carhops, still expecting to be served. People were not yet accustomed to waiting in line and getting their own food. Within a few weeks, however, the new system gained acceptance, as word spread about the low prices and good hamburgers. The McDonald brothers now aimed for a much broader clientele. They employed only young men, convinced that female workers would attract teenage boys to the restaurant and drive away other customers. Families soon lined up to eat at McDonald's. Company historian John F. Love explained the lasting significance of McDonald's new self-service system: "Working-class families could finally afford to feed their kids restaurant food."

San Bernardino at the time was an ideal setting for all sorts of cultural experimentation. The town was an odd melting-pot of agriculture and industry located on the periphery of the southern California boom, a place that felt out on the edge. Nicknamed "San Berdoo," it was full of citrus groves, but sat next door to the smokestacks and steel mills of Fontana. San Bernardino had just sixty thousand inhabitants, but millions of people passed through there every year. It was the last stop on Route 66, end of the line for truckers, tourists, and migrants from the East. Its main street was jammed with drive-ins and cheap motels. The same year the McDonald brothers opened their new self-service restaurant, a group of World War II veterans in San Berdoo, alienated by the dullness of civilian life, formed a local motorcycle club, borrowing the nickname of the U.S. Army's Eleventh Airborne Division: "Hell's Angels." The same town that gave the world the golden arches also gave it a biker gang that stood for a totally antithetical set of values. The Hell's Angels flaunted their dirtiness, celebrated disorder, terrified families and small children instead of trying to sell them burgers, took drugs, sold drugs, and injected into American pop culture an anger and a darkness and a fashion statement—T-shirts and torn jeans, black leather jackets and boots, long hair, facial hair, swastikas, silver skull rings and other satanic trinkets, earrings, nose rings, body piercings, and tattoos — that would influence a long line of rebels from Marlon Brando to Marilyn Manson. The Hell's Angels were the anti-McDonald's, the opposite of clean and cheery. They didn't care if you had a nice day, and yet were as deeply American in their own way as any purveyors of Speedee Service. San Bernardino in 1948 supplied the nation with a new yin and yang, new models of conformity and rebellion. "They get angry when they read about how filthy they are," Hunter Thompson later wrote of the Hell's Angels, "but instead of shoplifting some deodorant, they strive to become even filthier."

Burgerville USA

After visiting San Bernardino and seeing the long lines at McDonald's, Carl Karcher went home to Anaheim and decided to open his own self-service restaurant. Carl instinctively grasped that the new car culture would forever change America. He saw what was coming, and his timing was perfect. The first Carl's Jr. restaurant opened in 1956—the same year that America got its first shopping mall and that Congress passed the Interstate Highway Act. President Dwight D. Eisenhower had pushed hard for such a bill; during World War II, he'd been enormously impressed by Adolf Hitler's Reichsautobahn, the world's first superhighway system. The Interstate Highway Act brought autobahns to the United States and became the largest public works project in the nation's history, building 46,000 miles of road with more than $130 billion of federal money. The new highways spurred car sales, truck sales, and the construction of new suburban homes. Carl's first self-service restaurant was a success, and he soon opened others near California's new freeway off-ramps. The star atop his drive-in sign became the mascot of his fast food chain. It was a smiling star in little booties, holding a burger and a shake.

Entrepreneurs from all over the country went to San Bernardino, visited the new McDonald's, and built imitations of the restaurant in their hometowns. "Our food was exactly the same as McDonald's," the founder of a rival chain later admitted. "If I had looked at McDonald's and saw someone flipping hamburgers while he was hanging by his feet, I would have copied it." America's fast food chains were not launched by large corporations relying upon focus groups and market research. They were started by door-to-door salesmen, short-order cooks, orphans, and dropouts, by eternal optimists looking for a piece of the next big thing. The start-up costs of a fast food restaurant were low, the profit margins promised to be high, and a wide assortment of ambitious people were soon buying grills and putting up signs.

William Rosenberg dropped out of school at the age of fourteen, delivered telegrams for Western Union, drove an ice cream truck, worked as a door-to-door salesman, sold sandwiches and coffee to factory workers in Boston, and then opened a small doughnut shop in 1948, later calling it Dunkin' Donuts. Glen W. Bell, Jr., was a World War II veteran, a resident of San Bernardino who ate at the new McDonald's and decided to copy it, using the assembly-line system to make Mexican food and founding a restaurant chain later known as Taco Bell. Keith G. Cramer, the owner of Keith's Drive-In Restaurant in Daytona Beach, Florida, heard about the McDonald brothers' new restaurant, flew to southern California, ate at McDonald's, returned to Florida, and with his father-in-law, Matthew Burns, opened the first Insta-Burger-King in 1953. Dave Thomas started working in a restaurant at the age of twelve, left his adoptive father, took a room at the YMCA, dropped out of school at fifteen, served as a busboy and a cook, and eventually opened his own place in Columbus, Ohio, calling it Wendy's Old-Fashioned Hamburgers restaurant. Thomas S. Monaghan spent much of his childhood in a Catholic orphanage and a series of foster homes, worked as a soda jerk, barely graduated from high school, joined the Marines, and bought a pizzeria in Ypsilanti, Michigan, with his brother, securing the deal through a down payment of $75. Eight months later Monaghan's brother decided to quit and accepted a used Volkswagen Beetle for his share of a business later known as Domino's.

The story of Harland Sanders is perhaps the most remarkable. Sanders left school at the age of twelve, worked as a farm hand, a mule tender, and a railway fireman. At various times he worked as a lawyer without having a law degree, delivered babies as a part-time obstetrician without having a medical degree, sold insurance door to door, sold Michelin tires, and operated a gas station in Corbin, Kentucky. He served home-cooked food at a small dining-room table in the back, later opened a popular restaurant and motel, sold them to pay off debts, and at the age of sixty-five became a traveling salesman once again, offering restaurant owners the "secret recipe" for his fried chicken. The first Kentucky Fried Chicken restaurant opened in 1952, near Salt Lake City, Utah. Lacking money to promote the new chain, Sanders dressed up like a Kentucky colonel, sporting a white suit and a black string tie. By the early 1960s, Kentucky Fried Chicken was the largest restaurant chain in the United States, and Colonel Sanders was a household name. In his autobiography, *Life As I Have Known It Has Been "Finger-lickin' Good,"* Sanders described his ups and downs, his decision at the age of seventy-four to be rebaptized and born again, his lifelong struggle to stop cursing. Despite his best efforts and a devout faith in Christ, Harland Sanders admitted that it was still awfully hard "not to call a no-good, lazy, incompetent, dishonest s.o.b. by anything else but his rightful name."

For every fast food idea that swept the nation, there were countless others that flourished briefly—or never had a prayer. There were chains with homey names, like Sandy's, Carrol's, Henry's, Winky's, and Mr. Fifteen's. There were chains with futuristic names, like the Satellite Hamburger System and Kelly's Jet System. Most of all, there were chains named after their main dish: Burger Chefs, Burger Queens, Burgerville USAs, Yumy Burgers, Twitty Burgers, Whataburgers, Dundee Burgers, Buff-Burgers, O.K. Big Burgers, and Burger Boy Food-O-Ramas.

Many of the new restaurants advertised an array of technological wonders. Carhops were rendered obsolete by various remote-control ordering systems, like the Fone-A-Chef, the Teletray, and the ElectroHop. The Motormat was an elaborate rail system that transported food and beverages from the kitchen to parked cars. At the Biff-Burger chain, Biff-Burgers were "roto-broiled" beneath glowing quartz tubes that worked just like a space heater. Insta-Burger-King restaurants featured a pair of "Miracle Insta Machines," one to make milk shakes, the other to cook burgers. "Both machines have been *thoroughly perfected*," the company assured prospective franchisees, "are of foolproof design—can be easily operated even by a moron." The InstaBurger Stove was an elaborate contraption. Twelve hamburger patties entered it in individual wire baskets, circled two electric heating elements, got cooked on both sides, and then slid down a chute into a pan of sauce, while hamburger buns toasted in a nearby slot. This Miracle Insta Machine proved overly complex, frequently malfunctioned, and was eventually abandoned by the Burger King chain.

The fast food wars in southern California—the birthplace of Jack in the Box, as well as McDonald's, Taco Bell, and Carl's Jr.—were especially fierce. One by one, most of the old drive-ins closed, unable to compete against the less expensive, self-service burger joints. But Carl kept at it, opening new restaurants up and down the state, following the new freeways. Four of these freeways—the Riverside, the Santa Ana, the Costa Mesa, and the Orange—soon passed through Anaheim. Although Carl's Jr. was a great success, a few of Carl's other ideas should have remained on the drawing board. Carl's Whistle Stops featured employees dressed as railway workers, "Hobo Burgers," and toy electric trains that took orders to the kitchen. Three were built in 1966 and then converted to Carl's Jr. restaurants a few years later. A coffee shop chain with a Scottish theme also never found its niche. The waitresses at "Scot's" wore plaid skirts, and the dishes had unfortunate names, such as "The Clansman."

The leading fast food chains spread nationwide; between 1960 and 1973, the number of McDonald's restaurants grew from roughly 250 to 3,000. The Arab oil embargo of 1973 gave the fast food industry a bad scare, as long lines at gas stations led many to believe that America's car culture was endangered. Amid gasoline shortages, the value of McDonald's stock fell. When the crisis passed, fast food stock prices recovered, and McDonald's intensified its efforts to open urban, as well as suburban, restaurants. Wall Street invested heavily in the fast food chains, and corporate managers replaced many of the early pioneers. What had begun as a series of small, regional businesses became a fast food industry, a major component of the American economy.

Joan Didion

Joan Didion was born in 1934 in Sacramento. A renowned journalist, playwright, essayist, and novelist, she has focused much of her writing on her life in California. Her major works include *Play It As It Lays*, *The White Album*, *Where I Was From*, *Slouching Towards Bethlehem*, and the 2005 National Book Award winner *The Year of Magical Thinking*. Didion lives in New York City.

"Some Dreamers of the Golden Dream," about a woman accused of murder in the 1960s in the San Bernardino Valley, appeared first in *The Saturday Evening Post* as "How Can I Tell Them There's Nothing Left" and is included in Didion's 1968 collection of essays *Slouching Towards Bethlehem*.

Some Dreamers of the Golden Dream

This is a story about love and death in the golden land, and begins with the country. The San Bernardino Valley lies only an hour east of Los Angeles by the San Bernardino Freeway but is in certain ways an alien place: not the coastal California of the subtropical twilights and the soft westerlies off the Pacific but a harsher California, haunted by the Mojave just beyond the mountains, devastated by the hot dry Santa Ana wind that comes down through the passes at 100 miles an hour and whines through the eucalyptus windbreaks and works on the nerves. October is the bad month for the wind, the month when breathing is difficult and the hills blaze up spontaneously. There has been no rain since April. Every voice seems a scream. It is the season of suicide and divorce and prickly dread, wherever the wind blows.

The Mormons settled this ominous country, and then they abandoned it, but by the time they left, the first orange tree had been planted and for the next hundred years the San Bernardino Valley would draw a kind of people who imagined they might live among the talismanic fruit and prosper in the dry air, people who brought with them Midwestern ways of building and cooking and praying and who tried to graft those ways upon the land. The graft took in curious ways. This is the California where it is possible to live and die without ever eating an artichoke, without ever meeting a Catholic or a Jew. This is the California where it is easy to Dial-A-Devotion, but hard to buy a book. This is the country in which a belief in the literal interpretation of Genesis has slipped imperceptibly into a belief in the literal interpretation of *Double Indemnity,* the country of the teased hair and the Capris and the girls for whom all life's promise comes down to a waltz-length white wedding dress and the birth of a Kimberly or a Sherry or a Debbi and a Tijuana divorce and a return to hairdressers' school. "We were just crazy kids," they say without regret, and look to the future. The future always looks good in the golden land, because no one remembers the past. Here is where the hot wind blows and the old ways do not seem relevant, where the divorce rate is double the national average and where one person in every thirty-eight lives in a trailer. Here is the last stop for all those who come from somewhere else, for all those who drifted away from the cold and the past and the old ways. Here is where they are trying to find a new life style, trying to find it in the only places they know to look: the movies and the newspapers. The case of Lucille Marie Maxwell Miller is a tabloid monument to that new life style.

Imagine Banyan Street first, because Banyan is where it happened. The way to Banyan is to drive west from San Bernardino out Foothill Boulevard, Route 66: past the Santa Fe switching yards, the Forty Winks Motel. Past the motel that is nineteen stucco tepees: "SLEEP IN A WIGWAM—GET MORE FOR YOUR WAMPUM." Past Fontana Drag City and the Fontana Church of the Nazarene and the Pit Stop A Go-Go; past Kaiser Steel, through Cucamonga, out to the Kapu Kai Restaurant-Bar and Coffee Shop, at the corner of Route 66 and Carnelian Avenue. Up Carnelian Avenue from the Kapu Kai, which means "Forbidden Seas," the subdivision flags whip in the harsh wind. "HALF-ACRE RANCHES! SNACK BARS! TRAVERTINE ENTRIES! $95 DOWN." It is the trail of an intention gone haywire, the flotsam of the New California. But after a while the signs thin out on Carnelian Avenue, and the houses are no longer the bright pastels of the Springtime Home owners but the faded bungalows of the people who grow a few grapes and keep a few chickens out here, and then the hill gets steeper and the road climbs and even the bungalows are few, and here—desolate, roughly surfaced, lined with eucalyptus and lemon grove—is Banyan Street.

Like so much of this country, Banyan suggests something curious and unnatural. The lemon groves are sunken, down a three- or four-foot retaining wall, so that one looks directly into their dense foliage, too lush, unsettlingly glossy, the greenery of nightmare; the fallen eucalyptus bark is too dusty, a place for snakes to breed. The stones look not like natural stones but like the rubble of some unmentioned upheaval. There are smudge pots, and a closed cistern. To one side of Banyan there is the flat valley, and to the other the San Bernardino Mountains, a dark mass looming too high, too fast, nine, ten, eleven thousand feet, right there above the lemon groves. At midnight on Banyan Street there is no light at all, and no sound except the wind in the eucalyptus and a muffled barking of dogs. There may be a kennel somewhere, or the dogs may be coyotes.

Banyan Street was the route Lucille Miller took home from the twenty-four-hour Mayfair Market on the night of October 7, 1964, a night when the moon was dark and the wind was blowing and she was out of milk, and Banyan Street was where, at about 12:30 a.m., her 1964 Volkswagen came to a sudden stop, caught fire, and began to burn. For an hour and fifteen minutes Lucille Miller ran up and down Banyan calling for help, but no cars passed and no help came. At three o'clock that morning, when the fire had been put out and the California Highway Patrol officers were completing their report, Lucille Miller was still sobbing and incoherent, for her husband had been asleep in the Volkswagen. "What will I tell the children, when there's nothing left, nothing left in the casket," she cried to the friend called to comfort her. "How can I tell them there's nothing left?"

In fact there was something left, and a week later it lay in the Draper Mortuary Chapel in a closed bronze coffin blanketed with pink carnations. Some 200 mourners heard Elder Robert E. Denton of the Seventh-Day Adventist Church of Ontario speak of "the temper of fury that has broken out among us." For Gordon Miller, he said, there would be "no more death, no more heartaches, no more misunderstandings." Elder Ansel Bristol mentioned the "peculiar" grief of the hour. Elder Fred Jensen asked "what shall it profit a man, if he shall gain the whole world, and lose his own soul?" A light rain fell, a blessing in a dry season, and a female vocalist sang "Safe in the Arms of Jesus." A tape recording of the service was made for the widow, who was being held without bail in the San Bernardino County Jail on a charge of first-degree murder.

Of course she came from somewhere else, came off the prairie in search of something she had seen in a movie or heard on the radio, for this is a Southern California story. She was born on January 17, 1930, in Winnipeg, Manitoba, the only child of Gordon and Lily Maxwell, both schoolteachers and both dedicated to the Seventh-Day Adventist Church, whose members observe the Sabbath on Saturday, believe in an apocalyptic Second Coming, have a strong missionary tendency, and, if they are strict, do not smoke, drink, eat meat, use makeup, or wear jewelry, including wedding rings. By the time Lucille Maxwell enrolled at Walla Walla College in College Place, Washington, the Adventist school where her parents then taught, she was an eighteen-year-old possessed of unremarkable good looks and remarkable high spirits. "Lucille wanted to see the world," her father would say in retrospect, "and I guess she found out."

The high spirits did not seem to lend themselves to an extended course of study at Walla Walla College, and in the spring of 1949 Lucille Maxwell met and married Gordon ("Cork") Miller, a twenty-four-year-old graduate of Walla Walla and of the University of Oregon dental school, then stationed at Fort Lewis as a medical officer. "Maybe you could say it was love at first sight," Mr. Maxwell recalls. "Before they were ever formally introduced, he sent Lucille a dozen and a half roses with a card that said even if she didn't come out on a date with him, he hoped she'd find the roses pretty anyway." The Maxwells remember their daughter as a "radiant" bride.

Unhappy marriages so resemble one another that we do not need to know too much about the course of this one. There may or may not have been trouble on Guam, where Cork and Lucille Miller lived while he finished his Army duty. There may or may not have been problems in the small Oregon town where he first set up private practice. There appears to have been some disappointment about their move to California: Cork Miller had told friends that he wanted to become a doctor, that he was unhappy as a dentist and planned to enter the Seventh-Day Adventist College of Medical Evangelists at Loma Linda, a few miles south of San Bernardino. Instead he bought a dental practice in the west end of San Bernardino County, and the family settled there, in a modest house on the kind of street where there are always tricycles and revolving credit and dreams about bigger houses, better streets. That was 1957. By the summer of 1964 they had achieved the bigger house on the better street and the familiar accouterments of a family on its way up: the $30,000 a year, the three children for the Christmas card, the picture window, the family room, the newspaper photographs that showed "Mrs. Gordon Miller, Ontario Heart Fund Chairman..." They were paying the familiar price for it. And they had reached the familiar season of divorce.

It might have been anyone's bad summer, anyone's siege of heat and nerves and migraine and money worries, but this one began particularly early and particularly badly. On April 24 an old friend, Elaine Hayton, died suddenly; Lucille Miller had seen her only the night before. During the month of May, Cork Miller was hospitalized briefly with a bleeding ulcer, and his usual reserve deepened into depression. He told his accountant that he was "sick of looking at open mouths," and threatened suicide. By July 8, the conventional tensions of love and money had reached the conventional impasse in the new house on the acre lot at 8488 Bella Vista, and Lucille Miller filed for divorce. Within a month, however, the Millers seemed reconciled. They saw a marriage counselor. They talked about a fourth child. It seemed that the marriage had reached the traditional truce, the point at which so many resign themselves to cutting both their losses and their hopes.

But the Millers' season of trouble was not to end that easily. October 7 began as a commonplace enough day, one of those days that sets the teeth on edge with its tedium, its small frustrations. The temperature reached 102° in San Bernardino that afternoon, and the Miller children were home from school because of Teachers' Institute. There was ironing to be dropped off. There was a trip to pick up a prescription for Nembutal, a trip to a self-service dry cleaner. In the early evening, an unpleasant accident with the Volkswagen: Cork Miller hit and killed a German shepherd, and afterward said that his head felt "like it had a Mack truck on it." It was something he often said. As of that evening Cork Miller was $63,479 in debt, including the $29,637 mortgage on the new house, a debt load which seemed oppressive to him. He was a man who wore his responsibilities uneasily, and complained of migraine headaches almost constantly.

He ate alone that night, from a TV tray in the living room. Later the Millers watched John Forsythe and Senta Berger in *See How They Run*, and when the movie ended, about eleven, Cork Miller suggested that they go out for milk. He wanted some hot chocolate. He took a blanket and pillow from the couch and climbed into the passenger seat of the Volkswagen. Lucille Miller remembers reaching over to lock his door as she backed down the driveway. By the time she left the Mayfair Market, and long before they reached Banyan Street, Cork Miller appeared to be asleep.

There is some confusion in Lucille Miller's mind about what happened between 12:30 a.m., when the fire broke out, and 1:50 a.m., when it was reported. She says that she was driving east on Banyan Street at about 35 m.p.h. when she felt the Volkswagen pull sharply to the right. The next thing she knew the car was on the embankment, quite near the edge of the retaining wall, and flames were shooting up behind her. She does not remember jumping out. She does remember prying up a stone with which she broke the window next to her husband, and then scrambling down the retaining wall to try to find a stick. "1 don't know how I was going to push him out," she says. "I just thought if I had a stick, I'd push him out." She could not, and after a while she ran to the intersection of Banyan and Carnelian Avenue. There are no houses at that corner, and almost no traffic. After one car had passed without stopping, Lucille Miller ran back down Banyan toward the burning Volkswagen. She did not stop, but she slowed down, and in the flames she could see her husband. He was, she said, "just black."

At the first house up Sapphire Avenue, half a mile from the Volkswagen, Lucille Miller finally found help. There Mrs. Robert Swenson called the sheriff, and then, at Lucille Miller's request, she called Harold Lance, the Millers' lawyer and their close friend. When Harold Lance arrived he took Lucille Miller home to his wife, Joan. Twice Harold Lance and Lucille Miller returned to Banyan Street and talked to the Highway Patrol officers. A third time Harold Lance returned alone, and when he came back he said to Lucille Miller, "O.K....you don't talk any more."

When Lucille Miller was arrested the next afternoon, Sandy Slagle was with her. Sandy Slagle was the intense, relentlessly loyal medical student who used to baby-sit for the Millers, and had been living as a member of the family since she graduated from high school in 1959. The Millers took her away from a difficult home situation, and she thinks of Lucille Miller not only as "more or less a mother or a sister" but as "the most wonderful character" she has ever known. On the night of the accident, Sandy Slagle was in her dormitory at Loma Linda University, but Lucille Miller called her early in the morning and asked her to come home. The doctor was there when Sandy Slagle arrived, giving Lucille Miller an injection of Nembutal. "She was crying as she was going under," Sandy Slagle recalls. "Over and over she'd say, 'Sandy, all the hours I spent trying to save him and now what are they trying to *do* to me?'"

At 1:30 that afternoon, Sergeant William Paterson and Detectives Charles Callahan and Joseph Karr of the Central Homicide Division arrived at 8488 Bella Vista. "One of them appeared at the bedroom door," Sandy Slagle remembers, "and said to Lucille, 'You've got ten minutes to get dressed or we'll take you as you are.' She was in her nightgown, you know, so I tried to get her dressed."

Sandy Slagle tells the story now as if by rote, and her eyes do not waver. "So I had her panties and bra on her and they opened the door again, so I got some Capris on her, you know, and a scarf." Her voice drops. "And then they just took her."

The arrest took place just twelve hours after the first report that there had been an accident on Banyan Street, a rapidity which would later prompt Lucille Miller's attorney to say that the entire case was an instance of trying to justify a reckless arrest. Actually what first caused the detectives who arrived on Banyan Street toward dawn that morning to give the accident more than routine attention were certain apparent physical inconsistencies. While Lucille Miller had said that she was driving about 35 m.p.h. when the car swerved to a stop, an examination of the cooling Volkswagen showed that it was in low gear, and that the parking rather than the driving lights were on. The front wheels, moreover, did not seem to be in exactly the position that Lucille Miller's description of the accident would suggest, and the right rear wheel was dug in deep, as if it had been spun in place. It seemed curious to the detectives, too, that a sudden stop from 35 m.p.h.—the same jolt which was presumed to have knocked over a gasoline can in the back seat and somehow started the fire—should have left two milk cartons upright on the back floorboard, and the remains of a Polaroid camera box lying apparently undisturbed on the back seat.

No one, however, could be expected to give a precise account of what did and did not happen in a moment of terror, and none of these inconsistencies seemed in themselves incontrovertible evidence of criminal intent. But they did interest the Sheriff's Office, as did Gordon Miller's apparent unconsciousness at the time of the accident, and the length of time it had taken Lucille Miller to get help. Something, moreover, struck the investigators as wrong about Harold Lance's attitude when he came back to Banyan Street the third time and found the investigation by no means over. "The way Lance was acting," the prosecuting attorney said later, "they thought maybe they'd hit a nerve."

And so it was that on the morning of October 8, even before the doctor had come to give Lucille Miller an injection to calm her, the San Bernardino County Sheriff's Office was trying to construct another version of what might have happened between 12:30 and 1:50 a.m. The hypothesis they would eventually present was based on the somewhat tortuous premise that Lucille Miller had undertaken a plan which failed: a plan to stop the car on the lonely road, spread gasoline over her presumably drugged husband, and, with a stick on the accelerator, gently "walk" the Volkswagen over the embankment, where it would tumble four feet down the retaining wall into the lemon grove and almost certainly explode. If this happened, Lucille Miller might then have somehow negotiated the two miles up Carnelian to Bella Vista in time to be home when the accident was discovered. This plan went awry, according to the Sheriff's Office hypothesis, when the car would not go over the rise of the embankment. Lucille Miller might have panicked then—after she had killed the engine the third or fourth time, say, out there on the dark road with the gasoline already spread and the dogs baying and the wind blowing and the unspeakable apprehension that a pair of headlights would suddenly light up Banyan Street and expose her there—and set the fire herself.

Although this version accounted for some of the physical evidence—the car in low because it had been started from a dead stop, the parking lights on because she could not do what needed doing without some light, a rear wheel spun in repeated attempts to get the car over the embankment, the milk cartons upright because there had been no sudden stop—it did not seem on its own any more or less credible than Lucille Miller's own story. Moreover, some of the physical evidence did seem to support her story: a nail in a front tire, a nine-pound rock found in the car, presumably the one with which she had broken the window in an attempt to save her husband. Within a few days an autopsy had established that Gordon Miller was alive when he burned, which did not particularly help the State's case, and that he had enough Nembutal and Sandoptal in his blood to put the average person to sleep, which did: on the other hand Gordon Miller habitually took both Nembutal and Fiorinal (a common headache prescription which contains Sandoptal), and had been ill besides.

It was a spotty case, and to make it work at all the State was going to have to find a motive. There was talk of unhappiness, talk of another man. That kind of motive, during the next few weeks, was what they set out to establish. They set out to find it in accountants' ledgers and double-indemnity clauses and motel registers, set out to determine what might move a woman who believed in all the promises of the middle class—a woman who had been chairman of the Heart Fund and who always knew a reasonable little dressmaker and who had come out of the bleak wild of prairie fundamentalism to find what she imagined to be the good life—what should drive such a woman to sit on a street called Bella Vista and look out her new picture window into the empty California sun and calculate how to burn her husband alive in a Volkswagen. They found the wedge they wanted closer at hand than they might have at first expected, for, as testimony would reveal later at the trial, it seemed that in December of 1963 Lucille Miller had begun an affair with the husband of one of her friends, a man whose daughter called her "Auntie Lucille," a man who might have seemed to have the gift for people and money and the good life that Cork Miller so noticeably lacked. The man was Arthwell Hayton, a well-known San Bernardino attorney and at one time a member of the district attorney's staff.

In some ways it was the conventional clandestine affair in a place like San Bernardino, a place where little is bright or graceful, where it is routine to misplace the future and easy to start looking for it in bed. Over the seven weeks that it would take to try Lucille Miller for murder, Assistant District Attorney Don A. Turner and defense attorney Edward P. Foley would between them unfold a curiously predictable story. There were the falsified motel registrations. There were the lunch dates; the afternoon drives in Arthwell Hayton's red Cadillac convertible. There were the interminable discussions of the wronged partners. There were the confidantes ("I knew everything," Sandy Slagle would insist fiercely later. "I knew every time, places, everything") and there were the words remembered from bad magazine stories ("Don't kiss me, it will trigger things," Lucille Miller remembered telling Arthwell Hayton in the parking lot of Harold's Club in Fontana after lunch one day) and there were the notes, the sweet exchanges: "Hi Sweetie Pie! You are my cup of tea!! Happy Birthday—you don't look a day over 29!! Your baby, Arthwell."

And, toward the end, there was the acrimony. It was April 24, 1964, when Arthwell Hayton's wife, Elaine, died suddenly, and nothing good happened after that. Arthwell Hayton had taken his cruiser, *Captain's Lady*, over to Catalina that weekend; he called home at nine o'clock

Friday night, but did not talk to his wife because Lucille Miller answered the telephone and said that Elaine was showering. The next morning the Haytons' daughter found her mother in bed, dead. The newspapers reported the death as accidental, perhaps the result of an allergy to hair spray. When Arthwell Hayton flew home from Catalina that weekend, Lucille Miller met him at the airport, but the finish had already been written.

It was in the breakup that the affair ceased to be in the conventional mode and began to resemble instead the novels of James M. Cain, the movies of the late 1930s, all the dreams in which violence and threats and blackmail are made to seem commonplaces of middle-class life. What was most startling about the case that the State of California was preparing against Lucille Miller was something that had nothing to do with law at all, something that never appeared in the eight-column afternoon headlines but was always there between them: the revelation that the dream was teaching the dreamers how to live. Here is Lucille Miller talking to her lover sometime in the early summer of 1964, after he had indicated that, on the advice of his minister, he did not intend to see her any more: "First, I'm going to go to that dear pastor of yours and tell him a few things…When I do tell him that, you won't be in the Redlands Church any more…Look, Sonny Boy, if you think your reputation is going to be ruined, your life won't be worth two cents." Here is Arthwell Hayton, to Lucille Miller: "I'll go to Sheriff Frank Bland and tell him some things that I know about you until you'll wish you'd never heard of Arthwell Hayton." For an affair between a Seventh-Day Adventist dentist's wife and a Seventh-Day Adventist personal-injury lawyer, it seems a curious kind of dialogue.

"Boy, I could get that little boy coming and going," Lucille Miller later confided to Erwin Sprengle, a Riverside contractor who was a business partner of Arthwell Hayton's and a friend to both the lovers. (Friend or no, on this occasion he happened to have an induction coil attached to his telephone in order to tape Lucille Miller's call.) "And he hasn't got one thing on me that he can prove. I mean, I've got concrete —he has nothing concrete." In the same taped conversation with Erwin Sprengle, Lucille Miller mentioned a tape that she herself had surreptitiously made, months before, in Arthwell Hayton's car.

"I said to him, I said, 'Arthwell, I just feel like I'm being used.'…He started sucking his thumb and he said, 'I love you…This isn't something that happened yesterday. I'd marry you tomorrow if I could. I don't love Elaine.' He'd love to hear that played back, wouldn't he?"

"Yeah," drawled Sprengle's voice on the tape. "That would be just a little incriminating, wouldn't it?"

"Just a *little* incriminating," Lucille Miller agreed. "It really *is*."

Later on the tape, Sprengle asked where Cork Miller was.

"He took the children down to the church."

"You didn't go?"

"No."

"You're naughty."

It was all, moreover, in the name of "love"; everyone involved placed a magical faith in the efficacy of the very word. There was the significance that Lucille Miller saw in Arthwell's saying that he "loved" her, that he did not "love" Elaine. There was Arthwell insisting, later, at the trial, that he had never said it, that he may have "whispered sweet nothings in her ear" (as her defense hinted that he had whispered in many ears), but he did not remember bestowing upon her the special seal, saying the word, declaring "love." There was the summer evening when Lucille Miller and Sandy Slagle followed Arthwell Hayton down to his new boat in its mooring at Newport Beach and untied the lines with Arthwell aboard, Arthwell and a girl with whom he later testified he was drinking hot chocolate and watching television. "I did that on purpose," Lucille Miller told Erwin Sprengle later, "to save myself from letting my heart do something crazy."

January 11, 1965, was a bright warm day in Southern California, the kind of day when Catalina floats on the Pacific horizon and the air smells of orange blossoms and it is a long way from the bleak and difficult East, a long way from the cold, a long way from the past. A woman in Hollywood staged an all-night sit-in on the hood of her car to prevent repossession by a finance company. A seventy-year-old pensioner drove his station wagon at five miles an hour past three Gardena poker parlors and emptied three pistols and a twelve-gauge shotgun through their windows, wounding twenty-nine people. "Many young women become prostitutes just to have enough money to play cards," he explained in a note. Mrs. Nick Adams said that she was "not surprised" to hear her husband announce his divorce plans on the Les Crane Show, and, farther north, a sixteen-year-old jumped off the Golden Gate Bridge and lived.

And, in the San Bernardino County Courthouse, the Miller trial opened. The crowds were so bad that the glass courtroom doors were shattered in the crush, and from then on identification disks were issued to the first forty-three spectators in line. The line began forming at 6 a.m., and college girls camped at the courthouse all night, with stores of graham crackers and No-Cal.

All they were doing was picking a jury, those first few days, but the sensational nature of the case had already suggested itself. Early in December there had been an abortive first trial, a trial at which no evidence was ever presented because on the day the jury was seated the San Bernardino *Sun-Telegram* ran an "inside" story quoting Assistant District Attorney Don Turner, the prosecutor, as saying, "We are looking into the circumstances of Mrs. Hayton's death. In view of the current trial concerning the death of Dr. Miller, I do not feel I should comment on Mrs. Hayton's death." It seemed that there had been barbituates in Elaine Hayton's blood, and there had seemed some irregularity about the way she was dressed on that morning when she was found under the covers, dead. Any doubts about the death at the time, however, had never gotten as far as the Sheriff's Office. "I guess somebody didn't want to rock the boat," Turner said later. "These were prominent people."

Although all of that had not been in the *Sun-Telegram's* story, an immediate mistrial had been declared. Almost as immediately, there had been another development: Arthwell Hayton had asked newspapermen to an 11 a.m. Sunday morning press conference in his office. There had been television cameras, and flash bulbs popping. "As you gentlemen may know," Hayton had said, striking a note of stiff bonhomie, "there are very often women who become amorous toward their doctor or lawyer. This does not mean on the physician's or lawyer's part that there is any romance toward the patient or client."

"Would you deny that you were having an affair with Mrs. Miller?" a reporter had asked.

"I would deny that there was any romance on my part whatsoever."

It was a distinction he would maintain through all the wearing weeks to come.

So they had come to see Arthwell, these crowds who now milled beneath the dusty palms outside the courthouse, and they had also come to see Lucille, who appeared as a slight, intermittently pretty woman, already pale from lack of sun, a woman who would turn thirty-five before the trial was over and whose tendency toward haggardness was beginning to show, a meticulous woman who insisted, against her lawyer's advice, on coming to court with her hair piled high and lacquered. "I would've been happy if she'd come in with it hanging loose, but Lucille wouldn't do that," her lawyer said. He was Edward P. Foley, a small, emotional Irish Catholic who several times wept in the court-room. "She has a great honesty, this woman," he added, "but this honesty about her appearance always worked against her."

By the time the trial opened, Lucille Miller's appearance included maternity clothes, for an official examination on December 18 had revealed that she was then three and a half months pregnant, a fact which made picking a jury even more difficult than usual, for Turner was asking the death penalty. "It's unfortunate but there it is," he would say of the pregnancy to each juror in turn, and finally twelve were seated, seven of them women, the youngest forty-one, an assembly of the very peers—housewives, a machinist, a truck driver, a grocery-store manager, a filing clerk—above whom Lucille Miller had wanted so badly to rise.

That was the sin, more than the adultery, which tended to reinforce the one for which she was being tried. It was implicit in both the defense and the prosecution that Lucille Miller was an erring woman, a woman who perhaps wanted too much. But to the prosecution she was not merely a woman who would want a new house and want to go to parties and run up high telephone bills ($1,152 in ten months), but a woman who would go so far as to murder her husband for his $80,000 in insurance, making it appear an accident in order to collect another $40,000 in double indemnity and straight accident policies. To Turner she was a woman who did not want simply her freedom and a reasonable alimony (she could have had that, the defense contended, by going through with her divorce suit), but wanted everything, a woman motivated by "love and greed." She was a "manipulator." She was a "user of people."

To Edward Foley, on the other hand, she was an impulsive woman who "couldn't control her foolish little heart." Where Turner skirted the pregnancy, Foley dwelt upon it, even calling the dead man's mother down from Washington to testify that her son had told her they were going to have another baby because Lucille felt that it would "do much to weld our home again in the pleasant relations that we used to have." Where the prosecution saw a "calculator," the defense saw a "blabber-mouth," and in fact Lucille Miller did emerge as an ingenuous conversationalist. Just as, before her husband's death, she had confided in her friends about her love affair, so she chatted about it after his death, with the arresting sergeant. "Of course Cork lived with it for years, you know," her voice was heard to tell Sergeant Paterson on a tape made the morning after her arrest. "After Elaine died, he pushed the panic button one night and just asked me right out, and that, I think, was when he really—the first time he really faced it." When the sergeant asked why she had agreed to talk to him, against the specific instructions of her lawyers, Lucille Miller said airily, "Oh, I've always been basically quite an honest person...I mean I can put a hat in the cupboard and say it cost ten dollars less, but basically I've always kind of just lived my life the way I wanted to, and if you don't like it you can take off."

The prosecution hinted at men other than Arthwell, and even, over Foley's objections, managed to name one. The defense called Miller suicidal. The prosecution produced experts who said that the Volkswagen fire could not have been accidental. Foley produced witnesses who said that it could have been. Lucille's father, now a junior-high-school teacher in Oregon, quoted Isaiah to reporters: "*Every tongue that shall rise against thee in judgment thou shalt condemn.*" "Lucille did wrong, her affair," her mother said judiciously. "With her it was love. But with some I guess it's just passion." There was Debbie, the Millers' fourteen-year-old, testifying in a steady voice about how she and her mother had gone to a supermarket to buy the gasoline can the week before the accident. There was Sandy Slagle, in the courtroom every day, declaring that on at least one occasion Lucille Miller had prevented her husband not only from committing suicide but from committing suicide in such a way that it would appear an accident and ensure the double-indemnity payment. There was Wenche Berg, the pretty twenty-seven-year-old Norwegian governess to Arthwell Hayton's children, testifying that Arthwell had instructed her not to allow Lucille Miller to see or talk to the children.

Two months dragged by, and the headlines never stopped. Southern California's crime reporters were headquartered in San Bernardino for the duration: Howard Hertel from the *Times*, Jim Bennett and Eddy Jo Bernal from the *Herald-Examiner*. Two months in which the Miller trial was pushed off the *Examiner's* front page only by the Academy Award nominations and Stan Laurel's death. And finally, on March 2, after Turner had reiterated that it was a case of "love and greed," and Foley had protested that his client was being tried for adultery, the case went to the jury.

They brought in the verdict, guilty of murder in the first degree, at 4:50 p.m. on March 5. "She didn't do it," Debbie Miller cried, jumping up from the spectators' section. "She didn't *do* it." Sandy Slagle collapsed in her seat and began to scream. "Sandy, for God's sake please *don't*," Lucille Miller said in a voice that carried across the courtroom, and Sandy Slagle was momentarily subdued. But as the jurors left the courtroom she screamed again: "You're murderers....Every last one of you is a *murderer*." Sheriff's deputies moved in then, each wearing a string tie that read "1965 SHERIFF'S RODEO," and Lucille Miller's father, that sad-faced junior-high-school teacher who believed in the word of Christ and the dangers of wanting to see the world, blew her a kiss off his fingertips.

The California Institution for Women at Frontera, where Lucille Miller is now, lies down where Euclid Avenue turns into country road, not too many miles from where she once lived and shopped and organized the Heart Fund Ball. Cattle graze across the road, and Rainbirds sprinkle the alfalfa. Frontera has a softball field and tennis courts, and looks as if it might be a California junior college, except that the trees are not yet high enough to conceal the concertina wire around the top of the Cyclone fence. On visitors' day there are big cars in the parking area, big Buicks and Pontiacs that belong to grandparents and sisters and fathers (not many of them belong to husbands), and some of them have bumper stickers that say "SUPPORT YOUR LOCAL POLICE."

A lot of California murderesses live here, a lot of girls who somehow misunderstood the promise. Don Turner put Sandra Garner here (and her husband in the gas chamber at San Quentin) after the 1959 desert killings known to crime reporters as "the soda-pop murders." Carole Tregoff is here, and has been ever since she was convicted of conspiring to murder Dr. Finch's wife in West Covina, which is not too far from San Bernardino. Carole Tregoff is in fact a nurse's aide in the prison hospital, and might have attended Lucille Miller had her baby been born at Frontera; Lucille Miller chose instead to have it outside, and paid for the guard who stood outside the delivery room in St. Bernardine's Hospital. Debbie Miller came to take the baby home from the hospital, in a white dress with pink ribbons, and Debbie was allowed to choose a name. She named the baby Kimi Kai. The children live with Harold and Joan Lance now, because Lucille Miller will probably spend ten years at Frontera. Don Turner waived his original request for the death penalty (it was generally agreed that he had demanded it only, in Edward Foley's words, "to get anybody with the slightest trace of human kindness in their veins off the jury"), and settled for life imprisonment with the possibility of parole. Lucille Miller does not like it at Frontera, and has had trouble adjusting. "She's going to have to learn humility," Turner says. "She's going to have to use her ability to charm, to manipulate."

The new house is empty now, the house on the street with the sign that says

PRIVATE ROAD
BELLA VISTA
DEAD END

The Millers never did get it landscaped, and weeds grow up around the fieldstone siding. The television aerial has toppled on the roof, and a trash can is stuffed with the debris of family life: a cheap suitcase, a child's game called "Lie Detector." There is a sign on what would have been the lawn, and the sign reads "ESTATE SALE." Edward Foley is trying to get Lucille Miller's case appealed, but there have been delays. "A trial always comes down to a matter of sympathy," Foley says wearily now. "I couldn't create sympathy for her." Everyone is a little weary now, weary and resigned, everyone except Sandy Slagle, whose bitterness is still raw. She lives in an apartment near the medical school in Loma Linda, and studies reports of the case in *True Police Cases* and *Official Detective Stories*. "I'd much rather we not talk about the Hayton business too much," she tells visitors, and she keeps a tape recorder running. "I'd rather talk about Lucille and what a wonderful person she is and how her rights were violated." Harold Lance does not talk to visitors at all. "We don't want to give away what we can sell," he explains pleasantly; an attempt was made to sell Lucille Miller's personal story to *Life*, but *Life* did not want to buy it. In the district attorney's offices they are prosecuting other murders now, and do not see why the Miller trial attracted so much attention. "It wasn't a very interesting murder as murders go," Don Turner says laconically. Elaine Hayton's death is no longer under investigation. "We know everything we want to know," Turner says.

Arthwell Hayton's office is directly below Edward Foley's. Some people around San Bernardino say that Arthwell Hayton suffered; others say that he did not suffer at all. Perhaps he did not, for time past is not believed to have any bearing upon time present or future, out in the golden land where every day the world is born anew. In any case, on October 17, 1965, Arthwell Hayton married again, married his children's pretty governess, Wenche Berg, at a service in the Chapel of the Roses at a retirement village near Riverside. Later the newlyweds were feted at a reception for seventy-five in the dining room of Rose Garden Village. The bridegroom was in black tie, with a white carnation in his buttonhole.

The bride wore a long white *peau de soie* dress and carried a shower bouquet of sweetheart roses with stephanotis streamers. A coronet of seed pearls held her illusion veil.

Calvin Trillin

Calvin Trillin was born in 1935 in Kansas City, Missouri, and was educated at Yale University. A journalist, novelist, and humorist, he's been a staff writer for *The New Yorker* since 1963 and also frequently contributes to *The Nation* and *Time*. He is the author of twenty-two books, including *The Tummy Trilogy*, *Remembering Denny*, *Messages from My Father*, and most recently, *Obliviously On He Sails: The Bush Administration in Rhyme*. He lives in New York City.

"Todo Se Paga: Riverside, California, February 1979" was first published *The New Yorker* and later included in *Killings*, a collection of Trillin's essays about murder and other grim deaths. It describes a blood feud between two Riverside families in the 1960s and 1970s.

Todo Se Paga: Riverside, California, February 1979

The feud between the Ahumadas and the Lozanos, everyone agrees, began late one night in January of 1964, when John Ahumada, Sr., was beaten so badly that slivers of his skull were driven into his brain. It happened in Casa Blanca. Technically, Casa Blanca is a section of Riverside, California, a county seat sixty miles east of Los Angeles; spiritually, Casa Blanca is unto itself. Before the Second World War, when Riverside was still a quiet trading center for citrus growers, Casa Blanca had been isolated from the rest of the town for half a century—

a square-mile patch cut out of acre upon acre of orange groves. Mexican farm workers who settled on the East Side of Riverside, close to downtown, gradually learned to deal with Anglos and blacks and the city authorities; Casa Blanca remained something close to a rural Mexican village. In 1949, it had only two paved streets. In the years after the war, the citrus-packing sheds where many Casa Blanca men had worked closed or burned down. A double-lane deposited a strip of automobile dealerships next to one corner of Casa Blanca. Over the objections of many Casa Blanca residents, the local grade school—"the Mexican consulate," one former resident calls it—was closed as part of a citywide integration plan. Eventually, rising real-estate prices and increased industry in Orange County, the sprawl southeast of Los Angeles, began to turn Riverside into a bedroom community for what had itself been a bedroom community replacing the orange groves near one border of Casa Blanca with a middle-class housing development called Woodhaven. Still, Casa Blanca retained a feeling of being rural. Still, Casa Blanca remained unto itself—a place where uninvited strangers were challenged. Having never expected concern or justice from the outside, Casa Blanca remained a place that took care of its own territory and its own problems and its own feuds.

John Ahumada had been having some drinks with John Hernandez, whose wife was a Lozano. They had apparently been friendly enough in El Flamingo, where the drinking started, but some angry words were exchanged at the Casa Blanca Café, where they found themselves about one-thirty in the morning. Hernandez and Ahumada walked across the street to a parking lot next to the railroad tracks that form one boundary of Casa Blanca. They were joined eventually by two of Hernandez's brothers-in-law who lived nearby, Marcos and Roman Lozano—carrying tire irons, according to one account, or perhaps a part from a commercial ice-cream mixer. John Ahumada ended up in the hospital, on the critical list. Roman and Marcos Lozano ended up in court, where, contrary to the Casa Blanca tradition of not cooperating with outside authorities, John Ahumada testified against them. They were sent to prison for assault with a deadly weapon. Although everyone agrees that the fight across from the Casa Blanca Café was the beginning of the feud, it is not clear which family was left with a wrong to avenge. Was it the Ahumadas, one of whom had been beaten so savagely that his arm was partly paralyzed and his speech remained slurred? Or was it the Lozanos, two of whom served time in state prison because an Ahumada had broken the code that required Casa Blanca people to settle their arguments in Casa Blanca?

For twelve years after Roman and Marcos Lozano were sent to state prison, there were no incidents between the Lozanos and the Ahumadas violent enough to come to the attention of the police. In Casa Blanca, the explanation normally offered for that hiatus is simple: the next generation of Lozanos and Ahumadas, children at the time of the fight across from the bar, needed a dozen years to grow old enough to kill each other. In the meantime, there were some schoolyard fistfights. Apparently, Johnny Lozano Hernandez would tell Johnny Ahumada that his father was a snitch, and a fight would start. Words would pass between Richard Lozano and Danny Ahumada, Johnny's younger brother, and another fight would start. "The seeds were there," someone who knew both families said recently. "All they had to do was scrape the earth a little bit."

In those years, the most ferocious battles engaged in by the young men of Casa Blanca pitted them against the young men of some other *barrio* rather than against each other—Casa Blanca fighting people from the East Side who had dared to drive into the neighborhood in force, Casa Blanca fighting a crowd from Corona or Rubidoux because someone had stared too long at a Casa Blanca girl. When Casa Blanca was not fighting another *barrio*, it was often fighting the police.

There were a few years, beginning in the late sixties, when almost any Mexican *barrio* in southern California was dangerous territory for Anglo police. For those years, when confrontation was part of what seemed to be a unified movement for the betterment of La Raza, gang members were transformed into Brown Berets, street toughs began thinking of themselves as Chicano militants, and juvenile offenders learned to refer to the rest of the world as "the Anglo-dominant society" instead of "paddies." In the words of one former Casa Blanca Brown Beret, "We were rebels without a cause who became rebels with a cause."

Even when the movement evaporated, though, hostility toward the police remained in Casa Blanca, fed by the hostility toward outsiders which had existed for decades. Riverside police cruisers were able to drive peacefully through the Mexican or black neighborhoods of the East Side, but a policeman driving into Casa Blanca at night could consider himself fortunate to be met by a beer bottle instead of a rifle shot. One night in August of 1975, in a cornfield on the edge of Casa Blanca, sniping and harassment broke into what amounted to open warfare.

Five people were wounded. Two young men from Casa Blanca—Danny Ahumada and Larry Romero, a member of a family close to the Ahumadas—were arrested for shooting at a police officer. "Casa Blanca had a reputation for sticking together," a young man who grew up fighting there said not long ago. "Even if we had problems, we'd never think of killing each other."

They started killing each other on Christmas, 1976. Richard Lozano and a cousin who was visiting from Arizona, Gilbert Lozano Sanchez, were shot at from a passing car. Lozano was not hit; Sanchez was killed. By the spring of 1978, when James Richardson, a young courthouse reporter for the *Riverside Press-Enterprise*, pieced together court and police records to construct a chronology of the violence that the Lozanos and the Ahumadas had visited upon each other, three people had been killed, two people had been crippled, and any number of people had been sideswiped or shot at. Richard Lozano has been killed since then. Most of the shootings have been carried out with a sudden, dramatic ferocity. Danny Ahumada was grabbed by the hair and shot twice in the head point-blank with a .22-calibre pistol—an attack he somehow survived, although he was even more seriously disabled than his father. Johnny Lozano Hernandez was shot down before a dozen witnesses after a dispute during which, according to Johnny Ahumada, "he began to tell me my brother was a snitch, my brother was a dog." Ruben (Redeye) Romero—who, along with Johnny Ahumada, had been tried but acquitted in Johnny Hernandez's death—was killed at a Casa Blanca filling station by three young gunmen who shot him, knelt at his body, crossed themselves, and shot him again at pointblank range. When Richard Lozano was killed, seven weeks later, his uncle Raul Lozano, who had been tried but not convicted in the shooting of Danny Ahumada, was seen smearing the blood of his fallen nephew on his hand and tasting it, presumably as a symbol of vengeance owed.

The feud between the Lozanos and the Ahumadas lacks symmetry. There are family members who are not involved. John Lozano, the father of the recently murdered Richard, claims that he still has a friendly hello for John Ahumada, Sr., when they meet in Casa Blanca. Even those who are involved seem to go along for weeks, or even months, without retaliation. Most of the encounters that end in death or serious injury seem mere chance—a moment when someone is caught alone or when someone makes an insulting remark. "They're in no hurry," a man familiar with Mexican-American neighborhoods in southern California explained not long ago. "In the *barrio*, people say, '*Todo se paga.*'" Everything is paid.

In the *barrio*, the brutal simplicity ordinarily associated with a blood feud—an eye for an eye—is complicated by the element of pride. "You killed my brother, so I will kill your brother" sometimes seems to become "You killed my brother and that makes you think you are stronger than we are and can look down on us, so, to show that's not true, I will kill your brother." When Roman Lozano was asked recently why the feud had started again in 1976, he said, "They knew their dad was a snitch, and they had an uncle who was a homosexual. They had to prove that they were manly." People on both sides have complained of having their houses fired on from passing cars, but they complain even more bitterly of having carloads of their enemies drive by and throw kisses as a gesture of contempt. One of Johnny Ahumada's theories about the origin of the seventies violence is that the Lozanos were jealous because only Danny Ahumada and Larry Romero were singled out after the 1975 cornfield melee for having shot at the police. "They want to prove their heart," Johnny says. "They don't want to lose their pride. That's what makes them revengeful."

There are people in Riverside who believe that the violence between the Ahumadas and the Lozanos no longer has anything to do with the 1964 assault. "It's not like the Hatfields and the McCoys," a man who grew up in Casa Blanca said recently. "The underlying motive is drugs." Marcos and John Lozano have both been convicted on serious heroin charges at one time or another. There are people in Riverside who say that some of the younger Ahumadas—or their allies, the Romeros—may have pushed into Lozano drug-dealing territory while the Lozanos were in prison. There are people in Riverside who say that the argument between the two families is actually an argument between the two Mexican prison gangs that have emerged in California in the past several years—the Mexican Mafia and Nuestra Familia—one of which is supposedly challenging the other over control of drugs in Casa Blanca.

In the *barrio*, it is common to hear drugs offered as an underlying motive for any excess in violence or wealth. Members of the vice-and-narcotics squad in Riverside tend not to be believers in the drug-war theory. Redeye Romero, who is sometimes described as a "hard-core biker," was, like a lot of hard-core bikers, suspected of being a bagman in the heroin trade, but he was not thought to be in a position to challenge anybody for control of serious drug traffic. The only drug charge ever brought against an Ahumada was made when Danny was shot: the policemen who took charge of his clothing reported finding twelve balloons of heroin in the trousers. An investigator for the Riverside County district attorney's office who serves on a state task force dealing with prison gangs says that neither gang had anything to do with the shootings in Casa Blanca or control of the drug traffic in Casa Blanca. He says, in fact, that Nuestra Familia conducted its own investigation to make certain that the death of Johnny Lozano Hernandez, apparently a Nuestra Familia member, had been strictly a private affair. "If it's true," a Casa Blanca native said recently of the theory that competing gangs are involved, "it's just one more reason for hating each other."

Mary Ahumada, the wife of the original victim, sometimes speaks of the Ahumadas as respectable citizens who have somehow found themselves locked in a feud with criminals. When she was informed recently that her son Danny might be sent to state prison for having been caught with a stolen pistol while on probation for the drug charge and an old auto-theft conviction, she said, "My boys were never mixed up in that sort of thing." It is true that the Ahumadas have not served time in state prison, although they are familiar with the Riverside County jail. Mrs. Ahumada is a handsome, loquacious woman who, as Sister Mary, runs a small evangelical congregation that specializes in teenagers who have strayed from the Lord's path. The Lozanos sometimes speak of her as a hypocritical Holy Roller who goads her sons to violence. "People tend to pull you down," she says. "'Why doesn't she save her own sons? Why doesn't she save *their* souls?' Yes, I've had remarks from police officers in the past that have been cruel." (Sister Mary's ministry has not been completely without effect on her sons: Johnny wore a gold cross in his lapel throughout his trial for the murder of Johnny Hernandez.) Although the Ahumadas' ally Redeye Romero was known as a hard-core biker, he was also known as one of the founders of the Brown Berets in Casa Blanca—someone who showed up at meetings now and then as a spokesman for *barrio* youth. When he was killed, he was referred to in the press as a "street leader," although he was about to go to prison for an armed-robbery conviction. Policemen in Riverside are unimpressed by the prominence of the Ahumadas and the Romeros. In fact, to some policemen, particularly Anglo policemen who are not overly concerned about the effects of heroin on Mexicans in a remote *barrio*, serious drug dealers have the advantage over street leaders of trying to avoid incidents that only attract the authorities to their place of business—incidents like firing on police cruisers.

Some people in Casa Blanca believe that the Riverside police are not saddened by the sight of Ahumadas and Lozanos killing and maiming each other. The police have in fact made a lot of arrests in the shootings, but the closest thing to a conviction has been Raul Lozano pleading *nolo contendere* to a charge of having been an accessory to the shooting of Danny Ahumada. When Georgie Ahumada, the younger brother of Johnny and Danny, was released without charge after having been picked up for the murder of Richard Lozano, Mary Ahumada said she had told Georgie to trust in God, but most people charged with one of the shootings have trusted in the lack of witnesses willing to testify. After Georgie Ahumada went free, the deputy district attorney who has handled all of the feud shootings said, "This is the usual situation where twenty people see the killing and all of them say, 'I didn't see it.'" Even two of Richard Lozano's uncles who were present when he was killed declined to cooperate with the authorities. Richard's father, John Lozano, does not seem upset that his brothers would not help to bring his son's killer to justice. "They're the type that don't like to testify," he says.

Some people in Casa Blanca who are not related to either family have been unable to stay out of the feud. People who witnessed shootings have had their houses fired upon, making it necessary, in some cases, for their own young men to prove that they cannot be treated as weaklings. One of the young men who is awaiting trial for the murder of Redeye Romero seems to have got involved originally because his mother became friendly with Johnny Lozano Hernandez's mother upon moving into the neighborhood. ("They were the only ones who treated us with respect," he says.) A young man named William DeHaro, who was shot to death last September, may have been killed simply because he remained friendly with the Lozanos after a warning to avoid them. Some people in Casa Blanca—particularly older people—seem to be able to stay out of the feud. "You don't dare choose sides," one of them has said. "You talk to both. You go to the funerals for both."

Many of the Lozanos and Ahumadas and Romeros have moved out of Casa Blanca in the last year or so, partly in an effort to sleep peacefully through the night, but they return constantly. Everyone remains well armed; when the police search the house of someone involved in the feud, they invariably come up with a small arsenal. Complaining recently about some people having shot at his house the previous evening, John Lozano mentioned that he had taken the precaution of borrowing a machine gun. The Ahumadas and the Lozanos both say they would like the feud to end, but no one is optimistic that it will. A new generation is gradually growing old enough to kill each other. "You can see it in the ten-year-olds," Johnny Ahumada said recently. "They look at you, and you can see their hatred." Standing in the hall of the Riverside County Courthouse not long ago, John Lozano, who had just entered a guilty plea to possession of heroin for sale, was equally pessimistic. "I wish it would end," he said. "I'm facing four years, and I'll be out of the picture which, in a way, I'm glad."

Rowena Silver

Rowena Silver was born in Winnipeg, Canada, and educated at the University of California, Berkeley, in the 1960s. In addition to being a poet, she is currently an editor of *Epicenter*, a quarterly literary magazine published in Riverside. Her poetry has appeared in *European Judaism, Writer's Digest, Psychological Perspectives*, and many other journals, as well as in *Under the Fifth Sun: Latino Literature from California*. She lives in Riverside.

"That Dusky Scent" touches on the Inland Empire's seasonal forest fire problem.

That Dusky Scent

California
is dusting herself
in dream debris

Writers clutch scripts
veterans grab medals
atheists pray
coyotes howl
echoing sirens

In Rancho Cucamonga
burnt offerings
of native homes

quickly despair
into legend

We all dine on ash
as California,
twirls her fires
layering the sunset
in a glorious pied sky

Gina Berriault

Gina Berriault was born in Long Beach in 1926. Author of four novels and three short story collections, she was the recipient of numerous awards, including the National Book Critics Circle Award, the PEN\Faulkner Award, and the Rea Foundation Prize for the Short Story—all for her short story collection *Women in Their Beds*. She died in 1999.

Set in the mountains east of Los Angeles during a wildfire, "Wilderness Fire" is from Berriault's collection *The Infinite Passion of Expectation* and was later included in *Women in Their Beds*.

Wilderness Fire

A wilderness fire was raging in the mountains east of Los Angeles, and a great brown cloud of smoke, tinged copper by the sunrise, lay over the desert and the small towns she passed through on her way to her mother. The first few miles she was alarmed under the cloud. Only in a nightmare could the sky be like this. Or was it this bad only because she wanted to turn back and the smoke gave her a good enough reason? If she wasn't going to be forced over to the side of the road by the highway patrol and interrogated as to why she was driving so fast in this smoke, she just might pull over on her own, under that long row of eucalyptus up ahead, under those towering, dry, lonely, gray trees, and bend her head to the steering wheel and sleep. Sleep, to put off the moment when she would embrace her mother, bringing her news from the world outside the pink stucco bungalow on the desert's edge.

She went past the eucalyptus row and past the acres of fields planted with something she'd never remember the name for even if she were told twelve times; past shacks far away at the end of dirt roads; past a huge, dusty fig tree branching out over the highway; past a black dog ambling along in a ditch. On the seat beside her—the novel, untouchable, ominous, like an object stolen from a tomb. It slipped closer when she took a curve, and she hit it away with the side of her hand.

The folded letter slipped out from the book and fell to the floor, and it, too, slipped sideways. It was slipping close to the pedals and in another minute she could put her foot on it and grind it down. *All those who practice this profession betray. No, not all. Not the great ones. But maybe they betrayed, too. Just because everybody said "See how far they can see into the human heart," that didn't exonerate them in their own eyes. I have betrayed you, your confidences, your soul, and I will regret it for the rest of my life.*

She went faster past the entrance to a trailer park. Above the hedge the trailer homes swept by with their green awnings of rippled plastic. Oh, thank God her mother didn't live in a trailer park. She almost wept, imagining it. The heat of this desert edge was enough, and to have to live in a trailer with all its dinky built-in things, with plastic flowers planted in tanbark by the doorstep—that was the end. She had always wanted to be rich, not just for herself but for her mother, too. And she had never got rich and never would, not the so-so actress that she was, and married, not now but not long ago, to a man just as poor, though he was going to be less so, now, because his novel might elevate him into all kinds of upper brackets.

The scorched air, the dark clouds were almost left behind. The tall, tall date palms, acres of them, she was passing had always seemed from some far reaches of the earth, brought to a desert from deep swamps, and grotesquely lonely, out of place. She had told only her mother about how they looked to her. Who else would see they wanted swamps? And her mother had agreed they did look like prehistoric swamp plants, out of their element, enduring.

On the outskirts of the town where her mother lived, she slowed down past clapboard houses and stucco bungalows, low to the ground, some in weeds, some in squares of very green grass, one with the same silver porpoise-shape trailer out in back, one with the lemon tree; past the small, stucco school. And now the pink stucco house, small, too, boxlike, but showy in this place because it had two stories. Before it, a squat palm tree that never gave dates, just tiny, yellow, waxy droppings, and a midget fig tree; and, in the back, towering way above the house, one lone palm. All around the yard, a scalloped-wire fence, a foot high, protecting the house and the short dry grass and the three trees from nothing. *Oh, Mother, I had wanted an airy glass house for you by a blue, blue sea, say the Caribbean, lush plants all around with large, deep green leaves, always with drops of clear water on their surface. And birds, birds of miraculous plumage.* She parked in the gravel driveway, stuck the letter into the book and the book into her purse, and, swinging along, very erect in high heels, purse slung over her shoulder, she went up the paved walk to the front door.

For the moments of their embrace and the moments after, her mother couldn't speak, and then she went on ahead, leading the way into the kitchen, tossing her head from side to side with delight, like a child. Her mother was bare-legged and clopping along artfully on backless wedge sandals. Her flowered cotton dress had once been her daughter's in an awful movie, but it had been expensive and was kept neater now than its original owner had ever kept it. Her mother's short hair was tinted a pink-blond, like a faint reflection indoors of the exterior of the house. In the four months since the daughter's last visit, the mother seemed to have got quite a bit older. Or maybe it was the heat of the desert summer that shrinks the thin ones and expands the fat ones. And, coming along behind her mother, she said, *Mother, Mother, Mother,* just to herself. *If there was anything I did that made you get old, forgive me for that.*

"Penny, dear shiny bright Penny," her mother said, and here in the dim kitchen, the striped curtains closed against the heat swarming at the windows, here where her mother turned to clasp her again, the daughter felt again how much she was thought about in this house. Her mother's face in the shade of the room told her again how brief was the time of their knowing each other, only twenty-five years so far, and told her again of the unknowable limits of the time left.

"There's a fire in the mountains, if I smell of smoke," she said.

"You've brought me Chris's book," her mother said, hands palm to palm under her chin, like a child praying at bedtime. *Bless everybody, amen.*

"Oh, yes, that's right," the daughter said, tantalizingly wagging her finger under her mother's nose. "Patience, patience."

"You left so early," her mother said. "Shall I make you some breakfast?"

"Never hungry till two," she said. "Same as always. Let's just drink a toast. Some mineral water will do fine."

"Is he happy?" her mother asked. She had been an actress and had ·even got her name up on the screen—in much smaller letters than the leads. She had always played innocents, girls from small towns, from farms, and now, when she was called upon to express happiness, it came across like that of a girl who didn't know yet that happiness wasn't that simple. Her mother was a smart woman, but seeing her smile like that, you couldn't guess how smart she really was.

"Oh, he's happy, of course," she said, smiling at her mother the same sort of smile from the backwoods. "A novel with his name on it, what else can he be but happy? He's living with a friend of his—I guess it's a woman, he just says *friend*—at her or his apartment in New York. He's happy."

"He says that?"

"He says what?"

"That he's happy?"

"If he says so it must be so," she said, coming out smiling from behind her hands, as if she had spread them over her face only to rub away the soot or the dust or whatever that cloud of smoke had left. "He says he's going to write to you. You and he always had such wonderful discussions. Just about everything from quasars to cucumbers. He says he's going to mail you an autographed copy with something like 'Love to Melody, whom I thank for giving birth to Penelope.'"

"That's nice, but you're making it up."

The daughter was wandering around the kitchen, restlessly, as if she'd come to the wrong house and was going to have to leave at once. She came to the other end of the long kitchen, where there was a couch and a television and a sewing machine, and where, on a table, there were magazines and a row of African violets in little painted Mexican pots that had been hers when she was a little girl—a collection of sorts, and her mother brought over the misted glass to her, there.

"I made it up and it's not nice," she said. "He admires you for just being you and he loves you. It's easy, you know, to love you. He'll just write, 'To Melody, dear friend, all my love.' Let's drink to that. If he gets to be famous, your copy will be worth a small fortune." But how little love, none at all, he had shown in his novel for her mother; she wasn't mentioned, but what he had written about the daughter was to wound the mother beyond amends.

They raised their glasses.

"Chris has a good heart," her mother said.

"Chris has a great heart," she said. "Everybody's going to know that soon, not just you and me." But she couldn't drink, because the ice cubes were making such a racket she had to set her glass down.

"Sit down now," her mother said, sharply.

"Mother, it isn't me," she said. "The girl in his novel isn't me. He got it wrong. There's no resemblance whatsoever. I never gave him all that trouble and I was never loved like the girl in there was loved. Everybody will think it's me and it isn't me."

"Where is it?" her mother asked, afraid.

"Mother, he was always fascinated by women made of words. If you want to know their names I'll try to remember. Emma Bovary and Molly Bloom and Brett, and that girl who was mad over Heathcliff. Oh, and women in the flesh, too. Of course. But when he put me into words he got me wrong. It's not me, Mother."

"Sit down," her mother said, and the daughter sat down. "It's all made up," her mother said soothingly, sitting, facing her daughter. "Everybody knows that. That's what novels are all about."

"If I gave him trouble, Mother," she said, "it was because he gave me trouble."

"That's usually the way it goes," her mother said, stroking her daughter's arms, down and down again along the long silk sleeves. "And nobody ever knows who started the trouble."

"Mother, nobody can ever know what life feels like in another person. You only think you know. I never could know him, his desires for his life, his life in here," taking her hands away from her mother's to spread them over her chest, "and he could never know me. It's unknown territory. It's unknown in here, Mother. I don't know myself. All I hear is the uproar."

"Give me your hands," her mother said, reaching for her daughter's hands again and holding them down.

The daughter had been avoiding the mother's face. She had been looking everywhere, sideways and down, anywhere but at her mother, and now she looked at her mother's face, at the slack cheeks, at the waiting fear in the eyes. And the ears through the pink curls seemed comically large, waiting.

"Once I tried to kill myself," she said, and began to sob. She pulled her hands away and held them up, palms toward her mother, and the long sleeves slipped away from the wrists, exposing on each wrist the thin, pale line of an old scar.

They stood up at the same time and came together, clasping each other. She had betrayed this woman who had given her birth, betrayed this woman's hopes for her daughter to endure, endure against all the unsolvable puzzles life comes up with. She was taller than her mother— her mother, over the past few years, was getting smaller, and the daughter was wearing high heels—and her mother's face was pressed against her breasts, her tears wetting the blouse and the nipples under the cloth. Long ago, her mother had told her that when she was newborn and began to cry, the milk seeped out at once from her mother's breasts, wetting her dress. At once, though mother and child were rooms apart.

"Mama, I didn't die," she pleaded. "You see I didn't die. I'm alive. I'm alive." But her mother would not let go and would not raise her head.

With her arm about her mother, she walked her out into the yard, because the broad desert light might force them to calm down and to endure. Even the tall palm they stood beside might force them to endure. Way far to the west, the smoke was like evening at the wrong time of day.

Gayle Brandeis

Gayle Brandeis was born in Chicago in 1968. Author of *Fruitflesh: Seeds of Inspiration for Women Who Write* and winner of the Bellwether Prize for Fiction for *The Book of Dead Birds*, Brandeis has also been a writer in residence for the Mission Inn Foundation's Family Voices Project. She lives in Riverside.

In *The Book of Dead Birds*, Ava Sing Lo goes to the Salton Sea to volunteer to help environmental activists save birds poisoned by agricultural runoff; in this excerpt she is introduced to the gruesome situation.

from *The Book of Dead Birds*

Highway 111, as I come to know it, seems appropriately numbered—a row of three thin digits, each one almost invisible, spare and pale as the landscape it cuts through. Scattered patches of white—salt, I guess—gleam dully from the dirt like snow. Even the sky seems white, as if the blue had been taken by geese flying south, or, more likely, burned blank by the relentless sun.

I feel incredibly conspicuous in my shiny green car. The only other color along this stretch of the road comes from the occasional string of boxcars stopped on the Southern Pacific railway. The trains are pretty muted, too—dusty wine, dirty mustard, black sandstormed down to gray. The few cars I pass are equally eroded—pickup trucks painted with primer, twenty-year-old weather-faded sedans, eyes trained on me from inside, loaded with curiosity and threat. If I don't make some sort of decision soon, I worry that my own car, my own face might get sanded down to dust.

I crank the steering wheel and veer off the highway onto Desert Beach Drive.

The water spreads out before me, miles of flat shimmer. It looks refreshing, but as soon as I get out of the car, the heat and stench almost knock me over. An overpowering smell of bird and fish decay mixes in the air with something equally rank and environmental. I grab a piece of ginger to try to mask the scent, but the odor molecules still find a way to seep inside.

What planet have I landed on? I stomp a sleeping foot against the pavement, slap some life into my face, look around to make sure no cars have pulled into the lot behind me. The area is completely deserted. An empty fifties-style motel sits on the other end of the parking lot, all of its doors open, the rooms bare. The building is so utterly abandoned, no one has even bothered to vandalize it. Dusty tufts of overgrown bougainvillea seem incongruous against the walls, random bursts of fuchsia life.

A marina up ahead, partly underwater and long deserted, touts sandwiches and live bait from its sun-bleached awning. An old yacht club, shaped like a ship with broken porthole windows and faded nautical flags painted around the border, silently faces the water. It looks like no one has dined or danced there in decades. What happened here? *What happened?*

Holding my breath, I walk toward the sweeping span of water. As I get closer, the sea begins to looks less sparkly—it is the color of tea, the color of mud. The beach is not a sandy one, either, as it had seemed from the parking lot. The ground is completely heaped with barnacles, small white tubes that crunch beneath my sandals, making me shiver even in the intense heat. I remember reading somewhere that barnacles had been introduced to the area by WWII aircraft that used the sea for dive bomb practice. I feel like I'm walking across a bone yard.

Every few steps, I come across dead fish in various stages of decomposition—some still silver and wet with missing eyes, some dry and brown like the cuttlefish my mother buys in Koreatown, some dissolved down to bone, bleached white as the barnacles beneath them. Pale-green bird droppings offer the only other color on the ground. I walk up to an old swing set and steady myself against one of its hot metal legs. The end of a small slide disappears into a mass of barnacles nearby.

What am I doing here? I wonder, queasy from the rotten air. Then I see the jetty up ahead, covered with dead and dying pelicans.

The birds, dozens of them, are heaped against each other, a seething clump of beige and brown, long beaks jutting out like cactus spines. Some pelicans convulse violently, others have already started to decompose, their speckled breasts caved, split open. My eyes feel seared. Bile rises in my throat. I don't know what I expected—some ballet of languid wings, something remotely beautiful. Anything but this.

One bird lets out a horrible screech. Its head lifts briefly off the ground, then collapses, its beak wide open. I bend over and retch a small splash of orange onto the barnacles and fish bones, my contribution of color to the landscape.

I stumble back to the Sonata and blast the cold scent of Freon into my nose. My throat, my eyes are raw. I pop another sugary clump of ginger into my mouth, lean my head against the steering wheel, and take some deep breaths. It would be so easy to go home, so easy to hit the road and never look back. It would be so easy, but when I pull back onto the 111, I can't seem to drive toward San Diego. I find myself pulling off the highway again onto a street not far down the road, one I've passed three times already, a driveway with a sign that reads VISITOR'S CENTER.

A temporary structure is set up a few hundred yards ahead on the barnacled shore—chain-link walls covered with UV-protectant fabric. The air gets heavier, thick with the scent of something gone wrong, as I get closer. My stomach twists tighter.

Through the opening between two of the chain-link panels, I can see at least fifty people inside. Some tend pelicans in a child's wading pool, others unload trash bags full of dead birds. Some weigh the birds, catalog them, slit their bellies open, put hearts and livers into clear sandwich bags. In a small red tin structure adjacent to the enclosure, two men throw bodies into an incinerator that sends more heat into the sweltering air. A pile of dead birds taller than me stands in the corner. The stench is unbearable. I fan myself with the folded map.

"Can I help you?" A harried-looking man comes up to me.

"I'm looking for the hospital."

"You found it," he replies, then races off to the plastic pool full of birds, syringes of some kind spilling out of his vest pockets.

"This is the hospital?" I ask another man who is hefting a dead pelican onto a scale.

"You were expecting private beds?" he asks as he records the weight, then throws the bird in a pile.

"Running water, maybe." I look around. No sink, no fans. Dirt floor. Flies everywhere.

The man laughs and points to a long hose that snakes across the ground.

"Could you please tell me where I could find Darryl?"

"He's over there!" He points to the man by the wading pool, the man I had first talked to.

"Thank you." I try not to breathe. My voice sounds the way I've heard people speak after they've inhaled pot, all tight in the throat.

I walk over to the pool. A woman holds a pelican's floppy neck while Darryl squirts something from one of the syringes through a tube into its beak.

"Excuse me." I tentatively tap his shoulder.

He snaps his head around. Part of the liquid from the syringe squirts out, splashes against my jeans.

"Dammit!" he shouts.

"I'm sorry…"

"That syringe was measured out perfectly," he says. "This bird only got about sixty milliliters of electrolytes, thanks to you. Those forty milliliters on your calf aren't going to do you any good, are they?"

"I didn't mean—"

"Who *are* you?"

"My name is Ava. Ava Sing Lo. I'm here to help the birds."

"Well, then." He hands me a wet cloth. It is blessedly cool in my palm. He gestures to a pelican sitting at the edge of the pool, its neck draped languidly over the edge. "Wipe out this bird's eyes. I need to get more solution." He storms off.

I tuck my map into my pocket. "What do I do?" I ask the woman, stroking a pelican's head. The woman's light-brown hair is starting to come out of its hasty ponytail. Sweat streams down her forehead, trickles behind her glasses, down her freckled nose, over her chapped lips.

"Just wipe its eyes with the cloth," she says. "They fall down and can't hold up their heads, poor things. Their eyes get all full of mud and salt and crap before we can get to them…"

I swallow and walk to the other side of the blue plastic pool, which I now realize has circus animals printed all over it, almost mockingly festive. I kneel down beside the bird. Its eyes are so caked, I'm sure it can't see a thing. I tentatively raise the cloth to the pelican's head. I can feel the bird startle a bit, but it is too weak to do much. I gently touch the cloth against its covered eye. The bird flinches, shudders. A wing brushes lightly against my arm, sends a shiver down my spine. I wipe at the hardened crud, then run some water from the hose over the cloth so that I can loosen it some more. Eventually the dirt smears off. The pelican's eye looks right into mine. My heart starts to pound.

"It's okay," I tell the bird, then move over to the other side. The bird relaxes a bit as I wipe at the other eye. Once that one emerges from the layers of mud and salt, though, it is glassy, vacant. It takes me a moment to realize the pelican is dead.

"Oh, no," I whisper.

"We lose a lot of them," the woman says, raising her arm as if to signal someone.

"I have sort of a history of killing birds," I tell her.

The woman doesn't say anything, but I can feel her recoil.

A man in an olive-drab jumpsuit comes up to the pool and whisks the bird away without a word.

"How can you stand this?" I ask the woman.

"It doesn't get any easier," the woman admits. "Believe me."

"Are you a volunteer?"

"No, I'm with a wildlife refuge in Colorado. They shipped a few of us out here to help with the effort. I'm supposed to be here another two weeks, but frankly, I'm not sure I can hang on that long."

I wonder how long I can stand it myself. It would be so easy to just walk away. I know I can't, though, not yet.

"How many birds have been affected so far?"

"Over three thousand already—a few hundred brown pelicans among them. They're endangered, you know. It's kind of ironic, really—earlier this year, the browns were getting close to getting off the list, but now with this outbreak, it's possible we'll have to add the western whites to the list now, too."

I look around. The pile of dead birds is almost too awful to comprehend, big enough to fill the pages of several scrapbooks.

"I'm Abby, by the way," the woman extends her hand. "Abby Westin."

"Ava Sing Lo."

Abby's fingers are waterlogged and wrinkled against the back of my hand.

"Where are you staying?" Abby asks.

"I'm not sure. This whole thing was sort of a split-second decision. I figured I would find something once I got here."

"There aren't any hotels nearby," Abby says. "Not anymore, at least."

"I saw the one off Desert Beach Drive. It's like a ghost town over there."

"It's like a ghost town everywhere," says Abby. "If you want, you can bunk with me. They've set up big army tents for all the people who've traveled here to help."

"I'm just a volunteer."

"I'm sure you could stay with me," says Abby. "There's an empty cot. The gal who was sharing the place couldn't deal with all this. I was this close to leaving with her."

"No time for chitchat, girls." Darryl reappears. "We have to tube these birds. The van from the Pacific Wildlife Center is going to be here any moment to bring them to Laguna Niguel."

"What do they do with them there?" I ask.

"Rehabilitate them some more," he says, as he sticks a tube into a pelican's beak. The pelican is weak, but it has enough gumption to give him a bit of a struggle. "More electrolytes, then a multi milk solution— half milk, half water—eventually fish. When they're strong enough, up and preening, they get released." He hands Abby a tubed syringe. I watch her feed it to a pelican easily, like she has done it hundreds of times. She probably has.

"Darryl," asks Abby. "Would it be possible for Ava to bunk with me? She's not with the refuge—she's here as a volunteer—but she needs a place to stay."

"Don't see why not." Darryl tubes another bird. "We appreciate your help—it's the least we could do in return—not that the accommodations are all that spectacular."

"That's fine," I tell him. "Thank you."

"Welcome aboard." Darryl tosses me a syringe.

An hour later, after I struggle, and fail, to tube several birds, Abby tells me about a weekly boat tour for new volunteers and refuge workers. If I hurry, she says, I can make it. I have a feeling she just wants to get rid of me, but Darryl says it's a good opportunity to get a sense of the sea's expanse, its history, its flora and fauna. I stumble to the dock, where I am shuttled onto a boat with about ten other shell-shocked people. They sit like zombies, silently facing each other on the two benches that stretch the length of the boat. My arms feel raked by resistant pelican beaks; my biceps sting, but I can't find any scratches when I examine my skin.

A perky woman in a tan uniform hops on board and starts up the motor. As the pontoon pulls out onto the sea, she launches into her regular tour spiel like she has a boat full of eager vacationers, not a group of death-stunned workers.

"The Salton Sea," she says grandly, "was created by mistake! In 1905, water diversion dikes along the Colorado River collapsed, and water flooded into the ancient Salton Basin for almost two years, leaving behind the largest inland lake in California! Today the lake is about thirty-five miles long and fifteen miles wide and straddles two counties! It boasts one of the best fisheries you could ever find!"

She rattles off the varieties of fish in the sea as if they're all swimming happily in the depths, ready to be snared by some lucky wrangler's hook. As if they're not bloated and wasted by botulism, clotting the surface of the water.

When she mentions that the tilapia originally came from Africa, the whole crowd in the boat mutely swivels around to face me, as if I'm responsible for the slew of fish myself. I look down, my face hot. Brownish water seeps up through some little grommeted holes on the floor of the boat and slides over to my feet. I tense my toes inside my shoes. When the woman says that tilapia are mouth brooders, that their babies swim into their parents' mouths for protection, I can feel everyone stare at my lips.

I don't hear much else until the woman mentions gulf croakers. The fish actually croak when they die, the woman says, as the pontoon journeys toward the center of the sea; they make a froglike croaking sound. When they're alive, they make a sound like a drum. It's because of their modified air bladders. The woman sounds a bit embarrassed by this last word.

I try to listen for the fish drum, fish croak, but all I can hear is the motor of the boat. I never knew fish could make sounds. I'll try to record some later for my MIDI, maybe mix them with Kane's voice. With all the dead fish floating around, I'll probably have a better chance hearing them croak than I will hearing them drum, although I would much prefer something percussive. My hands feel restless for the skin of my *chang'go*. I thrum my fingers against the edge of the boat until someone shoots me a dirty look.

I started drumming on my first birthday. I can't remember the actual event, but I remember my mother's telling of it.

In Korea it's traditional to have a huge first birthday feast, during which objects are set before the child—coins, a calligraphy brush, a dancer's fan. The first object the child reaches for supposedly determines his or her life's path.

That day, so the story goes, my mother brought me to McDonald's. She set a few things on the table—some pennies, a shell, a small doll, a comb—but I reached for the chopsticks my mother had brought from home. She had been using them to eat her french fries, dangling each strip of potato in front of her mouth like a worm before she bit it away from the pinch of wood. I grabbed the sticks right out of her hand and banged and banged them against the yellow Formica.

Table drum, floor drum, chair drum, bed drum, knee drum, eardrum, heart drum, *ba dum, ba dum*, the whole world became a drum for me that day. When I was three, I got my first real drum—a feathered tom-tom my mother bought at a dime store. When I was six, she found a used set of bongos at a garage sale. Then, when I turned eleven, my mother gave me the *chang'go*, the drum that quickly became my home, my heart. That night was the first night she sang the *pansori* to me, the first night she began to let her story spill. Sometimes I think my whole life has been a silence punctuated by drum beats and MIDI samples and tae kwon do grunts. In between, I feel blank as the desert sky. Only sound can pull me into sharp relief.

A loud motor, like wire brushes on cymbals, whirs into earshot. I look up as an airboat speeds by, its floor heaped with pelicans, a man in an orange jumpsuit standing above them. The sight of the birds is sickening, but the huge caged fan mounted on the back of the boat sends a welcome blast of slightly cooler air across my face as it passes. Out in the water, the air is not quite so stifling, the stink not quite so lethal, but it is still hotter and smellier than anything I'll ever be used to. I'm grateful to at least have some space around my head, some open sky, after being walled in at the bird hospital for the last hour. The mountains that ring the sea are too far away to feel like walls.

The woman points out the line that cuts across the hills like a belt. A waterline, she says, from an ancient sea. This basin has been filled many times, with both salt- and freshwater. Freshwater snail shells can still be found up there.

The pontoon passes the top of a telephone pole that juts out of the water like a thick finger. The water level, the woman explains, keeps rising because of agricultural runoff from nearby farms. The sea won't reach those watermarks up in the hills anytime soon, but it does sometimes rise enough to cause problems. Several resort areas were inundated in the seventies. Whole buildings are now underwater.

"The Salton Sea has no outlet!" she explains to her catatonic audience.

The phrase sounds incredibly foreboding, even though I know the sea could be just the outlet I've been looking for. The boat passes some dead treetops pushing up through the wet surface. The branches are covered with birds. Living birds. Common cormorants, says the woman.

These birds are diving birds, she says, great fishers, but they're clumsy on the ground. They jump off trees to fly so that they won't have to run. See their legs, way back on their bodies, like they're coming out of their rumps? They'd tip over if they tried to run. In the Orient, the woman continues, people keep these birds as pets.

I expect everyone to turn and look at me again, but no one does. I am amazed they can't see my mother shining through my skin. My whole body feels like a watermark, a dark salty line left behind by the unknown soldier who fathered me. Only my eyes, my cheekbones, carry traces of my mother, like snail shells left behind, fragile memories of freshwater.

Marisa Silver

Born in New York in 1960 and educated at Harvard, Marisa Silver started her career as a screenwriter and film director. Her fiction has appeared in numerous publications including *The New Yorker* and the *Georgetown Review*, and her 2001 collection of short stories, *Babe in Paradise*, was a *New York Times* Notable Book of the Year and a *Los Angeles Times* Best Book of the Year. Silver lives in Los Angeles.

"The God of War," set near the Salton Sea and the Imperial Desert, was published in 2005 in *The New Yorker*.

The God of War

Ares couldn't help himself. He'd be standing in the circle, waiting for big Ernesto and the opposing oversized twelve-year-old center to fight it out for the jump ball, and he'd find himself yelling, "Irritation!" or "Horrible lack of judgment!," and the boy's hand would reach into the air a millisecond too late, by which time Ernesto would have slapped the ball halfway down the court with his big paw. Or, when the teams were lined up for a free throw, Ares would repeat the word "shame" in a low hiss until it sounded as though the nearby Salton Sea had broken its bounds and was roaring beneath the basketball court.

After a game during which Ares had flustered another player by screaming "Nightmarish thoughts!" just as the boy was about to dunk the ball and pull his team to a two-point lead, Coach Ortega called him in for a man-to-man sit-down talk. It wasn't the kind of talk that Ares had seen in after-school movies on TV, the kind where the coach turns a messed-up kid's life around with one meaningful sentence and a slightly too hard chuck on the shoulder.

"What the hell are you saying out there? What the hell is *wrong* with you?" Ortega said, and Ares got the feeling that if he had just yelled something about somebody's mother eating worms he wouldn't be sitting in the locker room after everyone else had gone home. But then his coach launched into something about respect and sportsmanship and how he had given Ares a chance on the team even though Ares wasn't particularly good at basketball and how Ares had let him down. How it wasn't just Ares who had to be embarrassed—Ortega had to be embarrassed as well, because of *his* horrible lack of judgment.

Ares felt the truth of the words like a river of warm shame coursing through his chest. It was a good feeling. Shame was as familiar and comforting as the pillow on his bed, which was emaciated and full of years of his own smell, and which he could not sleep without.

"Just cut it out, baby," Laurel said gently that night, after Ares had told her about the coach's talk. He had a habit of telling his mother all the bad things he did. He was like a dog in this way, showing up at the door with a half-chewed rat in its mouth, asking for approval. "You know what's right."

"O.K.," Ares said, deflated. Something about his mother's care seemed uncaring. There was too much acceptance in it, a disarming lack of judgment. She was stuffing a raw chicken with lemon halves and rubbing oil on its pimpled skin. Ares watched her hands. They were big, strong, and bumpy with knuckles. They spent their days rubbing and kneading the backs of her massage clients at a spa in Palm Desert. He couldn't imagine touching all those strangers, patting and slapping them like the chicken she was handling now.

He waited for her to say something more, but her head was tilted to the side as she focused on the back of a box of couscous. Her reddish hair covered her face. When she tried to pour the grains into a measuring cup, pellets flew across the countertop and onto the floor.

Malcolm let out his weird backward laugh, making the sound on the inhale, so that a stranger might have thought he was choking. He was five and did not talk. Or, as Laurel liked to say, he "chose silence." He also chose to organize all the videos according to which movie studio made them, and to pile up books in order of size, largest to smallest, then stack around the main room of the trailer: literary pyramids. Instead of putting the books back on the black metal shelves she had found in a dumpster a year earlier, Laurel simply used the structures as footstools or side tables for her smelly massage creams and clove-cigarette butts. Ares didn't know if she left the piles in place as a gesture of support for Malcolm or because she was the kind of person who didn't kill ants, even when they marched brazenly across the kitchen counter.

Malcolm's life was a head-bent, shoulders-hunched sidelong glance at the world. The only people he looked in the eye were Ares and Laurel. When Laurel wasn't around, Ares sometimes showed Malcolm a treasure—half a Mars bar he'd saved from lunch, or a dollar bill—waving it before his brother's eyes, then quickly hiding it somewhere in the trailer. Malcolm would search frantically while Ares watched, hoping that frustration and desire would compel words out of his brother's mouth. But Malcolm eventually lost interest in the treasure hunts, or he forgot what he'd been looking for in the first place.

The school had recommended that Malcolm be evaluated by a specialist. The district was obliged to offer the tests to learning-disabled kids. But Laurel had declined. She didn't want Malcolm to be labelled. "Labels are for boxes," she said. "So you never have to look inside them. You just say, 'Oh, I don't need any more of *that*.'" She wrinkled her nose and waved her hand dismissively, as though whatever *that* was had a terrible odor. "He'll talk when he has something to say," she said sometimes, as if Malcolm's critical faculties were so sophisticated that by the age of five he had judged the world and found it unworthy of his participation. That he had missed several developmental milestones on his way to being the obtuse, angular kid he was didn't seem to worry her. Or maybe it did worry her. This was the difficult place Ares lived in: the space between Laurel's seeming lack of concern, which felt somehow effortful, and his absolute conviction that she blamed everything on him.

"Typical," she'd say, mimicking the politically correct lingo for normal kids that Malcolm's special-ed teacher used. "As if being typical were something to strive for." She liked to hold Malcolm on her lap and stroke the place on the top of his head where he'd fallen. She'd circle the spot until Malcolm's hair became twisted around her finger. Then she'd extract her hand from the tangle and start over again. Watching her, Ares would become unbearably tense, convinced that one of these days she would come out and say what they were both thinking, what they had both been thinking non-stop for nearly five years. He waited for that moment with the kind of anticipation he felt on the slow ascent to the top of a roller coaster—knowing that what happened on the other side would be both painful and exhilarating, rich with the possibility of utter annihilation.

Two days after the "nightmarish thoughts" incident, Ares took Malcolm out of class early so that the two of them could ride their bikes to the clinic for a dentist's appointment. The other kids at school cut a wide swath around Room 23, the "'tard room," as if some force inside might reach out and grab them and suck out their otherwise normal brains. Some of the boys made gooney sounds if they heard laughter coming from behind the always closed door, and Ares had more than once heard his brother referred to as a "freak." He never defended Malcolm—a worse betrayal, he knew, than what he'd done to his brother in the first place.

When he opened the door, the room felt strange. It was too warm, for one thing, and slightly muzzy; Ares felt as if he were looking through a camera lens that had not been adjusted to focus. A boy in a motorized wheelchair hung his head down over his desk in a way that did not resemble either concentration or sleep. In one corner, a teacher led a group of kids in a song that sounded like "Yesterday," except that the words and the tune were stretched out like Play-Doh, and Ares couldn't be sure. Malcolm sat at a desk counting paper clips and putting them into piles of twenty.

"He's smarter than those other kids," Ares told his mother that night, after the dentist's appointment. "He's not learning anything in there."

"Malcolm is going to learn different things in his life than math or spelling," she said. "For instance, right now he's learning forbearance."

That night, Ares woke up falling. Even when his brain registered that he was secure in his bed, he continued to have the gut-inverting sensation that he had not yet landed, that the worst was yet to come.

Don't look at the clock. But it was too late. His eyes, those betrayers, shifted to the right and there was the electric-green warning—3:15. Immediately, he felt trapped in the night, and even though his mother and brother slept nearby—Laurel in her own tiny room separated from the main room by a curtain of playing cards stapled together in long strips, and Malcolm on the living-room couch, so close that Ares could have touched them if his fingers could magically pass through the laminated plywood walls of his room—he was alone. The nighttime quiet dulled the sounds of trucks and cars on the nearby highway, and the star-pocked sky obliterated the daytime lustre of golden arches and other neon enticements. Outside, there was only the desert—huge, an impermeable membrane.

Panic flooded his body and he sat up. He slid open the small window. It stuttered along its bent metal runner until it stopped halfway and wouldn't travel any farther. He inhaled deeply, smelling things he knew: the mesquite in the air, the leftover smoke of the next-door neighbor's barbecue, the distant chemical odor of the Salton Sea.

And there it was: the memory he woke with each night of his life at precisely this hour. *Go away.* But it insisted on itself. He lay back, a forearm slung across his eyes, and let it have its way.

It was always the same. Ares is eight. Laurel has pulled off the highway into the SoCo gas station in Niland, because Malcolm has just unloaded into his diaper and something yellow and foul-smelling is leaking out onto his clothes. Even Laurel, who loves everything about this baby from his shit to his snot, can't imagine making it home with this stench. The faded ducks on Malcolm's onesie look as if they were swimming in pond scum. Ares slides as far away from his brother as possible in the back seat of the Toyota Corolla hatchback, but it isn't far enough, and he starts to gag.

"Oh, come on," Laurel says. "Like you never messed your pants."

"Not like *that*," Ares moans.

The minute Laurel stops the car, Ares bolts and goes to stand on the concrete island between two gas pumps. He quickly scans the surroundings for the possibility of humiliation in the form of someone he knows from school. Laurel holds the baby in one arm. The travel wipes and a fresh diaper hang from her mouth like cat prey as she flips up the hatchback. She lays Malcolm on the ripped upholstery and goes to work.

"He's sick! What's wrong with him?" Ares says when he gets a glimpse of Malcolm's production.

"It's the heat," Laurel says. "It's giving him the runs."

It is late in the day; the warm air sits in place like a fat man in a lawn chair. Another five minutes, and Ares feels the kind of hot that makes him want to escape his skin. Laurel always tells him that his brown skin can withstand the desert better than her fair, freckled Irish skin, and that he should be grateful to his father for this. But Ares thinks that his skin is one more thing about his father that, as of yet, has no proven value—like his last name, Ramirez, which, along with his first name, serves as an instant invitation to ridicule. He is sure that his father, whoever he is, had no say in choosing the first name, especially since, according to Laurel, he had gone back to Peru by the time Ares was born.

Laurel carries the freshly changed Malcolm toward Ares, holding the befouled diaper before her like a gift.

"Are you kidding me?" Ares says, backing away.

"Can you just help me, please, and throw this out?" She gestures with her chin toward the garbage can that sits on the other side of the island.

"I'll take *him*," Ares says.

"Jesus," Laurel sighs. "It's just the body, honey. Everyone poops." She shifts Malcolm into Ares's arms and throws the diaper into the can, where it floats above the rim like a small iceberg on the lake of crushed taco wrappers and cellophane torn from cigarette packs. Ares is hoping that they will leave as quickly as possible so that no one will be able to associate them with this embarrassing thing, but to his horror Laurel heads toward the gas station's convenience store. Ares looks after her, seized with the fear he often has that she is walking away forever. His mother is a conditional concept.

But he is holding the baby, and she loves the baby, who is brown, too, darker than Ares, and looks like a Cahuilla Indian because that's what his father, whom Malcolm has never met, either, is. She loves this baby, and she stares into his eyes as if she were looking for a secret message in those black-bean irises, something that will tell her what comes next. She smells his skin and licks his hands and trims his fingernails with her teeth. Ares can't remember if she treated him with the same intensity when he was a baby. He is both horrified at the thought and desperate for it to be true.

Malcolm starts to squirm in Ares's arms. Ares bounces him up and down, trying to settle him, but Malcolm is getting frantic, looking over Ares's shoulder, and then twisting himself around so that he can look the other way.

"She's coming back," Ares whispers into Malcolm's sweaty neck. He makes shushing noises and even starts to sing whatever he can remember of the Barney song, looking around to make sure that no one hears him, because he has enough problems in school, with the kids asking him is he, like, a horoscope sign or something? He tells them he is the god of war, which makes them laugh but then grow glum, because they see him reading books in the hallway during recess, and they suspect that he's playing with their ignorance. That's when they get angry and start punching.

Malcolm screams, and even though Ares sings louder and switches to the SpongeBob theme song, which Malcolm loves so much that he rocks back and forth in his ExerSaucer like a spaz when the show comes on, the kid isn't having any comfort. He starts to kick Ares in the stomach. He's strong, and one kick lands right below Ares's ribs and, for a second, takes his breath away. Ares tells Malcolm to cut it out or else, and Malcolm puts his fat hands on Ares's chest and pushes himself away hard, and Ares drops him.

Malcolm goes down like a medicine ball. Ares hears the thud of his body as it hits the concrete before rolling lazily off the lip of the island onto the cracked pavement beside the wheels of the car. Next, the most terrifying thing happens: nothing. Malcolm doesn't move. He doesn't make a sound. It's as if someone had pressed the pause button on the universe and everything stood still. Ares can't hear the cars passing on the highway, or the sounds of the construction equipment going full tilt behind the convenience store. All he hears is the inside of his head, which sounds like water echoing through a pipe.

Then the finger lets go of the button and everything starts up at once—Malcolm screaming, Laurel running and yelling things that don't sound like words, her arms pushing Ares out of the way, the fat guy from the convenience store running from side to side, his red company vest flapping like useless wings. He screams, "Nine-one-one!," turns around, and does his jig back to the store while Laurel shouts, "No! No!," and gets into the car and starts the engine, not even stopping to put Malcolm in his car seat but holding him on her lap, one hand pressing him to her chest, so that a flower of blood appears on her shirt, the other gripping the wheel. She pulls out of the gas station so fast that the door closes on its own, trapping the end of her patterned skirt so that it waves back and forth as if bidding Ares goodbye. And Ares, because he doesn't yet understand what's going on, lifts his hand in response and waves to the Corolla as it disappears into its own cloud of desert dust.

Later, Victor, the convenience-store guy, drives Ares to Indio in his white Dodge Ram Charger tricked out with extra-large wheels. Ares knows that it's wrong to be excited to be in such a truck, but its height makes him giddy with a sense of power and safety that he rarely ever feels down below.

The hospital is the newest, cleanest place for miles. Ares feels like a smudge. Everything is quiet, and the nurses and orderlies move as though they weren't sure the hospital was theirs to keep. A nurse tells Victor to wait—the doctor will be out soon to talk to him and his son, at which point Victor gets nervous, and he tells the nurse that he doesn't even know this kid, really, and he'd better get back to work before he gets fired.

"Just"—he says, turning to Ares, his fleshy face settling into a perplexed look as he searches for something important to say—"don't move."

In the waiting room, the television hangs like a loose tooth from the ceiling. A Spanish-language soap opera plays without sound. A man and a woman stare silently at the TV. He holds a blood-soaked blue-and-white checked kitchen towel to his head. They look calm, and it occurs to Ares that the woman is the reason for all the blood. It's something about the way she won't look the man in the eye when she tends to his wound, and the way he pats her hand, as if to let her off the hook. There is forgiveness in the way they are together.

Ares tries to read one of the wrinkled car magazines that lie on empty chairs around him, but he can't keep himself from worrying about what his life is going to be like now that he has dropped his brother. Maybe Laurel will try to find his father and hand him over, even though she says she has no idea where the man is, and he was no one special to her anyway. Or maybe she will turn Ares in to the police and he will have to go to juvenile, like Rudolpho from the fifth grade, who set fire to the cactus garden after the whole school had come in on a Saturday to plant it for Pride Day.

After a couple of hours, Laurel comes through the swinging double doors that separate the waiting room from the rest of the hospital. A nurse follows her, carrying something that looks like a huge roll of toilet paper; Ares realizes that it's Malcolm, bandaged all over like a pathetic attempt at a Halloween mummy costume. When Laurel sees Ares, she bursts into tears and runs over to him. She pulls him out of his chair and wraps herself around him. She says, "I'm sorry. Oh, baby. I'm so, so sorry."

And, standing there with his head pressed into her soft chest, her hands stroking his head so hard that he thinks his hair may come out, he has the feeling that she is not sorry because she left him at the gas station, or because Malcolm is so banged up you can't see his face. She is sorry because she knows that, like his skin and his name, this new fact is something that will stick with him for the rest of his life.

Malcolm screamed in the night. Ares waited for the reassuring clump of Laurel's feet hitting the floor, for the sound of the card curtain fluttering noisily apart, for her groggy, soothing voice to calm Malcolm down. But then Malcolm screamed again.

"Mom!" Ares yelled, stumbling out of his bed and into the living room. His underwear was twisted around his hips, and he tried to straighten it as he felt for Malcolm in the dark. Malcolm was sitting up on his couch, hitting his leg with his hand.

"Spy, spy, spy," he said.

"Mom!" Ares called. Where was she? Why did *he* have to be the one to drag his ass out of bed in the middle of the night to take care of Malcolm? He gathered Malcolm in his arms and began to rock him, holding his brother tightly so that he couldn't scratch or hit himself, as he'd seen Laurel do countless times. When Malcolm's body began to relax, Ares risked letting go with one hand, and snapped on the light above Malcolm's bed. The card curtain was open, the sweep of it pulled to one side and caught by a hook, so that it resembled a girl's hair tucked behind an ear. Laurel was not in her bed. She was having sex with Richard, Ares thought. She'd come home at dawn, creeping into the trailer thinking that Ares had no idea she'd even been gone. This was the only information he had on her, but it was useless information, since he was sure that if he told her he knew about her nighttime jour-neys she'd simply smile and ruffle his hair and not even get mad. He turned his concentration back to his brother. Malcolm's eyes were wide open, but he was in a place that was neither sleep nor wakefulness. During these night terrors, Malcolm was somehow more present than he was during the day. He'd look at Ares or Laurel as though he were about to say something, perhaps even explain what he had been think-ing about all his life. But Ares knew not to make the mistake of hoping. Hope was only a selfish desire for absolution.

"There's no spider," he said, rocking his brother, although he knew it was unlikely that Malcolm was actually talking about a spider. He was used to taking Malcolm's sounds and gestures and inventing logic around them. That is what he and his mother did: they created Malcolm's world for him and pretended they were right. "He wants juice," Laurel would say if Malcolm smacked his lips in the direction of the refrigerator. But what if they were wrong? What if Malcolm wanted the opposite of juice? What if he didn't want at all? What if the fall had knocked desire right out of him?

When Malcolm's body was no longer a heavy lump in Ares's arms but something stiff with the architecture of will, Ares knew that the terror was coming to an end.

"Hey, buddy," Ares said.

Malcolm looked toward Laurel's room.

"She's not here right now," Ares said.

Malcolm craned his neck and looked back at Ares.

"You had a dream," Ares said, although he was sure that this was wrong. The terrors were not dreams. They were more like the moment when a cartoon character runs off a cliff—before he starts to fall; the terrors were a seizure of understanding. Ares thought that in these nocturnal moments his brother had periods of recognition, periods in which he realized that he was trapped by silence, by useless fixations, by the need to make the sound *pa* over and over again, or to count peas. Ares thought that if he were in his brother's situation he'd be frightened all the time.

By the time Malcolm fell asleep, Ares was fully awake. His body was wired, restless. He lay in his bed, staring at his bookshelf, another castoff that Laurel had picked up in Slab City, the old gunnery range where Richard, along with the other assorted snowbirds and wanderers, stayed every winter. Even in the dark, he could make out the dull, pseudo-gilded letters on the binding of "Gold and Gods of Peru," a stalwart hardback among the shorter, stubbier paperbacks in his collection. It was a library book, long overdue. Two years overdue, he reminded himself, and felt the familiar pinch of guilt he experienced whenever he caught sight of the book. He had checked it out of the school library in the fourth grade in order to write a report on Peru. Somehow, he had never returned it. It wasn't that he'd forgotten; he had thought about returning the book many times. But each time he did the idea seemed overwhelming, exhausting, as if the book weighed a hundred pounds and he would be required to carry it by himself. The book's absence had escaped the notice of Mrs. Pearl, the school librarian, and he had so far got away without paying a fine. But this made him feel even worse. Getting away with something was worse than suffering the consequences. He was too embarrassed to go into the library anymore. He had become a reader of Dumpster literature—books that other people didn't think were good enough to keep. In this way, he had read "Dianetics," a biography of Dolly Parton, some pretty good espionage books, and "East of Eden," minus twenty pages in the middle, which had been ripped out.

He had thought that Laurel might say something about the Peru book, but she didn't make a habit of engaging in Ares's school life, and it was unlikely that she would notice the book unless Ares pointed it out to her. He reached over and took it from the shelf. A month ago, he had found out from other kids at school that Mrs. Pearl's son had been arrested for murder. His own crime now seemed pathetic. He was an accidental hook thief. Mrs. Pearl was the mother of a killer.

The sound of tires crunching over the rubble driveway swelled and then stopped. The car engine cut out, and Ares heard the gentle ticking of the motor as the door squeaked open and slammed shut. He could barely hear Laurel's entrance into the trailer. He thought about calling out, letting his mother know that he was onto her. But what if that made her stop going out? Then he would never be able to experience the relief of her return. The card curtain made a noise like a thousand tumbling dominoes as she let it fall from its hook.

He carried "Gold and Gods of Peru" to school the next day, but when he approached Mrs. Pearl's desk he couldn't bring himself to take it out of his backpack. She looked up at him expectantly. Her hair was pulled back into a ponytail, but one strand had broken loose and she repeatedly tucked it back in, looking embarrassed, as though something more private than a lock of hair had escaped confinement. She had a round face and thin lips, and freckles spilling across the bridge of her nose. He thought she was too pretty to have a murderer for a son. She had no eyebrows, but she drew little arches above her eyes with a dark pencil, which made her look as though everything astonished her. Her nails had grown out beyond their pink polish, and little half-moons of natural color showed where the nail met the skin. Ares felt as if he were seeing a part of her that he wasn't supposed to see.

"Do you need help?" she asked.

"No."

A framed picture sat on her desk. It was of a boy, smiling. He had dark hair like Mrs. Pearl, and real eyebrows. Acne had made a rutted landscape of his face. He sat in front of the familiar blue sheet that the school photographers hung on the gym wall when they came for photo day. He was looking off to the side and up, as if trying to think of something. The name of the photographer was embossed in gold across the bottom of the photo. You could get the photo without the name on it, but that cost extra. Like his mother, he supposed, Mrs. Pearl had just kept the proof copy and thrown out the order form.

Ares had heard the talk about Mrs. Pearl's son, but there were many different stories: he had murdered someone in a botched holdup at a convenience store; or he was part of the gang that had been terrorizing towns around the Salton Sea. No one really knew what was true, but each kid pronounced his version of events with grave certainty, thrilled, for a moment, to be the one everyone else looked to for the truth. The photo on Mrs. Pearl's desk was in a heavy brown frame decorated with painted flowers. The words "For Mom" were stencilled on one of the petals. Ares knew that inmates made license plates, and he wondered if they made picture frames, too.

Mrs. Pearl saw where Ares's gaze had fallen. "There's a sign-up sheet for the computer," she said, pointing to an adjacent wall.

"I don't need a computer," he said.

She waited for him to state his purpose. When he remained silent, she sighed and looked mildly annoyed: another kid ruining her day. He left the library.

That afternoon, Ares's team played a team from Indio. Ares ran past the best player on the team and whispered "Typical" three times. The shooter missed, but Ares's team lost anyway.

Malcolm and Ares biked past the Gunnery Range checkpoint station. It was abandoned, but a beer can stood on the window ledge. Teen-agers came out here to drink and get high. Every so often, the cops would do a sweep, and then there would be an assembly about "Just say no." Ares and Malcolm rode past the station and on into Slab City, past the bar and an advertisement for a community talent show that was to take place in three weeks. Ares knew that Slab City had an unofficial mayor, and that it even had its own shortwave radio broadcast. But you had to bring in your own water and get rid of your own sewage, because Slab City wasn't really an official city. Laurel said that none of the people there paid for the land they lived on. There were people in Slab City who had big, expensive trailers and who could afford to pay taxes and live in a place with sewage pipes and fences, but they chose not to because, she said, they were also the kind of people who liked to get away with things.

The day was hot, and nobody lingered outside the trailers. Ares banged on the door of Richard's Airstream, an aluminum tube, shaped like a cigar, its surface a patchwork of cast-off material that he cobbled together whenever the trailer needed repairs. Richard had to stoop to fit his long, narrow body inside the frame. He shaved his head, and Ares could see two thick blue veins running behind his temples. He looked out at the boys through round wire-rimmed glasses.

Malcolm squawked happily. "You yell like that, someone's liable to come out of their trailer and shoot you," Richard said, though Ares could tell that he enjoyed Malcolm's enthusiasm. One of Richard's pant legs was tucked into a scuffed motorcycle boot; the other was hitched undecidedly halfway up the shank of its boot. A Chinese symbol hung from a leather thong at his neck. Richard claimed that he had once worked in Asia. He also said that he had fought, but not in a war. He was never specific about which country he had worked in or whom he had fought for, and whenever Ares tried to pin him down Richard was evasive. When Ares learned about the C.I.A., he decided that Richard must be an agent. But Laurel said that Richard wasn't good at keeping secrets—this was how she knew that he didn't really love her. She said she didn't think that he was someone the government would trust.

Malcolm couldn't contain his excitement. He reached for Richard's shirt, trying to pull him out of the trailer.

"O.K., O.K.," Richard said. "But I'm not paying this time. Business is bad."

"No fair," Ares said.

"That's my deal," Richard said, his voice so low it sounded as though it were rumbling from the back of a cavern. "Take it or leave it."

Malcolm loved the bumpy ride over the rock dunes. The jeep lurched forward and back and from side to side all at the same time, so that it didn't seem as if they were actually getting anywhere. Richard huffed and groaned, his cigarette bobbing between his lips. He made a big show of effort as he shifted gears with his right hand. The long fingers of his left hand gripped the frayed plastic cover of the steering wheel. If the wheel were a person's neck, Ares thought, that person would be dead by now. He wondered if Richard had ever killed a person with his bare hands.

A few minutes later, Richard stopped the jeep, and Malcolm and Ares scrambled out and ran off into the rocky foothills. "What's yours is mine!" Richard called after them.

When Malcolm and Ares went scrapping with Richard, Richard rewarded their finds: a nickel for small scraps; a quarter for something big. Richard said that in previous years he had found bombs, and that he'd pay five dollars if the boys came up with one, but Ares had never seen a bomb, and he wasn't sure what it would look like. Richard sold the scrap to a junker, who then sold it to a foundry in Mexico. At one time, he had been able to make a certain living off his finds—enough to carry him through a winter in the desert. But the Mexicans weren't doing much business these days, and scrapping had become more of a way to pass time than an actual job.

Richard threw a beat-up cowboy hat over his bald head, took his Geiger counter out of the jeep, and began to walk slowly. The machine gave off a soft hum that Malcolm tried to match with his own voice as he walked around in crazy eights. Ares was never sure that Malcolm understood what they were looking for; he presented rocks and pieces of metal to Richard with the same zeal. And sometimes he just wandered, head bent toward the ground, and Ares knew that he wasn't looking for anything at all.

Ares dragged his feet so that they displaced the top layer of soil. He was disappointed that Richard wasn't going to pay them for their discoveries, and he considered blowing off the whole search. But the truth was, even without the incentive of a reward, he loved studying the ground like this, directing his gaze and his entire mind onto minute bits of earth as they passed below him. When he was with Richard, Ares didn't think about Malcolm, or what he had done to make Malcolm the way he was. He didn't think about his mother, his library book, or Coach Ortega. He thought about dirt. The desert ceased to be the impervious, dry expanse that it usually was. It became the world writ small, miniature valleys and mountains, square inches of variegated detail. It became a place where you could see that you were not always right about what a thing was. It gave him hope.

Twenty yards from the jeep, the counter sent up a strong, insistent beep. Ares and Malcolm ran over to Richard, who stooped down, studying something on the ground. When Ares reached him, Richard held up a magazine clip. "This is a surprise," he said. "Thought things were pretty well picked over. Unless this is new. Meth addicts killing each other with machine guns now." He shook his head and handed the clip to Malcolm. "Put it in the box." Malcolm held the magazine to his chest like a treasured doll and ran to the jeep.

"He thinks it's something to love," Ares said.

"He wouldn't be the first person to love a gun, that's for sure."

"Mom says it's O.K., the weird stuff that he does."

"Well, the way I see it, when you're in a place you forget what it looks like from the outside. It's like how you never see yourself grow taller or older. You need other people to tell you the truth. That's how we all end up living the lives we do. Nobody ever tells us what we really look like."

Ares wondered if his mother had ever told Richard about Malcolm's fall. If Richard had been at the gas station that day, he might have caught Malcolm with his big, powerful hands. He might have saved him.

An hour later, Malcolm and Ares had found nothing. Richard had found an alloy bullet casing and some random pieces of metal. After throwing his finds into the box, Richard squatted down by the back wheel of the jeep and lit another cigarette. He took off his hat and wiped the sweat from his head with his palm. Malcolm picked up the Geiger counter and walked with it, waving it over the ground. It was turned off, but Malcolm made the sound of the motor, and then such a perfect replication of the beep of discovery that Richard and Ares both looked up expectantly.

"Should put that talent to good use," Richard said, exhaling smoke.

"How?" Ares said.

Richard shrugged. "Decoy. Could make a person think something was there that wasn't. You'd be shooting at a ghost."

Ares tried to figure out how this comment fit into his growing picture of Richard. Maybe he was a bounty hunter. Maybe he was a hired killer. Maybe he was a criminal, too.

Malcolm ran back to the jeep grinning. Richard reached into his pocket and pulled out two dollar bills. He gave one to each boy.

"You said you weren't paying," Ares said.

"For keeping me company," Richard said.

As Ares turned his bicycle into the parking lot of the store in front of the date farm, he looked back over his shoulder to make sure that Malcolm was following him. Only a few cars were still there at the end of the day—tourists collecting their prepackaged dates for the trip home.

Inside, Ares ordered two date shakes from the girl behind the deli counter; she looked like a drawing in the sex book that his mother used to keep by the side of her bed, but which was now the foundation layer of one of Malcolm's pyramids. The girl had dark eyes rimmed with black pencil, and her mouth was full and turned up at the ends, so that even though she wasn't smiling at Ares, even though she barely seemed to register him as she blended the shakes and yelled above the sound to the other, fatter girl behind the counter, he imagined her as one of those drawings, the outlines of her body formed from repeated strokes of a pencil.

Malcolm waited outside at a picnic table, patiently ripping a paper napkin into small bits. Ares handed him the shake and, to Malcolm's delight, blew the paper off the straw. After a few sips, Ares was sick of the oversweet shake, but Malcolm was stunned into pleasure by the drink. He didn't take his mouth from the straw the entire time he drank, not even to breathe. Malcolm was this way with everything he did; it was as if a given activity wiped out all thought of anything else. His entire existence narrowed in on the time and the physical space of one second. And then another. Ares knew that his brother's problem was exactly this disconcerting habit of fixating on one single, often meaningless thing to the exclusion of all other, more relevant information. But he sometimes wondered whether it would be a relief to be like Malcolm, and not have the whole army of your impulses and contradictory desires trying to crash the gates of your consciousness at once.

Malcolm reached the bottom of his shake with a wet slurp. He finally took his mouth off the straw and inhaled a laugh. He peeled the plastic lid off the shake and licked the underside.

"I guess you liked that," Ares said.

"Ma, ma, ma, ma," Malcolm said.

"No more." There was no end to Malcolm's appetite. He ate whenever food was offered to him, even if he had just had a huge meal. Laurel and Ares had learned to tell him when he was finished eating, and they were expert at distracting him so that his mind could tear itself away from the idea of food and land on a new obsession for a while. Of all Malcolm's traits, it was this hunger that upset Ares the most. It filled him with a great nostalgic sadness for lost things, the way a rich person might feel if he had to live as a pauper, always remembering the fancy cars and clothes of a bygone life.

Ares took Malcolm's cup, replaced the top, and tossed it into the nearby garbage can. Malcolm let out a piercing scream and raced to retrieve the cup. Gently, he wiped it off. "Pop, pop, pop," he chanted over and over. Ares knew that he would bring the cup home and add it to his menagerie of inanimate objects—rocks, sticks, empty envelopes, and soda-can pull tabs that he collected and often spoke to in strange murmurs and squeaks.

On the way home, Malcolm and Ares pedalled side by side. When they saw a flock of white pelicans making their low flight toward the sea, Malcolm looked at Ares with a huge grin.

"Do it, man," Ares said, encouragingly. "Go ahead and do it."

And Malcolm let out a caw that was so exact, so piercingly beautiful, that Ares felt his heart contract.

"What did he eat?" Laurel said, as she watched Malcolm bound up the trailer steps, screeching his uncanny pelican caw. Once inside, Malcolm spun around the living room, his arms spread on either side of him.

"A shake," Ares said. He knew that sugar, for Malcolm, was like a friend who was always urging you to do things that would get you into trouble. He waited for Laurel's admonition, but it didn't come. She simply stood, hands on hips, head tilted to one side. She watched Malcolm intently, waiting for the right moment to step in and grab him the way girls in the school playground waited to leap into the path of a swinging jump rope at exactly the right second, so that they wouldn't trip. When she did move in, she quickly wrapped Malcolm in her arms, holding him to her body. He laughed and continued trying to flap his arms, but she had him trapped.

"Let's have a bath, baby," she said into his hair as she moved him awkwardly toward the bathroom. "Help me with his clothes," she called back to Ares.

Ares reluctantly followed behind, reaching for Malcolm as his mother bent down to run the bath water. He grabbed Malcolm's T-shirt. "Arms up," he said. Malcolm didn't obey, and instead squirmed inside Ares's hold, grinning and laughing. "Arms up, dude," Ares said more forcefully, frustrated by his brother, and by the obviousness of his own unmentioned mistake.

"Don't yell," Laurel said over the sound of water slapping against the plastic-lined tub. "It doesn't help."

Ares got the shirt up and over Malcolm's head, then started on his jeans. He leaned down, and Malcolm draped his body over Ares's bent back, making it nearly impossible for Ares to move or to push the pants down Malcolm's hips. When he finally got Malcolm's pants to his ankles, Ares sat on the floor to untie his shoes. Malcolm sat, too, and then lay back on the bathroom floor, thrilled by his nakedness. His hands went to his penis.

"Cut it out, man," Ares said.

"That's why it's there," Laurel said, reaching under Malcolm's arms and lifting him up and into the tub.

"Fuck!" Ares exclaimed when the splash hit his shirt and pants.

"Lovely," she said.

"Sorry."

"That word coming out of those beautiful lips," she said. "O.K., baby." Laurel turned to Malcolm, sighing. "Want bubbles?" She showed Malcolm the nearly empty bottle capped with a plastic elephant head.

Ares left the bathroom, closing the door behind him. Still, he could hear the sound of Laurel struggling to quiet Malcolm. She sang "Hush Little Baby," and Malcolm droned along. Ares headed out of the trailer and walked to the edge of town, toward the beach. He found a fallen palm frond and dragged it close to the water. The Salton Sea, or the "sinkhole," as he referred to it, moved listlessly in the windless early evening. A few birds alighted on its surface, floated around in the water, then took off again, like people at a drive-through. Ares remembered when he was six, a time before Malcolm, when his own arms and legs were as thin and rubbery as licorice rope. He had pleaded with Laurel to take him for a swim in "my ocean." Then, the sinkhole had been his biggest treasure, a jewel as huge as he could imagine the world to be, its distant shore his unreachable horizon. Laurel had let him swim, although even then there were reports of fish dying, poisoned by the polluted runoff from farm irrigation that fed the sea.

Ares thought that Mrs. Pearl must really love her son—to keep his high-school picture on her desk like that, where everyone could see it. Maybe she didn't believe he was really a killer. Maybe she thought that if she took down the picture people would think that she had given up on him. Ares hoped that he wouldn't get acne when he was older. But probably he would, since he was a thief and also a trash-talker and there had to be some kind of payback.

He walked home, past the wood-frame houses and trailers, some derelict, some enlivened by cactus gardens and tangles of sagging flowers and date palms that resembled girls with long torsos and tiny heads. He passed the general store that sold cans of chili and sauerkraut, frozen dinners, emergency flashlights, and lengths of garden hose. The school bus stopped in front of the store each morning, carrying the young children to Niland and the older ones to the high school in Calipatria. By the time the bus returned each afternoon, there were only five or six kids on it.

He often wondered why he and Malcolm and their mother didn't live in Palm Springs or Palm Desert, someplace closer to his mother's work. Laurel said it was because they owned their trailer, and she could never afford to buy property in those rich-people places. But Ares thought there were other reasons, too. The sea, that repository of crippled nature, comforted Laurel. Sometimes he saw her there in the evenings, staring out at the flat plane of water while Malcolm wandered around the shore, stooping to inspect garbage. The Salton Sea needed its champions the way stray dogs needed rescuers, people who turned up their noses at the purchase of purebreds when there were so many abandoned frightened mongrels lurking beneath underpasses and beside freeways.

He wondered if his family would be able to survive anywhere else. Bombay Beach, like all the half attempts at towns nearby, was a place for people who had a provisional relationship to the world. Mecca, Niland—these towns were full of migrant laborers, drug dealers, snowbirds in their patched-together homes, like Richard. Daily, Ares watched Border Patrol cars speeding south along the highway, lights flashing self-importantly like some backward version of a police escort. Kids were pulled out of school all the time, and you never saw them again.

By the time Ares got home, Malcolm was asleep. Laurel was sitting at the kitchen table, knitting a hat.

"Sorry about the shake," Ares said.

"Maybe sugar isn't such a good idea unless we're really prepared for the consequences."

"You told me that before."

"You probably forgot."

"I didn't forget. I remembered it the whole time."

She looked up from her knitting. "Then why'd you do it?"

"I don't know."

"Everyone messes up," she said. "Look at me." She held her knitting out in front of her. "I messed up this whole row. I think I dropped a stitch. There's a big hole." She put the knitting to her face so that her eye lined up with the gap. "I see you," she said in a singsong voice.

"Is Richard leaving soon?"

She put down the knitting. "It's almost June. Pretty late for him to be hanging around, isn't it?"

"Maybe he's going to stay."

"Richard?" she said, laughing lightly. "No, no, no. He's not a stayer."

"Like you?"

"Me? Where would I go?"

He shrugged. "Nowhere."

"Nowhere that doesn't include my guys," she said, beginning to unravel a row of knitting. "Don't talk. I have to concentrate now."

That night, he woke up to the sound of a siren. He listened until its notes had been swallowed up by the desert. Someone was about to get caught. Perhaps it was someone from Mexico, or even Peru. Or perhaps it was someone who had killed someone else, like Mrs. Pearl's son. He looked at the clock. 3:15. He lay back. And there they were again at the gas station, on that hot, hot day.

His cheeks were filled with words. His skin felt tight, his muscles ached with the desire to release them. The players ran up and down the court. He told himself, *Don't do it.* But he couldn't hold it in. "Murder!" he yelled as an opponent lined up for an outside shot.

He was thrown out of the game. Ortega didn't even bother to yell at him. He just gestured with his head toward the locker room and Ares knew that he was finished. There was a can of soda sitting on a bench in the locker room. Ares shook it, popped the top, and let Coke spray all over the walls.

Ortega arrived in the locker room and surveyed the mess. "You're out of here, Ramirez," he said calmly. "You're off the team." He stood there for another minute, his hands on his hips, staring at his shoes as if he were trying to think of some final words he could offer. Ares wanted to tell him not to bother. It wasn't like in the movies. It wouldn't make a difference.

Mrs. Pearl was in the stacks, reshelving books from a small rolling cart.

"You know the Dewey decimal system?" Ares asked. He was still wearing his basketball uniform, stained now with Coke spray.

"Yes," she said, looking up. "You have to in order to be a librarian."

"That's cool," he said.

"Are you interested in becoming a librarian?"

"I don't know."

"It's a satisfying job."

"Do you have to go to college?"

"Yes."

"I don't know, then."

"You don't want to go to college?"

Ares shrugged.

"You have a lot of years yet to decide."

Ares wondered whether her son would ever get out of jail and go to college. Maybe they had college in jail. But what would be the point? If you were in for murder, you were never going to get out, and, even if you did, who would ever trust you again? Even a librarian had to be trusted not to steal the books.

Ares followed Mrs. Pearl back to her desk. As she sat down, she caught him looking at the photograph of her son.

"Do you want to ask me about him?" she said.

"No," he lied.

"Kids are curious. They hear things."

"Not me," Ares said.

"We're getting money for his defense," she said. "We sold our house."

"So he didn't do it?" Ares said.

"He was set up," she said.

He couldn't tell if she believed this or not. She absentmindedly rubbed her thumb across the glass, cleaning off a fine layer of dust. Ares could almost feel her touch on his own face. It felt like his mother's touch, when she bent down to kiss him good night, brushing her lips against his cheek, then pushing his hair back off his forehead with her palm, as if clearing the way for him to see his dreams.

Susan Straight

Susan Straight was born in Riverside in 1960. Currently the director of the Department of Creative Writing at the University of California, Riverside, she received her Master of Fine Arts from the University of Massachusetts, Amherst. She is the author of five novels: *I Been in Sorrow's Kitchen and Licked Out All the Pots*; *Blacker Than a Thousand Midnights*; *The Gettin' Place*; *Highwire Moon* (a finalist for the National Book Award); and *A Million Nightingales*; and one collection of short stories, *Aquaboogie* (winner of the Milkweed National Fiction Prize). Her work has appeared in numerous publications, including the *New York Times*, the *Los Angeles Times*, *The Nation*, and *Harper's Magazine*. She lives in Riverside.

This except from *The Gettin' Place* takes place in Rio Seco, a fictionalized Riverside that appears in many of Straight's stories. The novel is about an African American family's struggle to prove their innocence—on their own, without the help of the racially and socioeconomically biased local police—when two girls are murdered on their property.

from *The Gettin' Place*

The stairways were dim and steep, the night smell of cement still trapped by shadow, but when Marcus reached the courtyard of his apartment building and glanced back at his window, knowing he'd forgotten something, the wind had begun to clear the mist from the huge arched panes.

He hesitated near the curved wrought-iron railing that lined all the stairways. He'd already been to the gym when it opened at six a.m., walking the two blocks in the darkness. When he'd come back, his red message light flashed, and he'd known it could only be one of his brothers calling that early. Damn sure wasn't a woman. He was fresh out of females since Colette had moved back to Chicago. When he'd pressed the button, his mother's voice was, as always, uncomfortable on the machine. "Marcus? Marcus," she said. That was all she ever said to the empty space before she hung up.

Then he heard his oldest brother, Demetrius, after another beep. "Marcus. Marcus! Shit." His voice was ragged and impatient, as always, and he hung up, too.

Marcus didn't want to call either of them back. He was heading over there now anyway. And walking, goddamnit—he couldn't believe it.

He leaned against the railing for a moment. He'd left Demetrius's navy work shirt on the bed, the one he'd borrowed last week when he'd changed the oil on the Lexus at his father's place, more for show than anything else. "Hell," Marcus said softly, turning toward the courtyard. "I had that bad boy dry-cleaned just so Demetrius wouldn't talk shit, but I'm not carryin it all the way to Treetown."

He smiled at the thought of chemical creases and plastic wrap on the Dickies work shirt. Now Demetrius couldn't say, "Why you bring me back a dirty shirt and make more work for my wife, man?" Demetrius still loved to call Enchantee "my wife" in front of Marcus, even after eight years, because Marcus had loved her first. Marcus rubbed the razored line of his fresh-cut fade, remembering Demetrius dressing to go out, back when Marcus was in junior high and Demetrius was grown. The silky, long-pointed collars lay on the bed like bent wings, and Demetrius would spit from the doorway, "Don't let them grubby fingers touch nothin, boy. Only lady fingers touch them shirts." Marcus would watch the shimmering Qiana patterns stretch across the wide shoulders, feeling his own bony elbows hang from the plain white T-shirts all five boys usually wore. Marcus was the baby boy. That was what their lips popped scornfully all day: "*Ba*-by boy. Sissyfly. Go head on and bawl."

But when you thirty and he's almost forty, ten years ain't hardly nothin, Marcus thought, smiling again. Three negatives. Our favorite way to use em; that's what Brother Lobo used to say. Africans always emphasize.

He walked along the curving cement wall. Brother Lobo's black history class at Rio Seco High had changed his life, altered the way he saw everything from his father's chicken coop to his friends' insults. Lobo had been his idol for years, even after Marcus had come back from college to see him nearly blind at forty-five from glaucoma, barely able to play dominoes at Jackson Park. If Marcus didn't get any class assignments next week at Rio Seco High, where he'd only been teaching for a year, which of his flat-eyed freshmen would even remember him?

It could have been one of his students who stole the Lexus, for all he knew. He crossed the darkened courtyard, where the slow dawn hadn't reached through the three giant palms growing from circles cut in the cement. Las Palmas was the best apartment building in this historic downtown district. Marcus looked at the facade, the arches and gargoyles and hand-painted tile apartment numbers. It was taking him long green, longer than those palm fronds, to pay the rent on number 24 and the lease note on the Lexus, and now here he was walking, just like any wandering Treetown brother. Like his own brother Finis. The rest of them would bust up laughing when they found out about his car.

Leaving the arched entry, he moved his eyes casually up and down the street for patrol cars. A brother strolling this district at dawn was always an intriguing sight for law enforcement, even if he was wearing a J. Crew pullover and chinos, not sagging-to-the-sidewalk khakis. He stopped at the corner, thinking again of Demetrius's shirt. Demetrius talked big yang about Marcus's clothes, his apartment, his car. "My baby bro got him a *sherbert* car—a damn Lexus," Demetrius would laugh, and the men in the barn, working on engines and rims, would laugh, too.

"The ride's maroon," Marcus would say easily, knowing that the mangled pastel word didn't have a damn thing to do with the paint job.

As of yesterday, the ride was history, he thought, just like all this. He passed the museum, the newly renovated opera house, and the new coffee bars and bakeries catering to the crowds growing every month since downtown was no longer "redeveloping" but had become "The Historic Moorish District." The garden district had flowery yards, the Victorian district three-story gingerbread mansions; now the Moorish district had all its buildings and facades restored or newly faked with creamy plaster, red-tiled roofs, grillwork scrolling, and fountains.

The Lexus was history as of last weekend. Somebody else's story now, a quick tale to tell. Yo, man, we plucked this Casper's Lexus, from downtown, and you know that dude in San Bernardino needed him some Lexus parts? He got em now…

The only brother in the building, Marcus thought, and they gotta steal my hooptie. The insurance adjustor sure thought the thieves were brothers. In his halting-hard accent, maybe Boston, the man had said, "Mr. ah, Thompson?"

"Yes," Marcus had said carefully.

"Your Lexus was stolen from outside your residence on Las Palmas Drive?"

"Yes."

The voice shifted, emanating conspiratorial sympathy. "Well, the police found your vehicle stripped, in a lot off Olive Street. Do you know where that is?"

Treetown. Marcus played along with the clucking pity in the voice. "Way down there, huh?" he said, biting off his consonants.

"Not hard to guess some nice young riverbottom gentlemen have, ah, distributed the parts by now. Well, I'll send you the forms, and you'll get them back to me, right?"

"Sure," Marcus said, rounding that r hard. "Did they tow the car yet?"

"I'm not sure." The voice turned cautious.

"I'll take care of it. My father runs Arrow Towing. Off Pepper Avenue. *Way* down there by the riverbottom, about as way as it gets."

Marcus turned on California Boulevard, which ran the length of downtown and went all the way north past the university and the airport. He passed mouth after mouth of gated, dark parking caves. The brothers took my hooptie and didn't even check the glove compartment fulla tapes, he thought. Robin Harris. Richard Pryor. What white dude's gon have *Bicentennial Nigger* and some old BarKays and Cameo? No solidarity, man.

He was hoping his brothers wouldn't be at the yard when he asked his father to lend him a car. He needed transportation by Monday. Coming out of the chilled, ghostly corridor of banks and office buildings, Marcus blinked in the glare from the sliver of sun reflecting off the mirrored towers gathered at the corner of California and Pepper Avenue. The city was trying to attract companies to the newly built Los Arbolitos business park, with its spindly, just planted jacarandas and orange trees. Marcus listened to the fountain splashing around the huge concrete sign. A flapping banner advertised office space from one of the towers. The problem with vacancies, according to what Marcus read in the newspaper and heard in downtown conversations, was that although Los Arbolitos was attractive, it was at the edge of "a transitional area." In other words, this section of Pepper Avenue was too damn close to the Westside, and, even worse, to Treetown.

Down there. No, Treetown wasn't south, he thought. Due west. But it felt like down to them. He'd heard newscasters say the same thing about

South-Central L.A. "Down in the south-central part of the city today, robbery claimed a life…" And in Rio Seco, people in restaurants said, "You're heading down there through Treetown? Yeah, it's a shortcut to the freeway, but…"

Marcus waited at a stoplight on Pepper, looking at the blurred territorial edges. A long stretch of vacant lot, barely needled with winter grass among the broken glass and snowy Styrofoam bits, led to the slope of the arroyo that meandered through the city, spilling into the river-bottom not far from his father's place. Marcus and his brothers used to travel up the arroyo every day to find aluminum cans and other boys and fights in the Westside, sometimes even clambering up the banks and venturing downtown. Back then, downtown was half-deserted, but the cops still knew within a few minutes if a knot of Treetown boys walked up Pepper Avenue past a certain point.

He was near that certain point right now, he thought, smiling. It was a small, bare street marked with nothing but a scatter of green foxtails growing around the silver-edged hole where the sign pole had been knocked out by a car. The city had conveniently neglected to replace the sign, which used to read Gray Lane and lead down a long slant to the collection of houses called Gray Hollow, old shacks, really, that used to house citrus workers like his parents. Adjacent to the old houses, the last of which had just been bulldozed last year, was Jackson Park. The city had razed the houses and flattened all the tree-covered lots nearby, then fenced in the park with chain link and only one gate after a shooting that had wounded Brother Lobo and killed a young brother named Louis Wiley. Now some of the men that used to congregate under the pepper trees in the lot, playing dominoes and drinking, gathered in his uncle's barbecue joint.

Marcus crossed the street. The city was just as happy to leave this little lane to natives only, who had to want to get to the Westside this way. Commuters could stay on the avenue and go to work. They didn't need to venture down that slope. He grinned at the thought of his father and brothers watching the steady stream of cars passing their lot, remembering one day when traffic backed up and they sat in the yard laughing at the stoic, panicked faces briefly robbed of motion, almost out of Treetown.

The blue strip mall, a collection of tiny stores segmented like a long caterpillar crawling beside the avenue, was the uneasy outpost in this no-man's land. Marcus knew the businesses, a dry cleaner, a video store, a liquor store, nail salon, and doughnut shop, all depended on the commuters and downtown, and the owners were probably holding their breaths waiting for more commercial development between them and Los Arbolitos.

Marcus always stopped at the Donut Place, where the Cambodian owner, Som, made the best pillowy-soft glazed doughnuts in the city. But not today, he thought. Last week, Som had pushed forward a thin, sullen boy he said was his nephew. "Remember him, Teacha? He come last year from the camp. He go to the school, take your class now, okay? He need to learn so much." The boy had looked away. "He don't want get up one o'clock to make doughnut, he have to go to school, right, Teacha?"

I'm not a teacher today. I'm a walkin brother, Marcus thought. From here to the overpass, the sidewalk along Pepper was edged in another vacant lot. Everything in a long corridor had been torn down back when the city built the freeway, in 1960, the year he was born. His father and uncle said that Westside and Treetown used to merge together in one black neighborhood, and this was where the stores and barbershop and a bar had been. "Used to couldn't tell," his uncle Oscar would always say. "Niggas was niggas. But the Westside was city cats, lot of em worked for the aircraft plants. And Treetown was country. That's what they called us. But they came over here to drink, I'ma tell you that."

The overpass was a block away, as gray and curved as a huge rattler dusty from the hills. The pastel-pink bungalows of the Kozy Komfort Inn were like dollhouses from this distance, all in a straight line among short palms with fanned fronds. You'd expect to see the shimmering blue pool and girls in bikinis, way back in the fifties.

But the pool was filled in, the motel grounds defined by chain link topped with barbed wire. Usher Price sat on a folding chair outside the bungalow at the end that used to be the motel office.

When he saw Marcus, he slid through the propped-open sliding gate, squinting in the faint light under a palm. Marcus slowed his pace; he passed here driving every now and then, but never walking. He didn't know what to expect, what Usher might say or do, since it had been years since he'd seen him. Maybe since a few years out of high school, and Usher had smoked way too many Super Kools, cigarettes dipped in liquid PCP: same thing as his brother Finis.

"Say, man, Marcus? Hella long time," Usher said, close now, his eyes watery with what looked like weak tea, his thick hair combed straight back from his scarred forehead and patted down to a spongy flare at his ears.

"Usher," Marcus said, touching his palm to Usher's hard calluses. "What up?"

"You, man," Usher said, looking past Marcus to the street. "Seen you drivin to your Daddy's place in that Lexus sometimes."

"You see me walkin now," Marcus said, shrugging. "Midnight Auto Supply got my ride."

They both laughed, knowing that the young guys who stole cars now had nothing to do with the old Proudfoot brothers, the ones who'd stolen every vehicle in Treetown back in the seventies. But saying the three words to someone his age from Treetown made Marcus's heart unclench a bit.

"Where you stay now?" Usher fixed his eyes on Marcus's face, and Marcus heard the word float through his forehead. Stay. White people, downtown people, always asked, "Where do you live?" But growing up, he'd always heard the softer word. Where he stay now? She stay with her sister in Olive Gardens. Marcus smiled, knowing that Brother Lobo would love to talk about the origins of the word. Back after slavery, all those brothers drifting from place to place, until "Where you live?" became "Where you stay?" Temporary, fleeting. Where do you rest your head, for this moment?

"I'm stayin downtown, on Las Palmas," he said, and Usher nodded. He knew that for anyone in Treetown, no matter how long he'd been living elsewhere, his home was his father's place. Marcus pulled out a five-dollar bill from his front pocket, the money he'd put there because he'd known that walking would bring him Usher, or someone else from way back. He wondered who else he knew sleeping behind the dusty windows. The Kozy Komfort had gone from a seedy motel to a way station for the men so close to mental deterioration that they got government checks. In a few hours, figures would weave among the palm trunks or sit in the squares of shade cast by each tiny, peaked porch over the rooms.

Behind him, Marcus heard the short blip of a siren, like radar locating his spine, and he held himself perfectly still, the familiar prickle coating his forehead and spreading across his shoulders. That twirl of sound, lassoing him in one circle...the patrol cars stopping him and his brothers and friends whenever they'd walked where they weren't welcome with arroyo mud sculpting their shoes. "See some ID? You fit the description..."

He and Usher stared at the dirt between them. But the sound was swallowed by the powerful engine moving fast down Pepper. "Big shit goin on in the jungle," Usher finally said. "I seen lights goin past my window in the dark. Fire engines." His eyes were dreamy, sliding about in remembrance "Like red rockets."

Marcus looked toward the overpass. The wind was picking up now, and he could feel it much stronger here than in the protected slots between buildings downtown "You seen Finis?" he asked, the same question that rang in his ears each time he heard a siren.

Usher shook his head. "He come up here to hang, but he don't sleep here. Ain't he stayin at y'all place?" Marcus nodded, and Usher went on nervously. "Some dudes from L.A. here now. They always sayin they hate this country-ass place. Judge sent em out."

Touching Usher's palm again lightly, Marcus said, "All right, man, I'll check."

Walking toward the tunnel, he thought that no one in Treetown ever said good-bye. People he knew from the high school or downtown called out "Bye!" or even "Bye-bye!" But once, when he was about ten, he'd turned and said, "Good-bye, Aintielila," to his uncle's wife at the barbecue place, and she'd frowned deeply, her high forehead rippling with lines.

"Don't never say good-bye like that," she told him, "unless you really goin someplace. For good."

In Treetown, people said, "Next time, man," or "Later," or "I'll see you." They said, "All right-then brothaman," to finish their business. Or, "I'll check, man," drawing the thread already that would lead them to cross each other's paths again.

Marcus breathed lightly in the dank, chill air under the freeway and didn't look at the markings of Treetown and Westside and Agua Dulce and Terracina boys. When he came back out into the stronger light, he felt the wind gusting in steady currents, like it had all day yesterday. A fall wind rushing down from the nearby desert, shredding the remnants of mist that clung to the trees. Everything was stronger in Treetown: the fog rose from the riverbottom and held tight to the many branches. In summer, it felt cooler here, in the dusty shade. And the wind came straight down the desert pass, slicing through the hills and down the corridor of riverbed.

Downtown, the wind was silent, only a vision of dancing litter or struggling pigeons outside your glass. But Treetown was constant rustling and snapping of dead palm fronds from the tall trunks that lined Pepper Avenue, like all the old streets. Marcus looked down the avenue now and saw the pencil-thin trunks swaying together, fronds all blown west like a row of toothbrushes.

Marcus paused, watching the whole landscape shifting, swaying, as if he were underwater. The pepper branches moved like seaweed, and yesterday's vicious gusts had torn new, green leaves and twigs from pecan and carob and ash, piling them with bark and wood in drifts along the roadside like beach debris. While he stood, a plastic bag flew from the freeway overpass down toward him like a jellyfish.

The bag puffed onto the small sign and slithered off again. Marcus faced the back of the sign. He knew the front read CITY LIMITS—RIO SECO—POP. 342,000. But there was nothing facing this way to tell a stranger where he was headed. He better know, Marcus thought. Treetown. An unincorporated, poverty-stricken, high-crime, semirural area west of downtown. Those were all the descriptions the newspaper applied when rare stories about drug arrests or killings in Treetown went longer than a paragraph.

Even though the city had finally annexed Treetown several months before, noting that the several-mile-square area was completely surrounded by districts receiving city services, no one had gotten around to moving the sign. Marcus walked past the breathing, pale bag at his feet. His father and uncle had complained bitterly about the annexation, saying that code workers and all the other "government men" would come around to find everything wrong.

He could see in a long, unbroken line now, walking down the slight slope. The Pepper Avenue bridge used to span the river just past his father's place, and people had crossed the old bridge daily to the citrus groves where they worked. Marcus saw the wisps of mist pushing away from the riverbed and the two large piles of rubble along the treeline. The big flood in 1969, when rain had fallen for two weeks and washed boulders and sand and trees toward the ocean, forty miles away, had torn away the old bridge. No one crossed the river to work now, and most of the groves were gone, with rows of precision housing instead of trees.

Marcus walked along the long block wall built by the city to hide the flattened land and scattered rubble left near the freeway, after the county had razed buildings considered too close to the construction. Millard's Barber Shop, Good Time Liquors, Lonzo's butcher shop. Marcus stared at the webbed graffiti on the pale cinder block. His uncle always said, "Too many men. Too many black faces hangin out right there, that bothered them cops, them government people. They redeveloped that shit best way they knew. Clear it out."

Past the wall, scattered olive trees still sprung from the earth where old groves had been cultivated. The piles of rubble Marcus could see now at the edge of the field were dotted with tiny trees, wild tobacco and pepper and eucalyptus. A deep, rutted path was worn into the field here, leading to the part of Treetown closest to the freeway. He could see the scattered houses maybe a quarter of a mile across the vacant land, see the small wooden spires on Treetown's two churches, West Rio Seco Church of God in Christ and Standing Rock Holy Fellowship of the Lord. Marcus always thought of how big the names were, and how small the stucco buildings where heat and music and perfume floated from the windows when he had stood outside years ago. His mother was Catholic, and she went to the church in Agua Dulce, farther west.

The old Treetown\Agua Dulce school, condemned now and used only for adult education classes, stood past the houses in a field. It was tiny, too, a Spanish-style building sprawling low. The only two-story structures in Treetown were the Olive Gardens low-income apartments. That was where he assumed the police vehicles had headed, since that's where trouble usually happened.

Back when the old citrus housing used to flood, when parts of Treetown were under two feet of water during winter rains, the county had torn down the wood-frame houses and built the stucco boxes of Olive Gardens. Then, during the ten years when the bridge was destroyed, the groves were razed, and the Goodyear Tire plant closed, the men who used to live in the grove workers' housing and the small houses nearby had disappeared. Now mostly women and children peered from the windows Marcus could see in the distance. He knew they had heard the sirens, too. The sky was slowly lightening, but the yellow glow of the high windows floated in the dark like cats' eyes.

Only a single road led into the main part of Treetown now, Grove Avenue, and that was still half a mile away, to the left. But on the right, Marcus saw the dark belt along the freeway where it curved toward downtown, and the old olive-pressing place in the fallow two-acre field closest to the underpass. The ancient wooden shed was marked with silver and black writing, the low stone wall was crumbled, and the tiny stand built of river rock, where someone had sold fruits and vegetables years ago, was marked, too. Wild grapevines grew around the edges of the land, up to the start of the steep Los Olivos Hills that separated Treetown from downtown.

As he was walking slowly along the dirt near the plowed field that began his uncle's land he saw the yellow police tape and two patrol cars turned sideways across the avenue.

He didn't stop. They were far enough away that they probably couldn't see him yet, and his father's place was beyond the tape. He saw no figures out of their cars, strolling or running or staring at him, so he continued casually until he reached the three huge pecan trees in a hard-packed dirt circle. Leaving the road, he went into the swirling dark space under the trees, leaning against one trunk, waiting to see if they would come and question him.

His eyes were closed; he heard hissing leaves and another plastic bag skittering past, but he listened for tires or hard soles approaching. These were the jungle Brothers' trees. Right here. This was as far as any boy from the Westside or anywhere else could walk into Treetown before Marcus's brothers would confront him to find out if he and his friends were planning to look for Treetown girls or steal riverbottom fruit or find a Treetown fight. And the Thompson boys loved to fight. The Jungle Brothers. Demetrius would stand there, eyes moving from face to face, hands loose at his sides and slightly curled, like he was holding something even though he had only his fists, and he would chant one of Oscar's songs. "Ain't no use to stand there wit you eyes all red, cause I hit you so hard get yo gramma dead."

Marcus was the only one who wouldn't fight. Now he pushed off the pecan trunk and walked toward the stone bridge over the canal. Whatever was going on past the tape, he didn't want to mess with it. He didn't even want to know about it, which little Olive Gardens gang banger had shot somebody. Nobody rolled around in the dust under the trees now, punching each other out. They shot at each other from moving cars. The Jungle Brothers were old men. Even Sissyfly, the baby boy, was thirty.

He'd be out of the cops' sight in a few minutes anyway, and he breathed again, walking along the canal path between the glassy, sliding water in its moss-slick channel and the olive trees, remnants of one of the groves that now stood here and there in silver havens throughout the neighborhood. His great-grandmother's grove was the only one still harvested and watered, and that was where he was headed. The canal path would wind him around behind his uncle's land and his father's place, and he could avoid the red lights and the cops' gaze.

Sissyfly. That's what his brothers had always called him, when he wanted to tag along with them and see the *Superfly* and *Shaft* movies but didn't want to light in the riverbottom or the groves or at school. His father thought he'd hung out too long with his mother and sister after he'd had meningitis, way back when he was five. "Too much female coddlin," his father said.

But he'd loved his sister, although he didn't understand some of the girl things she did. He'd watched her prance along the pepper-tree roots, carrying an umbrella, her face intent on the fall of air she knew was below her. His brothers barely knew her; she wound around their legs like she was braiding ribbons to their knees, her long hair streaming behind her, and when she had collected candy and laughter, she retreated back to Mama, her face private and closed again.

Even though they rarely talked to her, his brothers fought for her every day, when she went to grade school turning pretty and girls pulled her hair, when she went to junior high turning beautiful and boys came to the yard looking casual, holding their raps just behind their teeth.

Now she only talked to him. She called him every Friday night, from L.A., where she lived some place she wasn't willing to tell him yet. For three months, she had called him, saying she had found his number from information and please don't tell anyone. Not Mama. No. And he had to watch his mother, who still spun around the place in a dreamy circle of longing, waiting for her baby girl to come home.

The canal began to curve at the base of the hills. To his right was the acre field that Mr. Lanier leased from Uncle Oscar, to grow blackeyed peas. Marcus walked to the left, along the chain link topped with barbed wire that ran along the back of his uncle's property. He listened closely for sounds of official voices or fighting; maybe the police had been called out for some leftover drunks at The Blue Q, but he knew scar didn't put up with fighting or customers who overstayed their welcome. Oscar and his big guys put them out in a minute.

The wind gusted sharply, tearing skeins of mist from the branches, and the slap of a short siren came at him again, pushing him against the fence. He smelled ashes then, and wondered if the riverbottom had burned like it had last summer. He waited for the sound of tires on the canal road; only official vehicles could enter the path at the gate off Pepper or at the water intake down the river. Someone had seen him. He fit a description.

But he heard car doors slam down on the riverbottom road, and voices there, near the storage lot. After years of listening for his brothers and father, trying to avoid work, he knew where every sound echoed. The cops had to be looking for something among the cars. Instead of heading down the fence and down the slope toward the gate, he crossed the two-plank footbridge he and his brothers always kept over the canal.

Bending to gain footholds on the steep, dry trail they'd worn into the boulder-strewn hillside, he waited until he reached the wide rock where a tobacco tree grew in the cleft made by dripping water long ago. Then he turned, hidden by the yellow tubular blossoms, the decomposed granite rough at his shoulders. Police cars were gathered on the river-bottom road, the gate was open, and he saw no sign of his father or brothers. Suit-jacketed strangers had gathered near a blackened smudge. Marcus frowned. The Granada.

He thought of Finis first, like they all did. From here, he could see the road to the storage lot, the path that led toward the olive grove, but the trailers were hidden by trees. The house and barn were barely visible, patches of stone and plaster through branches. But you could always see the courtyard, the gravel area under the arbor where his mother and great-grandmother usually sat. No one was outside.

The steady voices from the storage lot rose and fell like dogs barking and answering, and he slid down to rest his back against the rock and wait for quiet. No use in moseying down the riverbottom road, and worse to sneak through the back fence at his secret place, looking like a thief. His palms rubbed the sandy remnants of rock near his shoes. He and Finis used to sit here for hours, eating plums and then, later, drinking Uncle Oscar's home brew. Talking about girls and teachers and Daddy always wanting them to work. Marcus closed his eyes, picturing his brother's blurred eyes and weaving head, moving to the music, seeing powerful legs and the burned back of his neck. "Man, that's a walkin brother," people always said, seeing Finis striding loose all the way across the city. "He never get tired. Gotta keep movin."

Pinching quartz grains hard in his fingers, staring at the clear shards, Marcus hoped Finis was sleeping now, his feet buried deep in tangled blankets. He dropped the grains and brushed off his fingers. No one came up here now. The grandkids his mother was raising played computer games; they didn't hike up here in the hills. They weren't wild like the jungle Brothers.

But not far from his feet, he noticed a few empty bottles and a small paper bag. He pulled them toward him with a stick. Liquor he didn't recognize—the labels said "Southern Comfort" and "Crème de Menthe." Marcus looked inside the bag, pulling away from the seaweed-rank odor. Inside were two small, shriveled objects, burnt red and faintly glittered like ancient stones. And a sliver of something frayed, like a chewed matchstick, giving off the fishy smell. Marcus closed the bag, pushing it beside the thin trunk of the wild tobacco, and he lay his bare skull against the boulder, listening to the slamming of more car doors and new, rough laughter.

Two voices trailed closer to him now, and he knew from all the years he'd spent lying there, listening, that they were going up the sloping path through the olive grove. White male voices, low and punctuated with silence while he heard things being shifted around in his *abuela's* small olive shed.

"Jackpot, Harley," the first voice said. The clanging sound of an empty can echoed against the rocks. "Here's the gas. I guess the old man set it. Or somebody else on the property. Check it out—still got residue from where he poured it. See, right here where it dripped?" "Two females, right? In the car? Maybe transients." The voices began to move away. "Who the hell knows, down here. Anything goes." Marcus tightened his laced fingers around his head and felt his backbone rub against the rock. Old man? Females? He took in huge silent gusts of the damp air rising from the pebbles underneath him, waiting for the voices to subside. Abuela never kept gasoline in her olive shed. She hated the smell, and never needed fuel. Finis? Would Finis have set a fire? No....Finis couldn't plan anything but where his feet would go in the next block. Marcus pressed his fingers into his forehead, making dents, and the wind brought the acrid smell of burned tires drifting over him.

Scott Hernandez

Born and raised on a small farm in Yucaipa, California, Scott M. Hernandez is a recent graduate of the University of California, Riverside, with degrees in creative writing and Chicano/a studies. He is currently attending California State University, Northridge, working toward his master's degree. His poetry has appeared in UC Riverside's *Mosaic* and San Francisco State University's *Cipactli*.
"The Canal" was published in *Mosaic* in 2005.

Eastside Walls, Riverside CA 1999

Turning the corner, taking my usual walk
Through the Eastside, I run into sirens
Flashing red around a small crowd
Circling a crumpled man with thick black glasses.

He lays there in the alley,
Bleeding from a hole in his belly
The size of a quarter.

He was the one,
They called "El Leon."
Nightly At the *Café Libre*.
He read from a
Small red book
He had written, screaming
For change and blood.

He cried for his missing brothers,
Their names scrawled across the wall
Of poverty none could break through,
Before surrounding them taking their breath.

Remembering him and his words
That hit me like punches and slaps,
I grabbed the pen he dropped
And began to write on the walls
Of the alley around him and the
Crowd screamed at me, to stop, but
All I could hear was his voice

*Revolucion, Liberacion, Educacion, La Union es la Fuerza, la Fuerza es La
      Union, todos cantan en voz libre. Revolucion, Liberacion, Educacion,
      Tierra o Muerte, La Lucha*
Continua ...

These words spilled across the walls,
Around the corner into the open street,
Chased the people home, whispering in
Sleeping ears as they dreamt until
They woke in the morning's cold.

He is dead is all they heard,
That great mad man leaving
His words piled in the street
Like dark crumbling bricks.

Our sun is vanquished, the missing
Light leaves a black hole in our homes.

The Canal

In August
night cools the fields
we run to the water
and jump into the long canal
near rows of strawberries
and almond trees
like little brown fish
we laugh and bathe
in the orange moonlight
trying to wash the days grease
and dust from our bones
contented I fall under a
sea of shadows and starlight
then I am sad
that the season will turn
cold and we will leave
soon I will be kneeling
shivering in the used water
we all share
near the packing shed
at dusk as the sun falls
upon us in the migrant camp

Life Lessons

Before sunrise you wake me
promise me that it's for my own good
I will argue with you
before
I get up

I walk through the fields
headed for the vineyards
dressed in layers of your old clothes

I wear your heavy gloves
and hat that shields me
from the life of the fields

you go without any
you fear for me

I blame it on the sun
that hurts my eyes as it begins to rise
that's why I'm working so slow

the cold begins to lift and steam
begins to rise from my shoulders

I watch you

mi madre made from clay
fired under the blazing sun
you are the caramel color of onions
that stick to the pot after
they are cooked too long

my lessons are hard on you

It's better I learn them now
I must know your life
soon summer will be gone
our time is short

we cut the *uvas* from their vines
not the green ones though
I know, I know,

you say:

remember, you must remember
how you feel right now,
know how much it hurts

this is not the life for you,
you must leave the valley
and find a home far from
this harvest that
runs our lives

you will not spend your
life chasing crops up and down
this circuit we will call life

I know, I know.
A'ma.

E. J. Jones

E. J. Jones was born in Blythe, California, in 1972. He earned a bachelor's degree in English and a Master of Fine Arts from the University of California, Riverside. He teaches at San Bernardino Valley College, and his work has appeared in *Mosiac*, *Crate*, and *Faultline*. He lives in Riverside.

The main character of "Grass Green" is a young man sent to live with his grandparents in Blythe after getting into trouble in Pomona.

Grass Green

The heat created waves that made the blacktop basketball court at AppleBee Elementary look like an oasis, water floating over cracked asphalt. From the air, the entire city of Blythe probably looked like an aquarium with water-breathing human fish. I didn't give a shit though; eight-foot rims instead of the ten-foot regulation rims was the reason everyone played there. I had already dunked once and was looking forward to showing off my Barkley two-handed monster dunk. I saw myself immortalized on a poster.

Defense isn't really my thing, so I waited at half court for someone to rebound and throw me the ball, cherry-picking. With the game going on, no one saw my grandfather, Oscar, step onto the court. A six-foot-four, two-hundred-and-fifty-pound man in dirty blue coveralls should have been obvious, but he caught us all, especially me, by surprise.

A Mexican kid in cut-off khaki shorts and no shirt threw the pass I was looking for. I had to shield my eyes from the sun to catch the ball in stride. It would have been a pretty fresh dunk, but when I reached for the ball the wood of a bat came down on top of it first, inches from my fingers.

The ball's pop was gunshot loud, and I jerked my hands away and patted my body for holes. With no air or bounce, the ball looked like a busted pumpkin. I pulled in a quick breath when I saw Oscar's work boots; I knew I was in trouble.

One hundred and fifteen degrees suffocates, and standing still I tasted it in my mouth, choking me almost. Oscar stepped toward me and his heaving chest blocked the sun. Standing in his shadow made my skin even hotter. He raised the bat horizontal, about the level of my chin, and I saw *Birmingham Black Barons* seared in the pine. The wood was dented and chipped, and I wondered if he'd really use it on me, or if he'd used it on anyone else. I hadn't exhaled.

There must be some look, a set of words, a practiced reaction to get me out of this, I thought. But before an idea formed, Oscar grabbed me by the back of my tank top and yanked me off my feet. Someone was laughing, but with sweat running under my glasses and into my eyes, I couldn't tell who. I made him drag me, though, the rubber heels of my Converse being worn down by the concrete. Eventually my shirt ripped, and I landed on my tailbone. A vibrating pain shot up my spine. I blinked away my grimace, but didn't wipe away the sweat. Someone might have thought I was crying.

Most outward things about Oscar were sweet, despite his size. His face always seemed to be a moment from a smile, a simple boyish grin that drew people to his favorite counter spot at Denny's. But when he really smiled, the look seemed exaggerated. Disney happy. Not a face I was used to, not what I saw looking up at him after I fell. That look told me he'd dig his dirty fingernails into my flesh and drag my ass to his Ford, damn the shirt or anybody watching. It was the summer I turned fourteen. It was my first week living in Blythe.

Oscar's Ford had thin K-mart seat covers, and the sun-cooked leather bit at the backs of my legs. I heard the bat bump from side to side in the truck bed and knew not to complain. Two days earlier, I said the AC in his Ford felt like an old woman's breath over an ice cube. I thought it was funny, but he rolled down the window and spit. I hadn't figured him out yet and knew it was best to just shut up this time.

At the light on Broadway and Hobson, he mentioned that the price of dairy hay was too high and rising as if it was something we talked about all the time. I shrugged his comment off and eyed two girls on Beach

Cruiser bikes in the crosswalk, their dark sweaty legs shining in the sun. I heard him work the handle for the window and spit before shifting into first gear.

When he took the alley to the house, I sighed, knowing exactly where he was taking me. The Ford stopped and I opened my door, but he used his right arm and shoved me out anyway. If he noticed that I hit my head on the metal corner of the door, he didn't act like he was sorry.

"Pull 'em right." He licked the inside of his jaw like he'd found a piece of candy and pointed to the weeds along the chain-link fence in the backyard. You owe me a new damn basketball was all I could think.

Drops of sweat fell from my forehead watering what was supposed to be grass while I worked. I thought about walking into Ronald P's liquor on Indian Hill back in Pomona. I always came out with pockets full of munchies to give away. A serious under-bite and glasses meant I didn't look like a thief, and I had gotten pretty good. Everybody liked me.

Tap-tap, tap-tap. Oscar was staring at me from the window, a quarter between his thumb and index-finger pecking at the glass. I moved a little faster so he'd go away, but he stayed to watch.

Tap-tap, tap-tap. I heard it every time he thought I wasn't moving fast enough.

When I came inside, cocker-burrs from the yard like leeches on the fabric of my shorts and socks, dusk had already settled in the sky. My grandmother slid a glass of lemonade in front of me, the nasty kind with more pulp than juice. I sat, but didn't look at her or say thank you.

"What?" she said. "You think he wasn't gon' check?"

"He's not even growing real grass. I'm just pulling weeds from weeds."

"Boy," she said. "You just don't learn, do you?"

I picked a cocker-burr from my sock and flicked it on the carpet when she wasn't looking. I imagined my grandfather wincing in pain, pulling it from the bottom of his foot, then wondering if I'd done it on purpose.

"What am I supposed to learn from nonsense?"

I craned my neck to catch the cold air from the vent and saw thin strands of mangled black tape in the trash can next to me. It was my N.W.A. tape, snapped in the middle, bits of plastic still scattered around the can. I must have been staring at it for a while, because I didn't feel Oscar walk in and stand next to me.

My grandmother came over drying her hands with a dish rag and Oscar flashed her a Mickey Mouse smile. "Look at that Evey," he said. "Now, they're N.I.T....Niggas In the Trash."

It was the third tape he'd found and broken. His laughter echoed in my head, and I wished there was something I could do besides sit there and give him an ugly face. My grandmother took my empty glass, rinsed it in the sink, and they both disappeared down the hall.

"Pulling those weeds still doesn't make any sense," I said. Remembering he hated me using words he wasn't familiar with, I stuck my head in the hall. "It's nonsensical!"

Oscar was in his office and his rickety La-Z-Boy let out a whine as he shifted, deciding whether to get up or not. I pressed my luck and sure enough, footsteps were coming back down the long plastic mat protecting the carpet in the hallway. The steps got closer, and I wondered how hard hitchhiking the two hundred miles back to Pomona would be. And if Mom would let me in when I got there.

The week before, Mom insisted on packing everything herself for our annual trip to Blythe, knowing that if I saw all my clothes, I wouldn't have gotten in the car. And she couldn't have made me.

Once we got east of Indio, twenty miles away from anywhere I could walk to, she started bringing up all kinds of stuff I'd done.

"It's not just you coming home late. It's you thinking I shouldn't know where you've been. Like I don't have the right to ask. You're becoming…unruly."

"Don't have to sugar coat it," I told her. I clicked my seatbelt off and slid down so I could barely see over the dashboard. "Just tell me you're kicking me out."

"That's your biggest problem," she said, and waited for me to look at her. "You only hear what you want to hear."

"That's because you never say anything, but how I'm not doing this or should be doing that." I pulled a mirror from the glove compartment and mimicked the way she primped every morning. "Pull your pants up," I said, running an index finger over my lips. "Do your chores."

The car picked up speed and we passed a green and white sign that read Blythe, seventy-six miles. Mom had a look on her face I didn't recognize, so I told her I was sorry and that I understood. She didn't slow down; I've never been a very good liar.

"So," I said. "I'm gonna be there for the rest of my life?"

Her lips were pressed tight in a frown. "If you can prove to Daddy you can be trusted, then you can come home."

"You're trippin' like this cuz of the party?" Mom always overreacted. I got all A's in school, so who cares if I went everyday? I was learning, right?

"Marijuana, Sydney," she said, jerking her eyes from the road, to me, and back again. "And don't talk to me like I'm one of your wanna-be-gangsta friends. Two of those morons you had sitting on my couch had warrants. I looked into it."

"I ain't...I mean, I didn't even inhale. Really." I resisted telling her Metri and Logo weren't wanna-bes.

"I don't know what to think right now, but...this is what's best."

I was mad because she didn't believe me, especially since for the most part, I was telling the truth. "Best for you," I said, shifting in my seat to muffle the words. But she'd heard. And I was glad.

The car swerved some, coming close to a diesel we were passing. Her bottom lip jiggled in anger like Oscar's did when he was mad. "Yes, Goddamn it. Me!"

Her tone made me remember our old house in Chino Hills, the one with two stories and a big backyard, the one we lived in before my dad died, in the neighborhood where no one ever called me a 'white' black boy. I remembered her screaming about me dribbling my ball in her kitchen, imprinting NBA in dirt all over her tile. She hadn't been this mad in a long time.

"You don't give a damn about what I go through. That after all I do in a day I come home and cook for your ungrateful..." Mom took a deep breath and what she wanted to say shook from her mind, down through her shoulders, and she kneaded the steering wheel with her hands until she was calm. We both pretended the billboards just past Chiarico Summit were worth staring at for a while. "I'm sorry," she said. "But I am *too* tired."

Her words sounded like she was ending something, and I was kinda sorry about the party, but wouldn't say it. Mom didn't understand me and the homies were like family. I wanted her to look at me and see that what she was doing was wrong. That it was her and not me who was trip-ping. Remembering something Logo said all the time, I turned my face to the car window and whispered, "Fuck it, then." Mom readjusted her grip on the steering wheel, shook her head in disbelief, and I felt the car pick up even more speed. I ignored her and the speedometer, watching the mountain peaks instead. Not another word was said for fifty miles. Five off-ramps. Twenty-eight minutes by the clock in the dashboard.

The silence was getting on my nerves, and I reached for the radio dial since we were close enough to Blythe to pick up a non-Spanish-speaking station. "No," she said. I was just about to say something about the noise she was making tapping the steering wheel with her fingernails when I saw it. She'd stopped wearing her wedding ring and I'd never noticed before. The guy that called for her all the time, Jermaine, I think, popped in my head. She was serious about leaving me in the desert. I sat upright, put my seatbelt back on, and hoped she'd miss me.

When my grandfather came out to the car, Mom popped the trunk and didn't even get out. I probably wouldn't have let her hug me anyway, but still.

Mom called it restriction, but Oscar and Evelyn said I was on punishment. I couldn't leave the house without permission and when school started, it was there and straight back. Need to learn to do what I'm told, they'd said—a hard, but important lesson.

I could hear Oscar's Ford pull up even with the TV on, so after he went to work in the morning and while my grandmother took her daily nap, I roamed. There were three rooms, but I was only allowed in mine. Oscar's office door was easy enough to open. A butter knife and a little something Logo taught me before I left Pomona was all I needed. Old newspaper clippings of Oscar in a baseball uniform filled the desk drawers; dusty trophies and a copy of the Old Testament were on top. I couldn't figure out the lock on the closet door, but slid a ruler underneath and hit wood. I knew it was the bat, but I didn't really want it. And I was sure he'd miss it.

In about a week, I averaged Evelyn's naps at an hour and a half. Every day after, I got a little farther from the house. My grandmother and Mom were about the same anyway; they complained and threatened to tell Oscar, but two out of three times they were bluffing. If she woke up and I was gone, I told her I walked to Buy Rite to buy a Slushie. That's how I met Will.

He was seventeen and lived with his brother across the street and a few houses over. Will hung out in front of Buy Rite almost every day. He always had a starched and creased blue rag over his shoulder, or tied around his head, sometimes wrapped around his ankle, but it looked best folded over twice, hanging loose from his back pocket. I wanted one, but was too ashamed to admit I didn't already have one.

We started sharing beers and swapping stories in front of his house. I told him I was from P-town and he said he'd put me down with some real desert gangstas. I said cool, and asked if he liked to play basketball, but Will just laughed.

"I use to. But that shit don't make dollars." He flashed a wad of twenties from the pocket of his jeans. The money was wet with sweat and looked like something growing from his palm, grass green. I cringed, knowing there was only gray lint in mine. "So," he said, putting the bills to his lips, "for Chilly Willy it don't make sense."

Clothes were Will's big thing, though. He always had new ones. He pulled a joint from his shirt pocket one day like it was there when he'd bought the shirt. That Friday, Will said S.G.C. was having a party, and if I wanted to be put down, I'd go. He looked both ways before lighting, puffing, and then extending the joint to me. Will leaned against the chain-link fence and somehow made it look like he was in a lounge chair. I checked to make sure Oscar wasn't rounding the corner in his Ford and took it. I was a little nervous and pinched the center of the joint. An amber nugget popped out and fell to the ground, turning black once on the concrete.

Will sucked spit through his teeth. "Man, give it here. Thought you were from P-town, Nigga."

I pushed his hand away and reached for the lighter. Will smiled. His teeth were a decayed yellow, and even though I didn't want anything in my mouth that had been in his, I put the joint to my lips. The tip was wet with saliva and I tried not to cringe putting fire to the ass-end.

After the first pull inside, I couldn't breathe at all.

"Aaahhh," Will laughed. "You ain't shit."

Fire, not smoke, burned my throat and lungs. The sun was in my chest, and I couldn't swallow it or spit it out. The quick panicked air going inside was a ball of flame coughing out. I used the fence to keep myself from falling, the charred weed nugget on the ground staring up at me, calling me a punk. Pictures of black lungs from advanced biology class flashed in my mind, and I could hear Mom's nagging voice, *Told you, didn't I, but you think you know everything, don't you.*

I didn't even see Will go inside, but he was already coming out, one hand holding up his sagging pants, the other wrapped around the neck of a forty of Old English. Will was lying about his age, I thought; his hands were as small as mine.

Beer, water, even chilled blood, I would have drunk anything that stopped the burn and immediately reached for the bottle.

Until Will pulled it away, I didn't realize the joint was still in my hand. He examined it from saliva tip to ass-end, like there was a possibility of it doing to him what it had done to me. Through a few final coughs, I asked Will what was in the joint, because we didn't smoke this weak shit in P-town.

I took a few more hits, managing to brag more than cough. After sneaking back in the house, I got into bed and watched the bumpy white stucco on the ceiling, imagining another earth. A land where everything was possible, a place where Dads never died, a home Moms never made their sons leave, no matter how bad they got. This world was real to me, and I reached for it with both hands until the rumble of Oscar's Ford brought me back. I rolled over, closed my eyes, and tried to harden from the inside out; S.G.C., I whispered, Southside Gangsta Crip.

I'm not sure why I asked, probably because I'd done all my chores without having to be told for a few days, or it might have been that I'd pretended to read the Bible a few times, but it was a mistake.

"Boy, hell no," Oscar said. "Them hoodlums at that party will eat your butt alive."

Midnight darkness made it hard to tiptoe from my room to the front door, but I was determined. I wore my baggiest blue jeans, a wife-beater, and an XL white T-shirt over that. I found the navy blue rag my grandfather had taken from me a few days before in the garage, but couldn't wear it because he'd used it to check the oil in his Ford. There was nothing else in the garage worth taking, but I stuck a small Phillips-head screwdriver in my sock just in case. The party was three blocks away on Second Street. I perfected my stroll as I walked.

A yellow porch light out front made the four or five guys hanging out by the door look even meaner. I didn't see Will and waited at a distance with my hands in my pockets. "Gangsta, Gangsta" was boomin' from a fresh-ass black Camaro with Dayton rims parked on the lawn. I nodded my head back and forth trying to get into the music.

A kid about my size saw me, stepped out of the light and put both his arms in the air. In the dark his figure looked like a capital Y. A few other, bigger, and older guys left the light, too. I took tiny steps backward.

"You representin'?"

Will had showed me how to make the right sign. Cup each hand into a C, left hand over right so it looked like a big S. The smallest one ran inside, and Will stumbled out the door within seconds holding a forty of Old English.

"Oh shit," he said. "P-town in the house!"

After Will shook my hand, leaned in, and bumped my chest with his, I felt better. The guys at the door gave me the same one-armed hug, and then we all went inside.

The mix at the party was weird: women Mom's age dancing with guys a few years older than me. My glasses were in my pocket so everything was fuzzy. Will shoved a beer toward me and I took a sip. He chuckled, so I cocked my head back and titled the bottle vertical. After hearing a few cheers, I held it as long as I could.

An older woman, maybe late twenties, looked me up and down while picking up an ashtray from the arm of a couch. Her mouth twisted like she'd forgotten how to form words with it.

"And whose little boy are you?"

"Boy?" I said flexing every muscle I had. "Little?"

She got close, real close, the cigarette in her mouth a Fourth of July sparkler in my face. "Well okay," she said, blowing smoke. "Maaannn." Her fingertips ran across my skin from wrist to elbow, and every hair on my body grew stiff. I was half done with my forty, and without my glasses her brown skin seemed more like fur.

Will put his arm around my shoulder. "Ready to be put down, Nigga," he said in a voice so loud I was sure everyone there assumed I was.

The cigarette woman stood straight. "You ain't right, Will. You know he too—"

"Shut the fuck up, Shardeen," Will said and led me to the backyard.

Blue jeans, blue rags, and bare tattooed chests were everywhere. Will took a joint from someone and handed it to me. I faked a long pull like I'd done a hundred times in Pomona. My knees were already weak from the beer.

Someone pushed play on a tape deck and I heard the very first words from N.W.A.'s "Straight Outta Compton" tape, *You are now about to witness the strength of street knowledge.*

A man with chain links tattooed on each arm walked up. "Sup, Iron," Will said. I started to speak, but Iron drove his fist deep into my chest. The hardest thing that ever touched my body was his hand. The water in my eyes made everyone look like blobs, but I didn't want to put a hand to my face. I could lie, I thought. No one would know the truth. There was no fence to hold onto and lying on the ground, even through tears, I noticed that whoever owned the house had real grass in their backyard.

"Chill Will," Iron said. "Your man's looking mighty weak. I don't know if he ready."

"Nah, he's ready. He's a P-town nigga." I could feel Will pulling me to my feet. "Dog him!"

I thought about the screwdriver, but figured everyone would laugh because it wasn't a knife. I could barely breathe, but if I'd been able, I would have told them I was more than fucking ready.

I felt bodies surround me, but then a woman screamed and the music stopped. Will let go of my shoulders and I was on the ground again. I curled my body into a ball hoping they wouldn't break my glasses. Afterward, I'd be down and it wouldn't matter that I needed them to see. I'd be S.G.C., part of a new world.

A strong arm grabbed me by the back of my shirt and jerked me up. I was slumped over a shoulder and wondered what was going on. The blurry shapes that had circled me were backing away. I caught the scent of hay and saw the back of blue coveralls. Damn, I thought, not him. I squirmed trying to get free and felt a bat rise up and hit me in the ass. Oscar's grip tightened and he hit me even harder when I squirmed again.

"Iron," he said, "leave this one here alone. This here's family business."

Oscar started moving and I saw shapes jump out of his way. Shardeen, the cigarette woman, was staring at me, her eyes as large as cake donuts.

The bat rattled as it was thrown in the truck bed. I was tossed in the front, finally feeling the ease of air going in and out.

My grandfather's sentences were chopped up, his actions interrupting his speech. "I have," he said, slamming the driver's side door, "no idea." He stabbed the ignition with the key. "What the hell it's gon' take." He pulled something from his coverall pocket and placed it in his lap. "But damnit," he said, gunning the engine. "You gon' learn."

He went on and on about doing things the right way, his way. The ass whippin's I'd get by him and others if I didn't. Didn't I understand he was trying to help me? I should have been grateful, I guess, but when I saw the sparkle, the moonlight gleaming off the silver revolver in Oscar's lap, I could only think of what Iron would say after I started carrying a gun. He had to be hiding it in that closet. I'd get to it eventually.

Juan Delgado

Born in 1960 in Guadalajara, Mexico, Juan Delgado is a professor of English at California State University, San Bernardino. Educated there and at the University of California, Irvine, Delgado is the author of three collections of poetry: *A Rush of Hands*, *El Campo*, and *Green Web*, the winning manuscript for the University of Georgia Press's 1994 Contemporary Poetry Series. He is also the recipient of a Walter E. Dakin Fellowship. He lives in San Bernardino.

"Ofelia" is set in the Inland Empire and is from the 2003 collection *A Rush of Hands*. "Flavio's New Home" is about a move from Tijuana to Colton and is from the collection *Green Web*.

Ofelia

For OCD

I. Work Camp

She sits
In a chicken coop
Turned camp
And nurses her twins,
Blossom hungry and plump.
She walks between the rows
Of chicken coops,
And the camp eyes part their curtains,

Sheets strung up with clothespins.
Her can opener ran out of food,
So lock your door, Anna,
And play deaf, Ampara and Martha.
She picks a few oranges
Among the frost-bitten trees,
Their leaves tucked in,
Dark branches.

2. Hitchhiking

She travels the routes of gas pumps
And 7-11 diaper runs,
Leaving the lemons under the wet sun,
The ditches, and the splinters
Of ladders.
Her eyes are in his rearview mirror
When the yellow line veers
And sheds its skin;
Patting the seat, he asks her to sit
Up front with him, and her girls
Are drowned out by the tires' drone.
At the next stop
They will vanish behind a wall
Of eucalyptus, Santa Ana windbreaks,
Or stay in a gas station's restroom.
She will hold her girls until curses turn
To squealing tires.

3. Their Garden

Her girls' eyes are with the bees
Hovering among the blossoms.
They lie on a blanket
Made from old flour sacks.
One has learned to roll onto her stomach.
Ofelia walks between the rows,
Brushes against a web heavy with dew,
And glitters.
She checks if they are alone,

Singing so they can hear her voice.
Her song is a nursery, a grove
Of oranges not yet oranges,
Sweetening.

Flavio's New Home

Luz, Colton is not a big city or nice,
nor does it have a park where lovers kiss
as we did in Chula's backyard
the night I told you I was leaving Tijuana.
You will not find a lit fountain,
let alone a decent plaza where people can just be,
but this place has a great freeway
that laces through it, bringing cities closer.
How the freeway's ivy clings
and when I am thinking of you,
I am drawn to the fast lane,
the way it curls, spirals and bridges,
always leading back to itself
like a sacred serpent swallowing its tail.
All the way the arrows and green signs,
fluorescent, assure me of name and mile.
Luz, how easily you forget me here.
I am still your Flavio, the Flavio
who, when I couldn't use my brother's car,
rode his ten-speed through the dangerous shoe district
just to see you and who waited
until you flicked your porch light off and on,
the sign your parents were asleep,
and once together we never wasted time.
Now I have a job repairing flat tires.
Cash in my money order and come to Colton.
Sometimes, closing the door of my pick-up,
I imagine you beside me,
digging through your purse, looking around us.
You find your lipstick, pushing it up,

then tilt my mirror to your lips,
telling me of your hunger, unsure
if you want to eat at the open market,
or at your uncle's stand,
but like always you promise yourself
a fruit juice with crushed ice
and sprinkled brown sugar.

Alex Espinoza

Alex Espinoza was born in Tijuana, Mexico, in 1971 and raised in Southern California. He received his Master of Fine Arts in writing from the University of California, Irvine. Random House will publish *Still Water Saints*, his first novel, in 2007. He lives in Riverside.

"Santo Niño" takes place in a fictional town in the Inland Empire.

Santo Niño

My baby Lydia celebrated her second birthday last Saturday, and we threw her a party. My best friend Precious helped me get things ready around the house. We blew up balloons and stuck them to the ceiling with tape. We scattered confetti across the lawn and patio. We stuffed grab bags full of gum, jellybeans, plastic magnifying glasses, and whistles.

Out back, my husband Henry was threading twine between the branches of a tree to hang the piñata. Lydia was over with my parents, so the house was quiet, and everything was clean. I'd been up until two the night before catching up on all the laundry, mopping the floors, doing the dishes, vacuuming the living room and hallway and the bedrooms. I was drowsy. My head hurt from not sleeping. Already on my third cup of coffee, and the caffeine still wasn't hitting me. In a few hours the house would be full of kids running down the hall and through the kitchen, jumping on the furniture, fighting, crying, spilling all over the place.

Precious had spent a good part of the morning telling me how her man Frankie and her have been trying again to have a kid. Precious don't have none.

"Frankie wants a boy. No question about that."

"Why all of a sudden?" I asked.

"Been a while. We gotta try."

I wanted to ask why she thought this time would be different. Why this time she felt things would go right. She's had two miscarriages. The first one was right after we graduated, when Precious and Frankie'd only been going around for about a year. Her pregnancy was all good at first. Things were running all smooth. Precious giving me a hard time. Saying I'd better hurry and get that man of mine to get me pregnant too. That way we could raise the babies together, and they'd be like twins. She was so happy, getting all this attention. She started looking at baby furniture and toys. Her mom bought a sweatshirt that said *World's Greatest Grandmother* on the front. Then Precious got these pains like contractions early on. Next thing we heard she was in the hospital and the baby was gone.

The next one was about three years ago. A little boy, they said. Complications. Umbilical cord got twisted around his neck. He couldn't breathe. Little thing came out all blue. Skin looking like a raisin. It was touch and go with Precious, too. She lost a lot of blood.

Almost ten years married already, and she's got no kid. Doctors have run tests, say it's just that way sometimes. Say there's no real answer why she's miscarried. There were other ways, I tried telling her. You could adopt. Hundreds of kids out there being born to mothers who leave them by dumpsters or in bus terminals. Not the same, Precious said. Not flesh and blood. Besides they probably wouldn't even pass what with Frankie holding down odd jobs here and there—one or two months as a security guard, another three or four laying asphalt—and both of them only having high school diplomas.

"You scared?" I asked.

"You mean because of what happened last time?"

"Yeah," I said.

She unpacked the party hats and put one on. "Naw. I'm not scared. When you gotta go, you gotta go." She walked out to the patio with the grab bags and party hats in her hands.

Mainly it was our relatives at the party and some of the kids from the block whose parents I knew. My cousin Becky showed up with her five-year-old who likes to pull Lydia's pigtails when she thinks I'm not looking.

Becky brought her new boyfriend. This hood rat named Trey who drives a Toyota with fine rims and a loud system. He wore a Raiders football jersey and baggy cords. *Destiny* tattooed across his forearm.

"Who's Destiny?" I asked Becky when we were in the kitchen. "Some ex?"

"That's his shorty," she said. "Lives in Rialto with the mom who's a psycho bitch. Scratched the Toyota up. He put a restraining order on her ass."

Precious helped me with the hot dogs and punch and made sure none of the kids were fighting with each other or needed to be changed. When Lydia was opening up her presents, Precious walked over and stood by me. She was holding Jordan, this kid whose mother works with Henry. His face was all sticky from the punch he'd been drinking. One shoe was missing, and blond strands of his hair were sticking straight up from static.

"What?" Precious said when she saw me staring.

I pointed to Jordan. "Lookit," I said, laughing.

"Lookit what?"

"He kinda looks like Frankie."

"You think?" She turned his face around.

"Yeah." After a while she said, "Yeah. I think so, too. What a trip."

Precious didn't let up with that kid the rest of the party. She carried him around until it was time for Jordan to go home.

After people started leaving, we were doing some cleaning, picking up paper plates and tossing them in the trash. Precious took the two candles I'd helped Lydia blow out, and she wrapped them in a plastic baggie.

"You should save these," she said.

"I was gonna."

Then she asked me all of a sudden, "What do want for her?"

"What?" I said.

"What do want for her?" she asked again.

"Why are you scaring me for? What do you mean?"

"I mean what do you want for her? When she gets older."

"Never really thought of it. Too early, girl."

"Are you tripping?" She tilted her head. "What do you *see*?" She stuffed plates in the trashcan. There was frosting stuck to her fingers. Out in the yard, Lydia was playing with Henry. They were running around, chasing each other. Her party hat was on crooked, and Henry looked like a big old fool. All out of breath and laughing.

I told her, "I just take it day by day right now."

The wind had torn the streamers we'd strung across the patio. Some of the balloons had deflated. The purple ones looked like overripe grapes, the yellow ones like lemons when the skins crack and turn bumpy.

Lydia woke up cranky. She threw a big-ass tantrum. Kicked and screamed. Her face turned red.

"What do you want?"

The more I asked, the more pissed she got. I sat in my living room. Toys scattered all around the place. Naked dolls with frizzed out hair and spooky grins looking up at me. Blocks and books stuffed in between the cracks of the couch. The kitchen floor all sticky because Lydia'd smeared yogurt under the table when I was talking with Henry. First thing he does when he gets to the plant every morning is call me so that I can tell him "I love you" because he says it sounds more romantic over the phone.

"You think she's coming down with something?" he asked. "Everyone around here's sick."

"Hope not," I said. "I don't know what's wrong with her."

After hanging up, I fed and dressed the baby, then wiped down the kitchen floor and counters with a wad of wet towels, tossed some of the toys in the bin tucked behind the curtain, and shook crumbs out of the couch cushions. I was pulling out a blanket from under our dining table when she picked up the spill-proof cup to take a sip of orange juice, and the lid popped off because I hadn't screwed it on all the way. The juice poured all over her, the lid hit her on the forehead, and she was crying again. So I had to change her and calm her down before going to Precious's. She'd called me last night and said her mom was bugging, asking when I'd be by to pick up the birthday present she got for Lydia.

The extra diapers and wipes go in the pouch behind the stroller's seat. I take another pacifier in case we lose the first. Before locking the front door, I make sure I got my keys and wallet. I put the keys in the pocket of my sweats and stuff the wallet in the pouch behind the wipes.

Precious and me, we don't live that far from each other. It's a ten-minute walk from door to door. I usually wait until traffic's died down. Mornings, Meridian gets busy with trucks, school buses, and commuters taking the 10. Bumper-to-bumper drives lasting almost two hours for jobs out in Industry and L.A. Because it's later, there ain't many cars, so I can take my time getting over to the other side. I hang a left at the house on the corner where that same black pit bull growls at us from behind the chain-link fence, pawing through the dirt with those big-ass claws of his.

Precious is standing at the end of her driveway waiting for us. "Took you long enough."

To get to her parents' place, we have to take the number 17, which goes west down Central. On the bus, Precious takes her bracelet off and lets Lydia put it in her mouth. I didn't have time to do my makeup because of the spill and Lydia's second change. So I take my compact out and start by spreading foundation across my face, dabbing some liquid concealer to hide the circles under my eyes.

We get off on Pepper, cross Alta Vista, and go under the freeway. At Valley and Pepper there's a Mobil gas station with a convenience store. We stop there to buy a pack of peanut butter crackers because Lydia's hungry, so she's crying.

Precious's parents live in this new house that was built in a big empty lot sandwiched between an apartment building and a car wash. About a year ago, yellow bulldozers showed up. Then wood beams. Streets were paved. And six brand-new homes were there before anybody knew it. The front yard is a small green square with sprinklers that pop their heads out every night at ten. The numbers painted on the curbs are all still thick and black.

Inside, the couches are covered in plastic, and clear runners with bubbles on the bottom are all over the place, guiding you to the bathroom, the bedrooms, the coat closet down the hall. Everything's breakable. They got these lamps with gold shades. Big glass vases all over the place. Tabletop mirrors. Candy trays always empty. I have to watch Lydia, make sure she don't pick something up and bust it.

"She's getting so big," is what Precious's mom Jackie always says when she sees Lydia. And today's no different.

The present's one of those glowworms with sleepy eyes and round cheeks.

"Too cute," Precious says.

"Squeeze," Jackie says, putting it in Lydia's hands. The baby reaches for a glass bell on the coffee table instead. I take her hands and help squeeze the worm. The face lights up, and the head bobs to a lullaby I don't know.

"Say thank you, Liddy," I tell her. Only she's too busy fussing with the worm's tail. She points, tries to mumble something, and Jackie claps her hands.

"Like little parrots. Before you know it she'll be talking all the time," Jackie says. "I remember when this one turned two." She looks over at Precious, who turns away and walks into the kitchen. "I remember when she started making those sounds like words. Pointing. Mumbling. Recognizing things. Has Lydia started that already?"

"Kinda," I say. "She's been grouchy. I think maybe she's getting sick or something."

Jackie tells me I need to make sure Lydia's bundled up when we go out. "And don't take her out right after you've bathed her. The cold is bad for babies. And never put her down to sleep if her hair's wet. She'll get sick that way for sure."

Lydia drops the glowworm and picks up one of Precious's dad's hunting magazines. I take it away from her, and she throws a fit. "Lookit," I say, giving her the worm. Only she don't want it. She's trying to reach for the magazine and won't stop crying.

"Come." Jackie picks her up. "I'll take her outside for a bit."

When they go, I walk into the kitchen and see Precious leaning against the counter, staring out the window at her mom playing with the baby. She crosses her arms, shakes her head slowly.

"What?" I say.

"She's not gonna let you leave again."

Her mother holds Lydia, kisses her arms, pulls up her sweater and blouse and blows on her stomach. Lydia points her face up towards the sky. Laughs loud. Her face turning red again. Not pissed red. Happy red. Jackie puts her down and chases her around the yard, her high heels getting stuck in the grass.

After a while, they come back inside. Jackie's breathless and smiling big.

"Here it comes," Precious says.

"Are you girls going to be here a while?" Jackie looks at me.

"We should go, Mom," Precious tells her.

"Because, I was just wondering if you would let me take Lydia for a walk." Jackie laughs. "It's just that I'm always talking to Linda down the block about her. I'd like for her to see the baby."

Lydia holds onto my leg. Like she understands and don't wanna go. "Okay," I say.

After they've gone, Precious says, "Linda's a bragger. Always carrying around this photo album of her ugly grandkid. Old ladies, and they're still playing games. Trying to outdo each other."

"It's all good," I say.

"Yeah. I guess we should let her have some fun."

Lydia always naps from eleven-thirty until one or two. It's around noon when we get back to Precious's, so she's quiet, nodding off in my arms when we walk into the living room. I put her down to sleep on the couch. Precious and me sit in the kitchen listening to the radio and smoking cigarettes, talking about the days when we were still in high school and had all the boys crazy in love with us.

She's got some of Frankie's clothes to iron. Since they don't got an ironing board, Precious spreads a thick blanket over the top of the kitchen counter. She uses an old bottle of glass cleaner filled with water to spray his shirts, and when the iron passes over the wet drops, I hear the hiss, watch steam float around her head.

"Girl," she says, laughing. "Did you see my mom? Acting like a big-ass fool. Making those silly faces. Grandma Jackie Guzman." She presses hard on a shirt with the iron, making sure it's smoothing out the wrinkles.

Lydia's chest moves up and down. She kicks her legs like she's in the middle of some dream.

"Times like that I wish I could really give her a grandkid." Precious drapes some of the shirts over the dining room chairs by me. When there's no more room, she puts the rest on hangers, then reaches above and hooks them to the chandelier. They float above my head, reminding me of kites.

It's almost three, and Lydia's still out. I figure I'll let her sleep for as long as possible. Besides, Precious and me, we're having a good time thinking about high school and boys and the girls we knew and hated, the days we'd ditch class and sneak into the movies through the emergency exits behind the building or when we'd smoke weed in the park.

Frankie comes home early. Precious tells him to be quiet on account of Lydia still napping.

He goes to the couch and gives my baby a peck on the cheek.

Precious whispers, "You'll wake her up, *stupid*."

"I know what I'm doing," he says, keeping his voice low. "Chill." He comes back into the kitchen and puts his keys down.

Precious wraps the iron's cord up, and Frankie creeps up behind her. "You know what?" he says.

"What?"

He puts his arms around her waist. "You're going to make a great momma someday. You just wait. Wait and see. We're going to have a huge family."

Frankie's got six brothers and five sisters. They all still live back in Kentucky. There's a family picture of them hanging in the hallway. They all look alike with white skin and freckles and thick blond eyelashes. His sisters are in spaghetti strap dresses, their arms thin and sick pale. The older ones have feathered hair, and the younger ones have bangs that almost cover their eyes.

"Third time's a charm," Frankie says, sitting next to me and taking his boots off. "You'll see. Third time's a charm."

Lydia's still sleeping when I get going. Precious walks me out, and we stand at the end of the driveway.

"Come with me somewhere tomorrow, okay?" she says.

"Where?"

"Just this place. Could you come by around eleven?"

"Yeah." I push the stroller down the sidewalk. Lydia wakes. All I can see is her hand poking out the side of the stroller, pointing up to the streetlights.

We were in the bathroom, and Lydia was in the tub. I turned around for just one second, and she fell and hit her forehead. Next thing I know there's blood everywhere, and she's crying. Henry was at work, and I didn't know what to do. So I held my baby and squeezed her and tried to shush her. I panicked. There was so much blood. It dripped all over the bath mat. My head went dizzy and my legs felt rubbery and loose as I ran down the hallway to pick up the phone.

"Call 911," Henry shouted at me. "Why are you calling me for? Hang up and call 911."

When help came, I was sitting on the couch with her, holding a rag over the cut, pressing down on it real hard. I was so afraid to let go that the paramedic had to use both hands to pull mine away.

Outside the neighbors had come out of their houses, watching the big show, and I felt embarrassed when I realized everything was gonna be fine. I didn't even notice when Henry showed up. He shook the paramedics' hands and thanked them for saving Lydia's life even though she wasn't in any real danger.

I was still numb. There was so much blood. And Lydia was crying so hard and she was in so much pain that even thinking about it now makes me feel queasy and sick and shake from the fear.

That's the thing. About babies. You can't always be there to watch them. Even if you're in the same room. Standing only a few feet away. That's the thing that scares me the most sometimes. That keeps me up. I'm always thinking what if I'm not there the next time? What if she gets hurt real bad?

This is what Precious don't get. About timing. About how hard it can get sometimes with a baby. How real scary. That it ain't all about getting attention and making your mom feel good and giving her some reason to brag to her old lady friends about being a grandma.

When you have a kid, everything spins out of control. And you gotta let it and ride it out. Sometimes I think I'm not a good mom. Because I got pregnant too young. Because she wasn't planned. Because I let my baby down that one time in the tub. And in the back of my head I know there'll be more times just like that and I try to shake those thoughts away.

Precious asking me what I want for her gets me thinking too much about the future and what's ahead. I can't see that far. Part of me don't want to. Here's something I'll say that I'd never admit to anyone: Sometimes I'm jealous of Precious. Because she's still real young. Because she's still got time to do herself up and look all pretty. When we're walking down the street, she gets the whistles and the honks from the cars. It's never the one pushing the stroller.

All that you give up when you become a mom. And suddenly the world's a scary place. And it gets scarier everyday. Everyday there's something new and dangerous. Something waiting to snatch your baby away. An infection. Fists. Needles. Semi-automatics. A fall in the bath-tub. All of that's real simple and quick around these streets.

It was past midnight when Lydia woke up crying and couldn't go back to sleep. I thought for sure she'd be cranky this morning, but she's been good, real mellow. After eating her breakfast, she sat in the living room and turned the pages of a picture book, pointing at the cartoon drawings of puppies and ponies and kittens batting balls of yarn. I just left the dishes and sat there with her, saying the names of the animals in the book and pointing at them so she'd understand. We're both dressed and ready to go early today. I even had time to do my makeup before getting over to Precious's so I don't look all scary today.

As we walk down the street, Precious tells me their dryer finally died. Problem is they don't have the bills to buy a new one. Looks like she'll be drip-drying everything at least for a while, she tells me. It never ends, she says. Frankie's a little freaked, too. He's hoping the construction company he's working for'll keep him for the next job they got lined up. They'll be letting him know soon if he'll be staying on or not.

"You can dry at my place," I say.

We take Meridian straight down to the Prospect Shopping Center on Rancho. Lydia starts to fuss, so I give her the glowworm. Precious stops in front of the botánica at the very end of the building. I've never gone in, only seen it from the bus window on my way to the market. Behind the iron bars there's lace curtains with patterns of flowers and birds with long beaks and skinny legs. There are signs in Spanish on the door. I recognize only some of the words and phrases—*Velas, Religioso, Ayuda para su familia y su salud, problemas de amor y dinero.*

"Hold this." Precious gives me her purse. "Wait out here."

"Why?"

"Just because."

"Then why'd you want me to come?"

She crosses her arms, rolls her eyes. "Support, okay? Besides, there's all this stuff in there that the baby could break." Precious reaches for the door. "Just wait here. Or go get some coffee or juice." She points to the donut shop at the other end of the shopping center. "I have to do this alone. The lady said I needed to come see her alone."

"Do what?" I ask. "Why are you getting all secretive on me?"

"Lookit," she whispers. "She's just gonna do something to help me."

"With what?"

"With this whole getting pregnant thing, okay? Go and wait for me. Don't go nowhere far."

I get three donut holes and a small orange juice for Lydia and a maple bar and coffee for me. We take a seat near the window, and it's a straight view from the chair to where Precious is.

Lydia starts to fuss just as I think I'm gonna sneak over there and try to look through the window at what's going on. Instead I sit her down next to me. She only nibbles on the donut holes, puts them in her mouth and gets them all soggy, wipes the table top with one, then wants to eat it, so I snatch it away and get her another.

"Germs," I say. "Gimme."

Lydia's almost done with the donut holes when I see Precious finally coming out of the store holding a brown paper bag. She walks over and waves at me.

"What happened?" I say.

"Nothing," she says. "I need to go to San Salvador's now. Is that cool with you? If we do one last stop?" She looks down at Lydia. "It's still early. We'll be back in time for her nap. Here." She takes the stroller from me. "I'll push."

When we get to the church, it's empty except for a few nuns who are up front talking to each other and looking at a book. It's quiet inside. And cool. I sit towards the back, watching the nuns. Lydia cries, and her voice echoes across the room, up to the high ceiling, up to the stained glass windows.

Precious kneels at a railing in front of a statue of Jesus in a white robe. Gold beams shooting out of his heart and from behind his head. She's quiet for a few minutes before making the sign of the cross. As she gets up to leave, she takes a scrap of paper out from her pocket and sticks it to the railing with a piece of the gum she's chewing.

"I'm ready," she whispers.

"Okay." We get up and leave.

"I'm gonna run into the hall," she says when we're outside. "I've gotta use the bathroom. Wait here."

While she's gone, Lydia and me go back into the church. I reach for the note and slowly open it up, look up to make sure the nuns don't see me. She'd written:

Dear Jesus, my husband and I have been trying for years and can't get pregnant. Bless me with a baby as loving and sweet as you were. I also send this prayer to all the women of the world just like me who can't have kids and to all the orphaned babies in the world. I love you, Jesus.

Precious Guzman Dennis

I stick the note back on the railing and go out to wait for her.

A couple months later, I'm out back in the yard with Lydia. Even though it's late February, it's warm and sunny, and the sky's all clear. The San Bernardinos are white with snow and they don't even look like real mountains. I spread a blanket out on the grass and Lydia and me are sitting in the sun. I'm reading to her from this book that teaches the alphabet.

"A. Apple," I say slowly, pointing to the first page. "B. Bunny. C. Chair." I brought the cordless with us in case Henry calls. When it rings,

I answer, and it's Precious.

She says, "Hey. What are you doing?"

"Nothing. Here reading to Lydia."

"Come over," she says. "I need your help with something."

We're sitting in the kitchen with Lydia playing on the floor. Precious gave her some paper and a pen that's out of ink. Lydia holds it, passes it over the paper like she's really writing something. I make up words and letters out of her strokes. Crooked R. C.O.L. Backwards K.

"Remember how I went to the botánica?" Precious says.

"Yeah."

"The lady there massaged me. Said I have a good chance of getting pregnant."

"How does she know?"

"Something about how my stomach felt, she said."

"She a psychic?"

Lydia giggles.

"Sort of," Precious says. "Like some healer type."

"And *having* it? Did she say you could have it okay? Without nothing happening?"

"All she said was that I had a good chance of getting pregnant."

There's this kitchenette the woman has behind the counter, Precious says. Everything's miniature. Miniature fridge and coffee pot. Miniature sink and dish drainer and microwave sitting on a cart with rubber wheels. She had this table set up in front of these tall shelves. It was so cramped back there that Precious's feet tapped up against the microwave's door.

"It was embarrassing," Precious says. "I had to lift my blouse so that she could massage my stomach. She used this smelly oil she scooped out from a Styrofoam cup."

She told Precious her womb was twisted and needed to be put back into place. She gave her this tea to drink once a day for nine days straight starting from the third day after her period. The tea's supposed to warm up her womb and make it ready to carry babies.

"You believe this?" I say. "Because it don't sound legit to me."

She's quiet, then hands Lydia another sheet of paper. "Don't know. Maybe none of it. Maybe a little. Just thought I'd try. I've been drinking the tea just like she told me. And now I'm late."

"How late?"

"About four days. And you know me, girl. I'm never late. I haven't said nothing to Frankie."

She's scared. I can tell. Even Lydia knows. She gets up and sits on Precious's lap turns around and kisses her on the cheek.

"I went to the pharmacy yesterday," she says. "Bought a pregnancy test."

Lydia points to something make believe in the corner.

"And?" I ask.

"It's just sitting over there in the bathroom."

"You want me to help you?"

"Yeah," she says. "But later, okay? I don't feel so good right now."

I make her a piece of toast with butter, and she eats it slowly. Lydia's out in the yard, and I keep an eye out on her from the kitchen window. She comes in, mud caked all over her jumpsuit from playing in a puddle.

While Precious finishes eating, I take Lydia's muddy clothes off. Just after noon and she's rubbing her eyes, whimpering. I give her the pacifier, lay a blanket down on the couch, and in a few minutes she's napping.

Precious follows me out to the garage. The mud on the jumper's drying fast. I toss it in the washer and point the load size to "small" and set the time cycle to "short." While it washes, Precious sorts through piles of dirty laundry, separating everything by color. When the washer's through, I take out Lydia's jumpsuit and hang it in between a pair of Frankie's pants and his overalls that are hanging over a piece of rope that's stretched from one end of the garage to the other. Precious throws a load of whites in. She turns around and walks towards the back of the garage. Against the wall, there's a stack of books. I recognize the purple and yellow colors of our high school.

"Check it out," Precious says. "Our senior yearbook."

Even though I've flipped through it lots of times, can see the pictures if I shut my eyes and concentrate real hard, I go ahead and open it anyway. Page seventy-three. Me ten years ago. A tan backdrop. A royal blue robe. Frosted lipstick. Liquid eyeliner extending out the corners of my eyes. Hair teased out so high I had to use bobby pins just to keep my cap from falling off.

A few rows below me, same column going down, is Precious. She don't smile. Got that serious look on her face. She's got the future on her mind. Miscarried babies. Busted dryers. None of that's real yet.

What do I see? I ask myself over and over in my head. *What do I see for her?* I see my girl a professional businesswoman. The head of a powerful company that makes millions. She carries around a briefcase and wears a suit and orders people around. She works in an office in a building so high it dissolves into the sky when you're standing on the street looking up at it. She's married with a handsome husband who golfs. They go out all the time. Vacation in places I've never heard of. And kids. They got kids. Three or four. We're grandparents, me and Henry. And, on weekends and during the summer, they all come and stay with us.

Precious goes over to one of the piles of dirty clothes she's sorted. She pulls out one of Frankie's shirts, balls it up, and tucks it under her blouse, smoothes it out and shapes it with her hands.

She walks over to the mirror hanging on the back of the door and stares at her reflection, sweeping her hand across her stomach. Frankie's wet pants and my baby's jumper hang above my head on the clothesline, wet and wrinkled. Drops of water fall on top of my head, over and over.

Precious twists her hair into a bun. Uses a pencil to keep it from unraveling. I put the book away and watch her standing there. Blouse pulled tightly over her belly, her arm tucked underneath it, holding the weight, keeping it all from falling out.

Robert Gonzales Vasquez

Robert Gonzales Vasquez was born in Redlands in 1964. He is the founder of Inland Mexican Heritage, a community-based organization dedicated to preserving historic and cultural records of Mexicans and their descendants throughout Inland Southern California. He has a master's degree in history from the University of California, Riverside. He lives in New Mexico.

Comprised of both stories and images in various media, *Living on the Dime* is a project that takes a dynamic look at how the I-10— or Interstate 10 (nicknamed "the Dime"), which runs through the Inland Empire on its way from Los Angeles to Phoenix—has changed the cultural landscape of the Inland Empire. *Paved with Good Intentions*, an accompanying exhibition, has traveled to various cultural venues in the area.

from *Living on the Dime*

Introduction

Interstate 10 came to Redlands in 1964, the year I was born. I grew up along its concrete vastness and flat blacktop sometimes using the overgrown jungle at its edge as a playground. The freeway had been a part of my cultural geography long before I knew what that meant. At one point during a recent presentation I joked that the Interstate freeway system was authorized under the Eisenhower Administration, "a great decade for concrete." The irony was, in my studies of water and in my years as an oral documentarian developing materials on Mexican heritage, I had spent most of my time fascinated by dams, roads, and other things of a concrete nature.

Several years ago I was standing in the backyard of another home near the freeway, east of where I grew up. Amidst the chaos and noise of construction on the I-10 that living one block away can bring, I was having a party. The subject of the freeway came up in a conversation and one of my guests referred to it as "a river of technology." I felt the analogy worth remembering even if I had serious doubts that the freeway in all its useful ugliness should have such a pretty description attached to it.

In 2001 I founded Inland Mexican Heritage and later a website (mexicanheritage.org) to continue independent community research and develop cultural initiatives. In 2002 we began a journey that came to be known as *Living on the Dime: A View of the World along I-10*. For over two years a crew of photographers, videographers, and sometimes family and friends worked gathering stories and images in communities from San Bernardino Valley to the Colorado River.

In pursuit of highly selective notions of "beneficial use" the unholy, if traditional marriage between local governments and land developers is increasingly determined and quite skilled at articulating a quasi-religious doctrine of growth and progress, which generally occurs at the expense of rural communities, open space, and older suburban neighborhoods. For many along this two-hundred-mile stretch of the Dime, "progress" and "growth" are one and the same and tend to be accepted without much thought, or as an inevitable consequence of American cultural tendencies. Meanwhile the entire region continues to be deeply affected, for better or worse, by freeway construction and freeway-centered development.

Along the freeway, off the beaten track, during public programs, personal interviews, and chance meetings on the road, we visited the land and people that make up the rapidly changing area known as Inland Southern California, hearing stories and ideas about the past, present, and future of the region. Some of them are shared here for the first time in print.

RGV
Las Vegas, New Mexico
June 2006

Does Progress in Morongo Basin Mean the Death of Joshua Tree?

For thousands of years the Morongo Basin was a gathering place for groups of indigenous people who came down from the San Bernardino Mountains through Pipes Canyon to spend the winter, and others who traveled up from the lower Colorado desert for seasonal harvests. For much of the time since then, small indigenous populations maintained long-standing migration and settlement patterns within the region until Europeans arrived, bringing virulent diseases and strange customs, killing off many of the native inhabitants whose descendants became known as Serrano, Cahuilla, Mojave, and Chemehuevi. These groups lived and traveled extensively in the area now preserved as Joshua Tree National Park.

Historically, the Maringa Serrano occupied the village and Oasis of Mara until Chemehuevi bands moved into the area in the late nineteenth century. Colorado Desert Cahuilla territory extended across the southern section, and Mojaves passed through the area on journeys to and from the coast to trade goods and spend time with other tribes and clans on familiar trails that the I-10 follows today. By the 1800s, Morongo Basin was occupied by white settlers engaged in a number of occupations including mining and cattle ranching, which declined rapidly in the early twentieth century after despoiling the hillsides and decimating native plant life.

During the 1920s, motorized vehicles and tourism became more common in the desert. Minerva Hamilton Hoyt, a wealthy desert enthusiast from Pasadena, was shocked at the alarming scale at which areas like Devil's Garden, a vast and diverse native plant habitat along Highway 60 and 99 were being uprooted and stripped of vegetation to grace people's yards or simply to be vandalized and destroyed. Mrs. Hoyt and others urged the federal government to create a one-million-acre preserve to protect remaining desert habitat of which over 800,000 acres became Joshua Tree National Monument in 1936. In 1994 the monument was renamed Joshua Tree National Park.

Joshua Tree is considered to be an "urbanized" park, as the highly developed Southern California coastal plains and desert valleys put millions of people within a two-hour drive of the park's boundaries. Tourism is the lifeblood of Joshua Tree and the surrounding area, and after the change to National Park status more visitors arrived. The short-term effects have been a road and facilities improvement program, an increase in traffic, and crowded campgrounds during certain times of the year. The long-term effects are just beginning to show.

The park is home to a variety of wildlife and more than seven hundred plant species, as well as artifacts and sites significant to the entire human and geologic history of the region, and most anywhere in Joshua Tree Park today, the effects of air, water, industrial, and light pollution are felt. From development on the north and west border to the proposed Eagle Mountain landfill at the edge of its vast southern wilderness, Joshua Tree, referred to by park ranger Joe Zarki as the "barometer for the environmental health of the region," is at a critical juncture as outside forces vie for its soul and future.

Clear, clean desert skies have drawn people to the region for many reasons, yet air pollution is a serious problem at Joshua Tree, which has recorded high ozone levels throughout the park. Rising several thousand feet above the desert floor, Key's View overlooks the San Gorgonio Pass to the southwest; air pollution blown east along the I-10 follows this gap between the San Bernardino Mountains, frequently leaving a thick mantle of gray-brown crud hanging over the region.

Zarki also notes that the desert ecosystem and wildlife that depend on native vegetation are being overrun by invasive exotic grasses brought in by the most invasive species of all—*homo sapiens*. A new plant regime, some speculate, fed by air pollution deposited in the form of nitrogen, is rapidly changing the fire ecology of the park with the introduction of noxious weeds that are competing for precious resources and covering the ground with dry tinder during the hottest times of the year. In the last decade alone, tens of thousands of acres of Joshua Tree groves were charred by fast-moving wildfires. According to park geologist and air quality management supervisor Luke Sabala, a combination of factors including pollution and a larger human presence in the area are changing Joshua Tree National Park to the point that within fifty years, visitors might be lucky to find a Joshua Tree left in the park.

Desert Views

Today, as housing becomes increasingly unaffordable along the I-10, people have discovered the communities of Yucca Valley, Twentynine Palms, Pioneertown, Joshua Tree, and Landers out on Highway 62 in the Morongo Basin as an alternative to life in the crowded, busy, megalopolis inching its way eastward. Life in the basin revolves around

Nature and War, with the world's largest marine corps base at Twentynine Palms. Joshua Tree National Park and the Mojave Desert provide a dramatic backdrop for the many interests that lay claim to and play a role in shaping this changing, finite region that to many appears timeless and limitless.

When he was a kid, Howard Gross traveled with his family from New Jersey on a trip west. Amazed by the beauty and grandeur of it all, he grew determined to one day live in the vast, dramatic spaces he had encountered. Years later, he began working for the National Parks Conservation Association, an organization that helps protect public land and educate people about the importance of places like Joshua Tree National Park and the Mojave Desert. Although Howard loves the work and treasures the desert landscape, his task is large, as Joshua Tree is listed by the NPCA [National Parks Conservation Association] as one of the Ten Most Endangered parks in the National Park System.

Television producer and host Huell Howser works in Los Angeles, but he loves the desert for its peace, beauty, and open spaces. As the owner of several desert residences he understands the importance of desert preservation, but also sees that even his arrival heralds change for the basin. When new housing tracts began to build near his Twentynine Palms home he did what anyone who wants to preserve their view does: he bought the property in front as a barrier to further development.

At his studio and home, Chuck "Cowboy" Caplinger remembers moving to Twentynine Palms in the late 1990s after becoming increasingly disillusioned with life in LA. An artist who painted some of the town's many murals, Caplinger is also active in civic life serving on the City Planning Commission. Although cautious about how the city should grow, he believes that growth is inevitable. As to how the desert's scarce water supplies can support an exponential increase in population and use, he feels that there are sufficient reserves in the local basin for long-term, modest, well-planned growth, a view not shared by park geologists and environmental groups.

For Ethan Feltgef, a lifelong resident of JTree and the laid-back owner of Coyote Corner, the town's hiking, climbing, and general supply store, recent development in the area prompted him to declare, "We've been Starbucked" as chain stores and master-planned communities invade his quiet home. The area has changed so much and grown so fast, that Feltgef believes he may eventually have to move on.

Road and land development over the last fifty years has made the desert easily accessible to millions of people for recreation and increasingly to an exodus from coastal cities. As a result, desert inhabitants from the smallest animal to the dramatically beautiful Joshua tree itself are left to adapt to a serious intrusion into their home, or perish, to the detriment of us all.

I-10 & Aztlan: A Cultural Crossroads

Along the Colorado River in the sleepy town of Blythe a sometimes quiet, sometimes noisy cultural revolution of sorts is occurring. The agricultural town located in the Palo Verde valley has a history of corruption, anti-union violence, and racial prejudice that is almost a California agricultural-belt stereotype. Of the many people whose courage and perseverance is a hallmark of their dignity, the farmworker or laborer stands among the least recognized. For decades Alfredo Figueroa, first as a field organizer and folk balladeer, later as a community elder, activist, and scholar, has worked to reconnect people to their culture and their communities. To Figueroa, knowledge of Chicano and Mexica culture and identity go hand in hand with working to achieve social, environmental, and economic justice for all people.

Figueroa lives in the area of western Blythe known as "Barrio Cuchillo" and is a native of the Palo Verde valley. His neighborhood, once called Acacitli, or "Jackrabbit in the Reeds," has been occupied continuously by his family for six generations before and after land speculator and swindler Thomas Blythe arrived in 1875 with dreams of founding an American Nile along the lower Colorado.

While Blythe's dream was born on the backs of indigenous labor, the Figueroa family worked as independent miners, giving Alfredo a chance to learn the geography of the region and discover connections between the land and the people that have informed his life's work. About the connection between his work and the freeway, he commented, "The main trail through La Cuna de Aztlan runs parallel to the interstate"; people have traveled along the path of the freeway, for hundreds and perhaps thousands of years before the modern era.

Using information gathered in nearly fifty years of research, Alfredo Figueroa has opened new and highly controversial avenues of interpretation regarding the origins of indigenous people along the lower Colorado River Basin by declaring the Palo Verde and Parker valleys to be "La Cuna (the Cradle) de Aztlan," the home of the people who came to rule as Mexica in Tenochtitlan. Alfredo is among those who have worked to reawaken an indigenous consciousness among people based on knowledge of the past, fact, tradition, and the ancient concept of *tloque-nahuaque*, or "Among all, we do all, for the benefit of all."

Fifteen miles upriver from town are the Blythe Giant Intaglios, geoglyphs of giant figures, some over one hundred feet long, that were constructed on dark surface gravel known as "desert varnish" millennia ago. Part of a network of sites extending along the length of the Colorado Basin referred to by Figueroa as the "Omeyocan Diamond," the figures illustrate the creation story of indigenous cultures that arose along the river tens of thousands of years ago. The figures have inspired Figueroa to organize and lobby for special protection over this and other sacred sites in La Cuna de Aztlan. Figueroa's book *Ancient Footprints of the Colorado River*, now out of print, describes and interprets these and other sacred sites in the region.

Figueroa's upcoming work details the life and importance of Cuauhtémoc, the Eagle Descending, the last Tlatoani (speaker) for the Anahuac Confederation. Figueroa relates the story of Cuauhtémoc, who told the Mexica that with the fall of the Confederation to the Spanish it was their responsibility to maintain the knowledge, traditions, and other "treasures of Anahuac" within their homes and hearts and await the arrival of a new day. "Our sun has concealed itself; our sun is gone from our vision, the invaders have left us in total darkness. We know that it will return again to shine upon us...that one day it shall be that Anahuac shall rise again." For Alfredo Figueroa these words resonate deeply, and he believes that for the descendants of Aztlan their time has at last come.

Brandy Burrows

Brandy Burrows was born and raised in Corona, where she still lives. She is the author of three chapbooks of poetry, including *Mexican Breakfast*.

"Glitter" is taken from *Mexican Breakfast*.

Glitter

san bernardino county

   shines

in a moving car i watch
a field of broken glass
brilliant in the sun
she wears her roadside
tight as a girl going dancing

   now i remember

the story of how corona
my crown town
got its name

a king named joker
wore a broken beer bottle
on his head

like a crown
rubies falling into his eyes

his *novias* erected a statue
of him in memory

   places i have lived

have the luster of pretty
life

the sequin of sweat
hard work on the back
sparkle of chrome

and to all of my friends
who have moved away

we admire the stars
here
too

Dionisio D. Martínez

Born in 1956 in Cuba, Dionisio D. Martínez has received fellow-
ships from the National Endowment for the Arts, the Guggenheim
Foundation, and the Whiting Foundation. He is the author of several collections of poetry, including *Bad Alchemy*, *Climbing Back*,
and *History As a Second Language*, and his work has appeared in
numerous anthologies and magazines, including *The Norton
Anthology of Poetry*, *The Best American Poetry* (1992 and 1994), *The
American Poetry Review*, and *The Kenyon Review*. He lives in Tampa,
Florida.

"Hesperia" was originally published in the Spring 1992 issue of
Ploughshares.

Hesperia

Someone asked me once if the world changed whenever I crossed
from one language to the other. She said she noticed how my voice
changed. I listened to myself: it was the same voice, the same man
speaking a strange language. I wondered about my face—if a certain
look might be possible only in one language. But I could only speak to
the mirror in one language. I never went back. Lately I've noticed how
my anger grows only in this language; in the other, I have tried to kill
you but haven't found the strength.

I was coming down the San Bernardino Mountains last night, the half
moon riding east on my shoulder, the stained linoleum yellow of the

first desert towns spread out just beyond the foothills. This, I thought, is real desert. I wondered what geography might do to a man—if it changes him like language; if his face grows dull when the land is dead, for instance; if he laughs like mad in the mountains. Around here, the earth is flat by choice. It is a land without sky. A man with nothing to lose could live here.

Larry Kramer

Larry Kramer was born in Iowa in 1939 and grew up in Texas and Missouri. A graduate of Ohio State University and the Iowa Writers' Workshop, he taught English at California State University, San Bernardino, for over thirty years until his death in 2000. His poetry collections include *Strong Winds Below the Canyons* and *Brilliant Windows*.

Kramer's writer's statement from *The Geography of Home: California's Poetry of Place* celebrates the geography of his home near Cajon Pass. "Strong Winds Below the Canyons" is from his collection of poems with the same title.

from *The Geography of Home*

In the flat, desolate boom town of Amarillo, where I grew up, the great highway seemed to point only west, and the far towns appeared fabulous, even Barstow and San Bernardino. Years later, when I accepted a job in San Bernardino, Alice Notley, then a young poet and friend, who had grown up in Needles, expressed dismay, even fear. "Well, maybe it will work out," she said. My California is the shadowland of the glamorous coast, an inland, raw, dramatic place of rugged, delicate landscapes and equally outrageous human dissatisfactions and hopes. After arriving, I met the local writer. "There used to be some poets here," she said, "but they turned to writing pornography." When I laughed, she looked sternly at me, "There's not much difference you know." In time I have come to love this place, would be lost anywhere else. I have, I hope, become its voice, of the precipitous, craggy slopes of Cajon Pass where I live, with its fierce winds tossing semi-trailers like cardboard boxes; the desperate power of its citizens, who will try anything; yes, even the freeway, that reckless, wonderful, perverse river of life. I have found here what I most wanted, myself—a terrain twisted by immense forces of wind, water, and fault, folded, upthrusted, fantastic, a desertous landscape, strangely sweet-scented, of desire and love.

Strong Winds Below the Canyons

Like a rubber tire another
night bears down; the wind
turns around, now its first piston
striking the chapparal rolls back
the chilling fog. I come
toward the window, a moon
suddenly fills: how plain
my life has become, how terrible.
Below my city composes, a wheel
laid out by Latter Day Saints,
a Zion of accelerating violence
driving so many men toward murder;
on any week, behind the hills
coyotes dig up some vague remains,
a dog drags home a human skull:
thus even now as a snowy arm & fist
thrust skyward off Mount San Bernardino,
my face luminous through the broad window
impresses itself on thousands upon
thousands of low houses that descend
like steps toward the sea.
                    On ponds
we once appeared naked, & we shone,
then we suffered so easily a wind's
gentle erasure. Love, remember our
true country, we gathered blueberries
from puritan graves; my hat full
we turned back through the amber light

then softened into evenings
that were watery green. There, beyond
the congruence of old house
& rapids, on ancient ruts
of syrup wagons drawing us through
abandoned apple trees bears twisted
then tore into bonsai we found
a way, disconnected, often
completely obscured, that always
further on, doubling back, &
doubling back would appear again
would never, though losing purpose, end.
& when against the midnight cold
we made love, when rats began to drum
on the low tin ceilings, we heard
only each other.

              Tonight you hold
your face aside in strict profile
recalling the coins I collected
as a child; they were foreign—
the poor alloy of nations overrun,
one curiously large prewar cent:
like us they came to represent
values lost. Love, I press toward you
my own grave image struck on the smog
silvered air of San Bernardino;
now when we speak, or even touch,
it is metal, against metal.

Keenan Norris

Keenan Norris was born in 1981 in Fontana, California. He holds a bachelor's degree from the University of California, Riverside, and a Master of Fine Arts from Mills College. He teaches at the College of Alameda and other San Francisco Bay Area schools. His short stories have been published in the *Santa Monica*, *Evansville*, and *Green Mountains* reviews, as well as *Rhapsoidia* magazine, and he has been nominated for Pushcart Prizes. His short story collection *hap & hazard highland* is forthcoming, as is his debut novel. He lives in Oakland and Highland, California.

"hap & hazard highland" takes place in Highland, in San Bernardino County.

hap & hazard highland

Before he left, she gave him the anklet she liked so much, the one she wore every day, certain as sunrise. "You gonna come back later, right?" she asked.

"I already told you yes twice," Sharone lied.

Then she fell straight to sleep, her body on top of the covers, her face closed and serene, turned toward him. It was almost midnight now, the room was dark but moonlit and her face solidified, colored, bronzed. As he looked down at her, he thought how it was never beauty that attracted him but something beyond beauty, beyond the memory of beauty.

He felt like he should do something for her, this special girl. He looked around the close, oven-hot bedroom. It was too dark to see very well. The only window, positioned right above her bed, was closed. Sharone opened it and the night wind, cold with slanting raindrops, blew in on the two of them. He fiddled with her silly little anklet, still not leaving. He knew that this time when he left he would not return, at least not for a very long time. He gave her back the anklet, dropping it onto her chest in the shadowed valley between her breasts. Carefully, he pulled the white bed sheets from beneath her and wrung them out. Then he covered her with them.

That was the best he could do. He checked the time: 11:59, now. He left her bedroom, left the apartment and went silently down the cheese-grater stairsteps to his car. Then he went to L.A. and stayed there for five years. When the Angelenos would ask him where he was from, he would tell them "California's armpit"; "nowhere-nowhere land." He knew he was full of shit that whole five years.

When Sharone returned to Highland, he rode in on a bicycle. As he ped-dled up the Avenue, he saw the old Mexican who still emerged nights to collect cans. Sharone remembered talking to the man years ago, how up close he could see the man's rib bones and the evil-looking scars that ran the length of his forehead. He biked up to the Stater Bros. where he had been told Montilla still had a job loading whatnot and things all night long. Montilla was one of the few people still awake this late who wasn't either drunk or high. Late nights like this didn't go well with soberness: Sharone knew this and, in fact, he was still buzzing from some of his own midnight medicine. He had simply learned to master and function in his highs, if not his lows.

Montilla worked midnight to eight a.m. That was why the first thing striking to Sharone were the dark-bluish bags under his eyes: the flippin Filipino looked terrible, even at a distance. "San D'ego!" Sharone yelled across the empty store at him. Montilla was unloading cases of wine, which made a lot of noise, and he didn't acknowledge Sharone at first. Sharone had to yell two more times before his friend noticed.

Maybe he was happily surprised to see Sharone, but Sharone wasn't sure. It was hard to tell. Montilla just nodded an exhausted what's up and took the opportunity to stop working. Sharone remembered that Montilla had had a bad back since high school, when he'd lifted some weights incorrectly. Now he had to lift weights for a living. It had been at least six months and two days—the length of his prison sentence— since Sharone had sympathized with anyone. Jailing, he had cultivated self-pity at the expense of all the other primary emotions. But now he felt bad for someone.

Instead of asking him how his crap job was going, Sharone asked Montilla about their mutual friends. Montilla mentioned a lot of names but only a couple of them stuck with Sharone: Lil' Vit, who had joined the army to fuck Filipino girls and shoot at people legally, and Tease, the tease. "Still just a tease," Montilla laughed, "just a motherfuckin tease."

"Tyra McClain don't come around no more?" Sharone asked. He remembered that Tease was a pretty girl, but Tyra had been his. The memory of her flashed through his mind: a real sister, a straight sister; she didn't tease, didn't let you tease her.

"You know I don't associate myself with all that boojiness," Montilla answered. "I don't know. I'm sure she comes back sometimes, to see family."

Sharone changed the subject: "Don't you ever just get the urge to take one 'a them to the back with you, just down the shit?" He gestured at the wine bottles boarded up inside their wooden cases.

Montilla looked at him sideways. "Why don't you help me work," he said. "You been doin a grip 'a push-ups and crunches and all that shit. Even got the stamina to ride that bike in from wherever the hell you came from."

"You seen me ride up?"

Sharone helped with the wine cases, then moved on to the produce aisles and unloaded packages of ice-cold ribs that made his fingers feel frostbitten. A supervisor passed by. He frowned at Sharone's presence, then he shrugged as if to wonder given a chance in hell why anybody would volunteer for this work.

"He's a asshole," Montilla said, when the supervisor was safely out of range.

"Looks like one."

"Yeah."

"He fuck with you, D'ego?"

"Nah, nah. It ain't like that. But I think he embezzles."

"It's like standin in a freezer, idn't it?" Sharone said later, when it was almost three o'clock.

"You ain't the only one feelin it, man. There's guys workin back in the freezer right now. Now that's rough shit. We all dyin, ain't that bad."

Before he left, Sharone helped him unload the sausage. They talked some more. Montilla wanted to try a school closer to the coast, he said. That way he could hang out on the beach all day, meet new and interesting girls, have sex with them. When Sharone left, Montilla told him to get some sleep. "Not yet, man," Sharone sighed. "Gonna go see what's up with Tease. Lives in Colton now, right?"

"Just a tease!" Montilla yelled after him as he biked away.

Outside, a gentle, weak rain sprinkled him and the dawn-sun inched upward. There were specks of cloud in amongst all the darkness now. The trees didn't seem quite so solemn as when he had started out. Of course, he had been high at the time and the trees had looked a little like motionless C.O.'s. He rode from West Highland to San Bernardino and into a lighted alleyway wedged between the Federal Bank and the DMV. He took a minute to roll a spliff on his bicycle seat; he lit it and closed his eyes. He opened them again, a moment later: nothing had changed, he hadn't made like Rumple Stiltskin and nobody had a gun to his head or a hand in his pocket. But suddenly he no longer felt like visiting Tease. He had already visited her, just then, in the grip of the spliff: under a moonlight monsoon, she stood waiting for him. Her blazer and baggy Dungarees slashed back-and-forth on her slim body like they were fixing to fly away. Her hair, usually tied in a neat little bun, had fallen before her face. Its highlighted strands were not even curly anymore, just skewed. Her brown eyes bulged wide and seemed to jut out into the cold air. She had on nylon sweatpants that were too small for her now that she was pregnant. They came down to somewhere just above her bare ankles. She was barefoot and the arches of her naked feet, stiff with cold, seized up.

"I been waitin out here for five years, boy," she cried at him. "Five years." She paused, looking imploringly into his eyes: "Remember me? Tease?"

"Yeah, I remember. What do I owe you," he asked, "for waitin so long?" He fumbled around inside his orange jumpsuit and came out with a handfull of zags and three crumpled dollar-bills. He handed his possessions over to her.

She studied the zags, the money. "Whateva, Sharone," she said. "Long as you back for good." She played with the three dollar bills, exposed them to rain and moonlight: the elements penetrated the bills as if they were transparent. All of a sudden Tease leaned forward and hugged him to her and she became his old girlfriend, Tyra McClain. He looked into her eyes, different than Tease's eyes. He moved her into a dark corner and watched as her clothes fell from her, leafing away supernaturally. He watched as she bent over, grabbed her ankles, unlaced the anklet; she put it in her mouth, knelt down, blowjob.

Between the Federal Bank and the DMV, Sharone studied San Bernardino's skyline: light was gathering there, stars stood out against the dark, fogged firmament. The streetlight that illumined the alleyway died in spasmodic flickers crackling weakly out of existence. He looked down at his feet, where he had imagined Tyra to be, where pools of old rain had actually formed in the alley's divots like so many frozen tears. He rolled one last spliff, pushed his blunt guts off the bicycle seat onto the ground and tried to call back the image of Tyra McClain that had disappeared, he knew not where.

In the morning, Sharone Bonilla biked up the Avenue, rode public transportation north to the Jack-in-the-Box on Fifth Street. He walked from there, pushing the bicycle alongside him, up to where Fifth intersected with Center and ran down all the way to Carlos O'Brien's restaurant. Two Mexican chefs stood on the restaurant's red carpet and yelled something like, "Street full 'a niggers! Street full 'a niggers!" up the street.

Sharone heard them and became alert to his surroundings. He stopped in the middle of the sidewalk and looked back down the street: there were groups of smartly dressed children and older adults who were too busy erecting banners and makeshift bleachers to have the time to call him names. He looked back up the road: a long, windblown expanse; fallen tree leaves painted the sidewalk in reds and bronzes. The side street was narrow. One way in, one way out, a funnel for the erratic wind gusts and freakish voices. He looked from the parked cars to the backsides of buildings where nobody was working on a Saturday to begin with. Far down the street, he saw the chefs. The chefs stared right back at him.

Sharone bent down to tie his shoes, then remembered that the shoes had no laces. He wondered how far and how fast he could run in lace-less shoes. He wondered if his bicycle had potential as a weapon. On the one hand, he wasn't about to let a Mexican chef call him a nigger, on the other, he was up against two Mexican chefs calling him a nigger, and they were both burly-built types. Even in their white chef suits, white slacks and white aprons they still reminded him of the guys in County who exercised all day and never went to the prayer sessions and optional GED classes.

"Hey. Y'all got somethin to say?" he called to them. He continued down Center Street until he was a couple feet from the chefs. "I couldn't tell what you said."

"We wasn't talkin to you, homes," the first chef said. He was methodically adjusting his apron around his waist and didn't even trouble to look at Sharone.

The second chef nodded back toward E. Street where the banners and bleachers were still unfinished and smartly dressed persons were skittering back and forth like wet ants. "Look at them wiggers, aye. They stay clean until the Parade's over. That's all you can count on."

"Wiggers?" Sharone's eyes darted between the chefs. "Parade?" he asked.

The chefs stared back at him. "Yeah," the first said, "wiggers."

"You can always spot one," the second crowed, his laughter naked and thin as the wind that whined down the narrow intersection. "Dressed up or fucked up you can always spot a wigger. Only clean if they're fresh outta rehab."

"Don't matter, dry or high, they're still the same addicts." He whirled his spatula like a cheerleader's baton. "What, homes? You thought we said somethin else, aye? Nah, we don't get down like that. I mean, you didn't, you didn't know. It's Red Ribbon Day, like Thanksgiving out here."

Sharone ran his fingers through his natural: it was certainly natural, uncombed for days now. Biking into the city the night before, he hadn't thought about his hair. There were so many things competing for his attention now that he was back on the streets, around free people: it was like everything including body parts were novelties again. As a child, he hadn't cared how big his hair got, nor had he in jail, where he'd come to think of himself as an elderly infant. But now, under the free and streaming sunlight he was a man again, aware of his freedom and all it entailed.

He checked his watch: 8:20. He wiped the sweat from his forehead and jaywalked onto the opposite side of E. Street, where a throng of sleepy-looking women milled about at the extremity of the Parade, occasionally entering the A Cut Above barbershop where they worked.

They were each about forty, save for one, a girl who looked younger than Sharone even. Her dark eyes were big like strobe lights and brimmed with something forgotten yet familiar: hopefulness. She was the gopher to all the women, and therefore the liveliest and busiest of them all. She darted in and out of the barbershop collecting sodas and Red Ribbon pens for the beauticians and scotch tape for the Parade organizers. Only in brief snatches of time did she come to rest, and even then she was straddling the entranceway to the barbershop and talking with the beauticians or passersby. Sharone chained his bike to a pipe that ran between the barbershop and the bookstore. Then he went and took a seat in the barbershop's waiting area. He watched the girl. He listened to her. There was something forgotten yet familiar in her voice: that lazy, elongated twang, like the strings of a de-tuned harp had been lodged in her throat. "Ms. Shaw, Xavier's momma, she tol' me to come get my hair done by y'all. Said that's what she did on her wedding day, got her hair did by the people she trusted most. No nigga to marry, but whatever. First day at beautician school's important, right?"

"What about that Xavier?"

"Don't go there."

"You gonna like bein back in school, Kadeera."

"So how y'all plannin to pretty me up now? I made out this here list 'a suggestions and whatnot. But I ain't in charge. I'm in y'all hands. Them's just my suggestions from sittin up late last night."

"We'll do what we can."

"Wonder what that list'll look like on her wedding day."

"Whatever y'all do to my hair, remember: this shit is *tem-po-rary*, a one-day stand, that's it."

"I know it, dear. If you always looked as pretty as I'm bout to do you, you'd be too big-headed to be my gopher and clean the bathrooms. But I guess you bout to have more important work anyway. I'ma miss you, girl."

"An' all this time I thought y'all was just runnin me around to get me gone faster. I ain't realize how sensitive it could get up in here." Kadeera laughed. There was warm, general laughter among the women. There was a concentrated movement of high-heeled shoes and they escorted the girl like a bride into the recesses of the barbershop to begin her treatment.

Sharone was the only person in the barbershop who hadn't laughed when the girl mentioned the clock striking six p.m. Then again, he was also the only man in the shop. The beauticians completely disregarded his presence. This did not bother him. He was in no hurry. There was a male barber who had yet to arrive who dealt with the infrequent male customers at A Cut Above. Added to that, he had a perfect view of the Parade from where he sat at the front of the barbershop. Even if it was not his Homecoming Parade it was nevertheless colorful and joyous and all those other things that he had become unaccustomed to.

"I know you about to buy somethin from our ladies footwear display, handsome man like yourself. I'm sure you have a honey stashed somewhere needs her regular strokin." Sharone's eyebrows arched. He fidgeted in the rusted metal chair. He looked away from the Parade, to the speaker: it was the barbershop manager, Mrs. Simms. He remembered her from a long time before. He could remember being a teenager and bicycling to this same barbershop and how he had wanted to become a barber himself until Mrs. Simms told him that he needed to become a licensed beautician first. That was the end of one dream.

"People always say it's men that have the fragile egos and cain't get over themselves. They must not know any women," Mrs. Simms laughed. "It's the women who need the strokin."

Sharone stared at her, unable to be more polite. She was a big-boned, deep-shouldered woman. She had a big, high weave and red-white-and-blue fingernails and he wondered, hazily, why he had never really talked to her before.

He shook his head. "I'm out one girlfriend."

"You poor, poor child. No girl and no barber." She ran a painted fingernail along her cheek as if it were a tissue to dry her face. "I apologize. Kenny, our male barber, he's *still* a no-show. No-'count brotha. I hope you get places on time, young brotha?"

"I've had to be real punctual the last few months," Sharone said.

She nodded and whistled low and looked out the window past the shoe display onto the Parade. He followed her gaze: a high school cheerleading squad pranced up E. Street, their green-and-gold uniforms gleaming in the sun. The girls did front flips, back flips, girled it up. And after the cheerleaders, a fleet of police on motorcycles fanned across the two-way, four-lane street. Sharone could hear the light applause accorded the policemen. He remembered instances too numerous to recount and too vivid to suppress of he and his people on these same corners watching the moonlit policemen, who only patrolled in fleets after the sun went down.

"You don't like po-lice," Mrs. Simms judged. "I can see it all in your eyes."

He nodded.

"Yeaaah," she sighed, "I could tell. It was in your eyes. I got a sixth sense for some things. Just like I'm sensin that Mr. Kenny won't show up till past noon."

"I ain't waitin *that* long. It's only nine-thirty, though."

"Barbers are a finicky sort, them and chefs. I'm afraid our Kadeera will lose that sunny disposition soon as she gets along at that school. It spoils a person. But, tell me, why you so against some po-lice? You just back from jail or somethin?"

"I was locked up for a minute."

Her face registered no surprise. She didn't need to look into his eyes to understand this part of his past, apparently he had jail on him, flaunted it like good clothes. "For what? Not hittin on your ex-lady, were you?"

"Nah."

"What, then?"

"A bullshit possession charge, 'scuse my language."

"Possession." She nodded, and gazed out at the policemen profiling down the E. Street catwalk. "Don't worry," she assured, "the steppers'll come through any minute now, make everybody forget about these police. These steppers are the *truth*."

There was a dull, faint knock on the windowsill. Sharone and Mrs. Simms shifted their attention from the Parade to a raggedy dressed white woman with aqua green hair and a tiara balanced precariously upon her head. "Lord," Mrs. Simms sighed. She motioned that the woman could enter. She cut her eyes at Sharone, "Red Ribbon Parade." She sniffed. "Who's cured? I'ma be glad when these people are all pomped and circumstanced out."

The crazy lady entered: "Can I bathroom?"

"Sure you can," Mrs. Simms answered. She directed the woman to walk to the back of the shop and out the back door. She did so, stopping only long enough to offer her tiara to Kadeera, whom she mistook for a bride.

A minute later, the crazy lady had made her way back to the front window. She was making her dull knock once more, holding herself with graceless desperation this time. "Damn hophead," Mrs. Simms cursed. "If I let her use my restroom, I gotta let all the other hopheads in this city use it too. You know how them types can spread some good news."

Sharone nodded.

"You never tried any 'a that crazy, hard junk, have you?"

"Nah. No, ma'am."

He wasn't lying. He had been surprised how hard the police were about nickel and dime weed gates and lazy drug dealers like himself.

A beeper rang in the back.

"If that's Kenny," Mrs. Simms called, "tell him he's fired!" There was warm, general laughter once more.

But Kenny hadn't called. Time raveled away and away, just as it had most days in prison. The seconds, minutes, hours, days—more importantly, his irrepressible regrets seemed to lodge somewhere in the back of his mind, unresolvable, a persistent ache. He could tell time by listening to the boombox in the back of the barbershop. Each song lasted three to four minutes. Mrs. Simms brought him tissues. He'd been crying, something about listening to the divas sing and watching the girl steppers step past him, reminded him of Tyra. He had had other girls, homegirls, L.A. girls, but not personally, only physically. They only shared their bodies and when they separated and were done, he with them and them with him, they were separate as their separate bodies. There was no real sharing, no love. He felt the loss of his love, felt it somewhere below articulation. "Good lookin out," he said as he took the tissues from Mrs. Simms.

The football team rolled down E. Street in limousines, waving Hawaiian leis at the crowd. After them, the Mayor and Police Chief shuddered along in an old Oldsmobile, waving too, and the contenders for their respective positions followed in two more elderly cars.

But the Parade had blurred into insignificance like forgotten and irretrievable dreams of a weed haze. Sharone looked about the barbershop. There were other men now, sitting, waiting for the male barber who would apparently be fired as soon as he set foot inside the barbershop. The men were impatient and did not wait long. They seemed to leave as soon as they arrived. Only Sharone stayed and waited. When Mrs. Simms asked him why he hadn't left, he told her he had nowhere to go to.

She went over to the clear glass front door and opened it enough for the garish sound-blast of the Parade to flood in. She urged him up from his seat and into the street. "C'mon. C'mon now. You know bout the new place, right? Nah. Course not. How would you? You were away all this time, poor child. Well, look, it's that yellowish-goldish building with the ceiling that's kinda circular, kind of a dome. You see it? Point to it."

He pointed at a building that read J's in an elaborate scrawl.

"Yeah," she nodded, smiling now. "You got it. In between that Radisson's Inn hotel and the karate place. The roof looks like a bald-headed Puerto Rican if you stare at it too long. Anyway, now, just go on down there and tell 'em Mary Simms sent you, you hear?"

Sharone did as Mrs. Simms told him to do: he jaywalked across E. Street, weaving between rival high school marching bands, and walked through the open door of the tall and narrow and bowl-topped building she had directed him to. An elongated golden floormat lay across the entrance and led into the barbershop.

Music broke from the subwoofer and three twelve-inch speakers that roosted on shelves in each corner of the shop. First, he heard the light suggestion of the organ, then the disparate and distinct sounds that reminded him of the Baptist Church he had known as a child. It was just a few miles from here, but much further away in his vanished soul. The choral melody arose, lovely and full-bodied, so intimate in tone that he imagined the entire choir was hidden just behind one of the barbershop's closed doors. Then, suddenly, a succession of sonorous bells sheered through the song, replacing the voices, decapitating the rhythm. Then the song wandered toward its finale, silence, the bells tolling, tolling, on toward the final toll.

Silence. The music gone, if only for a minute, the barbershop's casual cacophony welled up: *Yes, 'a course the crazy lady can use the ladies room, ain't nobody turned away in this house, 'specially not on no Saturday morning. Saturday morning, ya heard, the barbershop's holiest hour. Some sassy-ass been diggin in what'shisface-movie star's pockets for diamonds and gold. Mr. Morgan wife gonna nag him all the way to the ER, 'n even if the Lord up 'n put all this land under liquidation again, she'a nag him underwater. It's a female God forever 'n bad times for a brother.*

"Mary Simms told me to come here," Sharone addressed the nearest barber.

"Right, right." The barber nodded. "Their dude Kenny didn't show, huh?"

"Uh-uh. Waited on him."

"Barbers will be finicky," he sighed. Then he called, "Cindy!" At the far end of the shop, in a corner shadowed by a high and imposing black mantle, Sharone saw a pretty, inconspicuous sister raise her head and rise from her knees. She'd been at work scrubbing between the oaken floorboards and there were soapsuds between her fingers. She rose and washed her hands, tied her long loose hair into a bun behind her head and started across the shop toward them. She had luminously black feline eyes, eyes that probably glowed when the clock struck midnight. She was a thick girl; she made that ankle-length, homemade dress curve in places. Tease, Sharone thought, I remember you, girl.

The next song began, plunging ahead organ first.

Tease smiled broadly and led Sharone to an open chair. She cradled his head in her plump, soft hands. "You remember me?" she asked softly.

"Tease."

"But my real name's Cynthia. They call me Cindy here."

"Cyn-thi-a." He let the name roll lazily off his tongue.

"Yeah, not quite as good and slutty as Tease." She laughed. Then she changed the subject: "You look like you've been through somethin rough, man." She moved her hand gently along his head until it felt soothing as a breeze.

He fell asleep—there was no intermediary drowse, no space of half-consciousness. He was dead in his sleep. And his sleep was cavernous. It had dark facets, ruptures in the dream down through which he plunged. But he remembered none of these travels, none of these travails. And when he awoke, his scalp and face were baby-bare; he felt newly clean. She administered precious droplets of a liquid solution made half from rum and half from something else onto his scalp. The solution burned like acid, but when she wiped it away he felt fresher for it.

She noticed he was awake and handed him a mirror. He looked at himself, then handed her back the mirror.

"You like it, or is it just a'right?"

"You're good," he said. "I should be payin you extra." He stilled her hands upon his head, holding them in his own. Then he turned and looked at her: she wore the crazy lady's rusted tiara off-kilter, like an inexperienced queen. "You know, I used to want to be a barber," he confided to her.

She wriggled her hands free from his and suddenly they were on her hips in indignant pose. "*Used to?* Like you still cain't?"

"I don't know if I can."

"You need to quit that act."

He nodded at her and hesitated to speak.

"You OK?" she asked, "You fully awake?"

He rummaged in his deep-sewn pockets and produced twelve crisp dollar bills, the standard fee. He handed it to her. She handed it back to him: "Nah, I'm no barber. No license. I cain't accept money for this."

He paused, money in hand. He was confused. In the near distance, he could hear the song's discrete interlude, a cluster of chimes. She took the money from him and put it back in his pocket. She dug around in the pocket and came up with an inelastic old anklet. "How nice," Tease said; she turned the anklet through her fingers. "You keep stuff girls give you?"

"Tyra," he said.

"This ain't Tyra's, though."

"Yeah, Tyra."

"Nah, she gone."

"I left first."

She handed the anklet back to him: "Yours now, anyway," she reasoned. When he didn't respond, she added, "C'mon, haircut's over. Raise up, let's give the dead some life."

He stared back at her, hesitant, staring.

"C'mon, raise up. You can walk me down to Jack-in-the-Box, how bout?"

He acceded to her will, or whatever hand it was that guided his steps. Outside, the Parade was over. The final encore had ended, debris littered E. Street and someone had thieved his bicycle. A skin-and-bones junkie went about collecting soda cans in a black trash bag. The Radisson's Inn pink and beige bell tower tolled the new hour. "I need to be back before it tolls again," Tease said. She looked up at the giant clock face with her midnight eyes, "There's things need to get done." Sharone looked skyward, too, chasing after those eyes.

Michael David Egelin

Michael David Egelin was born in 1980 in Fayetteville, North Carolina. He holds a degree from the University of California, Riverside, and currently lives in Corona. This is his first published piece.

"The Lost Generation" is set in Riverside.

The Lost Generation

We are ghosts. At least that what Jimmy says. They can't see us, he says, or at least they pretend not to. My head is throbbing, like it's been hit with a shovel. Funny—you'd think pain of a car crash drifts away after death.

We climb through his bedroom window. Even though he's been gone for three years, he says, mi mama no ha cambiado una cosa. She hasn't changed a thing. Posters of Alex Rodriguez hang on the wall; their corners have started to peel over the thumbtacks and a thin layer of dust has settled on the windowsill. He directs me to the bathroom. While Jimmy is scrambling through his mother's room, I cut my hair with a pair of orange-handled scissors and shave it to the skin with a straight razor.

He walks up behind me and dumps jars of foundation, charcoal eye shadow, and lip liner pencils.

Jimmy walks into his bedroom and turns on a lamp. Finally I get a good look at his face. *Jesus.* His face looks like a map and the scars running across it are intersecting streets. He walks around his bed, running his fingers along the comforter and hums something soft before walking over to his dresser. He pulls out a black T-shirt and a pair of blue jeans, and picks up a picture frame. Mi hermano Hector, pointing at the kid in the picture with a bowl hair cut. He's wearing a buttoned shirt that hangs off his body like a tarp, and he is holding a half-eaten popsicle in his hand. The kid is smiling so hard his cheeks push his eyes closed, bearing his silver teeth. Hector did not come back with us. Some things are too hard for children to bear.

His mother couldn't afford a proper suit so we have to cut him out of the grey polyester coat with brown elbow patches. Jimmy stretches out his arms and the sleeves end at his forearms. I run the scissors up through the back of his coat. He pulls the coat off by his sleeves and snaps off his checkered tie. His shirt is pressed against his chest like a second skin. He rips the shirt off. His jet-black hair falls to his shoulders, and he throws on a black Metallica T-shirt and slips on a pair of worn black jeans. He wipes up the mud from his feet with a towel and slips his feet into a pair of his father's shoes. I guess it doesn't matter what your feet look like when they look at you from the waist up.

Jimmy offers me some clothes. No, I say. I like my suit. It hides the scars.

I screw the lids off the jars and scoop the foundation into my hands, rubbing my palms together. I smooth the foundation on my face and over my shaven head. Jimmy hands me the eye shadow. I rub it over my eyes, my cheeks. The eye shadow sticks underneath my fingernails. Jimmy takes a pencil, draws teeth on my lips and carves a cross into my forehead. El padre. El hijo. El fantasma santo.

I follow Jimmy back into his bedroom. He opens his closet door, reaches up onto a shelf and pulls down a jelly jar filled with change. He screws off the lid and turns the jar upside down; the coins rain on the bed. Abra sus manos, he says, dropping two gold coins in my hand. Jimmy tucks the other two into his pocket. Para el paseo casero.

I thought I was home.

He scoops up the coins and drops them back into the jar and places it back on the shelf in his closet. He walks into the bathroom, cleans up the makeup, and scoops my hair in a pile.

His mother's house is filled with shadows. In the hallway, pictures stagger on the wall. Light from the streets shines in through the windows and bounce off the portraits.

I follow him into the kitchen, where he opens a cabinet door and pulls out three brown paper bags. He hands me one, opens up another with a swoop, and stuffs his torn suit in the bag along with my hair.

On the kitchen table there are three skull-shaped candles, a lighter, and skull cookies covered in pink and yellow frosting. Jimmy lights one candle for his father, who left his family ten years ago. Jimmy says he saw his father come back as a shadow six years ago. He closed his eyes when his father entered his room, sat on the edge of Jimmy's bed and ran his fingers through his son's hair. Mi hijo, tu estás creciendo, he said. My son, you are growing.

My father left my mom and I for a woman younger than my mother, a woman who hadn't lost her figure to childbirth. She lived in Newport. I was six. My father never came back. He sent mom a check every month, two in September and December till I was eighteen. Sometimes I would catch mom spraying his cologne in her bedroom. Sometimes she would stare at me, without saying a word, while I ate breakfast. She sometimes called him and hung up the phone without saying a word. And sometimes she would lock herself in her bedroom and cry or just sleep the day away.

He lights the second candle for himself and places the lighter on the table. Hector and Jimmy left their mother two years ago. This is his second visit. He came back with his father last year. They entered through the front door when his mother, a janitor at Riverside General, was working the night shift. Like us, they walked through the hallways, lit the candles, and ate the cookies.

Jimmy and his father waited in the shadows for his mother to come home. When the sun appeared over the foothills of Rubidoux, Jimmy's father grabbed him by the arm. It was time to go. Jimmy snagged his arm away.

What about mami? Jimmy asked.

It's time to go, his father said, standing up.

Mas un minunto, he said. Just one more minute.

No. He handed Jimmy two gold coins and they left the same way they entered. Jimmy's father didn't come with us.

Do you hear that? Jimmy asks.

What?

Children are knocking on the door. Trick or treat.

So what?

We came back early, he says. It's not the second. He paces around the kitchen. She must've put everything out early this year.

We got food, I say. What more do you want?

Jimmy hands me a cookie, looks at the photos on the wall, before disappearing into the hallway. He comes back with a Louisville Slugger. Hora de ir, he says. Time to go. He picks up his two bags and we leave through the window in his bedroom.

We take a shortcut through the orange groves. I hear the screaming and laughter of children on the street. They can't see us. Many of the oranges have fallen off their trees and black ulcers eat away at their skins.

My father and his brothers picked these groves, he says, peeling back the skin of an orange with his teeth. The Martinez men like to drink. You can't pay for shit when you got a family. Even the cheap shit's expensive. He squeezes the fallen orange and lets the juice spill into his mouth. They used to come here at night and pick the rotten ones from off the ground. On the weekend I worked clean-up at a restaurant. My uncle got me the job. He worked as a cook in the back. I'd come in at three in the fuckin morning and scrub the grease that built up behind the grill and fish out the fryers. You gotta clean that shit or it catches on fire. He reaches back and hurls the leftovers into the night.

He circles around a tree, looking for more oranges. I'd bring home empty pickles buckets. We'd peel the oranges and place em in a trash bag, then we put the bag in the bucket and mash em, then tie up the end. Every six days or so one of us would let the gas out of the bag and in a month, he said, peeling another orange, you get licor de naranja.

But we don't got a fuckin month.

That's why…He digs into the full bag and reveals a bottle with green cactus on the label. I snagged this.

Where'd you get that?

Mami leaves out a bottle on her nightstand for Papa every year, he says.

Then why did you drink the rotten oranges?

Because, he says, the Martinez men like to drink.

He screws off the cap and takes drinks until the tequila runs down his chin and spills onto his shirt. He hands me the bottle, turns to the moon, pushes back his shoulders, and lets out a yell that can only come from the gut. Heeeeya.

The tequila smells like burnt hair. Jimmy is staring at me. It burns going down and doesn't stop. It rushes back up almost as fast as it went down.

Aye Dios mio, he says. Don't tell me it's your first time.

My gut feels like a fire's been lit inside it and it's spreading through the rest of my body. Jimmy doubles over, laughing, pointing at me.

Pobrecito. Jimmy grabs the bottle and lurches back, tilting the bottle upside down.

He hands me the bottle. Save some for the fire, he says.

Jimmy sets down his paper bags in the dirt and chokes the bat with both hands. He laughs, runs into the groves, and smashes oranges off the tree. His face is hidden by the shade of the groves. I can only hear his laughter, the smack of the bat, and his body whipping through the bushes. He appears out of the shadows of the groves. His smile is ear to ear.

Jimmy juggles an orange in his left hand and drags the bat in the dirt with his right. He catches the orange and digs the balls of his feet in the dirt. The bat rests on his shoulder.

Jimmy deepens his voice. Jaime Martinez steps up to the plate. He has just been moved up from Triple A. This promising young talent from Riverside, California, has just signed a multimillion-dollar contract. The sky's the limit for this up-and-comer, he says. Jimmy adjusts his invisible cap, points to the sky, and throws the orange up, swings, smashing the fruit into pieces.

I laugh and light a cigarette.

Whooo! He throws his fists in air and jumps up and down; his shirt lifts up and I see the scars on his belly. Whooo! His voice cracks. Jimmy stops jumping. He turns around. His eyes are clinched and he swings the bat with such force that it looks like the bat is pulling him with it. He is biting his lip so hard that spots of red appear from behind the foundation. His eyes roll up and he snorts through his nose. He stops in mid-swing and his eyes drop on mine.

What the fuck are you lookin at? He charges me and raises the bat over his head.

I cover my face, waiting, but it doesn't come. He drops the bat; his chest is convulsing. Jimmy grabs the bottle from between my legs and chugs it. He is drinking too fast and he starts to choke. It sounds like he's drowning. The makeup on his face is now streaking away and his scars become visible. He pours the last of the tequila on the bag filled with his suit and my hair. He yanks the cigarette from my mouth and flicks it. The whole thing goes up in flames. *What a waste.*

My house is on the other side of Martin Luther King Boulevard. We jump the chain link. Palm trees hang over the blacktop. Children are running in the streets and knocking on doors or ringing doorbells with their bags held up to their chests. Demons. Angels. Ghosts. Soldiers. Princesses.

A kid dressed in a soldier's uniform three sizes too big runs up to me and points his plastic M-16 in my face. The sleeves hang over his ten-year-old hands, and his pant legs are bunched up around his clown-size military boots. He looks like he's shrinking. *Ka-ta-ta-tata*. The sound of his rifle winds down. Yer dead, he yells. Yer dead. His helmet falls over his eyes.

You got me.

Jimmy and I cross the street onto my cul-de-sac. People on my street don't close their doors when they're home. They sit in their recliners, watching television, waiting for someone to come knocking. Mom must be doing well because there's a new car in the driveway. Jimmy asks for a cigarette and sits on the curb, tapping the gutter with his bat, while I walk up the driveway to my house.

I knock.

Trick or treat. I look inside. She must've redecorated because the couch in the living room is now leather. I can hear the television on in the background. A woman in a denim jacket and cotton dress sits up from the recliner, and turns around. I take a step back and take a look at the numbers on the front of the house. Someone who isn't my mother walks down my hall and answers my door. She smiles when she greets me. Her hair floats like her cotton dress. She brushes the gray-streaked bangs hanging over her eyes. I wait for her to turn around and pick up the bowl of candy from the table before looking inside again.

My house has the same pearl tile outlined in an aqua grout and Santa Fe wallpaper; only the people inside it have changed. Next to the bowl there is a picture of the woman, her husband, and their daughter. They look happy.

What are you supposed to be? she asks.

Nuthin.

She drops a couple of pieces of candy in my empty bag.

No luck tonight? she asks.

Not yet, I say. I bet you can't wait to see your daughter's face when she comes home with her bag full.

She takes a step back and places her hand on my door.

Yes, she says. They should be back any minute.

I bet.

She closes the door but doesn't lock it. I can feel her eyes watching me from my window. I walk down the driveway and sit next to Jimmy. I pull out my pack of cigarettes, tap one out, and light it. I watch the smoke float away.

I mash my cigarette in the gutter. Give me the bat, Jimmy.

Jimmy says they can't see us or at least pretend not to. I walk back up the driveway with a bat in my hands. This time I won't knock. I don't think I'll be coming back next year. Even though we are surrounded, I am not scared.

Ruth Nolan

Ruth Nolan was born in 1962 in San Bernardino. She received her bachelor's degree in English from California State University, San Bernardino, and her master's in English and creative writing from Northern Arizona University. In addition to teaching English at the College of the Desert, she teaches poetry workshops and lectures on desert literature at various colleges in the Inland Empire. Her poetry has appeared in *Mosaic*, *The Pacific Review*, and *Dry Ground: Writing the Southwest*. She lives in Palm Desert.

   "Mojave Lullaby" and "Gated Community, Palm Springs" both discuss the desert climate of the Palm Springs area.

Mojave Lullaby

Our gravel has no color, and our flat scraped yard, no grass;
even the lowest deadpan desert of the Colorado River Valley
sinks to winter gloom, these days, a dull voice of dead nerves,
words frozen on the tongue, fingers glued shut to the bones.

I've hung the holiday lights on the sword armed cactus tree,
and I'm proud I've avoided a single puncture wound; I'd gather
armfuls of wailing blood red blooms in June, and sit in silence
as the fat hummingbirds suck them dry and dance with a mate.

But now the light is gone, and our world is stone at 4:00 p.m.
The sunset barely stutters; the daughter begs my frozen love.
A few colored stars punctuate the blank of this stiff-jerk world,
promising to last the deepest nights, our little Christmas tree.

Gated Community, Palm Springs

Some old homesteader once loved up here,
and chewed a deep well near the spring,
in the canyon that spines up the mountain,
past the leather-fruited pomegranate tree.

We have passed through barbed wire
looking for cool swimming hole and so
we are here, the cycle of life intact,
today's bald-faced golf courses below.

Someone tried to grow corn here,
but the old bamboo has taken over.
The well is deep with silt, littered with cans.
The ocean once rose all the way up to here,

leaving its mark with hermit crab shells,
punctuating the dry-rot air, guttural utterings
of the coyote, raspy crackle of rattlesnake.
They call this an alluvial fan, the spill of sand

from the teasing mountain peaks. I say
this is hard-skinned land, the steep climb
following your footprints, squeezing an old
tennis ball, tasting dust, spitting out seeds.

Mark Chapman

Mark Chapman was born in 1951 in Santa Ana. He was a glass-blower for eighteen years and is currently caretaker of eighty acres near Mecca, in the Coachella Valley.

"Farming Below Sea Level" is about Mecca and was first published in *Runes*. It won the 2003 Runes Award.

Farming Below Sea Level

This was once the Sea of Cortez.
Now the air is lousy with lost seabirds
and prayer. Viscous. Thickened
with the motions of the slowest angels,
as if they were swimming in sweet, heavy beer.

It's not thin air, into which things disappear,
it's pressurized. You can feel
that the ocean has changed its mind, turned around
and is now bearing down on this desert.
The ocean says you will be baptized.

To be baptized is to fall
like a meteor through a blue atmosphere
or to descend into a body
stair by stair, or into a field:
a round bowl full of green air.
Some wild sunflowers. A white owl

in the towering cottonwood. Night unwinds
like a bolt of black satin.

How can a farmer, kneeling in his field,
find himself both worn-out and unborn?
It's not a new life, or an afterlife,
but the one unlistened to he's farming now,
hands cupped: a chalice
holding air, as if listening
is what air is for.

No moon. Pitch black. If you like,
read: these are fearsome times.
We are falling through the air
and we are feathered on the inside.

The Tractor

You're not thinking
so much as rearranging your reveries
when a slack-key guitar on the radio
is subsumed by the omniscient voice of the diesel,
and its fumes. Thinking ought to have sequence,
an entourage, or retinue. A processional.
Like a bride dragging a gaseous white train.
Suddenly you've driven too far into the field,
the ground laying down eagerly under the harrowing.

The harrow's canted steel discs
churn clods into soft agreeable dirt, an egret
hopping alongside. She's tweezing unearthed field mice
with her long beak. Swallowing one,
she trains an eye on you and winks,
the way a farm boss might encourage
someone in their employ.

No other angel in attendance.
You aim yourself down the length of one row,
then the next—a faithful, if stupefied, weaver.

There's a tree in the distance you can use
as a landmark—a smoke tree, bluish-gray
and as far from here as the holy ghost,
a cloud of kicked-up dust trailing off behind you
like the luminous veil of a meteor.

Aris Janigian

Aris Janigian, a second-generation Armenian American, was born
in Fresno, California, in 1960. He is a professor of humanities at
the Southern California Institute of Architecture in Los Angeles
and he returns to the Fresno area annually to pack and ship grapes.
He is the author of the novel *Bloodvine*, from which the following
excerpt was taken.

   To supplement income from their farm in Fresno, Andy and his
brother Abe agree that Andy will rent land and plant tomatoes in
Perris. Things go well for a while, but they are unprepared for the
devastation caused by the powerfully hot Santa Ana winds.

from *Bloodvine*

By noon Andy had irrigated half of the field. The water flowed quietly
down the furrows. Andy sat against the shed in the shade with his
lunch. A wind swaggered over the land and cooled his body down. He
pulled his boot off, rolled down the sock, shook it loose of dirt and
draped it over his lap. He traced a finger over the scars that resembled
strips of dried glue, rips in a lady's stockings. He recalled how, when he
was a kid, he'd slather the entire foot with mud, honey, or wax, or put it
in a wooden vice, or clamp clothespins to his toes, as though that foot
was a kind of voodoo doll. As he massaged the bad foot he wondered
what he had meant to achieve through those rituals. Were they his way
of punishing the foot, or his way of befriending it? A truck threw up
dust on the access road. It didn't sound like Abe's truck. When the dust
cleared, he saw it was an old Dodge, not Abe's Ford, rolling up. Andy

stuck his boot on in a hurry, neverminding the sock. The truck pulled up parallel to the shack and stopped.

The man cut the engine. "Howdy," he said through his window.

"Howdy to you."

"Looks like yer puttin' in tumaytuhs here." The man flicked his chin at the land.

"Yes sir, I am."

"I passed by here a couple of times and saw it from the road. Just thought I'd see who was farmin'."

"I'm Andy Demerjian."

"What's that?"

"Andy Demerjian's my name."

"I'm Jules Ahearn. I farm 'round these parts myself."

"Pleased to meet you, Jules."

"If you don't mind me asking, them trellises are awful tall, ain't they? Plus, yer a little early on them tumaytuhs."

"I don't know, am I?"

"I don't farm 'em myself. But Clyde Boyd does, and so does Rocky Moss. Both of 'em are tumaytuh farmers. Maybe you use some special method, though."

"Nothing special, Jules. Just farming like I always farm."

"'Round here, do ya?"

"'Round Fresno."

"Fresno."

"Yes, sir."

"Well, son," he said with a chuckle, "this here's no Fresno by a long shot. Weather's got a different sort of constitution out heres."

"I've noticed that," Andy said, looking up at the sky. "What do you farm, Jules?"

"Cukes."

"They grow nice out here, huh?"

"I've been lucky. Last season, though, half the patch didn't size."

Andy shook his head sympathetically.

"Farmin's one of those kind of things, though. One year to the next."

"I've seen it myself."

"Five years back I got cukes where the insides was all seeds."

"Can't beat the dirt, though," Andy said, scooping up a handful. "I even like the smell of it."

"Minerals there, that's for sure. Hungry 'nough, dogs'll flat out eat it." Andy agitated the dirt around in his hand until it sifted away.

"Have a chat with them two boys Moss and Boyd."

"I plan to do that."

"Seeing the winds and all, I just never done seen anybody plant so early and up so high. But they're year-to-year too. Maybe you got a trick up yer sleeve."

Andy thought, What the heck is he talking about? "I appreciate it," he said. "Where do I find these guys?"

He gave Andy directions. Andy nodded his head.

"What'd yuh say yer name was again?"

"Andy. Andy Demerjian."

"What kinda name is it, Demerjian?"

"Armenian."

The man shook his head. "Never heard it. But I'm just a damn Okie, so my opinion don't mean hay."

"Thanks for comin' by," Andy said.

"Anytime."

Andy watched Jules's truck wobble back up the road and wondered what he meant by weather, winds. He could've planted one month earlier or later, but how could that matter much? True, maybe he might have gotten color a little earlier if he'd planted in April. Maybe I should look into this, he thought. He took a slab of jerky out of the sack and chewed on it absently. Then again, people are used to doing things a certain way out of habit and they get spooked when someone comes along and does it different. Still, he'd like to meet Boyd and Moss. In the future, if things go well, he might get one or the other of these locals to farm the place for a fee.[...]

Andy had been in the desert of Perris for two months now, and not once had Abe made it down as planned. First Abe couldn't go on account of that spinning sickness. Then the kids got sick, the barn needed repairs and Zabel's mother had to see the doctor. One thing after another. Andy would have made peace with working the Perris patch alone if only Abe and Zabel hadn't been hassling him to help with the raisin harvest too. As if all that weren't insult enough, Zabel called him once a week, wanting to know where their dough was going, down to the last nickel.

"We're right on budget," he told her.

"Budget? Since when do we have a budget?"

"Talk to your husband about it, Zabel. He'll fill you in."

"Where are you going to sell the tomatoes?" Zabel asked.

"I got a broker down here. Relax."

"Don't tell *me* to relax. You relax. Broker?"

"The guy who sells the fruit."

"How much does this so-called broker make?"

"A dime a box."

"Ten cents?!"

This kind of thing. Back and forth. It got to be that Andy felt like a hired hand, a kind of farm manager.

The tomatoes, though, they were coming in nice, heavy in number, and plump. They were so pretty, Andy was loath to leave them behind.

He told Abe, "Let's get the grapes down early so I can get back down to harvest these tomatoes."

"Don't want to get 'em down too early or they'll fry. How early?"

"Once the sugar is there. That's all."

Abe said, "Remember, *this* harvest is our bread and butter."

"You remember too, *this* harvest is our future."

Abe grunted.

"All I want is a little breathing room, Abe. As it is, I'm gonna be scrambling back and forth."

"Like I've got breathing room?"

"I don't know what you got. Anyway, Abe, turn the water off and work up the ground. That'll kick the sugar up a point more."

Abe said, "I'll give Gabe a call. We got our regular Filipinos."

"Weather?"

"Clear as a bell."[…]

They finished just past noon on the fourth day. Damn near five hundred tons of grapes lay in mounds on the terrace. The air around the vineyard was thick, syrupy with baking raisins. This accomplishment, which might otherwise have warranted a hearty meal and a few shots of whiskey, barely went acknowledged. Andy had to hit the road for another harvest ten hours away.

"Why don't you stay a couple of days?" Abe said.

"Naw. Better get going."

Though he'd been patient with his brother, somewhere along the line some resentment had seeped in. Now that the harvest was over, he could feel it. As taxing as the tomato harvest was looking, part of him couldn't wait to get out to the desert again.

"Nothin's gonna run away down there," Abe said.

Maybe I'm the one who is running away, Andy thought. From Zab, Abe, the farm. That's bad, Andy thought. When a man has an urge to flee his own land, something's wrong.

"Take care of the home front, Abe. I'll see you, God willing, in a few weeks."

The last hour's stretch of road was starting to blur, Andy was so beat. When he got back to the motel, he unloaded his bags in the room and sat on the edge of the bed, too exhausted to sleep. He decided to drive to Ike's and have a drink or two.

A great big silver moon lay a luminous silt over everything. There wasn't a single car in front of the bar when he drove up, no trucks across the road, nothing. The sign on the roof, it was missing. Had Ike closed the place down? He tugged on the door, half expecting it wouldn't open. Ike was sitting at the bar watching TV. Andy wondered whether Ike had been robbed, or maybe he'd lost his license.

Ike poured him a beer and set it in front of him just as he sat down.

"What's up, Ike? Things sure are dead around here."

"Always that way after the Santa Anas. How'd you make out?"

"Well, we laid 'em down. Now we'll wait and see."

The two men were talking about two different things.

"Lot worse than last year. Damn near threw this building on its butt," Ike said.

"What are we talking about here, Ike?"

"Santa Anas, what else?"

"What's the Santa Anas, Ike?"

Ike looked at Andy like he was the poor bastard who was the last to know his wife had cheated on him.

"Wind."

"Wind?"

"Andy, where you been?"

"Fresno."

"Came through here five days ago something vicious. Knocked out electricity. Tore everything apart."

"Don't fuck with me, Ike."

"I wish I was, partner."

Andy thought of the tomatoes. Ike was thinking the same thing.

"Probably them tomatoes of yours, too."

"Everywhere?"

"Like I said."

Back in the car, Andy could see himself shaking. He tried to calm himself. Had to be Ike was exaggerating. Andy couldn't fathom what such a wind might do to tomatoes, couldn't get a picture in his mind. What kind of winds was Ike talking about? A hurricane would've had to reel through here to do the damage he'd claimed. A fucking twister. He began to see signs of tumult he hadn't noticed on the drive to the bar. Tumbleweeds were climbing over each other against walls of buildings. He noticed sand clumped in the gutters, sand spread across the road. In spots, he heard his tires pick up loosened gravel.

Then he remembered the conversation he'd had with Jules. The words "trellises" and "weather" boomed in his heart. Here he was, thinking how clever he had been to jump ahead of the market. Shit! He drove up the back side of the acreage. By the light of the moon, he started to make things out. Harvesting buckets littered the entire yard. He cut the engine, got out of the truck full of fear, as if some rabid dog were near. Stakes were strewn over the silvery stretch of dirt. Everything was nightmarishly on the ground, almost buried with dirt. He dropped to his knees and picked up a vine in his hand. Sand shed off it in sheets. He could tell from its weight that tomatoes were still attached. He picked a tomato. It was wet. The skin broken. He threw it aside. He heard it plop somewhere in the dark. He stood up and started limping up the row. Beneath his boots he could feel tomatoes squish. "SON OF A BITCH!" he screamed at the moon that glowed lavishly overhead. He screamed it again, this time to whatever was beyond the moon, to whatever cruel being was behind it. What would Zabel say, what would Zabel do? He could see her pulling her hair out from its roots, and his brother's face go dumb. "Abe, it wasn't my fault!" He could hear Zabel: "Akhh, akhh! Akhh! Akhh!"

Andy hadn't the energy nor the will to make it back to the motel. He didn't want to sleep in a bed that night, the motel's or another. He felt as though he didn't deserve to sleep in a bed at all anymore. He was so tired he was nauseated. He lay down in the cab, curled up the way children do, and fell instantly asleep. He slogged around in muddy dreams.

Twice during the night he woke with the hope that, just maybe, what had happened out there had simply been a bad dream.

In the morning, the land was something to behold. Andy was less pained than astonished by what it had undergone. It reminded him of the Bible, of Moses and all those plagues. It looked like a tractor had first gone berserk down the rows, and after that the acreage had been crop dusted over and over and over again. Walking over it, he kept shaking his head and repeating to himself, What a shame. He could smell the tomatoes fermenting in the fields. He could hear flies sizzling. Tomatoes were barely visible under the mounds of ashy dirt. Other tomatoes were clumped together, getting shelter from each other. Tomatoes were all over, busted open, bleeding, naked and veined and exposed to the sun and flies that had now come to feast on them in droves. He almost wanted a camera to document it so that some day his kids could see what their father had lived through, what kind of fiasco he'd survived down south. He thought about getting some Mexicans in there to pick up what they could for slop for the pigs. But it didn't take a banker to calculate that, with the cost of labor, he'd barely break even. A few stakes somehow managed to stay bravely upright. He went and fetched a dozen buckets and started to pick what tomatoes he could off the vines.

Andy picked all morning. Never mind what he was going to do with them. It was something that he had to do, even if it was no more effective than panning for gold. He took extra care with what he did find, brushing it clean and shining it up against his shirt. He filled the buckets and set them next to the shack. When he'd filled them all, he sat, studying the tomatoes' ruby color, shapeliness. He picked out the prettiest ones and lined them up on a wooden board, sliced them into quarters with a pocketknife and proceeded to make lunch of them. The tomatoes were good and sweet, which made the situation all the more bitter. He munched and laughed. Fuck, he thought, these tomatoes taste good. FUCKING EXCELLENT TOMATOES! He pitied them, himself. He sobbed dryly. Over his shoulder he slung a big fat tomato. It landed with a "wank" on the shack's tin roof. He stood, assumed the position of a pitcher. "Fuck you," he hollered and hurled the tomato at the shack "blam." Again. And again "blam, blam"—juice was going everywhere. The side of the shack was all tomato juice and seeds. He emptied three buckets of tomatoes that way, until he was exhausted, until he couldn't see straight through the tears anymore. The senselessness of spending a better part of the day picking the very tomatoes he was throwing away hit him like a joke. Same as that guy—what was his name?—who can never get the rock up to the top of the hill, whose whole life was spent trying to get it up there. Just like him.

Lori Davis

Lori Davis, a native Southern Californian, was born in 1962. She has a degree in radio/television/film from California State University, Long Beach. Before becoming a writer and poet-teacher with California Poets in the Schools, she taught sixth grade in South Central Los Angeles. She hosts the Gneiss Poetry Series in Palm Desert and the annual Palm Springs Book Festival's poetry stage. She is the author of *White Dime*, and her poems have recently appeared in *Salt Hill*, *Atlanta Review*, *Hayden's Ferry Review*, and *Cider Press Review*. She lives in Palm Desert.

    I-10, or Interstate 10, goes through the Inland Empire from Los Angeles to Phoenix, passing through the cities of Palm Springs, Indio, and Blythe.

A Good Cry

"Climate is what you expect, weather is what you get."—Robert Heinlein

Days like this are unlikely. Unheard of, actually.
The dunes did not dissolve because of record rains.
They muddied into a mobile spackle on purpose,
varnish for a lackluster system. In the flood water,
I see a formula, where others might see the sky
floating by on its back or a puddle lit from underneath.
The arroyos are unabridged; the storm is incomplete.

The wash will soon be full of monkey flowers
and sand bells. A flute of Russian thistle.
Each seed has a long climb inside it.
Rainbows are not as portable as they appear.
A barrel cactus is done fasting inside itself.
It is overwhelmed by the slant of unending rain,
overcome by the staggering convenience.

Ambiance Report: 8:30 AM Off the I-10

A cough. A sip of tea, gone down wrong. A police car.
Cops eating at Coco's. Highway patrolmen, to be exact.
Splendid morning, slight breeze, rotten egg smell.
Birds chirp. Intermittently. An airplane powers overhead.
The freeway is fraught with freight. The bacon is crispy.
Birds. They chirp. The waitress walks out. For a cigarette.
Eggs dominate the menu at Coco's, a dozen miles
from the Salton Sea. I always thought it was Salt & Sea.
Either way. It smells of dead things, on breezy days.
Passing the parking lot and the restaurant. The waitress.
The cigarette butts. Here they are. Two cops, two toothpicks,
two car door slams. Birds scatter. The sea smell escapes
onto the freeway. The cops in pursuit. The birds return.
Chirp. The waitress pockets her tip. Coffee cups sit empty.
No busboy to clean up today. But there's bacon. And the sea.
And the cops with toothpicks, who protect us from ourselves,
intermittently. The birds chirp. I wonder if they can smell
the sick sea on the breeze. And the freeway, long & lean.
A siren in Sun City. A man in tan slacks chews a toothpick.
It tastes like the sea. A woman in purple pants gets one chirp
from the bird. You keep reading as if the stink is a new story.
The busboy is back. To clean it all up. He was outside, kissing
the waitress; a rush of sweet smoke still curling between her teeth.

Percival Everett

Born in Georgia in 1956, Percival Everett earned a Master of Arts in writing from Brown University. Currently an English professor at the University of Southern California, he is the former chair of the Department of Creative Writing at the University of California, Riverside. He is the author of fifteen books, including *Watershed*, *Frenzy*, and *Big Picture*. His 1997 *Big Picture* won the PEN Oakland-Josephine Miles Award for Excellence in Literature, and his 1990 *Zulus* won the New American Writing Award. He lives in Riverside County.

"909," whose title refers to the former area code of much of the Inland Empire (Riverside County changed to 951 in 2004), was published in *My California: Journeys by Great Writers*, edited by Donna Wares.

909

909 is a little like the name Bob. It's the same forwards and backwards. In fact, inverted, 909 is 'Bob', or at least 'bob'. There's a friendly ring to Bob, a familiarity. You don't call him Robert, you call him Bob. Bob is your plumber, your cable installer, your mechanic. In my case, my farrier. Bob is blue-collar, sweaty, down-to-earth. And that's how 213, 310, 714, 323 and 626 see 909. This is where I live, out in Riverside County about halfway to Palm Springs in desert hills known as the Badlands.

People in Los Angeles fight over area codes. They care what their codes are. I understand that the best one to have is 310 or maybe 213.

But out here we don't care. We live in towns called Banning and Temecula and Cabazon, separated not by an avenue, but by mountains or expanses of desert. We used to be orange groves and wheat fields, horse and cattle ranches. Now, we're tracts of affordable houses for people with too many children and jobs for people like Bob. We are known for meth labs and prisons and brutal summers and the occasional cougar wandering through town. Years ago the Mission Inn was the place where movie stars went to do whatever they later came to do in Palm Springs. Then someone discovered Palm Springs and so we became the space between Los Angeles and Palm Springs, the distance that made Palm Springs a getaway. The Mission Inn closed and remained closed for a long time and is now reopened. It is a kind of marker of what was, a luxury hotel in a place where no one comes. It's a nice hotel—beautiful, mission style and quaint and a place that no doubt sees its share of weddings and banquets. I'm sure it's where the president might stay during an election year visit. There is a chair in the lobby there made especially for William Taft, extra wide, and the story goes that he was, rightly, insulted by it. That might be the story of Riverside. Trying to fit in with the big boys by accommodating their oversized posteriors.

Out here, a lot of us have land and on that land we have horses. We're horsey out here. That's how we say it. We say, "This is a horsey area." And we have signs that depict basketball-headed silhouette humans seated on silhouette horses. That means go slow. We have feed stores and tack shops and desert, a really beautiful desert. It's the desert that has me here in 909.

Technically, the Badlands is chaparral. The hills are filled with sage, wild mustard, fiddleheads and live oaks. Bobcats, meadowlarks, geckos, horned lizards, red tailed hawks, kestrels, coach whip snakes, king snakes, gopher snakes. Rattlesnakes and coyotes. We don't see rain for seven months of the year and when we do we often flood. In the spring, the hills are green. They are layered and gorgeous. This is in contrast to the rest of the year when the hills are brown and ochre and layered and gorgeous. From my place I can see ten-thousand-foot Mount San Jacinto, sometimes topped with snow, most times not and occasionally hidden from view by some kind of inversion or smog. It is through all of this that I ride my mule. I can ride deep into the hills and I don't know there's anyone within a hundred miles of me. The trails are rough, steep, and sometimes a yard wide with long drops on either side. Of course this is why I'm alone back here.

Out here in 909, I saddle my mule while my neighbor to the north lunges a beautiful paint horse. I can hear the faint music of her radio. It's some kind of country music, not the same concertina music that wafted through the pastures from another house last night. My mule doesn't care about the activity. He stands with his big head low and awaits the saddle. It's August and the temperature will rise to one hundred eight. It's perhaps ninety-five right now at nine-thirty. If I don't ride now, I probably won't today. I'm using my cavalry saddle because it's cooler for the animal, though hard on my backside, and because I just think it's cool. I tighten the cinch and I listen. I want to know if there are any illegal dirt bikers out in the hills or whether someone is shooting at quail or cans or each other. Monk, that's my mule's name, and I climb the hill on the east side of the ranch and cross over onto a vast stretch of empty county and state land.

Before I head up, I swing south and around a crater that was caused by an exploded automobile. We speculate that car thieves destroyed the thing out here because it's so far away from anyone (except us). The explosion caused a brush fire that got squashed pretty quickly by firefighters, but it left a blackened and cleared area. I'm taking this opportunity to teach Monk to deal with strange and unfamiliar terrain. He doesn't like it. He dances off the charred ground and looks back at me, as if to ask, "Why would someone do this in our hills?" I tell him I don't know and guide him closer to a burned shrub and he sniffs it. I wonder what would have happened if I had come upon the criminals in mid-act? It sounds scary and all my city friends think of 909 as the wild outback, but I'm less likely to have a run-in with a crook out here than in 213.

Monk and I travel on, up and down and farther into the hills, past where I found the coyote den last year, past where Monk once shied from a balloon caught in a tree; there was an eye painted on it. We pause to watch a rattler cross the trail. Snakes don't bother Monk and I'm five feet off the ground, so I'm not bothered either. We watch him slither down the slope and into the high grass. There is no shade to speak of out here; the trees grow to nine or ten feet only in the bottoms of narrow arroyos that are so full of brush there is no getting close. We pop brush and make our way to a high place. The cracking of the dead weeds and shrubs is frightening. This stuff feels like it could ignite spontaneously. At the top I look down over the Moreno Valley, aptly named for this time of year, brown valley. Lake Perris is south. Also to the south is Mystic Lake, not a lake at all, but a huge wet spot that has diminished every year of the current drought. Around it is a wetlands area, an animal refuge.

Between the lakes and me, between my hills and the distant hills of Hemet and Perris, is the 60 freeway. It is ever growing and ever too small for the volume of cars it supports. When we moved here ten years ago, we would see only a few cars on the road. We drove to Joshua Tree often because it was a pleasant drive. But 909 is in-between. It's in-between where people live and where they want to be, apparently. Now on Sunday afternoons, the freeway is jammed with automobiles, platinum blondes in BMWs, SUVs pulling jet skis, Jeeps with three-inch lift kits, sporty purple cars with spoilers and decals of Calvin peeing on someone or thing. The traffic backs up like a bad septic system and does not move. I don't leave the ranch during these hours. I have come to believe that the highway must be their destination. All of those people have left home to be *there*, on the 60, in 909.

I can see them now, in their air-conditioned boxes, from where I sit on Monk. They are little specks and that's how I like it. For them 909 is the 60 or the 10. For me it's these rugged hills. Hills that defy human occupation. Hills that are not on the way to anywhere. Hills that will let you know if you're welcome. 909.

Sholeh Wolpé

Sholeh Wolpé was born in Iran in 1961. She holds master's degrees in radio/television/film from Northwestern University and public health from Johns Hopkins University. She is a poet and translator, and her book of poems *The Scar Saloon* was published in 2004. She is also the host and director of Poetry at the Loft, a cultural arts venue in Redlands. She lives in Los Angeles and Redlands.

In both "Morning After the U.S. Invasion of Iraq" and "And So It Goes…" the author learns of or thinks about events happening in her native Middle East while she is physically in the Inland Empire.

Morning After the U.S. Invasion of Iraq

It is as it has always been in Redlands.

At GFE on the corner of Cajon and Vine
people suck coffee from paper cups,
munch on muffins from Martha Green's Bakery.

The chatter is as always, quiet.
The smiles as always, broad.

But today the sun is concealed and the breeze
brings no news of the orange grove
down the road in Prospect Park.

Perhaps last night trees shed blossoms like sap
—trees grieve like that.

And So It Goes...

In the dusty market beneath makeshift canopies,
bodies captive in Baghdad's summer heat,
she tugs on her mother's chador, holds up a copper coin
in her tiny palm, asks *where to buy bombs to attack the Americans.**

My child cousin often marched around their round
mahogany table, fist punching air, chanting:
Marg bar Shah. Death to the Shah.

Months later, the Shah fled Iran.

Drought-empowered beetles, hungry,
killed countless old pines in San Bernardino Mountains.
                    Then came the fire
                                ruthless, sweeping…

A chador is a loose piece of cloth worn by Muslims as body veils.
*Quote from the *Los Angeles Times*, May 29, 2004

Dwight Yates

Born in Montana, Dwight Yates has been teaching writing at the University of California, Riverside, since the early 1980s. His 2005 collection of short stories, *Haywire Hearts and Slide Trombones*, is the winner of the Serena McDonald Kennedy Fiction Award, and *Bring Everyone*, forthcoming from the University of Massachusetts Press, won the 2005 Juniper Prize for Fiction. Yates lives in Redlands.

"A Certain Samaritan," first published in the *South Dakota Review*, takes place on Highway 243 in the Inland Empire. One couple picks up another couple having car problems, and the accidental companions discover they have wholly different views on many things—religion in particular.

A Certain Samaritan

Billy Stengel's daughters are asleep in their car seats, Jill sitting beside him up front, explaining how to rearrange the living room, get the sofa away from the window so that something more dramatic can be done with that spot. Billy listens but hears mainly the music in his head happily pumping as she repositions his favorite chair and the coffee table. He's caffeinated and content, just driving out of the mountains. Hardly any traffic and a moon ascending. Jill says, "Funny how getting out of the house makes it easier to see what has to be done and puts you in the mood for doing it." She is saying just this when he picks up taillights with his high beams and can soon tell it's a station wagon, an older one with a Jesus Saves sticker, and well over to the side with its hood up. He starts to slow.

"Not so sure you should," Jill says. "Mean that, honey."

He gears down going past it. A man and a woman both wave, the woman raising her arms and crossing them like a football referee. They look middle-aged and both of them husky. Billy pulls to the side, stops, and starts to back up.

"Honey," Jill says.

"Just folks," he says. In the side mirror he sees the man and woman walking toward him, the glow of his taillights on their legs. He rolls down his window.

"Don't get out," Jill says. "Keep it in gear."

"It's all right," he says, and his head music is backing those words with a reggae beat.

"Thanks for stopping," the woman says, bending to his window. "Everything just went out all of a sudden. The lights too, and we don't have flares." Billy can see her pretty well in the backwash from his head-lamps. Her blouse is a print of big flowers and hangs out over well-creased slacks. She's around forty with a turnip-shaped face. The man doesn't say anything but stands to the side and looks fed up. He looks mad and exasperated and tired all at once, the way only a big man can.

"Don't have flares either," Billy says, then adds "bummer," a word he feels too old for but seems to use when the reggae music is running through him. He doesn't really want to get out, although he had wanted to stop because he had been feeling good about everything, a feeling spilling over into compassion. Jill is massaging his knee. He can smell the resin from the pines above the cut bank, it has been that hot.

"Just coming down after taking our son to Lonesome Lake," the woman says, "and it suddenly died. Everything just quit."

"And not much shoulder," the man says. He is looking at his station wagon.

"I picked up your taillights from quite a ways," Billy says. "I don't think you have to worry." The man is looking back at his station wagon.

"Enough of a straightaway, you think?" he asks, still looking back.

"Enough of a straightaway, you think?" She passes it on from her husband. Her face wants so much reassurance, and Billy has that to offer.

"Maybe we could call somebody for you? Triple A? Would that help?"

"We tried that. The cell don't work in these mountains."

"I suppose," he says. "We could try ours down below."

She turns away to the big man in the dark. "What do you think? The Highway Patrol?"

"Or Tommy. Isn't Tommy working tonight?" he asks.

"I think so," she says. She returns to Billy's open window to rest her thick hands. "Excuse me, but we're thinking about our older son. He's at the 76 station. That they have a tow is what we're thinking."

"Just give me directions," Billy says. "Or maybe if you want to ride along. There's some room left in the back. We can work it out." His reggae comes in again on that, and he lets it refrain while the woman looks up at her husband. "It might be easier," the man says. "Faster." Jill exhales puffily and digs her fingernails into Billy's knee.

They pull both car seats out to the sides without waking the kids, and the woman squeezes in to sit sort of sidesaddle in the middle. Billy asks if this is going to be O.K., and she says fine and no problem and she even gets the belt buckled. She looks through the back window at her husband as they ease out. In the mirror Billy sees him bending over his engine with a flashlight. The woman smells like doughnuts.

"You were good to stop," she says. The way she is sitting it is easy to hear her, even though she holds her voice in on account of the kids.

"Don't worry. You can't wake those two," Jill says, turning around to make eye contact, which pleases Billy because one look at that face will relax Jill's mind about ax murderers.

"These are little doll babies," the woman says.

"Thank you," Jill says.

"Nobody else even slowed down. What's become of people?"

"He always stops."

"Well, God bless."

"I wonder if it's the generator or alternator," Billy says. "I suppose he checked the distributor. I wish I knew more about cars."

"Don't know what you could have done if a part was needed," the woman says. "I think it has to be towed. My name's Lucy. What's yours?"

"I'm Jill and this is Billy."

"A pleasure," Lucy says, and then she is quiet. He can sense Jill working on something to say, uncomfortable with the silence. He will just mind the road and the rhythms of the curves. He's feeling so very good here on old Highway 243, the descent from the San Jacinto Mountains. The day, a Saturday, had gone well: a lazy amble around Idyllwild enjoying the air and helping the kids collect pine cones, and then taking dinner at a restaurant serving waffles at any hour. Everything about their time there had been pleasant. He wonders what Jill will go with, and just then she swivels around, but Lucy speaks first.

"So what do you do for fun, Billy and Jill?"

"We have a paint store," Jill says. "Or do you mean fun fun?"

"I meant paint store. Your line of work."

"It's in West Covina," Billy says.

"I know where that is," Lucy says, and the conversation dies again.

"You say your son is at Lonesome Lake?" Jill asks.

"We took him up. It's the church retreat. He's been on about being a born again like his father. All this week it's what he's on about, so I told him honey, if you don't lose it, you don't have to find it again. Like your mother. I think he just appreciates the sound of 'born again.' So I said go ahead and be one by all means. Kids get strange in their teens."

"I guess we'll have to expect that," Jill says.

Billy checks his odometer mileage to tell the tow truck driver. He figures he has already gone about four miles, so subtracts that and memorizes the last two numbers. The doughnut smell seems to come and go.

"You don't know what to expect. You just don't. With Tommy, our older one, for instance. He is only nineteen and has our first grandbaby for us."

"Now that's getting an early start," Jill says, her chin all the way back to her shoulder. She's smiling, but Billy figures it has to be uncomfortable twisting like that.

"Too early, if you ask me. His young lady had to finish up in the special high school. Which is hard on them, but best overall. Did you know they do that?"

"I didn't know," Jill says.

"It's true."

Jill appears increasingly awkward trying to look and talk around her headrest. He feels lucky to be driving because he can come into this if he wants, yet he doesn't have to. Probably isn't fair to have stopped as he did and then saddle Jill with this woman.

"Tommy did the honorable thing. We saw to that. And now he's coming along as a father. It's a full-time what he has at the 76 station. Thanks to his daddy. And I tell you we wouldn't trade that grandbaby for the world. Not for the world."

"Of course not," Jill says.

"Now it's Christian rock. That's what Tommy's on about getting into. Got the guitar already. And the strange colored hair to go with it. That's where the money's at, so he says. I wouldn't know." She leans forward some more. "You're going to find," she says, "that these kids have got to have things we never needed. The DVDs and big CD players and ever so much else."

"I suppose," Jill says and tugs her seatbelt so that she can turn and talk better.

"It's very American," Billy says.

"Most of it's Japanese," Lucy says.

Billy was born in Canada and lived there until he was thirteen, so whenever he feels like it, he takes a comparative stance to talk about how Americans do things, and when the family visit his people in Calgary, he has it the other way. Jill pointed out that when he calls Canada on the phone he gestures with his free hand, reaching way out, but on local calls he keeps his hand on the counter.

"Tommy being our first born, we had high hopes. College at the very least, and I'm not ruling it out yet."

"Not at all," says Jill.

The woman seems very close—as if she were kneeling on the floor and not perched on the seat. Billy smells skunk and looks hard at the road so as to avoid hitting it, but the road is clean, and then he smells the doughnuts again and no more of the skunk.

"Skunk," Lucy says, and then she touches Jill's arm. "The thing is honey, the Lord has a design for our children, and you have to trust in that."

Billy comes into it then, saying all kids disappoint their parents some time or another. That's a given.

"A what?" Lucy asks.

"You take that for granted. You do what you can, I figure, but the kicker is they are bound to disappoint you in ways you'd not expect, but not in a big way, not in the long run, at least I hope not."

"So how do you know so much about it, Billy? You a professor?"

"Paint store," he reminds her.

"You're better off leaving it in God's hands."

"Leaving what?" he asks.

"Your children's future destiny."

"I'll do everything I can to control their destiny," he says. A banana-head Pentecostal, he thinks, but she's not going to destroy his good feeling tonight, the musical energy in him.

"Little lambs of God," Lucy says. In his mirror he can see her looking at his daughters, maybe feeling sorry for them having him as a father. Jill massages his knee some more, then Lucy turns forward again and puts her head between the front seats.

"The funny thing was we didn't even know Tommy was serious on girls. With him it was just cars and more cars. After that it was trucks. Who'd've thought? But she's a churchgoer, so we're real thankful on that score. For a time Tommy shut out Jesus, but now he's opened up his heart's doors."

Jill nods and is quiet, which is the way he is too when someone speaks reverently or patriotically, and he doesn't know what to say to it and really hopes a different topic will come up, yet he can still enjoy all this, just driving to his head music and not really having to talk but listening and trying to anticipate how Jill is going to react.

"Is your husband in the ministry?" Jill asks, finally. Her voice catches a bit, so she coughs to cover it and excuses herself.

"Security guard. But it was the Holy Bible cured him of drink when nothing else could. I told Tommy when they repossessed his truck, just look at your father, what he has overcome. There is no mountain too high."

"Good for you," Jill says. "I think that's what Billy meant about helping our kids to find their way."

"Without a vision, people perish," Lucy says. Billy remembers seeing that inscribed somewhere. "Have you two chosen Jesus Christ as your personal savior?" Lucy asks. Jill reaches out and pats his thigh. Neither of them turns or says anything, perhaps expecting the other to handle it. Lucy leans farther forward. "Don't deny Jesus. Oh, don't deny him. The Anti-Christ is on the prowl these later days. He runs the pornography shops and the abortion clinics. His mark is upon the land. Oh don't deny Jesus in these later days." She is breathing hard—agitated, seizure-like breathing—and in the close dark of the car she seems even bigger than she had been and the doughnut smell stronger. Jill's hand keeps worrying Billy's knee. "Almost to Banning now," Jill finally says, and Lucy subsides, her labored breathing coming under control.

The curves give way to a gentle downslope. Already Billy can feel the warmth of the valley floor through the vents and see the lights of the little city spreading to the north toward the San Bernardino Range. He had forgotten about trying his cell, but they are almost there now. At the edge of town, Lucy tells him all the turns in a businesslike voice. He is civil in response but wants her out of the car. His music has left him and with it the good feeling he had wanted to protect.

At what age, Billy asks himself, had he watched his father pummel a blasphemer on the streets of Lethbridge, British Columbia. Must have been eight. Pummeled him to death. The man was a drifter, clearly demented, screaming vulgarities about Jesus and the Virgin Mary—the kind of thing that today, on the streets of Los Angeles, you wouldn't even pause for. A crowd had gathered, someone called the police, but before they arrived, Billy's father had struck the man. People cheered and Billy's father kept striking, then used his logging boots before they pulled him off. He did a reduced sentence for manslaughter, served only eighteen months. Home again, he said, "We will not speak of this," and no one ever did. Billy hadn't even told Jill. He resents the memory coming to mind anytime and especially resents it tonight.

At the 76 station he parks to the side in front of the pay phone. Lucy thanks them over and over and stresses her thanks so much that he thinks she is going to cry.

"It was the least we could do," Jill says.

"And you two have a wonderful life with these little doll babies," she says.

Jill tells her they will and Lucy touches Jill's arm again. "God bless you and keep you," she says.

"It's easiest out my side," Billy says. Hysterical fucking woman, he thinks, and now the kids are waking up, whining out of sleep, so Jill starts explaining to them where they are, that they aren't quite home yet. Billy holds his seat forward and helps Lucy out. "I'll go with you," he says.

"No need to do that."

"Have to visit the john."

Two men on duty, older guys in white gas-station shirts, one finishing up with a full-serve and the other working an air wrench in the bay. Lucy waits for the full-serve attendant while Billy goes to the men's.

He feels suddenly tired, and it doesn't help much to wash his face in cold water. In the mirror, under that kind of light, he looks bloodless and altogether like his driver's license picture, which Jill says is ugly as sin. And then he hears one of the men shouting. "His goddamn hand in the till, lady!" Then it is Lucy's voice saying something, sort of sobbing it out, something about a seven-month-old baby and something else that Billy can't hear. "His goddamn hand in the till, lady!" That part is clear again, coming in through the transom. Billy slowly dries his hands, then runs the towel down and dries them again, and then washes again, dries again.

Lucy is slumped in a plastic chair between two vending machines, one with cigarettes, one with peanuts and Grandma's Cookies and assorted road food for seventy-five cents, her head in her hands, her big shoulders shaking, an unopened candy bar on her lap. The man leans on the half-door with the built-on counter where you pay. He's pink-faced and breathing hard, on his white shirt a plastic pin-on with his name, and below that "manager" in caps. He turns to Billy and says, "We'll see to it," which Billy takes to mean the station wagon out in the mountains. Billy nods but doesn't move and then does, taking a step closer to Lucy. She still has her head in her hands. He squats down so that he's eye level with her and just stays hunkered waiting for her to raise her face, which she eventually does. It's pinched and flush with piggy fat, and he wants to slap that face and keep slapping it, give into a wild wreckage of her face and wonder why later. Instead, he says, "The Lord has a design for our children, and you have to trust in that."

Outside, he stops by the pay phone for a deep breath, feeling embarrassed for being dramatic, wondering what prompted it.

Billy's daughters are fully awake and singing their ABCs, the older helping the younger over the hard part, the l-m-n-o-p hump, Jill singing with them and looking as pretty as he ever remembers her looking.

"Is everything O.K.?" she asks.

"Everything is going to be all right," he says, trying to get his reggae thumping again.

"Did you meet Tommy?"

"Just missed him," he says.

There is no traffic in Banning. He turns left at the light, then right for the access to I-10. Getting off the freeway and driving the mountain roads is what he likes about these outings, but after all the curves and the press of single lanes, it feels good to be joining the big artery again, heading into the heart of it, into L.A. In a few minutes the kids are asleep again, so he asks Jill to put in a CD, the music he'd been holding in his head long gone. "Anything," he says. "You're a good man," she says and pats his leg again. Very soon she is asleep herself, and he keeps looking over at her because she seems so sure of something and at peace. He is going to get everybody home, and tomorrow they will rearrange the furniture.

Someday he could tell her about his father. Or he will set it aside again along with all the other untolds, mainly confessions of times he wanted to cut and run, family and small business one big demand valve always open and sucking him in. What is it that keeps the telling from tumbling out, even this business just now about Tommy? In the dark he reaches out for Jill's hand, touches it without waking her. When the CD sticks, he drives on without that music or any generated in his agitated head. He thinks about Tommy's father and how it has to be getting cold out on the 243, help and bad news coming at him up those switchbacks.

And when his mind music does come edging back, it is gospel. *Will you walk on the water?* His own father's voice singing. *Will you fly through the air?* It's that Sunday in church, his father recently reunited with the family, welcomed by pastor and congregation, his father, champion of the faith, smiter of the blasphemer. *Will you rescue me Jesus?* His father's loud, wooden voice. *From this pit of despair.*

Looking ahead to where the Calimesa on-ramp feeds in, Billy sees a young man with what looks like orange hair, can't be twenty yet, standing next to a backpack and a guitar case and holding a hand-lettered sign on cardboard. "Bound For Glory" it reads—clear, crisp letters under the blue vapor lamp. The boy holds out his thumb. Billy slows.

Kathleen Alcalá

Kathleen Alcalá was born in Compton in 1954 and grew up in San Bernardino. A graduate of the creative writing program at the University of Washington, she is the author of three novels—*Spirits of the Ordinary, The Flower in the Skull,* and *Treasures in Heaven*—and one short story collection, *Mrs. Vargas and the Dead Naturalist.* She is the cofounder and a contributing editor to *The Raven Chronicles,* a magazine of multicultural art, literature, and spoken word. She lives in Washington.

"Gypsy Lover" is from *Mrs. Vargas and the Dead Naturalist* and takes place in San Bernardino.

Gypsy Lover

Every woman should have a gypsy lover on the side. At least that's what my sister said, with such conviction that I was inclined to believe her—my sister, who'd never even had a boyfriend.

When we were really little, our mother used to try to make us stay with her in a crowd by saying that if we wandered away, the gypsies would steal us. This made me hope that they would, and I had very specific ideas about the sort of gypsies I hoped would steal me. They would live in covered wagons drawn by big, gentle horses with heavy bells on their harnesses, and we would build a campfire every night.

I don't know that I ever discussed this with my sister, but we both seemed to have the same ideas about gypsies. It was quite a few years later when my sister made this statement, when she was in her early teens and I was about eleven.

"Every woman should have a gypsy lover on the side," she said, standing and looking at herself in the mirror, turning her head this way and that. She stood kind of sideways, trying to stick her hip out, I think, but she had no hips.

I remember that I was shocked to hear her use words like "woman" and "lover." It made her seem sophisticated and worldly, although she wasn't at all. My sister read Emily Dickinson and played the violin in the school orchestra. Maybe it was the violin that made her say that. Gypsies were supposed to play violins in the circle of light around a campfire while people threw heavy gold coins at their feet.

My sister was wearing a flowered shift when she said this, turning her head and looking at herself in an appraising way. The shift didn't look that great on her, the colors were wrong; I wanted her to give it to me. It was a hot September afternoon, maybe as hot as it got all summer. The room was stifling, and my sister looked pale in the heat, with large, tragic dark eyes, Anne Frank eyes —maybe the kind of eyes that would charm a gypsy.

"Why?" I said. "Why not marry a gypsy?"

She shook her head no, but otherwise didn't answer me. I would remember all this later, quite awhile after the night she didn't come home. Otherwise I don't think I would have remembered that day at all.

Once, the kids at the bus stop said some gypsies had moved onto their block. My neighbor Sylvia Gonzalez and I had to get up at five a.m. and walk seven blocks to catch our bus in a rough, all-white neighborhood. Sylvia was a year older and prepared to defend me to the death, since I was skinny and wore glasses and was generally assumed to be incapable of taking care of myself. This saved me from any serious fights all the way through high school in a city where people were commonly knifed or shot in school parking lots. Our bus driver, a black woman, kept a heavy pipe under her seat and was terrified of all of us—black, white, and brown alike. This gave us a sense of power and self-importance which evaporated as soon as we got to school, where city police stood at the high gates and on the rooftops watching us, nightsticks and cans of Mace at the ready.

I remember a boy, small for his age, who was supposed to be from the gypsy family. He had dark red hair and freckles, a first name that seemed to be short for something, and an Italian last name. He was quiet. The other kids teased him about his name being a girl's name— something like Sal—but they mostly left him alone. There was something about him that made me think he really might be a gypsy—his aloneness, as of someone who has had to move a lot, or some invisible mark about him, like the glint of an amulet under his shirt. He rode the bus irregularly for about three or four weeks, then he was gone.

That's how it was with my sister. One day she was just gone. She had walked to the library with some friends, and my mother was supposed to pick her up at 8:30, but she wasn't there. My mother came home, thinking she had gotten a ride with someone else, but as it got later and later, the evening turned into a night of loud conversations, of the phone ringing, and driving back to the library and around the neighborhood, and finally the awful calling the police.

We could all feel that something was wrong. A policeman came over and talked to my parents, then went out and looked for her. I don't remember everything that happened, just thinking that a police car, common in our neighborhood, was parked in front of our house, which meant that something bad had happened to us.

We found out that my sister had been offered a ride home with someone else's mother, but she had decided to wait for ours. It had been exactly 8:30, and she figured my mother had already left the house, so it was too late to call and say she had a ride.

I can almost see her standing on the wet lawn of the library in the twilight, the sun just gone down in the spectacular red and orange sunsets we got from the smog. She was wearing red slacks and a white blouse with little pleats on the front, and a baggy brown sweater. She always carried lots of books and a little square purse. Her long black hair was held back from her face with white barrettes. No one ever saw her again.

A thousand times I've imagined the gypsy cart as it turned the corner and rumbled slowly down the street, pulling to a slow stop in front of the library. How my sister stepped up to pet the snorting horses, and couldn't resist when the man on the seat offered her a ride. He would have had long black hair pulled back in a ponytail, green eyes, and one earring. He would have been wearing scuffed black boots and baggy pants and a full white shirt under a black velvet vest. A woman would lean out of the covered part of the wagon, which was lit from inside by a kerosene lamp, and smile at my sister.

"It's all right," she would have said. "We'll give you a ride just to the corner."

And my sister would have handed up her books and climbed onto the hard wooden seat, and maybe the driver let her hold the reins. That's how I imagined it happened.

By the end of the next day my parents were angry. They hadn't slept all night. My father went to work but came home early to drive around and look for her. My parents were angry because the police had suggested she might be a runaway. The police weren't taking it seriously. My parents were angry at my sister for disappearing, and probably would have killed her if she had come home that day or the next. Ours was not a happy home, but it was not one you would run away from. It would have been too much trouble if you were caught.

Besides, my sister had no reason to run away that I knew of. My parents kept asking me questions about her. What she said. What her friends were like. If she'd ever talked about running away. It made me realize that I didn't know very much about my sister. She was in high school and I was in junior high, so I didn't know her friends any better than my parents did. She was good and smart and all her friends were good and smart and came from families who lived in better neighborhoods—neighborhoods where Mexicans couldn't live.

I think my parents felt humiliated. They were worried, but they seemed to be as worried about what everybody thought as they were about my sister. They were from poor families, and had worked hard to establish themselves as decent, middle-class people. They had a lot of ideas about how decent people looked and acted, and they didn't include having your fifteen-year-old daughter disappear. Even if she had come back, her reputation would have been ruined. These were things my parents felt they understood. They did not understand the silence, the unspoken accusation that they had done something wrong to bring about my sister's disappearance. My mother cried constantly and her eyes were rimmed in bright red. She looked terrible.

During this time I remembered something that my sister had done when I was very little. She had entered a speech contest where she recited a poem about Scottish children who die while saving their kinsmen, by taking a message across a freezing stream. That was the first time I'd heard the word "kin." My mother and aunt, conferring with each other in Spanish, had coached her on their idea of a Scottish accent.

"The water is *cald*," I remember her saying over and over until they were satisfied. "The water is *cald*."

When she had learned it from beginning to end, they made her stand on a chair in the kitchen, where she recited, or more precisely, acted out the story of the poem with great feeling. I was so moved by the tragic fate of the innocent children that I cried. It wasn't until weeks after her disappearance that I remembered the remark about gypsies and figured out what happened to her.

They would have come around the corner from Eighth Street, the clomp-clomping of the horses and their bells audible for some time before she would have seen them. It was just getting really dark as the last light faded from the western sky, and the lamp inside would have made the canvas of the wagon glow a warm yellow. The man driving would have talked and whistled softly to the horses, which wore blinders. They would have pulled slowly to a stop in front of the library, giving my sister plenty of time to run away if she had wanted to. She would have stood transfixed by the sight, the lantern light shining on her pale face and big, dark eyes. And the gypsy couple would have seen that she was just the person for their son to marry when he grew up. They went slowly up the street, my sister on the buckboard seat, turning the corner just as my mother pulled up. She could have heard the horses' hooves and the bells jingling if she had only listened.

They would have continued north, up the quiet streets of houses lit only by the feeble glow of televisions, past the high school, past my junior high school, up past Highland Street and Sepulveda and Waterman, up to the foothills where their gypsy camp waited in a grove of eucalyptus trees. They would have camped on the old Coolie Ranch, a piece of property vacant and for sale for nearly thirty years. There would have been a big bonfire, and the woman would have put a warm black shawl around my sister's shoulders, and she would have seen her future husband for the first time—also fifteen, tall and skinny, with green eyes like his father. That's what would make her stay, that and the horses, which she would get up and feed early every morning, sometimes braiding flowers into their manes.

Our family was never the same after that. My father went to work and came home and watched television until it was time for bed. We ate dinner in front of the television, only speaking when necessary. Even though I was lonelier than ever, I joined clubs to get out of the house. My mother made me tell her exactly when I would get home, exactly how long it would take to do anything, until we were all obsessed with time. She never said, though, that the gypsies might steal me. I don't know if she remembered having ever said that to us at all.

I thought my sister might write to us, or at least to me. I imagined postcards from the Midwest, written with a cheap pen by the light of a fire, smelling of wood smoke. I imagined that they taught her how to juggle and how she and the boy, later her husband, would juggle flaming sticks that they tossed higher and higher in the air as people oohed and aahed. The boy wore a square-cornered hat which he doffed at the end and collected money in, always heavy gold coins, though I don't know where people got gold coins like that in this country.

I imagined that my sister, always a good writer, kept a diary about the life that she lived, and had kept an accounting of every day since the night she went away. She would keep it under her bunk in the wagon, in a secret drawer with her jewelry. My sister would have looked a born gypsy if dressed for the part. No one would have guessed where she came from.

I imagined that they went to different parts of the country depending on the season, and that they had many relatives who also lived in gypsy bands. Some of them were with circuses and lived in Europe part of the year. I watched Don Ameche's television show about the great circuses of Europe, searching the faces carefully for anyone who looked like my sister. Some of the gypsy families probably sang. My sister could have sung and played the tambourine. She could drop her shyness the way she dropped it to recite a speech or a poem, then step back into it like a cloak.

Sometimes after work, when it's too hot to go right home and there's nothing else to do, I drive slowly north from our part of the city, past Highland Street, Sepulveda and Waterman, up to where the new subdivisions start. I park on Rinconada, or Rodeo or Camellia, somewhere near where the old Coolie Ranch sign used to be, where the eucalyptus grove used to sigh and whisper in the wind. People out here aren't used to seeing a car as old as mine, so I have to park in different places to avoid suspicion. I watch the sun dull into gold and pink, sinking slowly into the Santa Fe railroad yards, although you can't see them from here. But I've known since I was a child that the sun always sets in the Santa Fe yards, and I've lived my life to the rhythms of its trains coming and going, coming and going—the whistle at noon, and the whistle at midnight.

I rest my chin on the steering wheel and picture the gypsy camp. I imagine that they sing and play music until very late around an open campfire; the children, dozing in the wagons, fight sleep to hear one last story or song. Then the adults drink wine or smoke hashish and fall into a sort of trance, perhaps sharing ancestral memories. My sister's ancestral memories would probably be pretty bloodthirsty, since we're Mexican and our ancestors practiced human sacrifice, so maybe she doesn't smoke the hashish. Maybe she just drinks red wine or thick Turkish coffee with lots of sugar.

When I think of my sister, she's lying back on a tasseled pillow in a gypsy wagon, not much older than she was ten years ago, watching people smoke a water pipe while she drinks from a brass cup. Her eyes are rimmed with kohl (aren't every gypsy's eyes?) and her lips are relaxed and reddened from the drink. No one around her knows that she once stood on a chair and recited a poem about brave Scottish children, and no one knows that she once played the violin as wildly and sweetly as any gypsy lover in her mind.

Gordon Johnson

Gordon Johnson, a descendant of California's Cahuilla and Cupeño tribes, was born in 1943 in New Mexico. Educated at the University of California, Santa Cruz, he wrote columns and features over an eight-year period for the *Riverside Press-Enterprise*; some of these are collected in his self-published *Rez Dogs Eat Beans*. Heyday Books will publish a sequel to this collection in the fall of 2007. Johnson lives in Pala, California.

"Rez Dogs Eat Beans" is a playful look at life on the Pala Reservation; "In the Stands for Improved Ramona Pageant" describes changes made to the now Indian-friendly annual Ramona pageant in Hemet (see the excerpt from *Ramona* earlier in this collection); and in "As the Spirits of the Old Ones Dance, We Sing," the expulsion of the Cupeño Indians from Warner Hot Springs is remembered (see Malcolm Margolin's article on the same subject, also included in this anthology).

Rez Dogs Eat Beans

Once my cousin Goose, who used to sport rich women in Palm Springs, brought an Afghan hound home to the Pala Indian Reservation.

My guess is that the dog was owned by some tanned, tennis-playing woman who decided to spend the summer sunning her wares on the French Riviera, and Goose couldn't abide just letting the dog mope in a kennel.

So he took pity on the thing. Pampered all his life, O.D. came high-stepping onto the reservation, silky hair brushed to a sheen, toenails clipped, teeth pearly white. A city dog.

O.D. was none too bright, either. Tell him to fetch, and he'd sit there looking goofy, as if saying, "Which way did they go, George? Which way did they, go?"

He ran like a thirteen-year-old boy who grew too fast. I can picture him now, all loose and gangly, padding down the dirt road toward Goose's house, singing, "I'm bringing home a baby bumblebee, won't my momma be so proud of me."

People used to make fun of O.D., myself included. It was plain he wasn't cut out for reservation hardships.

A couple of months later, you wouldn't have recognized poor O.D. Mud and twigs clung to his matted coat. He took to sleeping on the roof of Goose's car at night to make it harder for the other dogs to get at him. He seemed to have developed a nervous tic.

Needless to say, O.D. didn't last long on the rez. I'd like to think he's still loping across the desert, hellbound for his Palm Springs groomer. But more likely, he was hit by a gravel truck, or killed in a dog fight, or shot dead for chasing cattle.

Anyway, one day, he just disappeared.

Such is the fate of many reservation dogs, especially those not born to the life.

Nearly every reservation household has at least one dog. Many have two or three. With no fences, the dogs have the run of the place, free to do as they please.

In the morning, some chase rabbits through the willows and cotton-woods across the river. As the day heats up, they'll nap in the shade of the Mission San Antonio porch, or under the pepper tree behind the Pala Store.

Some dogs follow their kids to the mission school, where nuns throw blackboard erasers at them to chase them out of classrooms.

Others stick close to the back porch, ever watchful for a half-eaten tortilla roll tossed their way or a greasy frying pan that needs licking.

I get a kick out of dog food commercials, like the one where the guy's champion Weimaraners point quail and dive headlong into the pond to retrieve downed ducks.

With nutrients scientifically balanced, his dogs only eat the best, he boasts.

Reservation dogs eat beans. A dog that won't eat beans doesn't survive.

A woman who gossips too long at her friend's house and returns home to find her pot of beans scorched doesn't throw them out. She dumps them into the dog dish.

"That ought to hold you for a few days," she says. Eat or starve. That's the rule.

Reservation dogs are tough. They're known for it.

People will say when trying to saw through a fried round steak: "This meat's tougher than a reservation dog."

Or: "That Rosie sure is cranky, she's meaner than a reservation dog."

Or: "Joe's chasing that skirt like he's a reservation dog."

Dogs born on the rez have the playful puppy days to form alliances. They find a place in the pecking order, and hold to it, or suffer a whipping.

A top dog will usually have one or two sidekicks he's groomed over the years to back his play.

There was once a burly dog, mottled black and blue, named Shindig, who ruled the reservation for what must have been a decade. Shindig was pure mutt, but like I said, a brute. His backup was a dog named Duke, a German shepherd skinny as a razor blade with teeth just as sharp.

They liked nothing better than to rain misery on unsuspecting newcomers.

Shindig would launch the frontal attack, while Duke went around back for the huevos. More than one reservation dog went around with a half-empty sack.

So it went. And so it goes. A dog's life on the rez.

In the Stands for Improved Ramona Pageant

For as long as I can remember, my mother has been telling everyone she can corner how her father was a cousin to the famous Ramona.

We kids would fidget in the station wagon while Mom regaled the gas station attendant about Ramona while he pumped gas and squeegeed the windows.

I'd elbow my little brother, "There she goes." And we'd brace for the lengthy story while cars idled behind us waiting for a fill-up.

The Ramona thing is a running joke among us kids. But for her, it's a serious fascination. One she never tires of. When I've run out of gift ideas for my mother, a nice Ramona-related gift will always work. One year, I bought her a leather-bound, turn-of-the-century edition of Helen Hunt Jackson's novel. Another year, a Ramona video.

Mom loves all things Ramona. Once, we drove to Old Town San Diego just to see where Alessandro and Ramona married.

I reminded her: "Mom, these are fictional characters." It didn't matter. We had to wander the adobe hacienda where the storied marriage took place.

For seventy-seven years, the Ramona Pageant, a spin-off of the novel, has been performed at the Ramona Bowl in Hemet. But I never went. Never wanted to.

Long ago, I read *Ramona*. That was enough for me. I wasn't drawn in by the sentimentality, the melodrama, the frilly-skirted romance of the story. While I admired Jackson's desires for reforms, for her vehemence over the dishonorable treatment of Southern Californian Indians, couching it in a fictionalized, overwrought love story didn't work for me.

I'd also heard stories, about the cheesy campiness of the Ramona production, the dime-store Indian headdresses, the drug-store beaded moccasins, the pale-faced pretend Indians in wigs, and I didn't want to sit there and squirm in embarrassment.

So I stayed away.

But lately, the Indian grapevine reports a changed pageant. New sensitivities have spurred attentiveness to cultural accuracy. Local Indians have been invited to perform. And Cahuilla and Luiseño culture count for something in this evolving pageant.

Now, I was curious.

My son, Brandon, came home with news that he and his peon (Indian hand game) team had been invited to perform in the pageant. And my daughter, Missy, had been asked to dance with the Bird Song group.

On Sunday, the Pageant Association sponsored an Indian VIP day, inviting many local Indians to see the improvements. I got my invitation in the mail and I decided to give the pageant a try.

After seventy-seven years of improvements, the Ramona Bowl is quite a showpiece. The hacienda, resembling the adobe ranchos of early California, occupies center stage.

Climbing roses, palm tees, flowering shrubs splash the landscape with color. Ascending hillsides form the bowl, with trails winding through the granite outcroppings and native brush.

Brushy Indian dwellings perch on hillside ledges along with a one-room adobe hut where Ramona and Alessandro live.

The stands hold about five thousand people. And the cast of the pageant numbers about as many. That's an exaggeration, of course, but it's a huge cast, which requires several hundred volunteers to pull the whole thing off.

What made it most fun for me was seeing the pageant with other Indians.

When we first walked in, a friend of mine, Benjie Magante from the Pauma Indian Reservation, announced like a circus barker, "Shade pills for sale. Get your shade pills here."

And we cheered and booed in the appropriate places.

Even the small improvements matter. For instance, the pageant brought in Ernie Siva, an expert in Indian music from the Morongo Indian Reservation, to revamp some of the Indian songs. Now many of the songs are authentic.

And, I saw many old friends on stage, singing, dancing, rattling, and it felt good to see that finally local Indians were being included.

Yep, I'm sending Mom pictures.

As the Spirits of the Old Ones Dance, We Sing

A gossamer mist, soft and wispy, billowed from the branches of scrub oak and tamarisk as spirits of the night breezed by.

And the night sky, made starless by drifting clouds, seemed somehow expectant, waiting for some kind of deliverance.

On this night, thirty of us gathered in a small clearing at the foot of Hot Springs Mountain and stared out at the shadowy landscape, looking at nothing in particular, mostly listening to dead calm.

Then gourd rattles broke the silence, shaking out syncopated rhythms; and voices led by Leroy Miranda Jr. sang Cupeño bird songs, songs not heard by these mountains for some one hundred years.

We had come back to Kupa, our ancestral village at Warner Springs in north San Diego County, for a night of song and sweat to pay homage to the old ones who preceded us in death here.

Once this had been our land, where we birthed our children, prayed to our Creator, suffered our injuries, celebrated our triumphs and died our quiet deaths.

The hot springs here had been our power, the wild game and plants our sustenance. Our lives and this land were one.

But in 1902, we lost our land in federal courts. Seems we didn't have proper title, even though we had been on this land for as long as anyone could remember.

Governor John Gately Downey, who took over this land from John Trumbull Warner, who got it from the Mexicans, who got it from the Spanish, who grabbed it from the Cupeños, had plans for the land. His plans didn't include a bunch of red-skinned squatters messing up the place.

So in May 1903, armed soldiers encircled the thatched-roofed adobe homes and ordered people to pack what they could into mule-drawn wagons and leave. Simple as that.

Women wailed, babies cried, men resisted as best they could, but eventually most complied, except for the disconsolate few, who in fist-shaking rage, fled into the mountains, never to be heard from again.

It was a forty-mile trek from Kupa, down to their new home on the Pala Indian Reservation. To this day, Cupeños refer to it as the Trail of Tears.

And so we came to Kupa on this night to honor our dead.

Cans of Prince Albert tobacco, painted gourd rattles, bamboo clackers and a small hide-covered drum rested gently on the dirt mound at the sweat lodge's entrance. A short staff topped with an outstretched eagle's talon and two eagle feathers wrapped with red yarn stood guard over it all.

We smudged our bodies with smoke from dried sage, and one by one filed into the sweat lodge, the womb of Mother Earth.

Hot rocks, glowing red from the fire, were placed at the lodge's center, and the canvas flap was lowered.

The sweat leader, Tubby Lavato, poured water carried from the nearby hot springs onto the rocks. The rocks hissed, and the steam smelled of sulfur.

First came the prayers, offerings from the heart. Then came more songs, voices raised in reverence to the old ways and the old ones.

After an hour or so, the rocks were spent. So another batch was brought in, and the ceremony continued.

The heat was stifling, legs cramped, backs ached from leaning forward. But it was good to suffer for the people.

Sweat flowed in rivulets from the body, spilling into the sand to mingle with the blood, sweat and tears of our forebears.

When it was all over, we toweled off by the fire.

"It has always been a dream of mine to have a sweat up here," Miranda said. "It sure felt good." "I know what you mean," said Lavato. "I could see them, the women in long dresses, the men in white shirts and Levis, dancing and laughing. I think we made them happy," Lavato said.

Plates piled high with a meat and potato stew and fry bread were passed around. And the talk was quiet and the laughter gentle as we feasted.

From where we sat, we could see the cemetery below, where wooden crosses marked the graves of long-dead Cupeños.

Rest easy, my people, you have not been abandoned.

Mike Davis

Mike Davis was born in 1946 in Fontana. A social commentator, urban theorist, and sociographer, he received a MacArthur Fellowship in 1998. He currently teaches at the University of California, Irvine. His major works include *Ecology of Fear*, *City of Quartz*, *Magical Urbanism*, and *Planet of Slums*; he often writes about issues concerning his native Southern California. He lives in San Diego.

"The Inland Empire" was published in *The Nation* in 2003.

The Inland Empire

On the great world map in the Palazzo Ducale in Venice, California hangs upside down, close to Cipango. Geographical intelligence was, of course, a foundation of Venetian wealth, so unlike other contemporary maps in European courts, the ducal map correctly depicts the exotic land of Califa as a peninsula, not an island. There is an elegantly inscribed notation in the part that is today Southern California. It reads "Antropofaggi—Eaters of Men." Perhaps the cartographer was predicting realtors.

A month after admiring the Doges' map rooms, I was buying mangos from an illegal street vendor on Base Line Street in San Bernardino. West San Bernardino is an older Mexican and black neighborhood at the foot of Cajon Pass. It sits uncomfortably on the San Jacinto Fault, which is almost as dangerous as its nearby big brother, the San Andreas. Coyotes still prowl in the washes, and the Santa Ana winds periodically blow out of the pass like dry hurricanes. Hard times have reigned here since the railroad repair shops closed a decade ago. On most upscale mental maps of Southern California, this is still antropofaggi territory: the wild void that lies east of ethnic cuisine.

In fact, Base Line Street is the Euclidean progenitor, the *Ur-line*, from which all the glamorous movieland boulevards and drives—Wilshire, Rodeo, Sunset and so on—were originally derived. It was plotted in November 1852 by Col. Henry Washington, working under contract to Samuel King, the Surveyor General of California. The summer before, a survey point had been established on the top of Mt. Diablo, incorporating the Bay Area into the conquering Jeffersonian grid. Now it was Southern California's turn to submit to the geometry of Manifest Destiny. The colonel and his party of a dozen men first established a cadastral Initial Point on 10,000-foot-high Mt. San Bernardino, then laid down the Base and Principal Meridian lines. They are the absolute coordinates from which Southern California has been subsequently subdivided.

When Washington first ascended his mountain, he could see the smoke from Indian villages as well as the adobe houses of the Mormon pioneers sent to stake a claim on the Pacific for Brigham Young's independent State of Deseret. Now the lucky hiker who reaches the Washington Monument Initial Point on a smog-free winter day can survey a megalopolis sprawling from distant beaches to the furnace-hearts of the Mojave and Colorado deserts. More than 100,000 named streets have been cloned since 1852 from the platonic ideal of Washington's Base Line. Meanwhile, the surviving Indians own casinos, and local Mormons can drive to Salt Lake City in a day on high-speed Interstate 15.

From Santa Barbara to San Diego, what one local wag calls "Gross Angeles" is a bigger urban universe than many suppose. According to the 2000 Census, 19.3 million people now reside within Washington's grid: a population equivalent to Mexico City's and not far shy of Greater New York's. Graying "Anglos" are a bare plurality, about 40 percent of the population, and will soon yield demographic leadership to younger Latinos (already 7.5 million in 2000). This Latin Americanization of Southern California has been accompanied by equally epochal shifts in residential and economic geography. The congested coastal zone, where three-fifths of the population lives, is divided between the poor black and Latino flatlands and the lush thickets of white affluence in the foothills and along the beaches. Here land inflation is the most powerful law of nature. There is no more room to build, and the rule of thumb says that if you can smell the Pacific, the land under your feet is worth a million dollars per acre. Even shotgun shacks in Watts can cost more than a palace in Dubuque. So for the past generation, growth has been centrifuged eastward, across the Chino and Puente Hills, into western San Bernardino and Riverside counties. Although many Americans are hardly aware of its existence, this "Inland Empire" has a bigger population (3.2 million in 2000) than the city of Chicago or, for that matter, Detroit, Philadelphia and Seattle combined. By 2025 it will swell to more than 6 million: the entire population of California in 1935.

Two sociologically distinct streams of intra-urban migration are responsible for the boom. First, white-collar and public-sector commuters are ceaselessly moving eastward in search of affordable mortgages. The Inland Empire is the new promised land where "starter" homes, although still expensive by Midwestern standards, are $100,000 to $200,000 cheaper than in older coastal zone suburbs like Westchester, Pasadena or Torrance. The punitive trade-off is the grim three-hour daily commute between new homes and coastal office-parks and factories. As regional planners daintily put it, the Inland Empire suffers from a radical "jobs/housing imbalance." Long-suffering moms and dads routinely serve two or three years' aggregate hard time in traffic for each child raised in the sanctum of a spacious Moreno Valley or Temecula tract home. The long ride to work is even more of a burden for those who lack the compensation of a dream home. Soaring rents are relentlessly driving the families of low-wage workers toward the desert and far away from major job concentrations. The hard-core poor—senior citizens, the handicapped, parolees and families cut from welfare—are also being expelled to the hinterlands. This is the second, more pathological source of the Inland Empire's demographic dynamism. As one local economist complained recently: "What you are seeing is the exporting [of] the coastal communities' problems to the inland region." Indeed, during the 1990s individual poverty increased 51 percent in San Bernardino County and 63 percent in Riverside County.

One result is a Darwinian competition for the region's limited supply of low-skill jobs in Ontario warehouses or Perris mobile-home factories. Another is the nomadic homelessness diffused throughout the interior counties. The structurally generated stress levels of long-distance commuting and poverty, not surprisingly, often redline in family breakdown or addiction. The San Bernardino area, with perhaps the nation's largest concentration of over-the-road truckers and outlaw bikers, has long been the methamphetamine Medellín. It is not surprising, therefore, that some long-distance commuters have taken to starting each day with a booster-rocket of speed or crank with their cappuccino. More alarming, according to the *San Bernardino Sun,* their kids also consume drugs at almost triple the national average.

But the Inland Empire, if gridlocked and addled by speed, also adds something positive to the balance-sheet of civilization in Southern California. It may not have beaches, but it has the most democratic and racially mixed neighborhoods in the state. If you blended the 2000 California census in a Cuisinart, the result would resemble the multi-ethnic student bodies of Fontana or Perris high schools. Unlike much of Los Angeles, where diversity is often the transitional artifact of ethnic replacement, the blue-collar interior is a true rainbow. Affordable and, for once, racially unrestricted housing has attracted working-class whites following the eastward migration of warehouses and trucking companies, as well as African American families trying to save their kids from the carnage of LA's gang wars. Chicanos, more than a third of the population, follow in the footsteps of their grandparents, who toiled in the Inland Empire's orchards and railroad shops.

Base Line Street, from San Bernardino to Ontario, provides a fascinating cross-section of this new society. Unlike in the wealthy planned communities of the Ventura plain or southern Orange County, land use in western San Bernardino County has the capricious quality of a Chinese encyclopedia. Thus pager sales shops, Bible stores and barbecue places alternate with long lines of storage sheds, the ruins of 1920s chicken ranches and new subdivisions advertising "Still Low 100s." If some blocks now look like Levittown, others are still defiantly Appalachia. Enough debris, meanwhile, remains exposed—derelict cars, farms and steel mills—to suggest a Nochian flood event sometime in the area's recent past.

Cruising Base Line, in fact, is rather like watching a Jim Jarmusch movie. The dull moments are always promptly relieved by some new enigma or unexpected absurdity. The landscape here is fractally strange. At first glance, for example, a corner mini-mall looks like any other until you notice the hand-chalked sign promising "Fresh Gator" on its way from Lafayette, Louisiana. (Hard times along the Gulf Coast have propelled thousands of Louisianans to the Inland Empire, where Cajun accents and creole cooking now spice local culture.) Likewise, the dusty bramble next to a Mexican Pentecostal church on closer inspection reveals itself to be a ghostly fragment of a famous vineyard, once the world's largest, first planted in the 1850s. Exiled "Rollin' 60s" Crips graffiti, meanwhile, brazenly tags the protective wall of a new tract development preposterously called "The Village of Heritage."

In other suburban belts, artificial reality eventually smothers all intelligent life. But the Inland Empire's new commuter lifestyles must contend with a formidable quotient of traditional grit. The old blue-collar culture of the region, forged in the great Henry Kaiser steel plant in Fontana and in the freight yards of Colton and San Bernardino, has survived plant closure and deunionization. Harleys are still more common than Lexuses, and there are more gun shops than Merrill Lynch franchises. Although white-collar commuters during the week shelter inside their walled compounds in Rancho Cucamonga or Ontario, on Friday nights they mingle with the working classes at the local gridiron. High school football is the Inland Empire's ecumenical religion. The corridor of communities along Base Line compete in the famed Citrus Belt and Sunkist leagues. These are deceptively genteel names for some of the meanest prep football in the country. The pioneer generation of Kaiser steelworkers transplanted the gladiatorial football traditions of the Allegheny valleys to Fontana in the 1940s. Although the blast furnaces are long cold and dead, FoHi and its local rivals—A.B. Miller, Kaiser, Eisenhower, Rialto and Colton—still play ball with milltown passion. These Homeric battles over town honor frequently continue after the final whistle. In 1999, for example, FoHi players avenged themselves on an arrogant opponent by beating up the visiting coaches. Adults on both sides were scandalized, but many kids relished the payback.

Indeed, there is a populist element in the Inland Empire that bitterly resents the partial gentrification of once happy badlands. A few years ago, I visited the little house on Montgomery Street in Fontana, a half-block south of Base Line, where I was born in 1946. The current resident and his sons were in the backyard vigorously stripping down an automobile. I knocked on the door and was quickly confronted by big glaring men with socket wrenches in their hands. They became friendlier when I explained that I had stopped on sheer impulse to revisit my Fontana early childhood. As his sons returned to their demolition work, the dad shared his views about the population explosion in the Inland Empire.

"This used to be a good neighborhood." He gestured toward the sagging bungalow shaded by an elderly pepper tree across the street. "There was bikers and truckers. Regular people. Now," he said fiercely, "there's goddamn yuppies everywhere." He was obviously referring to the new "Falcon Pointe" subdivision a few blocks away. Although the dental assistants, schoolteachers and paralegals who live there are scarcely "yuppies" by West LA standards, I took his point. The new

Fontanans do tend to be intolerant of the old-timers' penchant for junk cars and biscuits and grits. "What's to be done?" I asked.

"Move to Victorville. I'm movin' to Victorville," he responded with the certitude of a new convert. Victorville is the nearest edge of the high desert, half an hour up the steep ramp of Cajon Pass from San Bernardino. Once a town of tough cowboys and gandy dancers, it is picturesquely sited where the railroad tracks (and now I-15) cross the mysterious Mojave River. Hollywood screenwriters with a tight deadline or a drinking problem used to be exiled to Victorville to finish their scripts without urban distractions. Herman Mankiewicz wrote the first draft of *Citizen Kane* there, although only a handful of English eccentrics like J. B. Priestley and Aldous Huxley genuinely seemed to have liked the Mojave and its relentless, howling wind. Now Victorville is the suburb of a suburb, the overflow basin for a rapidly urbanizing Inland Empire.

Most of the homes in the desert have space between them, the Jeffersonian antidote to the claustrophobia of folks like my Fontana informant who fear living cheek to jowl with "yuppies." For the moment, Victorville is still a sanctuary for loners and good old boys attached to a ramshackle sense of personal freedom and the right to squalor. For culture they have had the Roy Rogers–Dale Evans Museum and the Striptease Hall of Fame, not to mention gun shows and swap meets. But even the high desert—on the outer limits of LA commuter space—is rapidly growing strip malls and grassy subdivisions. Soon will come the day when the yuppies move in next door and a Starbucks replaces the Deadwood Saloon. Then it will again be time for the hardcore to load up the family Peterbilt and move further out, to Barstow, Baker or even Death Valley.

Indeed, Victorville is just one of the many pseudopods that the amoebic megalopolis is currently extending into its far-flung hinterlands. At the base of Grapevine Canyon, ninety miles north of downtown LA, developers have already used Washington's ancestral Base Line to plat thousands of home footprints on the dusty San Joaquin floor. Likewise, the chronic housing shortage in San Diego is turning agricultural Imperial County, two hours away over rugged mountains, into a dormitory for its blue-collar families. Without the rail infrastructure that weaves Greater New York together, and lacking any regional coordination of housing and employment, the outward expansion of Southern California—as urbanists have warned for a generation—becomes intolerably destructive of family life, community health and the natural environment.

Yet it also seems unstoppable. Opinion surveys consistently confirm that Southern Californians' hunger for affordable single-family homes remains insatiable, and that they are willing to endure truly purgatorial commutes to attain suburban heaven at the end of each workday. It matters, of course, that they have so few real alternatives to choose from. The celebrated "New Urban" vision of pedestrian-scale villages on light-rail lines has had negligible impact on local building culture. Regional planning, Southern California's eternal will-o'-the-wisp, remains little more than the desperate race to add more lanes to a rapidly petrifying freeway system. This side of the apocalypse, at least, the future belongs to the desert suburbs and their simmering discontents. Greater LA's deepest impulse is still infinity.

Permissions

Kathleen Alcalá. "Gypsy Lover" from *Mrs. Vargas and the Dead Naturalist* by Kathleen Alcalá. Corvallis, OR: CALYX Books. Copyright © 1992 by Kathleen Alcalá. Reprinted by permission of CALYX Books.

Juan Bautista de Anza. "Friday, March 18, 1774" and "Monday, January 1, 1776" from *Anza's California Expeditions* by Juan Bautista de Anza and translated by Herbert Bolton. Berkeley, CA: University of California Press. Translation copyright © 1930 by The Regents of the University of California. Reprinted by permission of UC Press.

Mary Austin. Excerpt from *Lands of the Sun* by Mary Austin. New York: Houghton Mifflin Company. Copyright © 1927 by Mary Austin. Reprinted by permission of Houghton Mifflin Company. All rights reserved.

Joan Baez. Excerpt from *And a Voice to Sing With* by Joan Baez. New York: Simon & Schuster. Copyright © 1987 by Joan Baez. Reprinted with permission of Simon & Schuster Adult Publishing Group.

Dick Barnes. "'At Barstow,'" "Few and Far Between," and "Willie Boy" from *A World Like Fire* by Dick Barnes. New York: Other Press. Copyright © 2005 by Patricia Barnes. Reprinted by permission of Other Press, LLC.

Horace Bell. Excerpt from *Reminiscences of a Ranger* by Horace Bell. Los Angeles: Yarnell, Caystile & Mathes, Printers, 1881.

Gina Berriault. "Wilderness Fire" from *Women in Their Beds* by Gina Berriault. New York: Counterpoint Press. Copyright © 1982 by Gina Berriault. Reprinted by permission of Russell & Volkening as agents for the author.

Gayle Brandeis. Excerpt from *The Book of Dead Birds* by Gayle Brandeis. New York: HarperCollins. Copyright © 2003 by Gayle Brandeis. Used by permission of HarperCollins. All rights reserved.

Larry E. Burgess and James A. Sandos. Excerpt from *The Hunt for Willie Boy: Indian-hating and Popular Culture* by Larry E. Burgess and James A. Sandos. Norman, OK: University of Oklahoma Press. Copyright © 1994 by the University of Oklahoma Press. Reprinted by permission of the University of Oklahoma Press.

Brandy Burrows. "Glitter" from *Mexican Breakfast* by Brandy Burrows. Copyright © 1998 by Brandy Burrows. Reprinted by permission of the author.

Raymond Chandler. Excerpt from *The Lady in the Lake* by Raymond Chandler. New York: Random House. Copyright © 1943 by Raymond Chandler. Used by permission of Alfred A. Knopf, a division of Random House, Inc.

Mark Chapman. "Farming Below Sea Level" by Mark Chapman from *Runes* Winter 2003. Copyright © 2003 by Mark Chapman. "Tractor" by Mark Chapman.

Erle Stanley Gardner. Excerpt from *Blood-Red Gold* from *Whispering Sands: Stories of Gold Fever and the Western Desert* by Erle Stanley Gardner. New York: William Morrow, 1930.

Robert Gonzales Vasquez. Excerpt from *Living on the Dime* by Robert Gonzales Vasquez. Copyright © 2006 by Robert Gonzales Vasquez. Reprinted by permission of the author.

Sumi Harada. "My Mother" by Sumi Harada. Copyright © 2006 by Sumi Harada. Reprinted by permission of the Estate of Sumi Harada.

William S. Hart. Excerpt from *My Life East and West* by William S. Hart. New York: Houghton Mifflin Company, 1929.

Scott Hernandez. "The Canal," "Eastside Walls, Riverside, CA 1999," and "Life Lessons" by Scott Hernandez. Copyright © 2006 by Scott Hernandez. Reprinted by permission of the author.

Villiana Hyde. Excerpt from "Going to Sherman" from *Yumáyk Yumáyk: Long Ago* by Villiana Hyde as told to Eric Elliott. Berkeley, CA: University of California Press. Copyright © 1994 The Regents of the University of California. Reprinted by permission of UC Press.

Helen Hunt Jackson. Excerpt from *Ramona* by Helen Hunt Jackson. Boston: Little, Brown, and Co., 1884.

Carrie Jacobs-Bond. "A Perfect Day" by Carrie Jacobs-Bond, 1910.

Edmund Jaeger. Excerpt from "Vultures" from *Desert Wildlife* by Edmund Jaeger. Palo Alto, CA: Stanford University Press. Copyright © 1950, 1961 by Edmund Jaeger.

Michael Jaime-Becerra. "Georgie and Wanda" from *Every Night Is Ladies' Night* by Michael Jaime-Becerra. New York: HarperCollins. Copyright © 2004 by Michael Jaime-Becerra. Reprinted by permission of Rayo, a division of HarperCollins Publishers.

John Jakes. Excerpt from *California Gold* by John Jakes. New York: Ballantine Books. Copyright © 1989 by John Jakes. Reprinted by permission of the author.

Aris Janigian. Excerpt from *Bloodvine* by Aris Janigian. Berkeley, CA: Heyday Books. Copyright © 2003 by Aris Janigian. Reprinted by permission of Heyday Books.

Gordon Johnson. "As Spirits of the Old Ones Dance, We Sing," "In the Stands for Improved Ramona Pageant," and "Rez Dogs Eat Beans" from *Rez Dogs Eat Beans and Other Tales* by Gordon Johnson. Copyright © 2001 by Gordon Johnson. Reprinted by permission of the author and courtesy of the *Riverside Press-Enterprise*.

E. J. Jones. "Grass Green" by E. J. Jones. Copyright © 2006 by E. J. Jones. Reprinted by permission of the author.

Laura Kalpakian. Excerpt from *Caveat* by Laura Kalpakian. Winston-Salem, NC: John F. Blair. Copyright © 1998 by Laura Kalpakian. Reprinted by permission of John F. Blair, Publisher.

Larry Kramer. "Strong Winds Below the Canyons" from *Strong Winds Below the Canyons* by Larry Kramer. Copyright © 1984 by Larry Kramer. Prose statement by Larry Kramer from *The Geography of Home*, ed. Christopher Buckley and Gary Young. Berkeley, CA: Heyday Books. Copyright © 1999 by Larry Kramer. Both selections reprinted by permission of Patricia Bywater.

Harry Lawton. Excerpt from "Orange Groves and Rice Bowls: A Narrative History of the Chinese Pioneers of Riverside, California 1869–1974" by Harry Lawton. Copyright © 2006 by Harry Lawton. Reprinted by permission of Georgeann Lawton. "The Walk to One Horse Spring" from *Willie Boy: A Desert Manhunt* by Harry Lawton. Banning, CA: Malki Museum Press. Copyright © 1960 by Harry Lawton. Reprinted by permission of Malki Museum Press.

W. Storrs Lee. Excerpt from "What Did I Do to Deserve This, Sergeant" from *The Great California Deserts* by W. Storrs Lee. New York: Putnam. Copyright © 1963 by W. Storrs Lee. Reprinted by permission of Ralph Lee.

José del Carmen Lugo. Excerpt from *Vida de un Ranchero* by José del Carmen Lugo and translated by Helen Pruitt Beattie from *Historical Society of Southern California Quarterly* 32.3 (September, 1950). Translation copyright © 1950 by Helen Pruitt Beattie. Reprinted by permission of the Historical Society of Southern California.

Norman Mailer. Excerpt from *The Deer Park* by Norman Mailer. New York: Random House. Copyright © 1955 by Norman Mailer.

R. S. Malloch. "When asked to put it on paper..." by R. S. Malloch from *Wong Ho Leun: An American Chinatown* edited and published by The Great Basin Foundation. San Diego: The Great Basin Foundation. Copyright © 1985 by R. S. Malloch.

Malcolm Margolin. "The Cupeño Expulsion of 1903" by Malcolm Margolin from *News from Native California*, Volume 5, Number 3, 1991. Copyright © 1991 by Malcolm Margolin. Reprinted by permission of Heyday Books and Malki Museum Press.

Dionisio D. Martínez. "Hesperia" by Dionisio D. Martínez from *Ploughshares* Spring 1992. Copyright © 1992 by Dionisio D. Martínez. Reprinted by permission of the author.

Carey McWilliams. Excerpts from "The Growth of a Legend" from *Southern California Country: An Island on the Land* by Carey McWilliams. New York: Duell,

Author Index

About the Editor

Gayle Wattawa made her way to California via the mountains of Colorado and the suburbs of Washington, D.C. She attended the University of California, Berkeley, where she received degrees in English literature and mathematics. She is currently the acquisitions editor for Heyday Books.

A California Legacy Book

Santa Clara University and Heyday Books are pleased to publish the California Legacy series, vibrant and relevant writings drawn from California's past and present.

Santa Clara University—founded in 1851 on the site of the eighth of California's original twenty-one missions—is the oldest institution of higher learning in the state. A Jesuit institution, it is particularly aware of its contribution to California's cultural heritage and its responsibility to preserve and celebrate that heritage.

Heyday Books, founded in 1974, specializes in critically acclaimed books on California literature, history, natural history, and ethnic studies.

Books in the California Legacy series appear as anthologies, single author collections, reprints of important books, and original works. Taken together, these volumes bring readers a new perspective on California's cultural life, a perspective that honors diversity and finds great pleasure in the eloquence of human expression.

Series editor: Terry Beers
Publisher: Malcolm Margolin
Advisory committee: Stephen Becker, William Deverell, Charles Faulhaber, David Fine, Steven Gilbar, Ron Hansen, Gerald Haslam, Robert Hass, Jack Hicks, Timothy Hodson, James Houston, Jeanne Wakatsuki Houston, Maxine Hong Kingston, Frank LaPena, Ursula K. Le Guin, Jeff Lustig, Tillie Olsen, Ishmael Reed, Alan Rosenus, Robert Senkewicz, Gary Snyder, Kevin Starr, Richard Walker, Alice Waters, Jennifer Watts, Al Young.

Thanks to the English Department at Santa Clara University and to Regis McKenna for their support of the California Legacy series.

CALIFORNIA
LEGACY

Other California Legacy Books

California Poetry: From the Gold Rush to the Present
Edited by Dana Gioia, Chryss Yost, and Jack Hicks

Under the Fifth Sun: Latino Literature from California
Edited by Rick Heide

Unfolding Beauty: Celebrating California's Landscapes
Edited with an Introduction by Terry Beers

Fool's Paradise: A Carey McWilliams Reader
Edited by Dean Stewart and Jeannine Gendar

Essential Mary Austin Edited with an Introduction by Kevin Hearle

Lands of Promise and Despair: Chronicles of Early California, 1535–1846
Edited by Rose Marie Beebe and Robert M. Senkewicz

The Anza Trail and the Settling of California Vladimir Guerrero

Death Valley in '49 William Lewis Manly

The Land of Orange Groves and Jails: Upton Sinclair's California
Edited by Lauren Coodley

November Grass Judy Van der Veer

And many more! If you would like to be added to the California Legacy mailing list, please send your name, address, phone number, and email address to:

California Legacy Project
English Department
Santa Clara University
Santa Clara, CA 95053

For more on California Legacy titles, events, or other information, please visit www.californialegacy.org.

Heyday

HEYDAY INSTITUTE

Since its founding in 1974, Heyday Books has occupied a unique niche in the publishing world, specializing in books that foster an understanding of the history, literature, art, environment, social issues, and culture of California and the West. We are a 501(c)(3) nonprofit organization based in Berkeley, California, serving a wide range of people and audiences.

We are grateful for the generous funding we've received for our publications and programs during the past year from foundations and more than 300 individual donors. Major supporters include:

Anonymous; Anthony Andreas, Jr., Audubon, Barnes & Noble bookstores; Bay Tree Fund; S.D. Bechtel, Jr. Foundation; Butler Koshland Fund, California Council for the Humanities; Candelaria Fund; Columbia Foundation; Colusa Indian Community Council; Federated Indians of Graton Rancheria; Wallace Alexander Gerbode Foundation; Richard & Rhoda Goldman Fund; Evelyn & Walter Haas, Jr. Fund; Walter & Elise Haas Fund; Hopland Band of Pomo Indians; James Irvine Foundation; George Frederick Jewett Foundation; LEF Foundation; Michael McCone; Middletown Rancheria Tribal Council; Gordon & Betty Moore Foundation; Morongo Band of Mission Indians; National Endowment for the Arts; National Park Service; Poets & Writers; Rim of the World Interpretive Association; River Rock Casino; Alan Rosenus; San Francisco Foundation; John-Austin Saviano/Moore Foundation; Sandy Cold Shapero; L.J. Skaggs and Mary C. Skaggs Foundation; Victorian Alliance; and the Harold & Alma White Memorial Fund.

For more information about Heyday Institute, our publications and programs, please visit our website at www.heydaybooks.com.